NECRONOMICON

NOIR
Publishing

PO Box 28
Hereford HR1 1YT
E-mail: noir@appleonline.net

Necronomicon Book Three
Edited by: Andy Black
ISBN 0 9536564 0 3
© Andy Black and all contributors 1999, all rights reserved.
First published 1999 by:
Noir Publishing
Copyright © Noir Publishing 1999
Necronomicon - an annual publication.
Cover Design:
The White Rhino Partnership
Photos from Salvation & Redemption Films, all additional visual
materials taken from the Noir Publishing Collection.
Cover Photo:
Le Frisson Des Vampires/Shiver of the Vampire, Jean Rollin
By courtesy of Redemption Films/Jean Rollin.

Editor's Acknowledgements
As with all such tome's many individuals assisted above and beyond the
call of duty and whilst it's unfair to single people out, heck, here goes ! -
thanks to all my contributors, Jean Rollin, Brian Yuzna, Lucas Balbo,
Richard Connole, Richard Larcombe & Rachael Marshall at The
Associates, Derek Mason, Rob Poole and GRC, James at Creation,
Clayton (even though he is a 'pool fan !) and the boys at Rhino, Babs,
Alex & Aaron for their patience, humour and support.

British Library Cataloguing in Publication Data:
A catalogue record for this book is available from the British Library.

CONTENTS

CONTENTS

FOREWORD

Well, amazingly, here we are again almost a year on from *Necronomicon* Book Two this time. As you all know by now, my original intention with the new book format was always to publish annually as opposed to sporadically and now we're finally getting there !

Once again I hope that you'll agree that *Necro'* contributors have scoured the globe in order to bring a gamut of varied and fascinating cinema to these pages.

Whether it's the compelling atmosphere and pulp plots which embellish the films of Mario Bava and Jean Rollin, or the visceral impetus which sees Jess Franco's work dissected alongside that of Georges Franju, or the arthouse exploitation which pervades Laurence Remila's feature, and just plain arthouse which imbrues Werner Herzog's **Nosferatu**.

And, just as this avowedly pro-European emphasis is deliberate and necessary in order to combat the prosaic product of the Hollywood system, then we also take a look at some of the more imaginative talents across the pond, inlcuding Brian Yuzna, John Carpenter and Roberto Rodriguez.

In addition, Ian Conrich investigates that filmic treasure on our own doorstep, the mesmerising **The Wicker Man**, we uncover that much neglected classic of seventies erotica, **The Story of O** and also look forward to new impetus being breathed into the Italian film industry through artists such as Sergio Stivaletti.

Before looking forward to *Necro'* 4 this time next year, I hope you will also check out the forthcoming titles from *Noir Publishing* which will span the wide spectrum of cult cinema and transgressive music.

Hope to see you then !

Andy Black (October 1999)

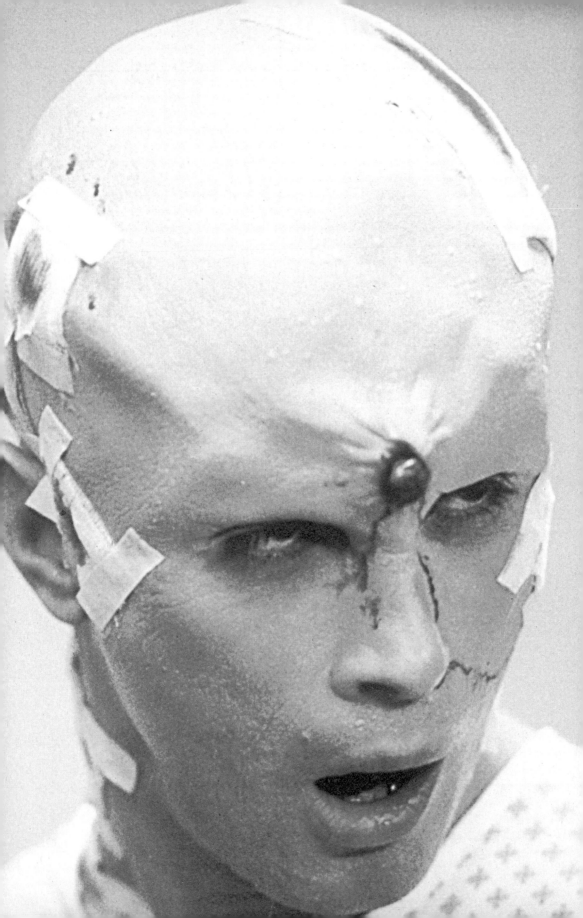

YUZNA SPILLS ALL

Rotting zombies, orgiastic couplings and Disney shennanigans in the diverse wold of Brian Yuzna.

Andy Black

On Society...

Iactually liked the project which was written by Woody Keith and Rick Fry. Originally I was attracted to it because of the paranoia aspect. I liked the idea of the guy who is really paranoid. and then my own sense of the ironic was that all of his fears were real (laughs). He's really paranoid but whatever he's paranoid of, it's worse than he ever thought. I kind of liked that idea. It's like hey, you've got a reason to be paranoid. So there's a sort of ironic sensibility that enjoys that. Originally I was working on a project called *The Men* written by Dan O'Bannon. We worked up *The Men* which was about a woman who discovers that all men are aliens (!) It had a real paranoic aspect and when that movie fell through I had already worked myself up into a lather over this paranoic thing. Then I saw the **Society** script and I loved this idea that this kid had everything going for him. The idea was to make him very privileged. And not only privileged, he's a nice guy, a good sport, good athlete, president of the class, he's very privileged, everything is going right for him and then to show how the paranoia takes over his life and that's what carries the movie at first. I also like anything that's bizarre or weird and surreal and I liked the idea. One of my favourite moments in the movie is when he first hears the tape and he hears his parents and sister saying and doing things which are so unlike them and so perverse, so hedonistic and it throws his world upside down.

Originally, it was a blood cult which they were involved in and that to me just didn't seem fun enough and so I tried to think of an idea we hadn't seen before and came up with the idea of melding and then tried to make sense out of it. Then I tried to interpret what I think was the inspiration of the script anyway which was implicitly the idea that the "under class" that **Society** called it, is really different from the rest of us,

From Beyond

it's not just that they have a lot more money. That they're actually different and so we tried to have fun with that and then of course there's this idea of incest that is a subtext to a lot of horror movies. Anything that is a really heavy taboo find's its way into a horror film. Even if it's not an explicit thing but an implicit thing and something like incest isn't something that you find movies about because it's not much fun, it's too threatening to us but often it's very much in the subtext so that was also something which I very much enjoyed, putting in a scene where he's very close to his sister but he accidentally goes into the bathroom and into the shower with her and the idea there was that it's like to accidentally walk into your sister in the shower is very Freudian (laughs). You don't accidentally do that but it could happen accidentally. I think the idea of being sexually attracted to your sister is such a taboo that I think it's expressed nicely when he sees her as being really strangely abnormal, sexually. Basically, her breasts and her ass are in the wrong place. So, that type of thing helps build his passion in a fun way that I think we all understand subconciously. Then I think the idea of making **Society** really perverse - to me I always wanted the studio to sell the movie as *Society - The True Story*, because I always thought that it was a true story - it's just that it's told figuratively. To me, I think it's like so what ? It's like at the end of the movie when he (Billy) escapes and goes charging off, the members of "society" don't bother chasing him because what's he going to do - go tell everybody that it's a big surprise ? (laughs). Nothing is going to change. So I really like to try and give shape to this incredible orgiastic perversion of the upper classes because I do believe it's true. I'm not saying that everybody is like that but when you get to the point where you have so much more than other people, so much power, so much privilege, there's a point where you don't believe you should, and often just don't, behave by the same moral and ethical code as other people, so called "normal" people.

*A similar conceit as found in Pasolini's **Salo** ?*

Yeah, it's kind of like if you're ever in a position of power you tend to abuse it. It's impossible because one of the things which holds back our appetite for abusing other people if you will, is the fact that physically we can't get away with it. And, at the point where you do start to get away with it and you see it all the time with people in a position, even briefly, of being powerful - say parents with children even, once you can get with lecturing, say a teacher in a school, they get so used to people listening to

Salo

them lecture that they adopt an attitude of self-importance and then they start abusing other people with their bullshit, because they're used to it. When you have a lot of money all of a sudden some of the main people you're around all the time are the people that you're paying. You've bought them so they put up with a lot of bullshit from you whether their your mate, or your driver or cook or shopkeeper. If you have a lot of money and go to the shops which cater to wealthy people then those shops will bend over backwards, kiss your ass and act like your best friend. If you and I go into those shops they'll actually be nasty to us.

It's like go fly on an aeroplane. It's packed with with people and they don't give you any room to sit and the stewards and stewardesses will treat you like shit sometimes. Or, go up to first class and you're paying for it and my god, then the same staff will be polishing your gonads (!) and I think that tends to make you look at the world differently. So, it's also very natural if you're in that sensibility that you use sex in a different way. Not that everybody doesn't but now you're in a position of perhaps being able to afford a lot of variation. And I think the whole idea of the "shunting", using a lower class guy and assimilating him, I liken that to a breed of dogs like say when you bred dogs like a German shepherd, all of a sudden they'll get hip displacement because the gene pool gets too limited and they gets lots of problems so they have to get another breed of dog that's similar and get it interbred to beef up the gene pool. So, that was the idea of them using the lower class kids in assimilating them in order to invigorate their own limited gene pool and of course to have fun and make a visual pun of the rich feeding off the poor. The idea of the movie **Society** is not just the rich but having to interbreed with wealthy families for many generations of family before you become a part of society, based on the idea of (the) nouveau riche. We know that even if you have a lot of money you won't be accepted into society. not even in the United States ! (laughs). The idea that you can't just have money and be accepted into society is what we tried to show by having society be a different race, a different breed and that you could breed into it really slowly if you were wealthy over generations.

On Reanimator...

We were lucky ! We (Yuzna & Stuart Gordon) had no idea what we were doing. To be honest I was just hoping that we wouldn't lose all the money ! (laughs) I was very careful to make clear when Stuart and I were

Reanimator

planning it, that he needed to indulge his own appetite for excess because I didn't want it to fail because it was too namby pamby. I'd seen enough amateur type horror movies that had tried to be respectable and I said that the one thing we won't do is to try and be respectable. We're going to go ahead and go for the guts though but who could've guessed that Stuart would turn out to be a brilliant director and the movie be good.

*The casting was ideal throughout the film but especially Jeffrey Combs who also put in an eccentric performance in **The Frighteners** recently ..*

Yeah, I think that was probably the best role he's ever played. Well, he was great as when we were casting it we obviously couldn't afford anyone who was a "name" and during shooting, Jeffrey was the one who just really knocked our socks off - and he was the wrong type as in the book Herbert West was blond-haired and blue-eyed - a sort of Germanic thing but when we saw Jeffrey read for it, bang, he was the one. There was no question for me and with Barbara (Crampton) we did see a lot of people but eventually she led the pack and she's beautiful. I thought she really was a great victim and Bruce Abbot a great straight man and of course David Gale, god rest

Alberto Grimaldi
presenta

Clasificada Ⓢ

Se advierte al público
que esta pelicula, por su
temática y contenido,
puede herir la sensibilidad
del espectador.

Un film de

Pier
Paolo
Pasolini

United Artists

SALO
O LOS 120 DIAS DE SODOM
Technicolor ®

EMEGE Dep. Legal: B. 440

From Beyond

his soul, for me was the classic villain. We had some options on Hill which were a bit more believable, more believable people but I was always a fan of horror and he was really a horror movie guy, so I really pushed for David even though he almost looked too much like a villain. For me, it was like making a Hammer movie. David Gale could be in a Hammer film.

What was it like filming the infamous severed head and oral sex extravaganza ?!

The "head giving head" scene we called it (!) and it was quite a distressing day for Barbara. It was a really hard thing for her to do and you just have to give her a lot of credit for doing it but it was pretty heavy. This is a terrible story but when we had the Horror & Sci-Fi Society give us some people to watch the rough cut and David Gale's wife at that time watched it and she left him then. Of course we had more of that scene then. We cut back believe it or not a lot of the gore and sex, not because of any censorship but because there was this build up of a thrill. The first one was that she was naked on the table. Well, girls are always tied down in horror films but usually they've got pants on - well, this guy is gonna' kill someone so of course he's not going to put pants on her. So, now she's naked and he comes up to her holding his bloody head and he sticks his tongue in her ear. Well, people start flipping then. They go, oh my god. Then it comes around and he kisses her nipple. Now the audience is starting to really go crazy because this is just getting pornographic. and then when you start moving the head down her stomach there's a moment where they realise what you have in mind and at that point they start freaking out. And as they recognise it and they see the head going down between her legs - at that moment you have to cut away. when you play it further what happens is that all of a sudden you've lost you're peak and a lot of the audience starts being uncomfortable. The trick with a movie like that is to take you up to the high point and then keep going because people always think that they see things that they never actually see on screen.

*On **Bride of Reanimator**..?*

From Beyond

I knew that with making a sequel you're basically celebrating the original and rarely is it any more than that. What I tried to do there was to keep the same tone as the first film but basically try to just go further with a lot of the things and use a lot of the material from the book which we hadn't used yet. So, there were certain themes in the book that we didn't use, For example the idea that Herbert West kind of likes to doodle with body parts. He got into the morbidity of it. The idea that they lived next to a cemetery and he put his failed experiments in the crypt and that at the end all of his failed experiments carry him off, so there were some of those ideas and the idea that they went to war was in the book except it was World War 1 there. At that time I was also reading Mary Shelley's *Frankenstein* and I was really impressed by it and so really the whole theme is **Bride of Frankenstein** and it's not really Lovecraft at all. The idea I really dug was that what made Frankenstein so great was this idea of the creator rejecting the created. That he created this creature and then rejected him. The creature wasn't good enough and the creature only wanted acceptance and I think that this is something that we all respond to because it's the post-religious reality - that whole Nietzschien universe where you say gee god, god abandoned us. We weren't good enough.

The strong will survive as in Nietzsche's "supermen" theories ? Yeah. we're not worth fooling with so just let us sink into our own shit. So that was the poignant moment in **Bride** where she's begging Dan to accept her and he won't and she just comes apart at the seams. She take out her heart and holds it and says is this what you wanted, but of course, all he wanted was Meg, he never liked her. Quite frankly, what is interesting is that if you're building a man in the mad doctor Frankenstein mythology it's always the brain that's the problem and when you're building a woman it's always the heart and I even found out in reading about the making of **Frankenstein** and **Bride of Frankenstein**, the James Whale versions, that originally Whale had the the bride of Frankenstein being built from the heart of Victor Frankenstein's new wife. That she gets killed and they actually use her heart to build the bride completes the movie but I don't think that scene survived. I thought that was very interesting because that's the same soloution that we had come up with. But of course, the things that I really love about Bride are the finger eye creature and Hill flying around on bat wings I think is absolutely ridiculous and I love it because of that. I love when he says "West, you bi-ped". Then of course, being able to have a head float up to the camera and talk to the audience at the beginning was always a dream of mine because I loved the William Castle movies like **The House on Haunted Hill** and **The Tingler** where he'd have everyone's head float up and talk to us, so here I thought when will I ever get the chance to do this again and especially in bloody colour, so that was fun.

On *Return of the Living Dead 3...?*

I really enjoyed doing that movie. It began with the title. When I was asked to do it I started thinking well, you think you've got trouble with **Bride of Reanimator** in trying to come close to an original, here we had a situation in which it was, if you think about it, the second sequel to an alternative sequel to a classic zombie movie. So basically you had **Night of the Living Dead** which had it's two real sequels, but because John Russo who wrote **Night of the Living Dead** had the rights to the name *Living Dead*, that all of a sudden Dan O'Bannon made that great **Return of the Living Dead** which was an alternative sequel, now what Dan O'Bannon did which I thought was absolutely brilliant was addressing the sequel issue right upfront - I love the opening when he says did you ever see **Night of the Living Dead** ? Yeah, well it was based on a real event so all of a sudden Dan was able to connect his movie to the original but still make the new mythology which he wanted to do.

Now with Romero's mythology it was basically that the dead were coming back to life. Now, I remember always assuming that if you got bitten by one of the dead you would turn into one as though their saliva was infected but on a close watch of the movie that's not the case. If you die you come back and I think in **Dawn of the Dead** he tried to give the reason that when hell is full the will walk the earth, but in the first one he played around the idea that maybe some satellite came back with something but who knows and he really didn't want to take a stand on that and I think it was the smart thing to do because the movie just worked on pure terror. But what Dan O'Bannon wanted to do was his own movie an an EC comics *Tales From The Crypt* type movie and quite frankly I think that **Return of the Living Dead** is certainly the most successful if not the only successful movie in that style and I think that he really captured that feeling, that look and black humour more than anyone else ever has and I think that his storytelling, I find that the very end of it with the chase when they're in the ceiling is a bit of a letdown, but up until then and certainly the whole gimmick of the guy blowing up the town is just brilliant and the way the story unfolds is brilliant. It really moves and I love the gratuitous nudity of Linnea Quigley where Dan O'Bannon rather than fooling around half-heartedly trying to get a little nudity into it which good horror movies should have and gratuitous sex !, but she just takes her clothes off and nobody will give her any attention so she just runs around naked and I thought that was great. So, it certainly is a great movie and he added the mythology which was that it was a chemical developed to eradicate dope.

Of course, when I came onto the scene I had to make the third sequel. Fortunately, unlike the second sequel, the people financing this didn't give a shit whether we carried on any characters and that was the first great advantage I had. You see the problem with **Bride of Reanimator** is that you have to carry on the characters but the story is already told. Herbert West was killed in the first one and Dr. Hill's head was smashed against the wall. But you can't do it without Herbert West so you're basically telling the story for some people that you've already told their story. With **Return of the Living Dead 3** they said we don't care if you carry over any of the story or any of the actors, but we do want to keep the brain-eating !

Now, the brain-eating was always a problem to me because in Dan O'Bannon's version it was just a goofy, EC comics style thing.... Yes, it was a gas that the military developed but what it did to you is it brought you back to life but you weren't growing, you were deteriorating, and the first thing that deteriorates is the nervous system. So, you're feeling a real void for your nervous system, you need to replenish it and of course, where are the most nerves - the brain is just a bundle of nerves - it is the nervous system. So, when they bite flesh as in the Romero version, they're biting it because flesh is is full of little nerves strewn though there, it's not really the meat that they are going for and there's a good reason for them going to the brain, so I settled that issue and then thought of how to make it different from the other thousands of living dead zombie movies is to make the main character a zombie.

I thought that would already change your point of view so much it would be fresh and then John Penny the writer came up with the idea of doing a "Romeo and Juliet" story, kids on the run and I thought that's great as a love story is always the best. Then he had the idea that the military had this magic bullet which would freeze them and I thought that was a great idea and I carried it even further by making this mechanical suit they can put them in. I thought,gee, what would happen if we really could bring back the dead. Well, immediately they'd see them as meat batteries and

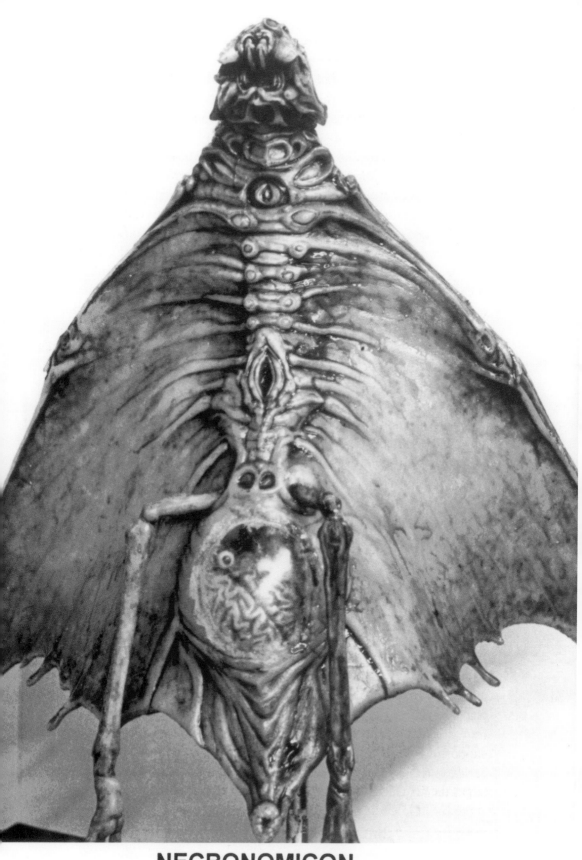

NECRONOMICON

what a great weapon it would be but how do you control it so that became a framing story, then ultimately at that point, especially which was early in this whole sort of modern primitavist movement. I was very interested in piercing, tattooing and scarification and so I went to some fetish clubs to research it and to find out how that would connect with this because I really thought that this should be an issue involved with this, so I came up with the idea that once Julie is brought back to life she is hungry all of a sudden and realises that she can't eat regular food, it's not satisfying but when she tastes blood, tastes flesh, there's something good about that, but she's ashamed of herself, horrified at herself and so the only way she can hold back the loss of her human identity and become this horrible cannibal monster is through the love of her boyfriend who she loves - that brings her to life but more and more the only thing that will stop it is pain so she starts pressing metal into her flesh and when she gets that pain it's better.

Of course, when she tastes brains she's way off the deep end and she's become a monster and I wanted her to look like a real cool monster so that she kind of had a rock in one hand to break the skull and scissors pushed through her other hand to dig out the brain ! And of course, in that particular movie there were certain shots which were actually deleted for the "R" rating which were actual stretchy flesh-chewing. That movie was actually cut back a bit and of course the zombies breaking through the doorway I did strictly because I felt that any living dead movie has to have the Romero homage - I think that any audience would've been disappointed not to see that. But I don't think that you can do any better than was done on **Night of the Living Dead**.

On Necronomicon...?

I think that it was kind of an experiment. What I really wanted to do was to see what would happen if you got an Asian, a European and an American making a movie together and everyone had quite a bit of freedom to do what they wanted. The only difference was that it was an uneven situation being co-produced by the French and the Japanese so basically, for example, *The Drowned* got as much money as the rest of the movie put together, because the French producer was very much into supporting his guy and the Japanese didn't give a shit ! I mean they gave a shit but they make their deal and not a dollar more. So, you have a situation for example where *The Drowned* has an orchestra of 75 and a score by Jo Deluca and then Dan Licked does the rest of the movie score with his synthesiser. I also think that it probably would've been a better idea to have conceived of all the stories before all the directors came into work on them. What I had wanted to do was to make it totally open, so I think that Christov did a great job with *The Drowned* - it certainly has a great atmosphere and great directing. I think as far as the narratives go the second one probably has the best, but it's probably the least interesting. I really like the mythology behind the third one and I really felt like it had to be something modern and a totally different feeling to the rest, especially as the first one was so classical and Roger Corman/Mario Bava-esque. I thought there should be a really different taste, a real dirty look. I like the idea of the unending horror and my favourite part of the movie is the opening wraparound. I just love it when Jeffrey Combs comes to the place and goes and gets the book, it reminds me of an old radio show and that's my favourite part as I think it has a great look and a great narrative starting up. But you're right about the trilogy movies - they're tricky but I'd like to do another **Necronomicon** and get three other directors because I think it's just fun to see what they do although I think if I did it again I would actually get the scripts written and then let the directors' re-write them.

*On **The Dentist..?***

From Beyond

It was a really tough movie because the moment they told me they wanted to do a movie called **The Dentist** my heart sank. I thought oh my god, it's **Dr Giggles** ! How do you do that and they didn't want it to be sci-fi or fantasy and they wanted it to be about teeth pain so I was really pulling my hair out, but I really felt that Stu' Gordon and Dennis Paoli came up with a great situation with the really up-tight clean-freak Dennis who sees his wife giving the pool guy a blow-job and starts falling apart because this would definitely be our fear - that we go to the dentist and he's having a bad day. So, that was a great set-up but it pretty much depended on a lot of gore scenes and then when Charles Finch came in and added a whole other sort of feeling to it, there was all of a sudden, the dentist started having some redeeming characteristics and so that's what I tried to focus on. It was a very difficult picture for me because I had to work within such limited situations and also it's all pretty much in bright light, you weren't going anywhere weird, it was just like a dentist's office and a pool.

There's nothing that obviously helped you make a horror movie so what I tried to do was really play up the bightness and I tried to be much more design-conscious about the shooting of it then I usually am. If you look at something like **Return of the Living Dead 3**, these kinds of movies. I'm basically more concerned with where I'm going, where'as with **The Dentist** it's a very vigorous framing in there. It's a very vigorous construction of the shots and I did that on purpose as I felt that it was just such a minimalist movie that it needed that and then to make fun out of these terrible scenes what I tried to do was to focus the whole movie on his interior landscape.

So the whole movie is based on what he thinks, what he's seeing, so when you take a scene like him diddling with the would-be starlet who's out on gas, that's a scene that generally would turn off an audience because it's not much fun, it's just perverse but by playing it with what he sees, the perversion, your seeing his wife, his mind and what's really going on all of a sudden, you take a very tawdry scene and suddenly to me it sings, it's really great, all of a sudden you get to enjoy the exploitative nature of it. You don't feel bad about liking the scene and of course, using the opera with him, it's almost that you like him because he has good taste (laughs). He's a very theatrical guy, the theme rooms are silly but really he's a guy who has a soul and he's just disappointed in love, that's all and he's killing about it, so a lot of these scenes, the way that it's shot is all based on his mindset at that time.

*On **The Dentist 2**...?*

It's your typical sequel - like **Stepfather 2**. You're stuck - the guy's got his escape from mental hospital and then he's got to get another identity and you've got to set him up so that he can do it again. Well, that's a real tough job because like in **Bride of Reanimator** , the story's already been told. But I guess it's my karma to do all these sequels (laughs) so I'm pretty used to dealing with those problems and avoiding the pitfalls. I tried to make it very comic bookish with a weird wipes style and it has a couple of showstopper scenes that really deliver and I think Corben Bernsen has three scenes in this film which are just him and the camera in which he's just dazzling and there's certainly one in particular which I just think is one of those scenes that you'll see in future compilations of horror performances - you'll just go my god this guy - it's just like watching Lionel Barrymore. He really takes off in this.

*On **Honey I Shrunk The Kids**...?*

It was a funny thing because Stu (Gordon) and I were getting ready to go to Rome and we had made **Reanimator** and Stuart's family were over because he's got kids and I've got kids and he was saying we should make a movie that our kids could go and see as they were pretty young at that time. I said that when I was a kid I used to imagine being really small so you could ride on a bug and you could fly on a bee, you could ride on an ant and even a blade of grass would be an adventure. So I mentioned that to Stuart and he thought it was a great idea and said well let's do a movie where kids get shrunk and so we immediately, gosh, in just twenty minutes (!) we came up with all the elements (laughs) - we called it *Teenie-Weenies* but Disney said it sounded like a low budget porno movie (laughs), so they came up with a great title and we worked on it for a year and Stuart was going to direct it and I went down to Mexico and built all the sets and we developed the whole thing and storyboarded it and designed all the scenes and there was a long history to it. We had the kids being taken by a bee into a beehive and having to hang-glide on a leaf to escape but it started being too expensive and they had this whole scheme where to get up on the table they had to shoot a pin across to the table and they decided that was too expensive so I suggested that they just end up in the cereal bowl, so there were other scenes but ultimately I think it was just a fun idea.

The idea that the adventure is in your own backyard and certainly it was a thrill to me to see the kid flying on a bee on McDonalds cups because I was thinking that no one else in the world probably knows this but that was my image from when I was a kid and there it is on a McDonalds cup, so it makes you realise that almost anything is possible.

*On **From Beyond**...?*

Well, that was supposed to kind of be the mainstram version of **Reanimator**. A movie that would work theatrically and be R rated and you notice we put Jeffrey Combs, Barbara Crampton and David Gale in there to keep the same actors, although David Gale didn't get to be the bad guy this time but Ken foree was a good addition and the idea was to do another Lovecraft and really try to hit one out of the park commercially. The idea to do **From Beyond** was that having a machine was a good idea as it gives you a little more to go on than just a straight horror, so the machine was cool and basically I wrote the story with Stu and Dennis (Paoli) and we used up the short-story before the titles because in the Lovecraft story the end of the story is where we end the titles of the movie. and then we came up with the idea of the pineal gland popping out as Jeffrey says "I'll never forgive you for putting a dog dick out of my head" (laughs) - "It's a pineal gland" I said - "It's a dog dick" he repeated ! And we got to do the whole business of what would be called a crude effects movie now but was cool then and I think it was a really neat movie and I did see it recently at a festival and I was really amazed at how good it looked. I think it was Max Ahlberg's best photography - the pinks and the blues, but it really holds up as a movie, it's really entertaining and different. I'd love to do something again like that with such a wild idea.

On the boundaries of taste...?

I guess I would have to define it the way it's normally defined which is that good taste is a mainstream value of something, I would guess is not exploitative and that somehow reveals a higher aesthetic, an appreciation for classical aesthetics and that bad taste is exploitation and the lack thereof. Of course, by making movies such as mine, most of which would be considered to be bad taste, you kind of get past that. You develop a good bad taste (laughs). I certainly know a good movie when I see it and I love exploitation stuff and it has more to do with how the entertainment fits together, how it really works, what kind of a ride does it give you. It doesn't really matter what the genre is.

On his plans for the future..?.

I also finished a movie last year called **Progeny** which is an **Alien/Rosemary's Baby** movie and I've been working on a few things. One was a movie called **Parasite** which was a Joe Stefano script but the rights to the script fell though with the distributor. I've been preparing this **Zen Intergolatic Ninja** for ever to shoot in Montreal and I've been

Necronomicon

working with a Dutch producer and writer to direct a ghost story which takes place in Amsterdam which I'm very excited about but the thing I'm doing right now is I'm making a deal with this Spanish company Filmax in Barcelona to produce and direct a series of English language, Hollywood style genre movies, low budget in Barcelona so right now I've been going through and picking projects to shoot next year. I'm hoping I can get three of them in next year starting in January. One of them is a circus horror horror movie written by Cats Vortburg, the guy who wrote **Angel Heart** and I'm hoping I can do this movie called **Dagon** with Stu' directing which would be a lot of fun. We expect to use a lot of English and American actors due to geography, so I'm really excited about that because this Spanish company Filmax really wants to put out a series of genre movies and I'd love to. They'll be cheap but that seems to be my lot in life (laughs) but at least I'll get the chance to maybe quit having these down periods as I feel I spend too much time inbetween things and I'm always ready to do a good horror movie.

STRONG ACID

The Killer Kool Kat of Scream and Scream Again

Martin Jones

"Like, Helter Skelter is a nightclub. Helter Skelter means confusion, literally. It doesn't mean any war with anyone. It doesn't mean that those people are going to kill other people. It only means what it means. Helter Skelter is confusion. Confusion is coming down fast. If you don't see the confusion coming down fast around you, you can call it what you wish."

- Charles Manson's Trial Testimony (19th November 1970)

Confusion is next. Charles Manson, that zenith of hippie destruction, may not be the most brutal full-stop in North American history, but his statements are packed with the incoherence of other would-be 20th century doom-merchants. Even a cursory examination of Manson's trial testimony reveals a monologue that makes James Joyce, in comparison, a very light read (see *Rapid Eye 1*). History has rightly consigned the majority of it to the bin and kept only the catchy pay-off (Prison's in your mind... Can't you see I'm free ?!). The remaining text shows Manson to be the mentally ill vagrant that he was, like the teeshirt worn by rebellious youth a few years back said: "he's not the messiah, he's a very naughty boy". With hindsight, Manson may have been more adept at popular music criticism; after all, isn't *The White Album* the only Beatles LP worth listening to ?

Whatever his role in the destruction of America's beautiful people, Charles Manson was - and always will remain, through his image alone - that most paradoxical of human beings: the dangerous hippie. More than any other cult of culture (bikers, skinheads, punks et al, the dangerous hippie draws a hell of a lot of fascination towards it's placid corner; "We come in peace, we leave you in pieces" as Gary Oldman remarked in **The Firm** (no way a relevant film but an appropriate quote).

North America in the 1960's endured what might be called a mild crisis of identity. The buy-now-pay-later sex & drugs crowd were at

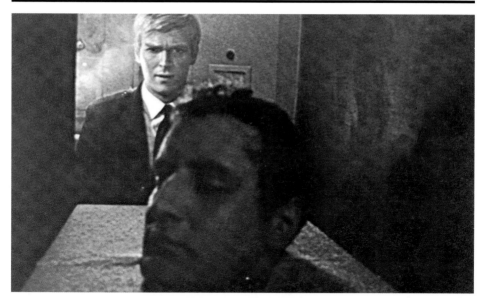

Scream and Scream Again

it like (white) rabbits, while on the other side of the world clean-cut young men were blown into dog food by the Vietcong. Both were literally dazed and confused, but it was more natural to expect a little animosity from the demaged veterans towards those free'n'easy peaceniks who never got blood on their fingers. With the roles reversed however, don't it look so much more appealing? A hippie who isn't afraid to get a little gore on his/her tie-dye teeshirt and hipster flares, a kool kat strangling the straights with love beads, a swinger who loves watching them swing....

"What's it all about ?"

Bar The Stooges back-catalogue, is there a more malevolent tune to emerge from the 1960's than Piggies by The Beatles ? Penned by George Harrison and adopted by Manson's followers as top of the pops for interior decorating inspiration, it rides precariously on the dangerous hippie ethic: lightweight song barely hiding its darker intentions, everything that could be found between its lines adopted by The Family as they dune-buggied around the Californian desert. Music (and literature) has offered guidance for crazies throughout history, but motion pictures have fewer role models for deadly drop-outs. The top kat of North American tie-dye psychosis is the Hitchhiker from **The Texas Chain Saw Massacre** (1974). Played by Edwin Neal, he has batty terrorism down to a fine art, which is unfortunate for the clean-cut group of kids who offer him a lift. With his greasy hair,

surplus clothes and extensive facial birthmark, the Hitchhiker is a long way beyond benchmark descriptions such as "far out" and "totally gone".

Self-mutilation, encyclopaedic slaughterhouse knowledge and inflammable rituals involving Polaroids serve to heighten the kids fear of their weird fellow traveller. When they finally get rid of him, the Hitchhiker leaves his mark by smearing blood on the side of their van, a sign to others as to how unhip they are.Although **The Texas Chain Saw Massacre** now resides in the "misunderstood" section of the Video Nasty Store, the Hitchhiker's mark is now permanent.

The confusion is coming down fast, so what about Britain ? Where are the paradoxical characters in the films that swam against such a carefree tide ? **Performance** (1970) can be viewed as an example of the end of that era, the culmination of seven years of intoxicating indulgence. But its psychadelic decadence falls short because of who we align our homicidal sympathies to. James Fox's dyed-in-the-red gangster-in-hiding is a much more dangerous prospect than Mick Jagger's preening fruitcake of a pop star ("D'you think I should wash my hair ?") Whatever The Rolling Stones' diabolic concerns were at the time, in **Perfomance** Jagger only walks the hot-knife edge when he sings; it's then that he becomes the dangerous hippie, literally intruding into Fox's mind.

Although on its last legs at the time, the British horror film industry provided a mantle for the Hitchhiker's transatlantic companion. Written by Christopher Wicking and directed by Gordon Hessler, **Scream and Scream Again** (1969) is a very strange film; not in a wacky Warhol kind of way, but considering the heritage it had emerged from, strange all

Scream and Scream Again

the same. It's 1968-69-70 home-grown competitors were flailing soft-core Hammers like **Lust for a Vampire** or illiterate psychadelia such as **Incense for the Damned**, tits and drugs thrills for straight society.

The initial appeal of **Scream and Scream Again** seems to be built around the novelty of having three prominent genre actors (Peter Cushing, Christopher Lee and Vincent Price) in one film together. But the unconnected order of each's scenes (Cushing has mere minutes of screen time), mirrors the complex and fractured plot: the film borrows from horror's past (mad scientists, vats of acid, vampirism) and splices it with the then present (visceral set pieces, international conspiracy theories, hip young killers). The confusion of the film acts as a fitting end to a decade coming down fast.

"Lovely mover..."

The homicidal hepcat of **Scream and Scream Again** is literally man-made. The film itself is a result of the (too late) shifts in power in Britain's family-orientated horror industry. One of the film's characters asks "what's it all about?" The plot concerns a surgeon who creates humanoids that install themselves in various positions of power around Europe: an Eastern-block torturer, a British civil servant, a disco-dancing hepcat. Coming into contact with them at various points is the cynical police officer in charge of a serial murder case, the idealistic young Dr. Sorel, the collapsed jogger who, each time he wakes in his hospital bed, finds another limb missing....

Scream and Scream Again fights its own battles, achieving a youthful victory over the old order, for the first half of the film at least. The dangerous hippie here is Keith, a disco-prowler who resembles Brian Jone's more malignant brother. Keith (played by Michael Gothard) is man-made, a product of the 1960's rather than a part of it; he has been created by Dr. Browning (Vincent Price), just like Konratz (Marshall Jones), the Eastern European official with a fondness for plier-induced torture. Keith may swing amongst the chicks on the dancefloor, but they are a means towards an end for his vampiric tendencies. Like Manson, he wants to take a part of these beautiful girls, his methods outwardly alluring, his motives entirely selfish.

The first time we see Keith in action (the police state that there have been others), the girl is effortlessly whisked away into his car. Touching the gearstick suggestively, she anticipates a night of free, uncomplicated sex, an activity that has become the bounty of her generation. Keith just grins. After a spot of outdoor foreplay turns rough the girl escapes, but Keith catches her, breaks her neck and drinks her blood.

Lovely mover.

Under his kool kat veneer, Keith is killing the 1960's, in the same way that Charles Manson set out to destroy the beautiful people in their beautiful houses. Every death is another nail in that freelivin' decade's coffin. Dr. Browning explains to Dr. Sorel that Keith has malfunctioned. Just like Manson, just like the Hitchhiker, his deeds don't fit with his outward appearance. It is fortunate for Keith that he is hip to the era he prowls in, just as, no doubt, Jack the Ripper was seemingly inconspicuous in the London of 1888.

"Yes, I'm a composite too."

As Keith is a Frankenstein's monster of the hippie era, so the England around him is similarly patched together. This 1969 is a celluloid flashing disco-ball detached from reality, not a million miles from the unsettling world inhabited by *The Avengers*. Helter Skelter may be a nightclub, but it isn't the one in **Scream and Scream Again**. There, music plays, and a band command the stage, but the two are not connected. The band is The

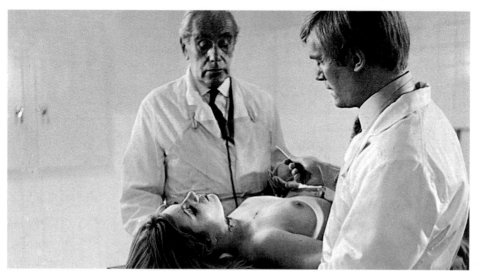

Scream and Scream Again

Amen Corner: the singer sways to the music, clicking his fingers, but he doesn't seem to be singing. In fact, no-one does. No-one dances in time either. In this confusion Keith prowls his chosen hunting ground, unaware that the police - that other authority of uncoolness - are closing in. They offer him live bait in the form of a female plain-clothes piggy and, after a car chase through the Green Belt, capture him. But again, Keith is not the complacent hipster they took him for: handcuffed to a car bumper, he wrenches his hand off at the wrist and escapes to Dr. Browning's country house.

It is here, in a barn, that Keith destroys himself in the only way possible: by jumping into a vat of acid. No chance of altered states, youthful poise intact, he has erased himself in the most lethal form of that decade's drug of choice. Manson rots way in jail, the Hitchhiker gor run over by a juggernaut, ugly turned uglier; Keith takes the one-way option of dissolving into nothingness, the best of his work done (could Manson have topped the Tate-LaBianca murders?)

Subsequently, other (unmasked) humanoids join Keith: Konratz, Dr. Browning, until only the civil servant Fremont (Christopher Lee) is left, the respectable government face that has destroyed the loose canons of this particular project. What started off as confused as lines in Manson's testimony has ended neatly tied up, like official paperwork in the filing cabinets of Fremont's office's. At the close of **Scream and Scream Again** Dr. Sorel asks Fremont if it's all over; "it's just the beginning" he replies, before the misguided theme tune intrudes. The malevolent love-child disintegrated in a vat of acid at the end of the 1960's, but other humanoids were ready to take its place.

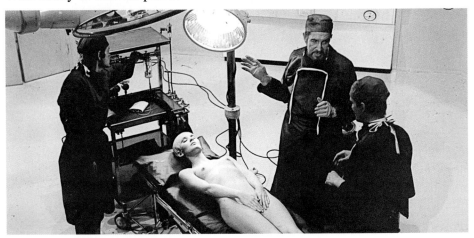

Scream and Scream Again

A MODERN WORLD WITH ANCIENT EVIL
Andy Black

T here is a valedictory moment in Mario Bava's **Baron Blood** where a psychic, Christina Hoffman (Rada Rassimov) admonishes the protagonists thus; "Mortals are such fools. Once you killed witches, now you bring murderers back to life."

It is a defining moment on one of the key perplexities which prevail Bava's ouevre -that somehow we in the so-called "civilised" world are steadily perpetrating the misconception that we are eradicating evil when all that we are really doing is fanning the flames in one area andpositively stoking them in another.

Take that twentieth century phenomenon the serial killer for instance. Yes, we may pursue such miscreants until they are behind bars and positioned on death row in certain cases. Yet we only succeed in fanning the flames by allowing them the maximum oxygen of publicity available through all media be it books, films, television, radio or the internet and so, effectively rebirthing them and stoking the fire for future generations to be drip-fed this diet of Warhol fame and serial fortune.

This insidious media influence is observed to varying degrees in contemporary Hollywood productions such as Gus Van Sant's **To Die For** [1], Oliver Stone's **Natural Born Killers** and Jon Amiel's **Copycat**, with the added nihilism in David Fincher's stark **Seven** and with revisionist originality in **Scream**.

For such a supreme stylist as Bava, these conflicts are presented with rather more subtlety if not sensitivity as he seeks to unveil the friction between the religious and the secular, often expounded by the collision of ancient myths with modern scepticism, human frailty be it greed or malice contrasting with childhood innocence (and sometimes guilt), and finally, the almost greek tragedy of his leading actors, their lot seemingly shaped as much by fate and destiny as by their own actions.

In many respects, two of Bava's films; **Baron Blood** and **Lisa and the Devil** offer the most salient appraisal of these central themes and as such, can be viewed as companion pieces, sharing a number of key

Baron Blood

similarities.

     Baron Blood was filmed in 1972 under Bava's direction and marked the first feature in a two picture deal with producer Alfred Leone (of which **Lisa and the Devil** formed the second). Partially derived from literary sources including Raymond McNally and Radu Florescu's account of Vlad the Impaler and his atrocities entitled *In Search of Dracula* and filmic sources, most noticeably Andre De Toth's Vincent Price starrer, **House of Wax** (1953).[2]

     Bava turns our attentions here to the titular figure of Baron Otto von Kleist, a sanguinary "Vlad"-styled warlock, previously responsible for an innocent woman being burnt at the stake as a witch over 300 years previously, only for her to put a curse on him before her death.

     The Baron himself perishes soon after, burnt in his own flames as fire engulfs his castle. Early on during the film, one of the Baron's descendants, Peter (Antonio Cantafora) jokes to his uncle whilst making a pilgrimage to the castle for the first time that; "Between us we might conjure up an ancestoral ghost or two." All he succeeds in doing though is to resurrect the now long dead Baron aided by Elke Sommer's mini-skirted National Trust worker, Eva.

The Baron's abode, "The Castle of Devils" being its chilling sobriquet, is an authentic medieval castle whose looming towers and shadowed battlements dominate the Austrian forest locale as Bava's prowling camera breathes life into every pore of the fortress. It becomes almost a character in much the same way that the inconquerable Egdon Heath permeates Thomas Hardy's classic novel, *The Return of the Native*.[3]

It is the castle itself which appears fully in control as Peter and Eva read out the witch's incantation to revive the Baron - all at the dead of night appropriately. Bava turns the screw and heightens the tension as doors creak, the wind howls and shadows form around the castle. The nearby church bells chime for midnight but ominously only two peals are heard as Eva recalls that the Baron's own death was rumoured to have occured at 2 am. Their looks of horror are intercut with a superb shot of the deserted churchyard, shrouded in fog and cloaked by a deathly silence save for the tolling bells.

Returning inside the castle, a door handle turns, the camera rapidly zooming in and Peter hurridly recants the verse and the handle now remains still as the camera draws back. Even the advent of morning however is unsettling as the camera pans out over the glorious sunlit views afforded by the castle, only for its' decaying walls to cast a malevolent shadow.

Foolishly brushing aside his uncle's protestations, Peter reads out the incantation again the next night in the castle room where the Baron was reputed to have died. This time there is no going back as we see a body stir and then writhe in the darkness. A sudden gust of wind forces the incantation scroll to fly into the room's raging fireplace and then the first of many pov shots indicate that the Baron is indeed alive. The cobwebbed interiors and gothic trappings of the castle then ebb away as Bava races into the film's most impressive sequence.

Eva, having rushed home to her appartment, now finds the Baron invading her room. She escapes him, only to be chased through the deserted village by the pursuing Baron. His grotesque, grue-covered features being only barely disguised by his long cloak and fedora-style hat. The image of him chasing Eva - a dark silhouette amongst the luminous mist [4], instantly recalls Vincent Price's figure in **House of Wax** (1953), only here, Bava makes the scene all his own as the pacing and lighting are uniformly excellent.

Eva runs from the Baron as a myriad of blue, orange and yellow shafts of incandescent light glimmers through the night. All the while, Bava's restless camera explores the claustrophobic alleys and wide agrophobic spaces of the village. Eva shelters in an archway as the Baron continues searching for her, walking right by her as she comes agonisingly close to being discovered, before running off to the nearest house for shelter. As she hammers frantically on the door for access, the camera closes in on the rapidly advancing Baron. The last drops of tension are rung out as she is finally admitted into the house, marginally escaping the clamouring clutches of the Baron.

The castle's new owner, via a property auction, a wheelchair bound Alfred Decker (Joseph Cotten), is then unsurprisingly revealed to be none other than the Baron during the film's climax. His own sadistic fantasies surface, as, with relish, he conducts a macabre tour of the castle's notorious torture chamber which he has now lovingly restored, complete with tape-recorded screams to complete the morbid ambience.

Then, Peter and Eva are shown the piece de resistance as they stare up at the castle turrets only to see human-like figures impaled there in an eerie tableau, in the Baron's finest sadistic tradition. It is Eva who saves them from the Baron's clutches when she drops an amulet (previously owned by the witch injustly burned by the Baron), onto the body of Fritz (Luciano Pigozzi) - a servant dispatched ingraciously by the Baron. As the trinket fumes and sizzles into his skin, he revives, and, along with a cadaverous army fromed from the tyrant's other victims, puts the evil von Kleist to death on his own instruments of torture, leaving Eva and Peter to escape.

In order to fully determine Bava's thematic assimilation here of ancient evil into a contemporary setting, it is necessary to outline the genesis of his companion film for Leone, **Lisa and the Devil** and its' own plot dynamics.

For Bava, **Lisa and the Devil** was very much his "wish" film as he had never previously had a producer willing to grant him the complete artistic licence to film exactly what he wanted to. When Leone offered him virtually "carte blanche" - "He told me the story of Lisa and the Devil and I told him to go ahead with it. I gave him all the freedom he wanted"

Leone reveals.

Having finally secured a guarantee of no inteference and the cast and budget to make his "dream" film, Bava wasted no opportunities in his development of the project, meticulously scouting for locations and incorporating some acutely personal tenets into the film. These included the proliferation of mannikins in **Lisa and the Devil** - something which Bava had grown used to from his formative years which were often spent in his father's sculpture studio, the choice of Elena for a central character - the name of his own sister and his daughter, and augmented by the use of dialogue and music from his own favourites, so elements of Dostoevsky's "The Devils" can be traced along with extracts from Joaquin Rodrigo's stirring orchestral score.

As with **Baron Blood**, it is Elke Sommer who plays a pivotal role as Lisa - "a displaced tourist on a voyage of self-discovery" and also as Elena in a dual/alter-ego performance which recalls Barbara Steele's finest role(s) in **Mask of Satan** (1960). Having studied a fresco depicting the devil, Lisa then confronts a real-life replica in the eccentric figure of Leandro (Telly Savalas).[5] The all pervasive use of mirroring and distorted viewpoints during the film continues as Leandro is seen holding a mannikin, only for Lisa again to confront the "real-life" materialisation in the guise of Carlos (Espartaco Santoni) who inexplicably "mistakes" her for an as yet unknown Elena.

Lisa's subsequent flight from the imposing, claustrophobic village locale leads her to flagging down a chauffeur-driven car where she is given refuge. Unfortunately, for all the occupants, mechanical problems necessitate their stopping at a nearby mansion for assistance. The bickering couple of Francis Lehar (Eduardo Fajardo) and his predatory wife Sophie (Sylva Koscina), the chauffeur George (Gabrielle Tinti), along with Lisa, are introduced to their impromptu hosts - the Countess (Alida Valli), her son Maximillian (Alessio Orano) and their butler.... Leandro.

What, with the all-encompassing azure-tinted fog and the sprawling estate enveloped by menacing woods , it is no surprise when Lisa, jolted upon discovering that the watch worn by Carlos on their initial encounter is now in her room, is then mortified at seeing his haunting face. [6]

The nebulous mood is accentuated as at dinner, Sophie confesses to the Countess that; "The entire setting is so right for a tall tale of gloom and perdition. We could make one up as we go along. We have all the right

ingredients. The dark night, this house, it's all so spooky. I prefer ghosts to vampires though, they're so much more human. They have a tradition to live up to. Somehow they managed to keep all the horror in without spilling any blood." Cue - a sudden crash upstairs, floorboards creaking and the sound of someone falling ? This provides a suitably tense and dramatic coda to Sophie's acutely-observed speech.

It is at this point that the surrealistic, often sedate tempo is radically altered as the bloodletting begins and we start to uncover an increasingly macabre web of deceit, betrayal, unrequited love, insanity, perversion and ultimately, death.

Having juxtaposed the guests' discovery that the Countess is actually blind (and yet apparently still all seeing, all knowing), with Lisa's first "flashback" which sees her as Elena courting Carlos in the estate grounds, Bava uses these revelations as the catalyst for further extremes of human behaviour. These involve the murder of the chauffeur outside as his throat is cut. The felicitous Sophie who, when distraught at the death of her clandestine lover then wreaks her own revenge by driving the car into her husband before running him over repeatedly - his body buffeted under the wheels like a discarded rag doll.

With the adrenalin still flowing we then glimpse Lisa with Carlos in a room full of mannequins only for Carlos to be struck by a gold staff. Sophie is a short-lived witness to this assault as, pursued through the house, she too is eventually clubbed to death - the camera pulling back to reveal the red-cloaked and now patently unhinged Maximillian/Max as the attacker.

The dark, deadly family secret is then unravelled as a sordid case of illicit affairs - of the mysterious Elena spurning Max's advances in favour of his own stepfather, Carlos. With Elena's apparent "rebirth" in the guise of Lisa, Max is unable to control his emotions and seeks to this time consummate their relationship by destroying all who endanger his plans.

Max's final thread of sanity is eroded however, with the discovery of his bedroom shrine to Elena - her atrophying remains adorning the bed, complete with grinning skull. That Max's ravishing of Lisa and his subsequent orgasm can only be achieved under the "watchful" gaze of Elena's decomposing corpse merely serves to confirm his descent into insanity.

The Countess' perceptive comment regarding Lisa; "That girl will be the end of us" proves to be prophetic, especially for her, as she finds herself impaled on a sword wielded by Max before the final grisly tableaux as all the assorted victims are seated at a wedding reception - complete with nuptial cake and Elena in black veil, whereupon the wounded Countess moves menacingly towards Max causing him to fall to his death from the high-level window.

We then cut to Lisa awakening on a foliage-strewn bed before emerging from the mansion grounds and entering the village again, only this time seeing Leandro with another mannikin - her own. Her speedy departure aboard a charter plane provides a fittingly surrealistic finale to the film - suddenly finding the plane deserted she hears a familiar voice imparting the passenger information over the intercom. Her worst nightmare is confirmed as she discovers all the victims now sat aboard the plane and her investigation of the cockpit reveals the pilot to be... Leandro, who cries out "Elena" whereupon she feints to the floor.

This then completes Bava's "fever-dream" vision and yet even this remained unseen in its' entirety until recent years due to the film's artistic and critical success but resounding commmercial failure.

As Leone himself explained to Tim Lucas regarding the film's premiere at Cannes in 1973; "There was a tremendous turnout and no one left the theatre during the screening. We even held additional screenings to packed houses but there were no buyers. I couldn't give the film away."

Like the similar problems encountered at the same time by the previously prolific (and hugely successful) Hammer Films, **Lisa and the Devil** was ironically, given its "timeless" quality, considered too subtle, too sophisticated in the wake of the astounding commercial success of **The Exorcist** (1973)[7] with its' graphic, special-effects driven portrayal of demonic possession.

So, having been consigned to virtual limbo and gathering dust in the studio vaults, Leone set about recutting the film and resurrecting its' commercial appeal and **House of Exorcism** was born in 1975. This hybrid version contained both Lisa footage and additional footage of Summer doing her best Linda Blair performance from **The Exorcist**, being strapped to a hospital bed, spewing forth toads, pea soup, profanities and impromptu levitations.

As Leone revealed; "There was a combination of scenes involving Elke that Mario refused to film. Mario's sister was a nun and he was a very superstitious man. At certain points during filming he would refuse to go any further. He would take Elke aside and tell her not to say those words, the profanity and what not. At such points I had to take over and he would go out and wait in the corridor. We had a falling out over this, eventually, so I had to complete the picture myself. Bava had nothing to do with the editing or the final assembling of the film."

As Bava himself later commented on the making of **House of Exorcism**; "It's not a movie of mine, although there's my name on it. It's the same situation, too long to explain, of a cuckold father with a son, who is not his own, but has his name and he can't do anything about it." Subsequently, Leone and Bava reconciled their differences and Bava's name was indeed restored to Italian prints of the film, **La Case dell'exorcismo** in place of Leone's pseudonymous director credit of Mickey Lion.

Given this torturous route to finally unveiling Bava's delerious original edited version, the fact that **Lisa and the Devil** is now generally considered by critics to be one of his most diverse and fascinating works provides a fitting (if postumous) coda to Bava's unique vision.

So what of Bava's personal obsessions and thematic components then and how do they synthesise within the cadre of both **Baron Blood** and **Lisa and the Devil** ?

As Leone's comments bear out, one of Bava's most overriding preoccupations concerned the profound irony of religious faith and secular belief being interwoven (albeit uncomfortably), into the diverse fabric of modern society. The notion that ancient myths and religious rituals could still prevail and influence in a seemingly agnostic contemporary society was one which captivated Bava throughout his career but most pointedly, in his duo of Leone collaborations.

Lisa and the Devil

As Peter's uncle, Karl (Massimo Girotti) succinctly observes in **Baron Blood** - "We live in an enlightened age, where science not only reveals the old mysteries as mere superstitions, but little by little discovers the true mysteries of the universe." He then sounds a germane warning that; "I would not play with the occult if I were you. One's obsession with it can be the real danger."

Given that this followed on barely three years after the notorious Charles Manson[8] murders and the subsequent growth in popularity of alternative religions, new age theories and homeopathic medicines, I'm sure that Bava would have allowed himself a wry smile if still alive today, at the prophetic nature of Karl's comments.

The fact that the Baron is resurrected by ancient incantations and not modern medicine - reinforced as the Baron ironically seeks out a doctor to "cure" his hideous wounds but contemporary medicine does not prevail whilst the Baron's sadistic force does, as he leaves the doctor lying bleeding to death and the on-rushing ambulance the doctor has alerted with a futile trip.

In a similar way, the incongrous sight of the death-black car set amidst the gothic mansion and medieval town in Lisa and the Devil suggests that modern conveniences are perhaps not what they appear and it is noticeable that it is the modern car's mechanical failure which draws the ill-fated protagonists into seeking help from the Countess' deranged family.

On a tangenital thematic level, **Lisa and the Devil** also questions our belief in fundamental aspects of our society. Bava's continual use of distorted reflections in filthy mirrors implies a distortion of our perceived "reality" as glimpsed in these surfaces, along with the suggestion that there is a parallel metaphysical universe to our own. Ditto, watches stop and we have a timeless limbo or twilight zone suggested to us, emphasised in the seemingly non-linear dream'flashback sequence Lisa experiences.

Lisa herself awakens during the final scenes in a verdant setting, her bed draped in fauna and shot through soft-focus filters which indicates a regression to the beginning, the genesis of the human race. It is also noticeable that in **Baron Blood** the childhood innocence of Gretchen (Nicoletta Elmi) is tempted by a fallen apple - only her "garden of Eden" contains the snake in the grass that is the Baron - his gnarled hand revealing his presence in the bushes, followed by his extended but fruitless pursuit of the frightened little girl.

Temptation, albeit in the form of modern greed and avarice are none better illustrated than in the death of Her Dortmund (Dieter Treder) in **Baron Blood**. His company's corporate raiders are seeking to transform the castle into a hotel and at one point, Eva goes to investigate "what your workers are destroying" within the ancient structure.

Dortmund however, gets his just deserts, having slotted his money into the neon-lit drinks machine garishly located against the arcane castle walls and the Baron strikes - strangling his victim. The presence of a treasure chest full of gold previously secreted away by the Baron no doubt has also fuelled Dortmund's "interest" in the castle.

Eva's own psychadelic wardrobe - mini-skirts and close-fitting sweaters exhibit an equally jarring visage when set against the drab walls of the castle, whilst in **Lisa and the Devil**, the regal, stately demeanour of the Countess appears at odds with the remaining participants who exude lust, greed and bewilderment in equal measures rather than civilised manners.

Given the strong sense of pre-ordained fates which seemingly envelop the doomed characters, it is interesting to note the influence of one of Bava's contemporaries, the Belgian director Harry Kumel. Kumel only made two full length features during the early 1970's - the sapphic **Daughters of Darkness** (1971) and the outre **Malpertuis** (1972)[9], before then bizarrely consigning himself to the relative backwaters of working in Flemish television.

It is the latter entry which most interests us here in relation to Bava. **Malpertuis** revolves around an eccentric collection of guests gathering in an old dark house, who are revealed to be greek gods, sewn into human skin for the amusement of explorer/taxidermist Cosavius (Orson Welles) for his own delectation.

As Steve Guariento [10] has noted, Cosavius bears a striking resemblance to the role of Telly Savalas' Leandro in **Lisa and the Devil**. Both figures are seen as toying with the mortals fate has earmarked for their collection, in the same way that Bava is toying with his characters in order to create his (and our ?) playthings.

The numerous life-like mannequins which we see Leandro carrying in **Lisa and the Devil** are literally his toys - his collection of "souls" if you will as in repeated scenes, the distinction between human and mannikin is deliberately blurred by Bava.

The very opening titles of **Lisa and the Devil** also indicate

Leandro as the "puppetmaster" as we see (his) white-gloved hands playing tarot cards - life becomes a game, a game of chance or fate. Take your pick. Bava then cuts immediately to the figure of Leandro in an antique shop - his face a replica of the fresco-depicted devil glimpsed only moments earlier by Lisa.

The continual use of mannikins or "dummies" in Lisa and the Devil reaffirms the sense that the characters are mere playthings, porns on a human chessboard. In the same way, just as Leandro is associated with the devil, so too is the Baron the personnification of evil in **Baron Blood** as he gradually decimates the cast list.

Again, as with **Lisa and the Devil** there is an overwhelming feeling from the beginning that the Baron will re-emerge, only Bava provides the characters with both his means of resurrection and the amulet to herald his destruction.

Both films also lend credence to the notion that the sins of the father will be visited upon their children. From the very opening scenes of **Baron Blood** we can glean that Peter has an unhealthy interest with his infamous ancestor - "I'm particularly fascinated by the ghoulish Baron on my father's side" he confesses and his later barely concealed glee at acquainting himself with the Baron's macabre torture chamber leads him to conjecture; "I wonder how many victims the Baron tortured with these trinkets".

As soon as he is familiar with the legend of the curse placed upon the Baron, Peter is seemingly hell-bent on reciting the incantation in order that his nefarious ancestor will materialise. Common sense and rationale fly out of the window and the fact that Peter has just gained his degree at university emphasises that modern "intelligence" can still be hamstrung by ancient beliefs.

Likewise in **Lisa and the Devil** we see the haunted family skeletons of the Countess' lineage displayed eventually for all to see - any hereditary status and breeding sacrificed on the heady altar of human weakness and perversity.

The sins of the stepfather Carlos' indescretions with Elena not only infects the Countess with feelings of guilt, but transfers them to her son, Max, who out of some misplaced sense of loyalty to Elena, maintains her grisly shrine and attempts to recapture her image as embodied in the flesh by Lisa.

Such instances of family rifts, dysfunctional behaviour and their perverse actions not only inform much of Bava's output but also epitomise some of the most salient motiffs throughout the Italian horror tradition.

Bava also exhibits his own zeal for the anti-hero, the miscreants in both **Baron Blood** and **Lisa and the Devil** at the expense of the (by comparison) vapid "heroic" leads. Thus, in **Baron Blood** Bava enjoys building up the Baron's history and reputation in classic horror movie style before the mangled one's dramatic entrance serves to increase the tension.

Leandro's wicked sense of humour is a constant theme running through Lisa and the Devil, whether he is breaking the legs of a corpse to cram it into a coffin and joking "Say it with flowers" and nonchalantly rearranging the numerous mannequins/corpses as is his want, to the oneiric denouement where he assumes the role of aircraft pilot on the charter flight which belongs in the realms of nightmares.

Ultimately, the charge generally levelled at Bava (and many other directors working specifically within the horror and sci-fi fantasy genres) is that his films betray a sense of style over substance. Whilst there is certainly an argument to consider that style can be of pre-eminence, this is not the time to argue such polemics as I believe that Bava demonstrates sufficient substance, even with the often penny-dreadful scripts he frequently worked from, to refute such claims in any case.

One can certainly see from the prevalent themes outlined above that there is plenty of sub-textural work going on in Bava's films if you are prepared to dig deeply enough to locate it.

Baron Blood

That said, both **Baron Blood** and **Lisa and the Devil** illustrate Bava's acute understanding of the mechanics of horror and the dynamics of terror and also demonstrate just what can be achieved when a director maintains his distinctive style whilst simultaneously attempting to to delineate lapsing moral standards and expanding "ethical" boundaries.

With this in mind, Bava's camera is ever zooming, rapidly arrowing in on characters as if to identify them as "victims" in direct violation of the more considered framing of the classical close-up shot. When Bava uses a close-up it is often to gain maximum impact from the latest pool of blood to encompass the screen as we are awash with murder, mayhem and bloodshed. Wipe away the gossamer strands of the gothic milieu and you will see the utilisation of almost de riguer horror motifs in energising fashion by a master at work.

So, the ancient castle looms large in **Baron Blood** whilst in **Lisa and the Devil** it is a sprawling, remote mansion. In the former film we are informed of the locals' fearful suspicion of the Baron and his legend in a thinly-veiled correlation with those two bastions of the gothic genre; Baron Frankenstein and Count Dracula (via Vlad the Impaler), whilst in the latter, the sheer isolation of the nebulous family estate suggests a haunted past if nothing else.

Eva and Peter's invocation of the malevolent Baron - is a triumph of the classic horror tradition transcending common sense as is also so expertly satirised in Wes Craven's Scream. [11] So, the couple blindly recant the script knowing full well that if the curse prevails, then the Baron will return in all his bloody glory. It is demons of a different kind which are invoked from ancient tomes in Sam Raimi's kinetic **Evil Dead** series.[12]

In **Lisa and the Devil** it is a classic combination of "don't run into the forboding woods at night" and "don't flee aimlessly down corridors in expansive houses" which spell danger for Lisa in the first instance and death for Sophie in the second.

Bava's love of German expressionism also punctuates both of these films to a high degree as both feature snaking, narrow alleyways, full of menace and towering ancient buildings which soar skywards, especially given Bava's low-angle camera shots to accentuate the intimidating, claustrophobic confines of the locales. That the same arcane streets in both films stretch away into the distance, unnervingly recreates the style of surrealist artists such as Giorgio de Chirico and the use of mannequins in

Lisa and the Devil, besides recalling Bava's father, also evokes the spirit of Chirico again and Rene Magritte. [13]

That a permanent incandescent fog swirls around both locales also heightens the gothic atmosphere, as does the cogent scene in **Baron Blood** where the psychic is introduced, partially to explain the gaping holes in the plot (!), but also to provide the characters with the modus operandi (an amulet) for destroying the Baron, but mainly to recapture the vertiginous gothic heights of his earlier films. Bava even has one character, Fritz (Luciano Pigozzi) impaled in an iron maiden in **Baron Blood** in homage to Barbara Steele's spiked face mask demise in **Mask of Satan** and the aforementioned "face at the window" in **Lisa and the Devil** conjures up poetic moments from both Bava's **Black Sabbath** and **Curse of the Dead**.

Bava also adds a decidedly surrealistic edge to the proceedings in both films - a style he is not readily noted for. This is mainly evinced in **Baron Blood** during the Baron's pursuit of Eva at night - the ominously silent streets and kaleidoscopic use of colour lending the scenes an ethereal quality.

The even more enigmatic **Lisa and the Devil** recalls surrealism-guru Alain Resnais' **Last Year in Marienbad** (1960) [14], in parts with its' fragmented narrative and its' lack of a final interpretation - an insoluble enigma in effect. The "wedding reception" scenes here also recall the supreme surrealist of them all - Bunuel with their "Last Supper" connotations. Staple horror film accoutrements including grisly killings and death by sharp implements are capably realised in each film for the cognoscenti to revel at.

After the careful cultivation of the reborn Baron in Baron Blood his anticipated killing spree is probably rather more rapid than one would expect but then Bava was always willing to pre-empt the "slasher" films phenomenon of the late 1970's and early 1980's. His groundbreaking double-impalement of victims in **Bay of Blood** later reappeared to more commercially viable effect in **Friday the Thirteenth** (1980).

So, the dramatic hanging of Dortmund in **Baron Blood** was to later inform Dario Argento's **Suspiria** (1976) - only this time with a double death, and Lucio Fulci's **City of the Living Dead** (1980) as a priest swings limply in his own cemetery, a rope around his neck.

Echoes of such violence resound in **Lisa and the Devil** where the sight of an up-raised arm with murder weapon poised to strike spells doom for more than one victim and the macabre "wedding" tableaux resurfaces to chilling effect in Michel Soavi's ably-crafted **Stagefright**.

Crimes of passion coupled with the dead returning to life have always skirted the uneasy taboo of necrophilia and with this brace of films, Bava confronts the thorny subject to varying degrees.

In **Baron Blood** there is no overt mention of such evil deeds but the climactic confrontation inside the torture chamber - with an alternative outcome - the Baron triumphing, wouldn't stretch the imagination too much to see the Baron make advances on the nubile figure of Eva before, during and after torturing her !

With the case of **Lisa and the Devil**, partly "inspired" by an unrealised project about necrophile Viktor Ardisson, the references are far more overt - especially during Max's molestation of the drugged Lisa, lying adjacent to the rotting remains of Max's beloved Eleanor.

Although Max's obsession is convincingly portrayed, the seminal work in this disquieting area remains Riccardo Freda's macabre hymn **The Terror of Dr. Hitchcock** (1962). [15]

So, enough of these undoubted Bava successes in merging ancient evil with the modern world but who can we now hold up as his most fitting successor. His own son Lamberto flickered brightly with his debut feature **Macabre** before then being sucked into the artistic quicksand of Italian television.

Of Argento, the gialli remains more of a driving force than the gothic and Soavi still produces inconsistent and erratic work concerning both his choice of projects and the differing style he assumes for each one.

What price then someone who can take the memory of Bava's gothic flair whilst still inaugurating modern ,fantastical thematics to propel the Italian gothic cinema forward into the next millenium and beyond ?

NOTES

1.   Media manipulation in **To Die For** centres around Nicole Kidman's small town girl Suzanne Stone, with a big time dream - to become a famous television personality. This dream in reality, becomes an obsession as well as a salutory observation on modern society as events are only deemed to be of "importance" if bestowed with the oxygen of tv exposure. The reality here is that if it's not on tv it doesn't exist.

Stone's **Natural Born Killers** caused an almost inevitable furore upon its' release with its' duo of deranged psychos lining up and (sporadically) hitting a multitude of targets in contemporary American society and especially the media, though the film is instantly burdened with the "condoning what it purports to condemn" tag.

Amiel's inveigling **Copycat** explores a serial killer at large who is literally replaying infamous serial murderer's including John Gacy, Ted Bundy and Jeffrey Dahmer and using their individual modus operandi as the "inspiration" for his crimes, aided by the global media attention given to these miscreants.

The show trial mentality of increasing media coverage is alluded to by Sigourney Weaver's protagonist who declares pointedly; "We spent 8 million dollars on executing Ted Bundy. Wouldn't it have been better to spend the money on studying him scientifically."

As writer Poppy Z Brite has also observed; "...violent films and publicity given to serial killers can provide a blueprint for nascent killers."

In David Fincher's unremittingly bleak **Seven** the sadistic killer John Doe (Kevin Spacey), has read too many newspapers and watched too much television as he puts his own distorted interpretation on the "diseased" society he inhabits, leading to his eventual atrocities which are carried out with religious conviction.

Wes Craven's knowing **Scream** manages to segue a number of horror movie cliches with media exploitation as portrayed in Courtenay Cox's news reporter who hounds the potential victims almost as much as the Munchian-masked killer.

2. Price stars as a mad sculptor who turns human corpses into wax exhibits and his pursuit of Phyllis Kirk through gaslit streets is the film's most effective scene and a clear inspiration for Bava.

3. The omnipresent Egdon Heath represents a sprawling landscape which dominates Hardy's novel, its' natural beauty and its' hidden danger continually guides the plot development to a greater degree than the protagonists do. The Heath's enigmatic qualities are encapsulated in one line of Hardy's prose; "In the heath's baroness to the farmer lay its' fertility to the historian."

4. The cloaked Baron shambling through the eerie night mist is affectionately parodied by Bava fans Joe Dante and Allan Arkush in their debut feature HollywoodBoulevard.

5. Savalas also starred alongside Peter Cushing and Christopher Lee to good effect as a zombified cossack in Eugene Martin's energetic **Horror Express**, before going on to fame as the lollipop-sucking detective in the *Kojak* tv series - his sweet-sucking habit formed during his Leandro characterisation in **Lisa and the Devil.**

6. The haunting image of a face looming from out of the darkness to peer in at a window was pioneered by Bava in "The Wurdalak" episode of **Black Sabbath** and later in his **Curse of the Dead**.

7. Linda Blair's tour de force as a 12 years old girl Regan possessed by a demon

included urinating on the carpet, vomiting green bile over a priest and masturbating violently with a crucifix, all aiding the confrontational film to become the (then) most commercially successful horror film of all time. The use of such graphic special effects and make-up heralded the onset of the special-effects driven film as opposed to the period gothic's of Bava, Hammer et al.

8. Charles Manson, the notorious American cult leader of the drop-out group known as the "Family" and the mastermind of the graphic murders on the 8th August 1969 of actress Sharon Tate (and her unborn baby), along with companions Jay Sebring, Voytek Crycowski, Abigail Folger and Steven Parent, at the house in Cielo Drive, LA owned by Tate's husband, the film director Roman Polanski.

9. Kumel's **Daughters of Darkness** is a heady cocktail of surrealism, camp and lesbian chic courtesy of Delphine Seyrig's compelling performance as the infamous Countess Bathory via Marlene Dietrich ! Malpertuis adopts an approach of flamboyant fantasy which somewhat dilutes Jean Ray's original source novel which fuses the idea of Greek gods with the perverse world of the tawdry characters within the film and so loses the horror generated by the juxtaposition of the two seemingly incompatible worlds.

10. A three issue feature in Samhain magazine.

11. Craven's phenomenally successful revisionist **Scream** includes elongated scenes of characters stepping out of relatively safe, well-lit houses and into dark, forboding areas immediately outside, in outhouses and in garages with predictably fatal consequences.

12. Sam Raimi's **The Evil Dead, Evil Dead 2 - Dead By Dawn** and **Army of Darkness** feature possessed characters returning as demons following incantations and tape recordings read/played out aloud from (in this case) the ancient tome "The Necronomicon" or "Book of the Dead".

13. Such surrealist artists as Chirico and Magritte influenced numerous continental directors such as Jean Rollin and Alain Robbe-Grillet whose La Belle Captive (The Beautiful Prisoner) was based on Magritte's painting of the same name.

14. Alain Resnais' **Last Year in Marienbad** was one of the quintessential art films of the 1960's - a suffocating melodrama where even the minutest of details appears crammed with significance.

15. **The Terror of Doctor Hitchcock** is probably Freda's greatest horror film - a confrontational period melodrama concerning a necrophile, the titular doctor (Robert Flemyng), haunted by his dead wife (Maria Teresa Vianello), when he returns to the family home with his new bride (Barbara Steele) as a highly fetishistic mix of sex and paralysis ensues amidst a supremely gothic atmosphere.

The Modern Fantastic
Michael Grant

The contemporary understanding of fantastic literature is in large part the result of the account of it given by Tzvetan Todorov in The Fantastic, first published in Paris in 1970. On this view, membership of the literary fantastic requires a novel or story to be so structured that it induces a certain hesitation, leaving the reader suspended between two distinct ways of understanding the events depicted: The fantastic requires the fulfilment of three conditions. First, the text must oblige the reader to consider the world of the characters as a world of living persons and to hesitate between a natural and a supernatural explanation of the events described. Second, this hesitation may also be experienced by a character; thus the reader's role is so to speak entrusted to a character, and at the same time the hesitation is represented, it becomes one of the themes of the work - in the case of naive reading, the actual reader identifies himself with the character. Third, the reader must adopt a certain attitude with regard to the text: he will reject allegorical as well as "poetic" interpretations.[1]

The first of the conditions Todorov specifies is sufficient to establish a work as belonging to the genre, while the second need not be fulfilled. The third is a consequence of the first. Typically, then, the fantastic takes the form of an exclusive disjunction, in which the events of the fictional world may be explained in terms of either the supernatural or the natural, but not both. The fantastic exists for as long as there is uncertainty as to which of the two kinds of explanation should prevail. In George Romero's film, **Martin** (1978), the inner experiences of the protagonist are so presented that the viewer is unable to decide whether he is truly a vampire, remembering events that actually took place over a hundred years previously, as his fanatically Catholic elder cousin, Tata Cuda, believes, or a victim of psychotic delusions. The first kind of reading Todorov characterises as 'marvellous', the second as 'uncanny'. It follows from this first condition for establishing the fantastic that allegorical and poetic interpretations are to be excluded. Allegory implies the existence of at least two meanings for the same words: a literal meaning and a second meaning-a division indicated explicitly in the work.

Martin

If what we read describes a supernatural event, yet we take the words not in their literal meaning but in another sense, which refers to nothing supernatural, there is no longer any space in which the fantastic can exist.[2]

A similar prohibition holds in the case of poetry. The fantastic requires a response to events as they occur in a depicted or fictional world, but for Todorov, following Mallarme and the Formalists, poetry is without reference to anything other than itself. It is a pure interplay of rhythm, sound and ambivalence of meaning, leaving no space in which the fantastic can appear. As Tom Gunning has noted, there is a distinction between the self-referential language of poetry and the explicit double meanings of allegory that corresponds to the initial division in Todorov's analysis between the marvellous and the uncanny [3] and the fantastic is suspended between them.

Two problems arise at this point for the idea of the modern fantastic. First, in the literature of the twentieth century, words have gained an autonomy that in earlier literature they lacked. The created or depicted worlds of fiction have been subordinated to language as such, and as a result a seemingly fatal blow has been dealt to the fantastic. Second, a question arises as to religious belief and the plausibility of supernatural explanation, both of which, according to Todorov, have been undermined, notably by the emergence of psychoanalysis. Without recourse to a supernatural explanation of narrative events, the hesitation definitive of the fantastic simply becomes impossible. The question concerning the existence of a modern fantastic is therefore essentially a question concerning the possibility (or otherwise) of the narrative of the supernatural in the twentieth century, and Todorov considers it in the closing pages of his book. Kafka's Metamorphosis provides an answer. The supernatural event is announced in the opening sentence of the story: 'As Gregor Samsa awoke one morning from uneasy dreams he found himself transformed in his bed into a gigantic insect'. There are at first brief indications of hesitation. Gregor thinks that he is dreaming, and though he is soon convinced that this not so, he continues to search for other rational explanations for his condition. However, as Todorov points out, 'these succinct indications of hesitation are drowned out in the general movement of the narrative, in which the most surprising thing is precisely the absence of surprise with regard to the unheard-of event which has befallen Gregor Samsa'.[4] Hesitation has no further role to play.

Metamorphosis begins from a supernatural event, which, during the course of the narrative, is deprived of all supernatural colouring. There is a process of adaptation, which naturalises the inexplicable event, until in the end it becomes unremarkable. It is as though the ordinary and supernatural had fused into a single genre, uniting the uncanny with the marvellous. The story obeys a logic like that of dream or nightmare, constituting a system of its own, unconnected to the real world. Sartre has argued that a writer such as Kafka has no concern with extraordinary beings. For him there is only one extraordinary or fantastic object: man. And what is understood by 'man' in this context is the man of the modern world, the 'normal' man whose values are those of his society, and who adheres to its norms and customs. Such is Gregor Samsa, a commercial traveller, working to support his father, mother and sister. The "normal" man is precisely the fantastic being; the fantastic becomes the rule, not the exception.[5] This is the modern fantastic. Here, the fantastic swallows up the whole world of the book, and the reader with it. The impossible appears as the ordinary, and the monstrous as the everyday. What in the classic definition of the fantastic was an exception becomes, in the modern fantastic, the norm, the rule.

The exigencies laid upon Gregor Samsa are emblematic of the

paradoxical conditions determining the existence of literature itself.

According to the tradition within which Todorov situates himself, a tradition deriving from Hegel, and whose exemplars include Mallarme, Valery and Ponge, the act of writing is inseparable from death-the death of things as things. The act of naming, of substituting a word for a thing or sensation, delivers things to us, but only at the cost of subordinating them to concepts and so depriving them of their being. To write is therefore to murder, and every poem is-as Eliot has it-an epitaph.[6] Maurice Blanchot makes the position clear: For me to be able to say, "This woman" I must somehow take her flesh and blood reality away from her, cause her to be absent, annihilate her. The word gives me the being, but it gives it to me deprived of being. The word is the absence of that being, its nothingness, what is left of it when it has lost its being-the very fact that it does not exist.[7]

Todorov takes a similar view. He argues that literature cannot be simply a tracing or image of reality, of what is not itself. Words do not have their life in relation to the things to which they refer; for writing to be possible it must be born out of the death of what it is speaking about. And yet this death makes writing impossible, since there is no longer anything for writing to engage with. Literature can become possible only insofar as it makes itself impossible. Either what we say is actually here, in which case there is no room for literature; or else there is room for literature, in which case there is no longer anything to say. [8]

The conclusion is inescapable: for writing to be literature it must be literature, and, at the same time and in the same sense, not literature. It seems obvious enough that a statement of this kind amounts to a violation of the law of non-contradiction, that is, that a proposition and its negation cannot both be true. Todorov would thus seem to have committed himself to a genuine contradiction, saying of the same thing that it exists and does not exist. It is, however, a contradiction that is more apparent than real.

The position derives from an identification of a Kantian concern for the possibility of meaning with the 'transcendence' of meaning, with that which is taken to lie beyond meaning. It is an identification-or slippage-that serves to locate the possibility of meaning in its impossibility, and the resulting equivocation, while important for Todorov's critical endeavour concerning the modern fantastic, is fundamental to Blanchot, especially in relation to his exploration of romantic, symbolist and post-symbolist poetry, a poetry he encounters crucially in the work of Hˆlderlin, Mallarme and Rilke. What contradiction amounts to here is the proposal that within the actual practice of specific poets a set of conflicting assertions is put into play, and the resulting self-conscious juxtaposition of different perspectives on what is represented calls the status of literature into question. As Eliot puts it, in Burnt Norton: 'Words strain,/Crack and sometimes break, under the burden,/Under the tension, slip, slide, perish,/Decay with imprecision, will not stay in place,/Will not stay still'. It is this idea of writing that Todorov draws on for his discussion of the modern fantastic, and by so doing he finally effects a synthesis between the fantastic and poetry, despite the fact that his earlier definition had depended on a clear distinction between the two. The modern fantastic does not induce hesitation concerning what it represents; it stands in a hesitant relation to itself. It is an art based on equivocation and ambivalence, and like the poetry of symbolism it attends above all to the process of its own coming into being. In this sense, it may be said to articulate its own impossibility. As Rosemary Jackson has noted, the fantastic understood in this way is based on a split between things that have no names ('It', 'The Thing', and so on) and empty signs, which are devoid of meaning (names such as Lovecraft's Cthulhu or Nyarlathotep, or Poe's 'bobok'), and whose only reality derives from their own palpability as words.[9] Jackson quotes Sartre, who considers the modern fantastic, as exemplified by Blanchot's Kafka-like recit, Aminadab, to be a language of non-signifying signs, which lead nowhere. They are means without ends, which appear full and yet are capable of achieving only a terrible emptiness.

The law of the fantastic condemns it to encounter instruments only. These instruments are not...meant to serve men, but rather to manifest unremittingly an evasive, preposterous finality. This accounts for the labyrinth of corridors, doors and staircases that lead to nothing, the innumerable signs that line the road and that mean nothing. In the 'topsy-turvy' world, the means is isolated and is posed for its own sake.[10]

*

The conception of language as essentially a matter of naming, and the related notion, of the word as the murderer of the thing, underpin both Blanchot and Todorov's ideas on literature. However, there are problems here. As Wittgenstein has pointed out, naming is only a preparation for something else:

Naming is...not a move in the language-game? any more than

The Thing

putting a piece in its place on the board is a move in chess. We may say: nothing has so far been done, when a thing is named. It has not even got a name except in the language-game.[11]

In learning to speak we learn what can be said. We learn, however uncertainly and hesitantly, what it makes sense to say. A child comes to have an idea of how different remarks have something to do with one another, how they are interconnected, and in this way can be said to be learning the language-game. As Rush Rhees makes clear, as the child is learning to answer you and ask you things, and beginning to follow a conversation or to carry on a conversation herself, she is getting a sense of how remarks bear on each other.[12] Because the child learns this, she can go on speaking and go on learning. While not all speech is conversation, it seems clear that there would be no speech or language without it. As Rhees remarks, if there were someone who was unable to hold a conversation, who had no idea of asking questions or making any comment, then it seems unlikely we would say that this person was able to speak. We learn from a conversation, and we learn from what is said in it, and this fact of intelligibility, the fact that we understand each other, is the unity that language has. Not only this, but in order understand people we must understand more than the language. We must understand what people are talking about, what matters to them, what values they hold to, what experiences they share, and so on. We do not talk to each other in order to make ourselves intelligible. Intelligibility is found in the ways we talk to each other-in what we say. Hence, naming only takes place in the context of understanding other people and the lives they lead. It makes no sense to think of it as the foundation of this understanding, or of language in general.

Blanchot and Todorov assume that words take the place of something else, the objects whose lack or 'death' they stand in for. Words are exchanged for objects in the way coins are exchanged for commodities in a financial transaction. However, if one considers the exchanges that take place in a currency, it is clear that no exchange of a similar kind takes place in a conversation. Words and sentences do not have 'value' in the way coins do, and they are not taken in exchange for anything. Furthermore, our understanding of what people are saying to us depends on the fact that we share a way of living. There is an intimate relation between the language people speak and the fundamental assumptions they have in common. As Wittgenstein remarks: 'Knowledge is in the end based on acceptance'.[13] A child learns things by accepting what she is told by parents and teachers, and as adults we rely on what we are told by others, what we read and hear.

Must I not somewhere begin to trust? That is to say: somewhere I must begin with not-doubting; and that is not, so to speak, hasty but excusable: it is part of judging.[14]

The child can only learn by trusting the adult. Doubt is something that comes later, and it presupposes belief. It is in this context that Wittgenstein raises the question of how this sense of trust and shared assumption about how the world is would be affected if some extraordinary event took place.

What if something really unheard-of happened? - If, say, I saw houses gradually turning into steam without any apparent cause; if the cattle in the fields stood on their heads and laughed and spoke comprehensible words; if trees gradually changed into men and men into trees. Now, was I right when I said before all these things happened `I know that's a house', etc., or simply `That's a house', etc.?[15]

For Wittgenstein, one possibility is that an event of this order would take away his ability to make any judgements at all. His entire sense of what judgement is, of what thinking is, would be undermined: 'But what would make me doubt whether this person here is N.N., whom I have known for years? Here a doubt would seem to drag everything with it and plunge it into chaos'.[16] In Metamorphosis, the unheard-of occurrence is responded to as if it were an inconvenience, a distressing nuisance that interferes with the everyday course of life. Normality is asserted in the face of an event by which judgement and normality have been wholly undermined, and yet it is a subversion whose totality is nowhere acknowledged. The narrative continues to employ established modes of intelligible ordering: there are conversations, descriptions, a clear presentation of emotional response (of shame, humiliation, anger, and so on), and a coherently presented sequence of events. And yet it is as though the world had somehow been turned inside out, with the impossible becoming not merely the possible but the ordinary. If we are to find the possibility of literature in its impossibility then it is here that we should look. One might say of Kafka what Hugh Kenner has said of Eliot, that his is a 'difficult art, the art of creating with an air of utter precision concepts one cannot localize'.[17] We are at once inside a world of intelligible meaning, and beyond it, in a place where meaning gives way to a silence, a silence in which, as Blanchot would have it, nothing speaks.

In art of this kind, words become divorced from our common practices of using them. In this it exhibits a similarity to that exile of language, or threat of it, that for Wittgenstein was induced by the aspirations of metaphysics: When philosophers use a word-"knowledge", "being", object", "I", "proposition", "name"-and try to grasp the essence of the thing, one must always ask oneself; is the word ever actually used in this way in the language-game which is its original home?- What we do is bring words back from their metaphysical to their everyday use.[18]

The clarification of philosophical confusion depends on our coming to see how words, such as 'pain', 'grief', 'I', 'name', 'proposition', and so on, are woven into the texture of our lives. One can imagine an animal angry, frightened, unhappy, happy, startled. But hopeful? Why not? Can only those hope who can talk? Only those who have mastered the use of a language. That is to say, the phenomena of hope are modes of a complicated form of life.[19]

For Wittgenstein, a philosophical problem takes the form of not knowing one's way around. One loses one's bearings in language, and words leave one at a loss. The arguments of scepticism, for example, are couched in a speech that denies the importance of our shared forms of life, inasmuch as the sceptic seeks to establish an inhuman and unconditioned certainty concerning the existence of other minds and the world. To repudiate in this way our common life in language is to deprive oneself of meaning and the power of coherent speech, and it is a repudiation that follows from what Stanley Cavell has called a 'chronic distrust of the ordinary'. It is the cardinal sin of philosophy, and he comes upon it not only in scepticism but throughout modern thought, most especially in certain kinds of radical modern sensibility, notably that of deconstruction, but widespread beyond it, and he thinks of it 'as a horror of the common, expressed as a flight from the banal, typically from banal pleasures. It stretches from a horror of the human, to a disgust with bourgeois life, to a certain condescension toward the popular'.[20] It amounts to 'a modern inflection of the prideful human craving to be God, of the perennial human desire to deny one's own humanity'.[21]

It is a craving that finds expression in the modern fantastic, and it is clearly evident in Blanchot's powerful evocations of loss and error, as he explores the attempt of literature to go beyond language and our

The Thing

common way of living, in order to 'take the side of things', and return to the origin, to the silence and materiality of the world before the act of naming annihilated it in its being. What Blanchot is committing himself to is not only an effect of the truancy of words brought about by the philosophical misuse of them, words like 'nothing', 'being', 'origin', 'writing', and so on. More crucially, he is repudiating our common life in language. For Blanchot, everyday speech itself lacks meaning. Our belonging to language is only possible because our words present things through the absence that determines those things. Writing is an attempt to go beyond the bounds of sense in an effort to recapture that absence. The artist does not aim at mastery over things, a mastery acquired from the strangely annihilating power of language. His concern is not with dread in the face of death (the Heideggerian notion of dread) but dread in the face of the existence of things. Death is a power that humanises nature, and gives dignity and meaning to human life. But to enter the night, as did Gregor Samsa, only for the night to end in an awakening and the realisation of one's metamorphosis, is to lose through death the possibility of being mortal. Another man, 'knowing he is dead, struggles in vain to die; death is over there, the great unattainable castle, and life was over there, the native land he left in answer to a false summons; now there is nothing to do but struggle, to work at dying completely, but if you struggle you are still alive; and everything that brings the goal closer also makes the goal impossible'.[22] To experience this is to experience what Blanchot calls 'the impossibility of dying'. It is a sense of irremediable errancy and loss that for him characterises the experience of writing, and one finds exemplary realisation of it in the post-symbolist poetry of *The Waste Land*:

> *Here is no water but only rock*
> *Rock and no water and the sandy road*
> *The road winding above among the mountains*
> *Which are mountains of rock without water*
> *If there were water we should stop and drink*
> *Amongst the rock one cannot stop or think*
> *Sweat is dry and feet are in the sand*
> *If there were only water amongst the rock*
> *Dead mountain mouth of carious teeth that cannot spit*
> *Here one can neither lie nor stand nor sit*
> *There is not even silence in the mountains*
> *But dry sterile thunder without rain*
> *There is not even solitude in the mountains*
> *But red sullen faces sneer and snarl*
> *From doors of mudcracked houses*

The poetic unit of the passage is the line, identified with half-completed sentences or completed sentences that stand in an uncertain relation to the context surrounding them. This emphasis on the line as such means that there is not the subordination of phrase to phrase or line to line that we tend to encounter in earlier poetry, where syntax runs over the line, building up larger rhythmic or rhetorical wholes, based on the strophe, the verse paragraph, and so on. Instead, sentences turn back on themselves or transform themselves unexpectedly into other sentences, a process accentuated by the lack of punctuation. The wavering, uncertain movement this sets up constructs an antiphonal structure that seems to echo-or parody-that typical of certain books of the Old Testament, such as the Song of Solomon, Ecclesiastes or the Psalms, as statements are made, retracted and repeated in other forms, creating an effect of circularity from which there is no clear escape. What is expressed and the means of expression are inseparable. This is poetry comparable to that of St.-John Perse (whom Eliot was to translate in 1931), in which syntax has become like music, fulfilling a function quite different from the role it normally plays in assigning and fixing meaning.

The aim of such writing is that meaning should give way to opacity and ambivalence, only for the loss of meaning to return as a meaningful lack of meaning, an absence of meaning possessed of the force of meaning. The attempt to escape the dominance of meaning is definitive of the poem's project; at the same time, the failure of that project is no less constitutive of it. It is this order of doubling or conflict that indicates what truth in post-symbolist literature amounts to-an experience of irreducible ambiguity. In *The Waste Land*, the oddly hesitant yet insistent rhythms and repeated negations, with their potent evocation of drought and sterility, work to induce a sense of something close to what Blanchot calls 'the error of infinite migration'. He is referring here to what he sees as the obligation placed on the poet to make a world of what is outside the world, and to transform 'error', or the displacement of meaning, into the origin and principle of a constantly renewed and self-critical practice of signification. It is the obligation fundamental to writing, and its central thrust is to force the writer to recognise 'the truth of exile and his own dispersion'.[23]

Seeing *The Waste Land* in these terms, one might say of it what Blanchot has said of literature in general, that its end is to 'maintain the movement, the insecurity and the grief of that which escapes every grasp and all ends'.[24] The purpose of the poem is to open a space 'where what approaches is the nonserious and the nontrue, as if perhaps thence sprang the source of all authenticity'.[25]

*

There is in art, as Blanchot accounts for it, a repudiation of the human and an inevitable return to it. It is a conception that accords high value to equivocation and apparent contradiction. The resulting conflict of elements brings to the fore assumptions that would otherwise remain implicit, and which more conventional forms of expression tend to gloss over. Hence, Blanchot's understanding of art is one that seems peculiarly compatible with the horror film, where ambivalence with respect to established norms is a staple of the genre. I give three examples, the first being from Murnau's **Nosferatu** (1922).

When Hutter crosses the bridge into the land of the demons he is met by a coach, which approaches him at an impossible speed. It stops and he boards it, at the command of the oddly vampiric coachman, only to be carried off at a similar pace. Panic-stricken, he appeals wildly from the coach's window to the coachman, who ignores him. There is a reverse angle cut, and the coach comes towards the camera, this time in slow-motion, and in negative. This shift in the image signals an irruption of loss, which will not be confined to the land of the vampire, but will invade Hutter's home city of Wisborg, carrying with it plague and dereliction only the self-sacrifice of Ellen (Hutter's wife) will have the power to end. Later, when Nosferatu leaves his castle, he needs to load the coffins carrying his native soil onto a wagon before he is able to depart. Hutter, who is locked high inside the castle and unable to escape, looks down on the courtyard below. He sees what we see: the coffins loaded onto the wagon by stop-motion. Similarly, in the hold of the Empusa, the ship carrying Nosferatu to Wisborg, the vampire rises from his coffin by means of superimposition and reverse motion. His death also is a consequence of special effects, as he is dispersed at cockcrow with the rising of the sun, transformed into smoke by means of a superimposed dissolve and fade-out.

The nature of the vampire's existence is made evident by the film's most famous image. When Nosferatu climbs the stairs to Ellen's room, at the end of the film, he appears as a huge shadow, stretching along the wall, and it is as a shadow that he reaches out his hand towards her door, to open it. The identification of the monstrous figure with shadow, slow-motion and other effects and devices of cinema serves to set him apart from the other characters in the film, and yet at the same time it renders him ludicrous. The obviousness of the devices subordinates the originating potencies of the supposedly demonic figure to an all too evident contrivance. However, against this backdrop of artifice the deaths in Wisborg gain in realism. The emptiness of the streets, the grief of the bereaved and Ellen's awareness of what is required of her possess the poignant significance that comes from having a place in a comprehensible, human world.

The ludicrous aspect of what lies outside the human order is an explicit element in the transformation of Norris in **The Thing** (1982). After Dr Copper has applied a defibrillator to his chest, Norris's ribcage opens, revealing a set of teeth which close on the doctor's arms, cutting

The Thing

them off, as tentacles and yellow slime spill out of the rest of the body and shoot up in a spectacular display to form a leering parody of Norris's head. Not content with this, Norris's neck stretches down the side of the table his body is lying on, and his head shoots out a long tongue to pull itself under another table, which is close by. Now upside down, the head acquires two eyes rising on stalks on each side of it, at the same time as it generates spider-legs. The insect-like entity now scuttles off, while the men are attempting to burn what remains on the table. As Palmer sees it disappearing out of the door, he utters the defining line of the film: 'You've gotta be fucking kidding'.

Anne Billson wishes to assimilate the spider-head to psychoanalytic notions of castration, backing up her case by reference to Judith and Salome, femmes fatales of the decadent movement, whose castrating power derives from their painterly association with the severed heads of Holofernes and John the Baptist, respectively.[26] However, neither Judith nor Salome plays a role in late nineteenth century art that is any way comparable to that of the alien shape-changer of Carpenter's imagination. Nor is there any comparison between the iconography of the film and that of, say, Moreau's *The Apparition*, which might justify the reference. In addition, there is something spectacularly unserious and meaningless in the spider-head transformation, to which Palmer's response is entirely appropriate, and it is this that points to an ambiguity, as between what has meaning and what is without it, that underpins the whole film, and which Billson's psychoanalytic reading misses.

The human community of the research station is faced with an impossible and paradoxical entity, The Thing, each of whose parts is identical to the whole, a condition incommensurate with logic. Furthermore, The Thing cannot die. As we learn at the beginning of the film, it has survived in the ice for tens of thousands of years, and lived for eons before that.[27] Its mode of existence is not that of a virus or parasite. It is-as the film presents it-wholly incomprehensible.[28] And it is precisely this unheard-of being the film's characters are forced to acknowledge. In order to struggle against it, MacReady and the rest of the crew have to strive to understand an entity, a thing, beyond language and inaccessible to the image, which nonetheless is able to transform itself into a perfect imitation of living flesh and speak with cogency and point.[29]

The impossibility on which the film is based comes to a focus at the end, as MacReady and Childs sit opposite each other in the ruins of the research station, drinking from the same bottle of whiskey. The fires consuming the buildings are beginning to die down and the cold is starting to penetrate. Either one of them-or neither-may be, or may yet become, The Thing. What The Thing confronts them with is not death, however, but the dread of being possessed by something that will not die and cannot be killed. It is a possibility Poe describes in *Premature Burial* as the ultimate horror, that of being confined within an inescapable experience of existence, with no way out.

Critical writing on the fantastic and on the horror film has drawn on Julia Kristeva's discussion of abjection, in support of the view that what in these types of cinema brings about a transcendence of meaning is bodily disintegration and the cadaver. The corpse, seen without God and outside of science, is the utmost of abjection. It is death infecting life.'[30]

Kristeva is here pointing to the body as such, the body without a soul and outside the realm of religious or spiritual recuperation. Cannibal movies are clear examples of this, as are films of possession, such as **The Exorcist** or **Rosemary's Baby**, vampire and zombie films, or films like **Psycho** or **Carrie**. The ambiguity of the object of defilement disturbs identity and system, threatening to engulf us in what is undifferentiated and meaningless. This family of ideas undoubtedly owes a considerable debt to Blanchot, and yet for him the corpse does not simply lie outside, in the beyond of abjection. More disturbingly, he sees in the condition of the corpse a condition which is also that of art. The cadaver is reflection making itself master of the reflected life, absorbing it, substantially identifying itself with it by making it lose its value in terms of use and value and change into something incredible-unusual and neutral.[31]

It is as the cadaver falls out of the world of identity and affection that the dead person comes to resemble himself. The corpse is an image of the man who was alive, and yet it is an image whose physical density seems to have absorbed him into itself. No longer related to the world, in which nonetheless it still appears, the corpse offers itself to us, but only as it withdraws into its own elemental strangeness, taking with it the man whose image it still is. The corpse is a reflection that reflects nothing and no one. The condition may be compared with that of a damaged tool, whose connection with use and function has been ruptured. The broken implement appears as an image of itself, abandoned to a pure resemblance, behind which there is nothing. No longer obscured by its use, it simply appears. So with art: the image serves to absorb what it depicts into its own material density, so that what has surrendered itself to the image appears as what it is, imaginary. Hence, the image of an object is not the meaning of that object. The image 'tends to withdraw the object from its meaning and to maintain it in the immobility of a resemblance that has nothing to resemble'.[32] The image appears as image.

In **Twin Peaks: Fire Walk With Me** (1992), David Lynch establishes image and threshold as categories no less fundamental to the film than those of psychology and narrative. One might instance this by reference to the framed photograph acquired by Laura Palmer, about halfway through the film. While Laura is engaged on the mundane task of loading meals-on-wheels into a station-wagon sometime one afternoon, an elderly woman emerges out of the woods surrounding Twin Peaks. She is

accompanied by a mysterious boy, his face covered by a white mask, with a sharp, extended nose and lacking eyeholes. The woman beckons to Laura, and hands her the photograph. At dinner that evening, Laura is submitted to a violently abusive verbal onslaught by her father, Leland, for not washing her hands before sitting down to eat. Leland is possessed by Bob, who is both a demonic presence and a projection of his incestuous desires. Leland has committed the first murder in the film, that of Teresa Banks, a waitress of Laura's age, whom he beat to death. He will murder Laura in the same way.

Later, in bed, Laura watches a painting on her wall, showing an angel looking down on three curly-headed children. It is a work of considerable sentimentality. As she watches, the angel disappears from the painting. Laura rises, and takes it off the wall, staring at it in disbelief. She then hangs the photograph in its place. It shows a half-opened door, with light from a source somewhere over the threshold. Laura goes back to her bed, and stares at the photograph, before falling asleep. There is then a cut, to what seems to be a subjective shot, from Laura's point of view, as the camera, now within the space of the photograph, tracks towards the door. As it passes over the threshold, another space opens up, invisible from the photograph, with a further door beyond. The elderly woman is waiting, urging Laura on, and the camera continues slowly forward, through a second door. A boy (presumably the boy with the mask, though he is now unmasked) is positioned on the far side of it. He raises his right arm, and clicks his fingers.

The scene is gradually transformed, by means of a colour change and slow dissolve, until the screen is filled with the image of a red curtain, which in turn gives way, through another dissolve, to the Red Room itself. The camera moves along the floor, patterned in black and white zigzags, until it tilts up to a gilt-legged table, with a green ring lying on top of it. Dale Cooper enters through a red curtain, and confronts a small man, dressed in red, whose mode of speaking is curiously protracted and contorted. The small man holds the ring up towards Cooper, who then turns to look directly at the camera, as he says, with emphasis and deliberation: 'Don't take the ring, Laura, don't take the ring'. We cut back to Laura in her bedroom, and Cooper's words carry over into this space also. After a nightmare confrontation with a dead girl, Annie, who is lying in her bed, Laura is aghast to discover that she is holding the ring in her right hand. She goes to the door of her bedroom, and looks out, after which she turns towards the photograph, where she is pictured returning over the threshold. We then cut back to within the photograph, and see her looking out at herself as she stands by her bedroom door.

After her death, Laura finally appears in person in the Red Room, where Cooper stands over her. No longer bearing the marks of her traumatic beating and murder, her hair is permed, and her face and lips heavily made up. She has the look of a corpse prepared by a funeral parlour for an open coffin. She gazes sadly into the distance, and then stares up at Cooper. A flickering light suddenly illuminates her, as a hand reaches out to her from beneath a white satin gown. It is the hand of an angel, resembling the angel in her painting. There is a low angle shot of the angel floating above her.

This may be a reminiscence of the previous sequence, in which Leland was seen floating above Bob, a sequence also set in the Red Room. If so, Laura's relation to the angel is like that of Bob to her father, and it becomes hard to say which sequence is a parody of which. At this point, Laura begins to laugh, though her voice is not audible on the soundtrack. As her laughter grows, tears run down her cheeks, and the music becomes more prominent, sounding a religious motif. The camera gradually draws up and away from her, with Cooper still standing beside her. As the camera continues upward, Laura bends forward and holds her head in her hands. The image of the angel is superimposed on the upper right of the shot, and this too begins to flicker, until the screen fades to white, the music continuing over the credits. There are two worlds in the film and it is in the Red Room that they penetrate and transform each other. The photograph is an image of the threshold across which they meet and at the same it is that threshold, a threshold Laura has already crossed, entering the world which will claim her on her death.

Throughout the later sequences of the film, the anticipation of her death comes increasingly to absorb her, as she is sucked into crime, perversion and madness. After her death, the two worlds merge inextricably. As Michel Chion has remarked, 'it becomes as impossible for the film to distinguish one world from the other or to signify their separation, as it is for the spectator to locate himself or herself in the interval between them'.[33] Chion sees the black and white zigzag patterns on the floor of the Red Room as representing this interval, inasmuch as it is impossible to say whether the floor is white with black stripes, or black with white stripes. In addition, the floor is flat, and yet it creates an illusion of rising and falling.

We cannot say because the Red Room is the double setting of

Carrie

this interval. It is a hell or a heaven, depending on the moment, and we cannot identify the moment.[34]

Chion writes of the Red Room in terms that seem intended to evoke Blanchot. Although Laura has been murdered during the course of the narrative, the Red Room is somewhere outside the world of the narrative, and ambiguity holds sway there. As Chion sees it, she is to remain where one never dies, but to what end one cannot say. The angel may be an image of redemption, or a tawdry parody of all such hopes. Laura's laughter may express joy, or horror and despair.

At the heart of **Fire Walk With Me** is a desire to escape the human world, and to experience the duplicitous and unstable point of an impossible origin, located somewhere in relation to the pre-linguistic density of things. There is something in this that touches on the extremes of human experience, and in order to make clearer the significance of what is involved here I will suggest a parallel between the condition explored in Lynch's film and that which we find addressed by Hugo von Hofmannsthal in 'The Letter of Lord Chandos'. Chandos is an Elizabethan aristocrat, writing to Francis Bacon to explain his failure to produce the literary works expected of him. He tells Bacon: 'I have lost completely the ability to think or to speak of anything coherently'.[35] And yet it is not a simple doubt about the value of words, or their legitimacy, which disturbs their significance for him. It is that they have undergone a radical transformation. They have ceased to be signs and have become, as Blanchot puts it, 'gazes, an empty light, attractive and fascinating'.[36] His condition is one in which words 'congealed into eyes which stared back at me and into which I was forced to stare back-whirlpools that gave me vertigo and, reeling incessantly, led into the void'.[37] Words have become 'a presentiment of unknown relations, of another language', another language capable of 'enclosing the silence that lies in the deepest recesses of things'.[38]

I felt, with a certainty not entirely bereft of a feeling of sorrow, that neither in the coming year nor in the following nor in all the years of this my life shall I write a book, whether in English or Latin, and this for an odd and embarrassing reason....to wit, because the language in which I might be able not only to write but to think is neither Latin nor English, neither Italian nor Spanish, but a language none of whose words is known to me, a language which inanimate things speak to me and in which I will perhaps one day, from the depths of the tomb, have to justify myself before an unknown judge.

Condemned to a language whose words are unknown to him, and which he will speak only from the depths of the tomb, Chandos nonetheless writes, in a style composed of swelling and melancholy periods, a statement and justification of the verdict against him. It is a verdict whose paradox Poe captures in the condition of M. Valdemar, when Valdemar utters-in all truth-the impossible sentence: 'I am dead'. It is also the paradox of **Fire Walk With Me**. Despite being done to death by her father, Laura has not escaped him, because she has not got free of Bob. As we see, prior to her entering it, the Red Room is Bob's world, as her home was his world also. During her life, Laura was condemned to experience within her home an utter homelessness, an extreme of spiritual and moral degradation. And after her death, we are unable to determine whether or not she will be forced to savour this degradation to the bitter end, in a place where there is no ending. Her brutal slaying is only intermittently revealed by the film. And her ultimate torments-if torments are what await her-likewise remain uncertain. Like Gregor Samsa, Laura is a figure of ambiguity. Her sufferings embody the film's essential darkness, as it enacts, alternating between the intelligible and the nonsensical, the serious and the ridiculous, the conditions that characterise the modern fantastic.

NOTES

1. Tzvetan Todorov, The Fantastic (New York: Cornell University Press, 1980): 33.
2. Todorov: 63-64.
3. "'Like Unto a Leopard': Figurative Discourse in Cat People (1942) and Todorov's The Fantastic", Wide Angle 10:3 (1988): 34.
4. Todorov: 169.
5. Todorov: 173.
6. 'Every phrase and every sentence is an end and a beginning,/Every poem an epitaph.' From Little Gidding, in The Complete Poems and Plays of T.S. Eliot (London: Faber and Faber, 1975): 197.
7. Maurice Blanchot, The Gaze of Orpheus, trans. Lydia Davis (New York: Station Hill, 1981): 2.
8. Todorov: 175.
9. Rosemary Jackson, Fantasy: The Literature of Subversion (London: Methuen, 1981): 38-40.
10. Jackson: 41. Cited from Situations 1 (Paris: Gallimard, 1947): 130.
11. Philosophical Investigations, trans. G.E.M. Anscombe (Oxford: Blackwell, 1986): ß49.
12. Discussions of Wittgenstein (London: Routledge & Kegan Paul, 1970): 79.
13. On Certainty (Oxford: Blackwell, 1979): ß378.
14. On Certainty, ß150.
15. On Certainty, ß513.
16. On Certainty, ß613.
17. The Pound Era (London: Faber and Faber, 1975): 136.
18. Philosophical Investigations, ß116.
19. Philosophical Investigations, p. 174.
20. Stanley Cavell, "Notes and afterthoughts on the opening of the Investigations", in Hans Sluga and David G Stern (eds), The Cambridge Companion to Wittgenstein (Cambridge: Cambridge University Press, 1996): 286.

21. Stephen Mulhall, "Introduction", in Stephen Mulhall (ed), The Cavell Reader (Oxford: Blackwell, 1996): 9.
22. Maurice Blanchot, The Gaze of Orpheus: 56.
23. The Space of Literature: 70.
24. The Space of Literature: 247.
25. The Space of Literature: 247.
26. The Thing (London: BFI, 1997): 74-75.
27. The ways in which the film brings us to accept this reading of events is discussed by Steve Neale, in "'You've Got To be Fucking Kidding!': Knowledge, Belief and Judgement in Science Fiction", in Annette Kuhn (ed), Alien Zone (London: Verso, 1990): 160-168.
28. Stephen Prince has seen The Thing as a parasite and as a virus like that of AIDS (though viruses and parasites are two very different kinds of being), arguing that the crew decides to commit a ritualised mass suicide at the end in an attempt to deny it hosts. Prince draws on Mary Douglas and Edmund Leach to suggest that the film is reinforcing notions of taboo in order to sustain the distinction between the human and the non-human, and so to preserve our sense of what is human. However, parasites and viruses do not threaten our humanity, though they may threaten our lives. Furthermore, his descriptions of The Thing as a "horribly anomalous animal", "cosmic pollution", and so on, presuppose the conclusions he seeks to establish. The anthropological positions his case is based on distinguish between the edible and the inedible, the holy and the profane, the clean and the unclean, and the human and the non-human. However, The Thing has no place in the categories of intelligibility and orders of being these arguments take for granted. It is not a "creature". It is the impossible: a creation of Carpenter's film. And Prince has yet to establish that The Thing fulfils a role even analogous to that of religious ritual. See: Stephen Prince, "Dread, Taboo, and The Thing: Towards a Social Theory of the Horror Film", Wide Angle 10:3 (1988): 19-29.
29. One of the crew members asks if he would know if he had become an imitation of himself. But this prompts the further question: do I know I am who I am? Is the fact of my being who I am a matter of knowledge at all? Wittgenstein speaks of certain propositions "as not accessible to doubt". There are certain facts that are withdrawn from doubt and assertion. The remark I cited earlier from On Certainty is relevant in this context also: "Here a doubt would drag everything with it into chaos" (ß613).
30. Julia Kristeva, Powers of Horror, trans. Leon Roudiez (New York: Columbia University Press, 1982): 4.
31. The Gaze of Orpheus: 83.
32. The Gaze of Orpheus: 85.
33. Michel Chion, David Lynch (London: BFI, 1997): 157-158.
34. Chion: 158.
35. Hugo von Hofmannsthal, Selected Prose, trans.Mary Hottinger and Tania & James Stern (New York: Pantheon Books, 1952): 133.
36. The Space of Literature: 183.
37. von Hofmannsthal, Selected Prose: 135.
38. The Space of Literature: 135.
39. von Hofmannsthal, Selected Prose: 140-141. Translation modified, after Blanchot.

DARK PASSIONS

The seductive charm of Soledad Miranda

Andy Black

Just like such famous icons before her as Jane Mansfield and Marc Bolan, Soledad Miranda met her premature death by speeding to her appointment with destiny from behind the wheel of a car on a Lisbon highway during the final months of 1971.

Prophetically, only months before, her "dying" breath as the title dominatrix in Jeff Franco's **Eugenie De Sade** (1970) rasped that "Je suis morte", only for her character to be deliciously "tickled" back to life ! Unfortunately, life did not imitate art as no such resuscitation was possible in reality.

Born to Portuguese parents on July 9 1943 in Seville, Spain, Miranda was actually christened Soledad Redon Bueno or "good solitude" and spent the formative years of her life performing song and dance routines in San Fernando talent contests. As Franco once commented on Miranda; "She had a rather unfortunate and difficult life, which began with flamenco dancing and lead to small roles in films". As one of her fellow countrymen Franco's insight into the marginality of Spanish cinema and its paucity of opportunities is revealing, especially when considering Miranda's own neglected talent - "It is very difficult for actors in Spain to achieve any kind of recognition", Franco observed.

Miranda's film debut, aged 16, reflected her prowess on the stage as she portrayed a ballerina in Jose Maria Elorrieta's **La Bella Mimi (The Beautiful Mimi)** in 1960.

Her film career blossomed as she then appeared in Franco Giraldi's spaghetti western **Sugar Colt** (1966), before starring in a brace of international productions, **Cannons for Cordoba** (1967) and **100 Rifles** (1968).

More universal recognition however, followed her work for US producer Sidney Pink in Javier Seto's **The Castilian** (1963) and Julio Coll's **Pyro** (1963). In the former, Miranda appears briefly, but to noticeable (!!) effect as one of a dozen young nubiles who strip off their clothing and bathe in a public stream in order to distract a unit of invading

soldiers!

Her role in the latter, as a sensitive, caring innocent, the daughter of a carnival worker who has a love for dogs, induces a certain degree of pathos in the audience in Coll's somewhat underrated Spanish horror.

This exposure to the prolific fear genre undoubtedly acted as the catalyst for her eventual partnership with horror auteur Jess Franco. Although she made a total of 31 films (perhaps even more), it is for the mercurial Spanish director's work that she is best known and indeed, fondly remembered.

After a brief hiatus when she gave up films and started a family with a Portuguese racing driver, Miranda then returned to life in the cinematic fast lane via her role as Mina in Franco's **El Conde Dracula (Count Dracula)** in 1969.

Although much-touted (mainly by Franco !) as being the most accurate and reverential adaptation from Bram Stoker's seminal vampire novel, **El Conde Dracula** is certainly light years away from being the definitive version of the source work.

All this, despite the appearance of Christopher Lee in his favoured role as the Count, with the eccentric Klaus Kinski as a manic Renfield and with Herbert Lom as Professor Van Helsing. In fact, the only real authenticity that Franco recreates from Stoker is in accurately portraying the arch vampire as a silver-haired and moustached figure who, upon suckling the elixir of blood from each successive victim, becomes

Vampyros Lesbos

progressively more youthful in appearance.

Miranda certainly made her mark on this picture in more ways than one - her supposed seduction by Lee's demonic vampire being almost overturned by the actor's reaction to her - "I've played this scene many times, but this woman is giving me something no other actress has ever had" - praise indeed !

Lee's initiation into Miranda's mesmerising aura is part-explained by Franco's appraisal of her; "When she began working in my films, it was like watching her undergo a transformation". He continues; "She told me it was the first time in her life (that) she felt so fulfilled".

As if to echo this physical transformation, Miranda also took to utilising a pseudonym when appearing in Franco's productions, as a cross-fertilisation of the producer of **The Thief of Baghdad** and the author of *Valley of the Dolls* gave birth to Susann Korda !!

Then came a trio of Miranda (or Korda!) appearances in the films Franco directed for Liechenstein productions; **Sex Charade** (1970), as yet unreleased with Miranda as a woman held captive by a sadistic maniac who has escaped from hospital. She is forced to tell him a story (!) in order to keep the fugitive awake which she does, but it is a self-revelatory, allegorical premise which mirrors her present situation - quite a departure from Franco's requisite flesh and fear oeuvre.

Next came **Les Cauchemars Naissent la Nuit** (1970), only marginally better known than **Sex Charade** as it did receive a solitary film release in Belgium (!) and which saw Franco return to one of his earlier film plots - **Miss Muerte** (1966) as a nightclub dancer unconsciously commits murders for somebody else who is controlling her, and, enjoying her actions vicariously.

The last of this triumvirate **Eugenie De Sade** (1970) is at least more widely seen which is appropriate as it showcases perhaps Miranda's definitive work as the titular and truly modern sadist.

As Eugenie, the daughter of Albert de Franval (Paul Muller), an acclaimed psychologist and who under the name of "Radeck" is researching into sexual perversion - good work if you can get it !

Given that Eugenie's favourite book is the story of Saint Theresa you could be forgiven for thinking that she is a shy and retiring violet - not so ! She is incestuously attracted to her father and provokes his desire by strangling to death a nude model they have hired for a kinky S&M photo session (played by another Franco regular Alice Arno).

Along with the sadean perversions on show, **Eugenie De Sade**

The Devil Came From Akasava

is also noticeable for the outre costumes which include go-go boots, cape and floppy hat (all red), and white framed, blue-lensed and oversized shades ! Pyschadelic or what ?!

Of Miranda's final trio of Franco films, **The Devil Came From Akasava** (1970) is the least well-known - a real potboiler of a story based on a Bryan Edgar Wallace krimi and liberally borrowing from mystery/crime writer Mickey Spillane's *Kiss Me Deadly* - filmed so memorably by director Robert Aldrich in 1955.

As Jane Morgan, captain of the British Secret Service no less, Miranda poses as a prostitute in London and is recruited as an exotic dancer in Akasawa with a mission of getting closer to the thieves suspected of stealing a lethal "philosophers" stone - a glowing mineral which turns metal into gold but burns men to cinders. Draped in crimson scarves and flamboyant costumes Miranda cuts a stunning figure - aided and abetted by Scotland Yard detective Walter Forrester (Fred Williams).

For Franco, Miranda's performance obviously had a lasting impression as her role was virtually reprised in Lina Romay's character of Countess Irina in the later **Female Vampire** (1973).

Rather more well known, thanks to Redemption Video's release of the two titles, are **Vampyros Lesbos** and **She Killed in Ecstasy** (both

1970). In both films, Miranda's smouldering sensuality is utilised to great effect as she literally embodies the persona of a cogent femme fatale - her nebulous, piercing pools for eyes and pouting lips merely the veneer to lure her "prey" before ensnaring them in her hedonistic web of perversion.

As if to reinforce this seduction theme we even see a butterfly symbolically snared inside one of the fishnets which adorns Miranda's coastal "fortress" in **Vampyros Lesbos**. As Princess Nadine she makes a startling entrance - decorated in a translucent black neglige she caresses then kisses a full-length mirror to the accompaniement of an almost funereal sounding Hammond keyboard, before then turning her attentions to the naked figure of Lucy (Ewa Stroemberg) as the two cavort on the floor, writhing in orgasmic ecstasy!

Given that this graphic display takes place within a darkened night-club, some of the intimacy is lost in favour of an avowedly exhibitionist atmosphere created by the "performance".

Princess Nadine's fortified retreat eschews the trappings of the gothic in preference to similarly extravagant displays imitating the Princess' own exotic nature - so fishnets rather than cobwebs ensnare unwary visitors, kites rather than bats fly overhead and luxurious poses on sandy beaches or aboard a sun-kissed boat replaces the traditional vampire pose rising from a coffin and such like - no such obvious images permeate

Vampyros Lesbos

the Franco imagination for his own unique sanguinary predator.

Princess Nadine's taloned fingers beckon the camera closer in one memorable scene as, outstretched on the floor, her (blood) red scarf unfurls in front on the lens, flowing in an imaginary breeze, at once capturing the erotic, cloying actions of the Princess.

Having succumbed to and then overcome "death" the Princess is quick to turn her amoral desires towards the blonde beauty of Lucy again - eventually supplying her with an authentic "love-bite" after Lucy's long blonde tresses have fallen dramatically in front of Nadine's equally long stockinged legs.

The triumphant finale relocates Nadine and Lucy to the familiar nightclub dancefloor as the Princess masquerades briefly in a latex peek-a-boo bra, matching panties and thigh length boots, before turning her attentions to the statue-esque Lucy - draping her own discarded lingerie onto the prone blonde to create the ultimate erotic frisson.

As a very "loose" interpretation of Bram Stoker's *Dracula's Guest*, **Vampyros Lesbos** doesn't really cut the mustard but as a highly-charged, kinky and kitsch curio the film excels, especially with the bravura dance/striptease sessions and psychadelic jazz score which rates almost as highly as the visuals.

For **She Killed in Ecstasy/Sie Totete in Ektase** (aka **Mrs. Hyde**), Franco returned again to his earlier epic **Miss Muerte**, but if anything, **She Killed in Ecstasy** is a far more explicit work with Miranda as the avenging widow Mrs Johnson - reaping punishment upon those she believes drove her scientist husband to death - his revolutionary ideas meeting with almost the same kind of hostility reserved for Baron Frankenstein !

Utilising the **Vampyros Lesbos** sets the familiar jutting coastline and imposing castle residence is the ideal backdrop for Miranda's character as she glides down the stone steps cut into the island, her raven hair flowing in the wind, along with her purple cape which (barely) conceals a tight black dress beneath.

Appearing very much as the "castrating feminine" figure that the psychologists would have us believe, Mrs Johnson proceeds to graphically sow the seeds of her enemies destruction - first, by seducing her victims, then by stabbing them in a homicidal frenzy, her phallic knife-thrusts appropriately aimed at her victim's genitalia.

Her final victim fittingly is Franco himself (as Dr Donan) - tied to a chair and left helpless as his wide-eyed tormentor traces first her lips,

then the knife-blade over his bare body before his bloody demise ensues.

In one telling scene we see one victim lured to his doom by admiring Mrs Johnson's reflection in a mirror - a direct reference to her alter-ego/dual nature - seductress one minute, killer the next.

Her own demise - at the wheel of a car which careers over a cliff, unfortunately proved prophetic in the extreme. As Franco himself lamented after Miranda's tragic death - "The day before she died, she received the greatest news of her life. I visited her appartment in Lisbon with a German producer, who came out to offer her a two year contract with CCC, which would assure her of at least two starring roles per year in big budget films. She was going to become a major star in Germany". And all this, a mere two weeks after **Vampyros Lesbos** had opened to rave reviews in cinemas in West Berlin.

Miranda's death was also seemingly the catalyst for Franco's obsessive, workaholic approach to film-making - literally throwing himself into projects as if to expunge her from his memory. As Franco noted in a final tribute; "She left behind an incredible legacy. All of the women who acted in my films after her were deeply affected by her legend. Lina Romay, for example, has had moments in which she was completely possesed by Soledad. She became Soledad Miranda !"

That being so, there really was only one Soledad, and at least now some of her finest works are becoming available to view again for new audiences to share in the mystique that was Miranda.

T & A the Arthouse Way
Laurence Rémila

Most *aht* film connoisseurs have long figured something that certain porn slackards are only just beginning to realise : that you're more likely to get your fist some fine nekkid poontang by hiring yourself a videotape of some impenetrable - the plot, reader, the plot - arthouse epic, than some softcore potboiler hacked to decency by the British Board of Film Classification. In their wisdom, the Board know that the only thing the British want shoved up their actresses is lines of unfathomable tedium. The Board is happy to watch thespians shovelling turd all over themselves at some crazed banquet - Pete Greenaway, come on down ! - while shying away from the showing of full-on intercourse.

So. Wily fratboys and aging, aged ahthouse cronies, you have but two choices. Either give it all up, find a good woman and settle - settle ! - down. (Sorry. That's not one of the choices, just an impossible dream.) First choice : haunt Soho's ghastly, ghostly jizz shops and its deathly parlours, walking with the word 'Loser' tattooed to your sappy forehead, having given up on life, pride, and the faintest hope of ensnaring a compliant bit of poon - that is, one who won't make you pay through your yellowing teeth to snatch a peak at her snatch. Yours will be an existence that spells out : "This is what I live for. I might as well be dead." Or. Or you could - You ? Me ? Us ? No. Him. That sap sitting over in the corner.

This whole feature's written for his benefit - he could say, through teeth none more gritted : "Yes, I love that foreign film stuff. Yes, I love spending what little time I have on this Earth watching hours of interminable, incomprehensible bilge. You know, it's by some clown whose name I can't spell - let's call him Coco - and he's the one filming clouds in slo' mo', sixth form discussion groups ten in a row, an ascetic neanderthal yogi flossing his toes, unexplained flashbacks to William cleaning his bow, or was it Blind Willie Jo gleaming his mojo ? Uh. Yes, I love this stuff... Especially the bits where they show some broad nekkid ... I can watch two beautiful, intelligent-looking women getting it on, and assuage my guilt with the thought that, Wow, this was written by Buñuel's long-term, oft-overlooked, collaborator.

The arthouse T & A drooling, dripping, fanboy has an

abundance of video choices with which to both get his rocks off and feel intellectually satiated. The number of nude scenes is astounding. ("Astound away," mutters the conspirational VCR.) You'll be happy to learn, reader, that these scenes are now such a staple of the arthouse film that if you hire one and none exists, you can infer that the director reached some zen-state, or it was filmed somewhere ridiculously cold. They're all at it, bless, no matter how old. Antonioni returns after a decade , and what does he do ? Gets Sophie Marceau naked. Perhaps he had intimations of mortality and thought, It doesn't get much better than a woman's beauty. Perhaps she figured, Pops there's as good as gone, his films are notoriously boring, what's the harm, let's pep up this ponderous bunkum with some good old nekkidness, let's make this old buffer happy and let's have them gazing at more than their navels.

So. Fratboys. Dirty old men. The lot can walk into Prime Time, Blockbusters, Virgin and, with their ugly heads held high, they can walk straight past the Special Interest and Adult aisles, mentally tut-tutting the drooling creature stooped there, as he lets all know of his abdication from Living, as he stands there choosing between Pandora Peaks and Tifanny Towers, between a rock and a silicone-hard place. The dirty old/young man can walk with something resembling pride to the Arthouse display, and look sophisticated - cultured even - as he chooses. He might even smile at the woman stood nearby with the Buñuel in her hand - unbeknownst to him, she's a lesbian - safe in the knowledge that he can get one of these without the sense of Where's-the-bridge ? or I-may-as-

The Cook, The Thief, His Wife And Her Lover

well-move-back-to-Mother's-(and-spend-the-rest-of-my-life-making -comp-tapes-for-maladjusted-penpals). Safe in the knowledge that somewhere, amongst the cloud formations and terminal discussions, amongst the cack-handed politics and ham-fisted observations, there will be poontag. Nekkid poontang. Without the sense of shame. Hazzah. Of course, there's something faintly disturbing about some poor wretch fast-forwarding through **Apocalypse Now** to freeze-frame on some Playmate's poster.

It seems the arthouse film is now a product dependent on the following components : the faint veneer of respectability provided by certain directors and actors ; a certain faux-impenatrability to make college-boys feel cultured, and the requisite amount of nudity (about the same percentage as that found in any straightforward straight-to-video release) to sell the confounded thing. And, like those videos, the scene containing the nudity is the one that ends up plastered all over the poster or the video-box. (This is, admittedly, nothing new. Even some of Bergman's film-meditations would be sold on their nudity. For proof, the salacious posters advertising **The Silence** in 1963.) What rankles is that arthouse practitioners and promoters are more dishonest about it. Try getting them to admit that Antonioni's last film would have had a hope of a British release without his star stripping her All for his Art. These actresses are as essential to the success of arthouse films as the Vanessa Angels of that world are to straight-to-video titles. And for the same blessed reasons : for their T & A. Where would art *et essai* film be without its T & A ?

This has been the case since cinema's unexpected birth. From its earliest experiments to current produce, film has gorged itself on female nudity. In 1896, **The Kiss** satisfied the audience's prurient desires porn-like, without the arthouse accoutrement of an accompanying story. And nearly ninety years before La Belle Noiseuse, Painter and Model (Undressed), a 20 m spool, could be procured from Pathé. Its synopsis reads : "A painter and a model who feels disgust at getting undressed. The painter manages to convince her and touches her suggestively."

If you go by Umberto Eco's criteria for judging whether a film's pornographic - admittedly, Eco is read by the kind of people who drool over Juliette Binoche : middle-aged and middle-brow - then a lot of arthouse T & A is pornographic. What it comes down to, according to Eco, is whether a film is full of "wasted time". Which accounts for two thirds of arthouse films. Eco writes : "If, to go from A to B, the characters take

Lair of the White Worm

longer than you would like, then the film you are seeing is pornographic."
(*How To Travel with a salmon and other essays*, Secker & Warburg, 1994,
p. 207.)

     Certain directors choose to temper their films' nudity with bouts
of sickening visions and , in the case of Peter Greenaway, mathematical
equations. Minutes into **The Cook, The Thief, His Wife and Her Lover**
(1989), Willie Ross is lying on the ground covered in dog turd, getting
pissed on by Alan Howard. The film then goes on to feature plenty of
nudity, very little of it arousing. It seems directors believe they can
assuage their guilt at featuring female nudity by adding lots of gore to the
film. Alain Robbe-Grillet's **The Other Side of Midnight** (1977) has the
ravishing Marie-France Pisier in a number of nude scenes (some very nice
and featuring oil and cubes). But just as the long-macced intellos are
getting off at the sight of her breasts, they also have to endure this pretty
object performing a domestic abortion with the aid of a coat-hanger. Most

of the films made by the father of the *nouveau roman* contain oodles of old-fashioned nudity.

One way of conferring some sort of respectability on these sexploitative features is to adapt works by well-known erotic authors, hence the plethora of adaptations of books by Miller, Nin, the Anon of O, etc. In these, there's still plenty more female nudity than male. Something we should be thankful for when we consider that Rip Torn plays Miller in **Tropic of Cancer** (1970). Similarly, **Venus In Furs** (also 1970) shows plenty more of Maria Rohmer than Klaus Kinski. The culmination of the muddled adaptation of the erotic novel is Annaud's David Hamilton-like mangling of Duras' L'Amant.

Henry and June (1990), an Anais Nin adaptation features former French porn star Brigitte Lahaie in a cameo, appearing opposite Maria de Medeiros. This crossover between arthouse and porn occurs more frequently than might be expected. Ginger Lynn Allen, US porn star, has tried breaking into straight cinema via independent features and Ken Russell's **Whore** (1991). The OTT director's **Lair of the White Worm**

Lair of the White Worm

(1988) features British top-shelf lovely Linzi Drew as a maid/nun. She also appears in Russell's **Salomé's Last Dance** (1987) as a slave. His championing of her is similar to John Water's attempts to help Traci Lords in her reconversion. The appearance of these adult actresses is but a logical development. If the arthouse film is going to ape the adult film's cynical but necessary use of its starlets' nudity, it might as well go the whole hog and poach the actresses themselves.

And, just like in porn, the actresses denuded in the arthouse film are often being directed by boyfriends and husbands. Nic Roeg, for example, is an odd fellow who films Theresa Russell getting undressed a mite too often. They are but one couple of arthouse cronies wanting to be taken seriously ; and they think of themselves, I'll warrant, as partners in Art. However, the frequency with which these directors sell their films on their spouses' questionable charms suggest a rather less glorified relationship : that between the Page Three Girl and her boyfriend-cum-personal manager. And the indignities these directors put their bitter halves through ! "Dahling," Mr. Roeg sheepishly whispers, " in this one you're doing the double-backed beast with, uhm, Art Garfunkel." And, with a look of consternation, Ms. Russell asks : " Oh, can't you make the scene a bit more tasteful ? Maybe intercut it with some tracheotomy footage ?" And he does ! (**Bad Timing : A Sensual Obsession**, 1980.)

But where the arthouse film comes into its own is in its simultaneous critique of the nudity. It is with regret that I inform you, this is where it can become more than merely exploitative. Oh, the irony ! The greats can make you aware of the futility of your pursuit of nekkidness (and, by implication, of most human endeavour) by dishing up hours of it. (Which explains why Pasolini's **Salo**, for example, containing all kinds of naked depravity, manages to be completely unerotic, leaving a queasy feeling in the stomach rather than a creamy liquid in the hand. This is due to **Salo** containing two of the things cinema audiences find hardest to digest : excrement and literature.)

But in most cases, what these nude segments in arthouse films most resemble is the striptease described by Barthes in *Mythologies*. The rest of the film, the extraneous fully-clothed sequences, proffers the "alibi of art" on the nudity, just as the dance in a strip-show does. The rest of the film is the equivalent of the stripper's dance and its superfluous yet essential gestures. Going by Barthes' argument, your true - authentic - porn is equivalent to the amateur striptease Barthes contrasts the professional with. Like porn, these amateur shows deny "the woman the alibi of art and the refuge of being an object, imprisoning her in a condition of weakness and timourousness".

If art's alibi can transform these actresses into objects, that's probably why, despite the acres of bare flesh available in the genre, so little provides you - sorry, him - with your genuine porn thrill. The sad truth is, let's face it, that what truly gets him off is the amateur stripper's or pornographic scrubber's condition of weakness and timourousness.

More Rats Than Bats: Werner Herzog's Nosferatu
Daniel Bird

Werner Herzog's **Nosferatu** occupies a curious place in the history of cinema: a-remake of an illegitimate version of the "Dracula" story with a grotesque disguise. Given the spate of high profile horror films (not to mention remakes) during the 1970's, It's easy to dismiss "Nosferatu" as just a commercial excursion by a usually ferociously independent director - but it pays to look closer.

The most immediate difference between Herzog's film and it's silent predecessor is the use of colour photography. Whilst Herzog's documentary films are assured and perhaps somewhat stylized (Herzog belongs to the tradition of Chris Marker as a globe trotting cine-essayist) his feature films, by contrast have a very bizarre and unnerving quality indeed. All of Herzog's features have a similar form, where actors deliver their lines as if half asleep whilst the camerawork suggest that the film is a documentary of it's own making. The effect can be fascinating (as in **Aguirre, Wrath Of God**) or it can be vacuous, to the point where an actual documentary of Herzog making a film becomes infinitely more interesting than the film itself (e.g. Les Blank's documentary of the making of **Fitzcarraldo**). Colour photography seems essential to Herzog's conception of film-making, based on a gloriously naive idea grounded in a primitive belief in the moving image.

A more subtle difference is the intermediate steps Herzog's makes to identify his work as a decedent of the Bram Stoker story. Herzog gets rid of the names Murnau used to disguise his script. Gone are Hutter, Dr Bulwer, Ellen and Knock, instead Herzog uses the original character names from the Stoker novel - but with a bizarre twist. Mina and Lucy's names are switched. It's not clear why Herzog switched the names of the two female characters, however, this is not the only twist in Herzog's film.

The dynamics between the main characters is also distinctly different. Van Helsing's character as the scientist - vampire killer is made almost redundant, here his stake through the heart business seems almost

Nosferatu The Vampyre

superfluous. Jonathan Harker - the traditional protagonist seems particularly alienated in Herzog's version, plucked from his comfortable job and family and dwarfed in the Captherian mountains and incarcerated in Count Dracula's castle. The real shift in emphasis is towards the relationship between Dracula and Lucy.

It is clear that Herzog's motives form remaking **Nosferatu** were not to return to the source material to provide the definitive "film" of the book - the ludicrous idea that most filmmakers drift away from the literary source material because they either lack respect for the author or because they don't have sufficient skills as a filmmaker to translate the original text to the screen - and that it requires filmmakers like Francis Ford Coppola and Kenneth Branagh to set the record straight. Nor does Herzog's motives seem purely aesthetic. It could easily imagine Tim Burton wanting to remake **Nosferatu** because Murnau's film looks "nice". In fact, Herzog is concerned with establishing a link between contemporary German Cinema and Murnau's era:

"We are trying in our films to build a thin bridge back to that time, to legitimize our own cinema and culture. We are not remaking **Nosferatu**, but bringing it to new life and new character for a new age." (Werner Herzog quoted by Nigel Andrews in *Dracula in Delft* (1978).

As unlikely as it first seems, Herzog has made two other genre films: **Heart Of Glass** (1976) and **Cerro Torre: Scream Of Stone** (1992). Both films belong to the mountain film genre which developed roughly at the same time as the expressionist hey day of the UFA studios, Lang and Pabst. Pabst even co-directed a mountain film with Arnold Fanck (the genre's most prolific director) **The White Hell Of Pitz Palu**. Nigel Andrew's (in Kracauer mode) describes how Murnau's **Nosferatu**: "prophesied the rise of nazism by showing the invasion of Germany by Dracula and his plague bearing rats."

Indeed, Murnau's film wasn't the film of that era which seemed prophetic in hind sight: Murnau's **Faust**, Fritz Lang's **Dr Mabuse** cycle being the two most obvious examples. On the other hand, the mountain films progressively embraced nazi ideology. The blonde star of many mountain films was one Leni-Riefenstahl and she even directed one of the genre's best films: **The Blue Light**. Even if (as Herzog claims) he is transposing a pre-fascist film into contemporary circumstances (the same could be said about **Heart Of Glass** and **Cerro Torre**), his **Nosferatu** has little to do with politics.

The author of the *Haunted Screen* (and not to mention Herzog's mentor) Lotte Eisner described Murnau as "the greatest film-director the Germans have ever known" and Herzog's **Nosferatu** cannot be interpreted as anything other than an elaborate homage to Murnau. Herzog goes to great lengths to recreate scenes with precision (the most obvious example

Nosferatu The Vampyre

Nosferatu The Vampyre

is the reconstruction of the shot of Max Shreck walking across the deck of the boat carrying his coffins into town) but as a whole the film doesn't feel out of place in Herzog's filmography. Murnau's **Nosferatu**, like all of Herzog's films is concerned with a journey both literal and spiritual from the known to the unknown (Judith Mayne: *Herzog, Murnau and the vampire* (1985). In all of his films Herzog essential plays the mad romantic visionary, coming somewhere in between Conrad and Bruce Chatwin (Herzog made a literal adaptation of a Bruce Chatwin novel with **Cobra Verde** in 1988).

　　The final third of Herzog's **Nosferatu** skips between a melancholic and apocalyptic note. Lucy and Dracula act out their own bizarre love affair, both each other's angel of death - their final kiss of death entails a kind of mutual surrender of life (both in the world of the living and of the dead). The most spectacular imagery in Herzog's **Nosferatu** involves the plague of rats taking over the town of Delft. Indeed, in another one of Herzog's twists on Murnau's orginal , animals represent a prevailing life force of which human characters are mere playthings. Kittens toy with Lucy's portrait during the opening sequence of the film, the plague of rats do the real damage and wipe out an entire village whilst slow motion shots of a bat punctuate the film during the opening and closing segments of the film. Arguably the most surreal shot

in the film is when the town folk submit to the plague and invite Lucy to their "last supper" - fully dressed for the occasion eating an infected banquet on a long table set out in the town square. Rats cover the cobbles of the town square and after a toast, in a disturbing jump cut Herzog shows exactly the same composition except with none of the diners there and with the table covered with rats.

Nosferatu also benefits from some imaginative casting. As well as Herzog regulars (and technical crew members - even Herzog plays a monk in one sequence) is the Panique and Fluxus artist Roland Topor as Renfeld, Wender's regular Bruno Ganz and Isabelle Adjani. Herzog claims that he had not seen any of Adjani's films and that he cast her on the basis of an image of her on the poster of Truffaut's *Story Of Adele H.* Her icy beauty works well, Lucy remains virtually unobtainable throughout the film. Despite the cumbersome makeup, it's hard to imagine anyone other than Kinski playing **Nosferatu**. Kinski wrestles with both Herzog's ambitions and the every present danger of the whole film degenerating into a parody of both Murnau's film as well as Herzog's oeuvre.

As usual in a Herzog film, music plays an integral role in **Nosferatu**. There was no score composed specifically for **Nosferatu**. Herzog had completed the rough cut at roughly the same time when Florian Fricke of "Popol Vuh" had completed a studio album for release. Herzog immediately asked to see whether he could use the music on the soundtrack of **Nosferatu** and the "Popol Vuh" album was immediately repackaged as a film soundtrack. The meditative moog drones and resoundingly epic quality of Popol Vuh's earlier work seems to work in perfect synchrony with Herzog's style of filmaking.

To conclude, Herzog's **Nosferatu** is not a mere commercial excursion into the mainstream by an idiosyncratic film director whose work is more comfortable either on the festival circuit or on late night television. The passion which Herzog has for Murnau's work can be felt on the screen, and the rigor with which he executes this homage seems to curb the indulgences that are usually to be found in Herzog's films. Whilst never horrific, Herzog's **Nosferatu** is undoubtedly a haunting experience a wash with images which are difficult to forget.

The Story of O
Andy Black

"The innate desire to humiliate, hurt, wound or even destroy others in order to thereby create sexual pleasure in one's self." **Richard von Krafft Ebing** defining sado masochism.

"There's no way it would ever get a release at the moment. It's that sort of film where if you cut a minute you would cut twenty. (It's) the overall approach and the image the film portrays rather than anything specific and the whippings wouldn't go down too well with the censor." (spokesman for Angel & Nouveaux films).

Rather like Leopold Sasher Masoch's seminal slavery tome, *Venus in Furs*, filmed literally by Massimo Dallamano in 1970 and liberally by Jess Franco in 1969, Just Jaeckin's **The Story of O** (1975), seeks to explore the feral landscape of slavery and dominance, subjugation and supremacy as meted out to the eponymous O (Corinne Clery) in the litany of sexual perversions and tortures she endures/enjoys.

Still bouyant from the wave of commercial success which Sylvia Kristel brought him in the enjoyable soft-core romp **Emmanuelle** (1974), Jaeckin sought to visualise Pauline Reage's rather more transgressive source novel, where O is initiated into a new life of sexual servitude by her lover Rene (Udo Kier), and subsequently, the masterly Sir Stephen (Anthony Steel).

Having been brought by car to the singular Roissy chateau, Rene instructs O that; "You must get out of the car and ring the doorbell. You will follow whoever answers. You will do as they say. You will obey."

Once inside, besides noticing the opulent interiors of the mansion, O rapidly discovers the patriarchal structure of command within. Having waited "for an hour or two, it seemed like a century", the darkened room is then bathed in shimmering light as two female "servants", dressed in white gowns greet her, undress her and pamper her, before then applying make-up and lipstick, declaring that; "You mustn't keep your legs together, it's forbidden."

As O is then ritually led into a room full of people, she is then arbitrarily used and abused by the male contingent - "Has she been chained..or whipped...if you had, it might have given her pleasure. What we had to do is get tears out of her" one guest calmly suggests.

With O now wearing a symbolic dog collar, she is taken lasciviously by one guest, silhouetted in front of a roaring fire - "I want to hear her scream, right now" he zealously shouts, whereupon O is then tied up and whipped, the lashes seemingly strikng each pore of her naked body in a lengthy, squirm-inducing scene as the cane repeatedly strikes her. When Rene partially intervenes, O announces triumphantly; "You see. I managed to stand it." This heralds the embryonic seed of her subsequent accession to further "masters" later in the film, accentuated when she spurns the opportunity to escape the chateau of her own free will - even having been ordered to wear the same (slit) dress code as the other girls, being informed that; "They are very practical. The women all dress in this manner. And so you remain constantly at the disposition of anyone who wishes to use you. Any way he wants or whenever he wants."

O's compliance with this life of subordination is complete as we see her personal valet Pierre (Jean Gaven), chain her up to a post at night, before then sumarily awakening her from her sleep later for a bout of

The Story of O

The Story of O

impromptu flagellation.

There's one teasing shot from Jaeckin where we see the intricate archways of the building give way to a black and white checked floor, evoking the image of a chessboard with perhaps O and her companions the "pawns" in this game of sexual strategy.

"You are mine" Rene orders at one stage and whether it be Pierre or any number of other male (or female) partners, if Rene wishes it, then O will indulge him as we see her in a succession of carnal couplings under Rene's active (and sometimes voyeuristic) guidance.

Dispensing with the often gloomy interiors of the chateau, Rene then takes O into the bright sunshine outside, ratcheting up the stakes in her sexual compliance as she meets sir Stephen, who we learn, "is like a brother" to Rene, with them "sharing everything." Sir Stephen announces; "You'll continue to have only one master. A most exacting one because I have a penchant for rituals. I think you'll learn quite a lot."

Having pleasured himself with O, Sir Stephen offers his rather damning verdict; "You are easy. Does Rene realise you want every man who desires you ? He gives you an alibi for your sensuality...you love Rene but you're an easy conquest" he concludes as he strokes her pussy. "You confuse love with obedience...you will obey me without loving me and without me loving you" he orders before then indulging in some anal sex with O.

The anguish of the emotional and sexual politics then begins to fully develop as Rene informs O that "first you belong to Sir Stephen" with O now protesting to Rene for the first time that "tonight I want to be with you." When O is subsequently taken to Sir Stephen's house later that evening, we learn that Rene betrays her by informing the host of her protests, whereupon Sir Stephen punishes her so much for her "disobediance" that she loses consciousness.

O's compliance remains however, despite, or because of this punishment - she readily cultivates a lesbian relationship with her friend Jacqueline in order to initiate her into the ways and sexual mores of the Roissy chateau and to enable Rene to control Jacqueline who he now desires, so leaving Sir Stephen with O.

Whilst Sir Stephen's lofty, pretentions embody Focault's notion of sado masochism being power delegated from the monarchy, to beaurocrats to ordinary citizens, the "right to punish"and the "power to punish", O herself embodies Freud's theories of sado masochism being the result of displacement, most striking of which being how "It's active and passive forms are regularly encountered together in the same person." Witness O's behaviour when she attends Anne-Marie's (Christiane Minazzoli) finishing, read "punishing" school where having been whipped herself, O then reverses roles on her tormentor and zealously lashes her victim who is tied between two posts, almost to the point of death before remorse sets in and she pleads "forgive me" to her victim.

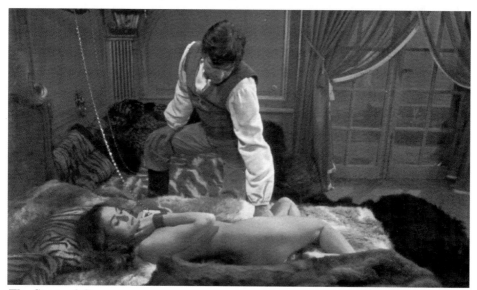

The Story of O

The Story of O

Despite this, Krafft-Ebing's assertion that women are to blame for male dominance - "It seems probable that this sadistic force is developed by the natural shyness and modesty of women towards the aggressive manners of the male", is partially reinforced as O allows herself to be branded with a hot iron delineating Sir Stephen's mark - a cattle-market analogy not entirely at odds with the previous "bartering" over "ownership" of O which Rene and Sir Stephen indulge in. To complete his ownership, a pair of clitoris rings also adorn O's body as sir Stephen is literally now "under her skin."

As Sir Stephen's escalating feelings for O burgeon ironically beyond his usual control, he is forced to turn away in disgust during a trip to Brittany when he allows a business acquaintance to take O from behind.

Hurriedly exiting, Sir Stephen then escorts O to the Commadores party - her dramatic entrance, dressed in an elaborate owl mask (and precious little else !), is then completed as she stands naked in the centre of the darkened room leaving the other guests gasping in awe. "Was she made of stone, of wax or was she a creature from another world. Sir Stephen watched O triumphant in her insolent nudity and was enthralled by the measure of her power" a narrator informs us.

The revelatory denouement sees the slave perhaps becoming the master as O enquires mischieviously of Sir Stephen; "You say to me you love me. But just say I demand it, that you bear only a few of the same

histoire d'O

punishments as me. you would accept it wouldn't you ?" "I believe so" he responds, continuing that; "One of the few things that a man in love learns...", his words abruptly halted in pain as O buries Sir Stephen's lit cigar into his own hand - O may spurn the Monica Lewinski method of cigar abuse here, but the tangible inference here is that it is *she* and not Sir Stephen who is now the dominant partner in their relationship.

With **The Story of O** being one of those all-too rare examples of an "intelligent" adult film, the plot may be rather pedantic in places but it is the psychological aspects of the central characters and their behaviour which provides the most riveting aspects, together with the stunning locations brought to screen by Robert Fraisse and Yves Rodallec's vivid photography.

What is most intriguing here is observing the "economic problems of masochism" as Freud would have it, namely the degree to which the masochist partner is really "controlling" the "dominant" partner in a relationship. Thus, just as in Dallamano's afore-mentioned **Venus in Furs** where we see the masochistic Severin (Renate Kasche) and the sexually liberated Wanda (Laura Antonelli) sour their relationship by deliberately inciting infidelity and the jealousy it brings, so too in Jaeckin's opus do we see the initially introvert O transformed by the conclusion into a sexually emancipated figure - flagellating her foes and manipulating her "master".

For Jaeckin, his training as a photographer in the army, architecture and interior design experience in Paris, art direction work on glossy magazines such as *Marie Claire*, *Elle* and *Vogue*, plus his work in tv advertising, all serve to inform his stylish approach to the subject matter. From the energetic fashion shoots which O herself photographs, to the sensual, semi-clad madame's and mistresses in cut-away dresses who decorate the picture, **O** is an exquisite film to look at and yet perversely, remains perhaps almost *too* painterly to capture the almost religious fervour of the source novel.

Jaeckin's greatest legacy with **O** however, was in popularising a new form of eroticism which reflected his own fashion experience - his films being glossy and escapist, refined and yet approachable, especially so for couples with the sexual fantasies on display.

Whilst some maintain **O** to be something of a failure - almost too polished and lacking in immediacy and compromised when compared to the novel, with Gerard Damiano's **The Story of Joanna** (1975) better representing a woman as sexual slave, Jaeckin's film still retains a

The Story of O

heightened erotic charge throughout and convincingly portrays the concept of pleasure in slavery - a problematic concept in other films with a nazi slant such as Liliana Cavani's **The Night Porter** (1974). In fact, one (then) member of the French National Assembly, Eugene Claudius-Petit, remarked that "...it was perhaps futile to fight against the theories of Nazism if we are prepared today to accept what Mr. Himmler dreamed about as long as it is presented in an attractive way." The fact that any eroticism was vetoed during Hitler's reign in power and that such product was actually banned from German cinemas' during the nazi rule, shows the ultimately misguided nature of Claudius-Petit's argument.

Reage also wrote a sequel to **O**; *Return to Roissy* which furnished film-makers with further erotic material to visualise, with Shuji Terayama's **Fruits of Passion** (1981) being based upon this with the inimitable Klaus Kinski in the Sir Stephen role and Isabelle Illies essaying O, "the excruitiating pain of endless pleasure" being the hyperbolic ad-line for the film.

Eric Rochat's **The Story of O Part II/Histoire d'O** (1984) offers yet more visual splendour with Sandra Wey starring this time as the tormented O. Neither film however, can boast the assured direction of Jaeckin or the visual elan he imbrues his work with - only some lame dialogue in the opening scene - "They stroll along a luminous road surrounded by dark, endless forests. Twilight is approaching and autumn is in the air" the narrator gushes airily, or Rene's risible dialogue during the opening car ride with O - "How are your panties?" (!) and "Your flesh and the seat have to be touching", somewhat intrude on the more sensual couplings and sexual polemics later, but otherwise Jaeckin's film stands the test of time rather well thanks to its' stylised milieu and hedonistic concept, plus the renewed interest in the S & M scene which has gradually increased in the last decade, only adding to the longevity of this "great masochistic hymn."

For Your Viewing Pleasure: The Sadean Aesthetics of From Dusk Till Dawn

Xavier Mendik & Graeme Harper

She was placed like an actor in a theatre, and the audience in their niches found
themselves situated as if observing a spectacle in an amphitheatre . . . At the
back of each niche was a little door leading to an adjoining closet which was to
be used at times when . . . one preferred not to execute before everyone for
whose execution one has summoned that subject.[1]

Introduction

In Robert Rodriguez' recent film **From Dusk Till Dawn** (1996) a pair of gangsters named the Gecko brothers and their hostages hide out in a sleazy bar named The Titty Twister . Here, they and the assembled audience of road house rogues are treated to an erotic dance routine performed by the club s star entertainer Satanico Pandemonium. Satanico's dance signals that both the fictional as well as the film's audience are about to be inculcated in a new, transgressive rhetorical structure. These spectators are, as is the Madame Duclos in our opening quote from the Marquis de Sade's *120 Days of Sodom*, placed in niches as if observing a spectacle in an amphitheatre .

As Satanico dances, she and Rodriguez's trucker-bar dogs

transform into vampires, in so doing the structure of the narrative suddenly and dramatically changes from tough heist/road drama to offbeat comedy.

This sudden textual transformation mirrors the transitions in Sade snovel, where a trio of whores begin to narrate a series of stories which radically alter the flow of the implied author s established narrative. These stories, which belong both to the whores and to the actual author, Sade himself, directly share rhetorical positioning with the transformations that occur in **From Dusk Till Dawn**. They strike the audience as absurd and disturbing not merely on the basis of their convoluted nature, but because they conflate extreme acts of eroticism with bizarre and violent actions. In the case of *120 Days of Sodom* these include the consumption of excrement in company with seemingly eroticised sexual molestation, as well as the violation of the body by destructive acts based almost entirely on extravagant and convoluted philosophic intentions.

In **From Dusk Till Dawn** there is, simultaneously, the sexual pleasure of Satanico s performance presented alongside the text's sudden acceleration into a grotesque vampire orgy.

During this ensuing mayhem Quentin Tarantino (delightfully playing the psychotic Richie Gecko) is bitten and eventually killed (as are the rest of the now formerly human cast). The film's frenetic finale finds Seth Gecko (George Clooney), his former hostage Kate (Juliette Lewis) and the film s audience left bewildered in a welter of blood, puss and body

From Dusk Till Dawn

organs.

Such are the extremes of the film s textual and bodily violations that neither depicted/ watching audiences can remain external to its alteration of narrative structure or be spared the excesses of its physiological transgressions. These are texts which both invite and require a proactive reception from the spectator. Yet, the multiple mode of engagement that a work such as **From Dusk Till Dawn** offers its viewers has primarily been discussed only as a postmodern reflection of the cinematic whims of its key creators: Rodriguez and Tarantino.

While we would agree that the film s convoluted narrative and in-house, in-joke movie references and pop culture comments do reveal a great deal about the concerns about both the director and screenwriter/actor, it would be naive to presume that our interpretive works stops with the postmodern. As an alternative to this mode of analysis, we wish to employ Sade s ideas about the liberation of both text and body via dramatic, sudden and disturbing narrative shifts and excessive depictions. By using Sade we wish to define **From Dusk Till Dawn** as a movie with both a narrative mode (the opening heist segment) and a display mode (everything that is absurdly altered following Satanico s dance). While it is obvious that the ground of the film begins to shift in The Titty Twister scene, we wish to consider not only its resultant generic confusions (horror with a touch of blaxploitation, western, comedy) but also how it implicates the internal and external audiences in its cross-textual and inter-generic referencing.

In these ways we will argue that it is possible to identify in Rodriguezs film the thread of Sade s own work. That is, in endeavouring to shift the banal into the lap of the audience, Rodriguez inculcates the audience in dramatic social transformations. The audience must respond to Sade's transgression. In these works, they must actively identify constantly shifting definitions of good and evil, as well as sudden alterations in accepted story structure.

Now that's what I call a f***g Show : Libertines and Story-tellers** [2]

In the Sade's *Sodom*, the narratives that the whore trio detail are organised in the manner of a theatrical production which demands the direct involvement of the assembled libertines. The narratives of the whores, presented as they are to a captive, indeed captivated, audience in turn open up the possibility of further narratives, further stories, each of which draws

From Dusk Till Dawn

the viewers and listeners further into the web of the text. To receive the work of Sade and his narrators just as to receive **From Dusk Till Dawn**, is to release a large element of socialising and, as Sade would have it, politically right-wing self control. As Timo Airaksinen has pointed out, the construction of a reflexive and staged dialogue between narrator and audience is central to the vignettes that dominate *120 Days of Sodom*, *Justine* and Sade's other works. Here:

> *The key task is to create variety by translating the creatures*
> *of the imagination into the language of reality by means of*
> *stageproductions. the standard etiquette is set aside*
> *momentarily, the workers erect a stage and direct a play, the*
> *masters join their victims and slaves and create something new.*[3]

From Dusk Till Dawn follows this Sadean ideal, exemplifying what is a symbiotic relation between audience and text s performativity. Fundamental to this is a definite mode of storytelling constructed for active interpretation by an informed, contemporary film audience. We can, likewise, see this same kind of focussed film avid appeal in other Rodriguez films, such as **The Faculty**; and in **The Misbehavers**, Rodriguez's short in the Rodriguez/Rockwell/Tarantino/Anders ensemble film **Four Rooms**.

The film avid is that core of the contemporary Western film audience,

The Faculty

aged between 17 and 24 years, who buys around 40% of cinema tickets, visits a cinema on average once a week, and therefore forms the commercial hub on which a corporate film industry like Hollywood s depends. This audience is hedonistic, an audience whose primary aim is pleasure seeking. It is aware of the constructive dimensions of the film texts it watches (that is: the behind the camera actions and events which are regularly reported in popular teen and tabloid press). And it is accepting of the fact there that there is not one mode of representation or one mode of interpretation available to them; rather there are multiple modes. In other words: it promotes the ideal that individualism and self-flexivity are preferable to central or hierarchical modes of engagement offered by intellectual or social elites. In these ways, the film avid audience is a Sadean audience.

In **The Faculty** the relationship between this Sadean audience and the film itself is obvious. There are, for example, the regular appearances of TV and PC screens and PA systems so that what is going on on-screen is placed within the context of other narratives, other stories occurring elsewhere. Each character enters the narrative with their names slashed in red across the frame, effectively signing themselves onto the film. When Mr Tate, **The Faculty**'s history teacher, attempts to start a discussion of chapter 4 of a history books his class quickly informs him that we covered that last week and that they therefore need to move to chapter 5. The storytelling, of course, must not stall; it must continue.

Hedonism, after all, is about the regular and concerted renewal of stimulus.

In **The Misbehavers** Antonio Banderas opts to abandon his children in his hotel room rather than miss out on having fun with his girlfriend that night. He presents himself as hard man, a strict father. When negotiating with the bellboy, Tim Roth, to look after the kids, Banderas (trying to get Roth to accept not the £500 initially offered, but £300) says: What you say last counts. What Banderas says last in this film, the last words in fact, are: Did they misbehave? And, of course, they did.

When **The Misbehavers** concludes, the hotel room is on fire and Roth is holding the leg of a dead whore that the kids have just found in the bed. The kids have been drinking, smoking and watching the nudey channel. Roth is holding a syringe found in the bedside table and Banderas s girlfriend has passed out. The image is obviously one of mayhem, but it is also an image of excessive pleasure seeking. On finding the body of the whore, Roth vomits immediately and excessively. There is no technical transition to soften the image of this vomiting, and its inclusion would be gratuitous if not for the Sadean ethos of discovery through excess which is the story discourse employed here. These are the realms of storytelling in which both Rodriguez and Quentin Tarantino consciously participate.

In a similar way, **From Dusk Till Dawn**'s curious construction results not only from the convergence of generic types that dominate post-classical cinema but also from the presence of such iconic contemporary cinematic storytellers as Tarantino within the film's production. As Paul A. Woods has noted:

" . . . *Hollywood helped to shape the sensibility of a movie maker who loves to celebrate the medium s cheap thrills and glamour, validating it with a knowing, referential context.*" [4]

What has become central to the formation of the Tarantino's cine-literate reputation is not merely the fact that his movies are collections of other filmic references, but that his characters frequently suspend narrative progression in order to assume a story-telling function. Within Tarantino's own directorial efforts, the role of story-telling would appear to take two distinct forms. The first pattern focuses of a single transgressive event which is repeated, retold and renarrated by different

Reservoir Dogs

implicated sets of characters. This trope is clearly evident in a movie such as **Reservoir Dogs** (1992). Here, a flashback device is used to reveal different criminal characters recollections of the ultimate heist that goes wrong. The second type of storytelling function in Tarantino's work is via a complex overlaying of different narrative structures which work to unite an otherwise disparate set of protagonists. The interlaced composition of **Pulp Fiction** (1994) which retroactively ties all its oddball characters together provides the ultimate example of this second strategy.

While a storytelling function is thus central to Tarantino s work as a director, it is given even more impetus by the cameo appearances he has himself made in the works of other filmmakers. For instance, in his brief appearance in Rodriguez' **Desperado**, (1995) Tarantino briefly appears as a hustler who attempts to win favour with a group of Mexican hoodlums by demonstrating his skill in obscene joke and story renditions. Indeed, the movie is significant for its use of the theme of a vengeful gun-toting guitar player (or Mariachi) as a framework for multiple storytelling.

As with Sade's example from *One Hundred and Twenty of Days of Sodom* (as well as the later **From Dusk Till Dawn**), **Desperado**'s recourse to multiple modes of narration characteristically takes place before an assembled audience who are able to participate in the story under discussion.

This function is established in the film s pre-credit sequence. Here, a nervous stranger (played by Steve Buscemi) arrives at a Mexican

bar and unsettles the assembled rogues with the story of the mythical and indestructible guitar player (Antonio Banderas) he claims to have seen annihilate the inhabitants of a similar bar in a neighbouring town.[5] Buscemi's recollections (which are cinematically realised via a flashback of the event) are subject to frequent audience intervention - firstly in the form of ridicule and dismissal from the bartender (Cheech Marin), before this is replaced by nervous realisation that the guitar player is heading their way.

As with Sade's narrative digressions, the opening of **Desperado** locates its storytelling function at an axis of both textual and violent bodily alteration. This is seen by the fact that the Mariachi does arrive at the bar to inorgurate the orgy of violence that Buscemi's rendition has predicted. In the ensuing mayhem, not even Tarantino is not spared the violence that engulfs the bar in the latter part of film. Firstly, his companion randomly executed by the barman because his story doesn't check out , before a bullet to the brain provides the director's own abrupt exit from the narrative proceedings. Such examples indicate that in the contemporary Sadean text, narrative alteration works in conjunction with acts of extreme or unmotivated violence a way of both titillating and disturbing the text's audience. In this way:

".... the text works not only as a pornographic story, a scandalous novel, or an incoherent philosophical treatise, but also as an instrument of torture which is directed by Sade against the reader."[6]

Aren't These Things Supposed to Burn up? Audacious Audience Knowledge Testing.

As with the Sadean ideal, the cinematic dialectic is indeed a performative aesthetic: it always requires, simultaneously, both an act and an audience. This dialectic is culturally attuned and, in the case of contemporary cinema, increasingly sophisticated. Tarantino's own cameo appearances in both his and Rodriguez' films add to his status as a Sadean libertine whose actions are spurred on by the assembled audience whose individual desires become, in the act of voyeurism,communal. The audience here is the location of communal as well as individual desire and is not, as is often suggested, necessarily an audience harbouring unseen responses. However, the examination of this dialogic relationship - between informed private/public viewer and contemporary Sadean text -

From Dusk Till Dawn

has largely been ignored.

To cite one instance: the broadly psychoanalytic approaches employed in James Donald's *Fantasy and the Cinema* figures horror cinema as a subversive medium which allows the re-emergence of repressed material in sublimated form.[7] Several papers in this volume follow, largely without development, a Sadean critique in their analysis of filmic modes of physiological punishment and their radical effect on the construction of subjectivity.[8] What remains undeveloped, however, is a direct discussion of how orgiastic moments occur and are contextualised by differing audiences. In so avoiding this discussion Donald's essayists point to an overdetermination of a universal and timeless theory of psychic spectatorship constructed in direct relation to the cinematic apparatus.[9] In effect, they are responses looking for an audience rather than the responses of an audience.

Modern hedonistic film audiences, film avids, insist upon a high degree of emotive involvement. Sophisticated in their knowledge of cinematic effects, techniques and positions they are capable of responding outside the primal responses of their sensations. And yet the work of Tarantino, for example, has been said to be instantly unemotive and rational, more concerned with elements of sharp dialogue and the fusion of exploratory and actions scenes, with a cold fetishistic deployment of gunplay and masculinity. What is interesting about Tarantino's involvement in **From Dusk Till Dawn** is that the film uses its generic shift between realist narrative mode and fantastical display mode - a shift initiated by Tarantino's script - to greatly strengthen the emotive elements of the film's appeal to the audience. It is, in this sense, an extremely audience- responsive film and, thus, in confrontation with the notion of Tarantino as detached boy auteur..

From Dusk Till Dawn's narrative depicts the activities of the Gecko brothers, played by Tarantino and George Cloony. In its initial sequences the film clearly establishes its preoccupations with previous Rodriguez and Tarantino productions. For instance, the film reveals that the brothers are on the run following a botched bank raid - recalling similar Tarantino tactics in **Reservoir Dogs**.

Further engagement with a pre-established audience position is provided by the Gecko brothers decent into squabbling and recrimination for the mounting loss of life which occurs during their flight to freedom, and by the opening sequence in which a gas station is destroyed in extravaganza of gunplay directly reminiscent of Rodriguez' **Desperado**. In addition the brothers, now heading for Mexico, take a family hostage. The family is headed by a burned-out preacher played by Harvey Keitel, a key performer in earlier Tarantino productions.[10] Decisively, however, **From Dusk Till Dawn** uses the position of audience familiarity to eschew generic expectations around its primary evolution as a violent heist/kidnap drama.

The narrative trajectory is radically undercut, and the film s reception given an emotive charge, when the kidnappers and their captives find themselves marooned in the sadistically named Titty Twister bar. Here now established characters are attacked by vampires who, soon to perform their own transformations, nevertheless inhabit the bar as archetypal rock musicians or exotic dancers. The radical alteration in narrative drive, premised by Satanico's dance, soon after begins in the fatal wounding of Richie Gecko/Tarantino.

In the sudden generic shift, **From Dusk Till Dawn** problematizes the reception of the real and the unreal, the normal and the pathological, the pleasurable and the painful, the loveable and the hateful. This chaotic environment redoubles Sade s parodic positioning of morality and codes of social power by forcing the oppressors, the Geckos, and their former hostages to band together to defeat the undead. Audiences, struck by the incongruity of this movement, reach out therefore for the position not unlike Madame Duclos in Sade's *Sodom*: they become actors in a theatre, both part of an informed cinematic community and individual's in their own right.

Such works are both sadistic in the extremes of bodily alteration and punishment they produce, as well as playful in their manipulation of narrative drive and audience comprehension of the transformations occurring. In both narrative and physiological formulations, texts such as **From Dusk Till Dawn** reference simultaneously both creation and destruction.[11]

Tarantino, who plays psychopathic Richie in the film identifies the supreme pleasure seeker as both Creator and Destroyer. Richie's pleasure (as indicated in his random execution and molestation of helpless victims) is the pleasure of the obscene and the orgasmic. It represents the actual experience of the moment of transition from life to death, the very moment of psychic transformation, the point at which creativity and destruction meet.

It was de Sade who suggested that evil without enjoyment is banal. Tarantino's work, whether **Natural Born Killers** (1994) or **Pulp Fiction**, whether **True Romance** (1993), **Reservoir Dogs** or **From Dusk Till Dawn** have not backed away from this Sadean projection. These films display evil as undesirable only if unimaginative. If, however, it is strong or grand or creative or spectacular or humorous then it becomes a new type of problem, something to be privatized and enjoyed. What we as viewers enjoy is both the extension of spectacle beyond its generic origin and the turning inward to egotistical pleasures, a much misunderstood self-scenery of terror and violence.

So you think that s funny ? : Obscene Humour and the Horror of the Hole

In her rejection of **From Dusk Till Dawn**, Lizzie Francke has argued that : *"The film is pure juvenilia that should have remained true to its origins . . . Stretched to a big budgeted feature film, with its Vampire stand-off second half going on for an eternity, it tests the viewers patience."* 12

The problems Francke has with the film point to its provocative positioning of scenarios of evil, elements of spectacle, thrill and visual excess for the contemplation of the spectator's pleasure. It is possible to argue that the sudden textual transformation into **From Dusk Till Dawn**'s display mode is all the more dramatic because of earlier attempts to not only separate but to suppress elements of generic and bodily excess in the film's opening guise as Tarantino bank/ heist drama.

Here, Richie Gecko is wounded in the hand after the brothers destroy a bordertown gas station and its inhabitants. At this point the film playfully prefigures the use of special effects in the latter part of the film. At this point, Tarantino is shown looking through the hole in his hand that results from his injury as the special effects team s credits appear on screen. However, the wound is taped at the point at which the special effects team s credits disappear from screen. The wounds disappearance behind the taping at this point reiterates the need to suppress excessive physiological textual elements from the causal based modes of narration that dominate the former part of the film.

Importantly, it is in The Titty Twister that Richie's wound is reopened when is attacked with a knife by Satanico's henchmen. The assault on his hand provokes both the transformation of the bar's inhabitants into vampires, as well as the alteration of narrative flow. In fact, the hole (which is held as if it is evidence of crucifixion, in centre-frame) is a portal linking the inside of the body with the outside. The hole represents a challenge to his state of mere insideness and a call for interaction from both the assembled audience and the film's spectator.

In the next few minutes **From Dusk Till Dawn** provides an insight into the Sadean metamorphosis where the disillusion of established body boundaries is reciprocated by a transformation in the text's structure and audience engagement. Both text and blood flow, instead of life and death there will be multiple lives and multiple deaths, a truly chaotic and orgiastic replication of text and subjectivity.

It is pertinent that de Sade identifies the notion of the hole as a paradoxical entity for both text and body. It is the proper source of death, as well as birth, and it is the source of climax .13 It thus represents a void which in the form of wounds or lacerations disturb the stability of the external body image, while functioning as a break or alteration in the text's depiction and its established mode of narration.

Effectively, the second injury that Richie sustains functions as a symbolic wound, not only does it compel the Titty Twister inhabitants to transform into vampires, but alongside physical alteration comes a transition in narrative structure. This is a hole which shifts the text from causal based narration into one where a plurality of audience desires are gratified.

We will see, in the next few minutes of the film, how **From Dusk Till Dawn** becomes inter-generic as both subjectivity and formal structure change. It is not merely that the text shifts from realist heist drama to body horror narrative but in that shift the film accelerates to take in divergent elements of Kung-fu, Western, Blaxsploitation and eroticism alongside the vampire narrative. In this relentless shift and transformation, the narrative structure replicates the chaotic construction of the Sadean narrative.

Although the film began its narrative mode with a tightly constructed diegetic frame by exploring the interrelations of Richie and Seth Gecko, The Titty Twister becomes a site where these concerns widen to take in the multiple characters emerging in the small group of survivors gathered at the bar. Importantly, these characters such as Frost played by Fred Williamson and Sex machine played by Tom Savini are not only characters, but story tellers who narrate their textual and non deigetic pasts. In this respect their placement in the text replicates the multilayed nature of the sadean text. Here:

A story teller has free access to novelty and variety. Everything possible is bought up, told and explained. The stories are shared by listeners as if they were real life possibilities. Because the grammer of routine and conventional etiquette is broken, a new twisted grammer emerges where the relations of peoples, ideas and things are contorted.[14]

The introduction of these two protagonists indicate that in the Sadean work, not only narrative drive but also processes of characterisation are open to sudden change and transformation. This fluidity of identity is marked through a split between the discrete fictional role and the actor's past status. In the case of **From Dusk Till Dawn** the (undeveloped) character of Frost becomes a reference point for all the other roles

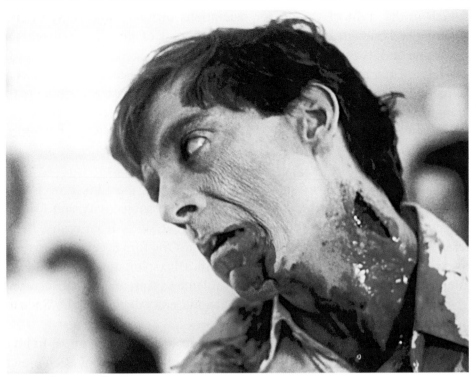

Dawn of the Dead

undertaken by Fred Williamson. These characterisations were initiated in a number of blaxploitation films such as **Mean Johnny Barrows** (1975) and **One Down Two to Go** (1982), which Williamson also directed. These cast him as a disaffected kung-fu fighting Vietnam vet who has to defeat inequality with physical prowess. From **Dusk Till Dawn** parodies these roles by showing how ineffectual his brand of martial arts is, when attempting to use Kung-fu against a vampire. Equally, in one comic scene, Williamson provokes his own death by, delivering a Vietnam vet remembers speech which prevents him from noticing that his friends are transforming into vampires around him.[15]

In Rodriguez' film, this construction of characterisation points to subjectivity as a fragile shell. In the same way de Sade offers his readers heroes with which they cannot identify, Rodruiguez' film reproduces a series of mutually exclusive types, each person represents a conglomeration of attributes.[16] Here, identity is reduced to a object, to be marked, disguarded and destroyed. The ultimate reducability of identity is seen in **From Dusk Till Dawn**'s casting of Tom Savini in the role of Sex Machine. This clearly draws on his earlier role as a biker in George A.

Romero's zombie film **Dawn of the Dead** (1979). Again, this intertextual reference is taken to the point of parody for humorous effect. Whereas the Savini character in **Dawn of the Dead** was depicted fetishising a flick knife with a comb blade, Sex Machine's toy is a gun mounted cod piece which opens to repel potential assailants.[17] Equally, Savini s depiction in **From Dusk Till Dawn** not only replays his established cameos, but also extends upon them. Whereas his status in **Dawn of the Dead** was of a special effects man performing a cameo, in Rodriguez' film his performance literally is as a special effect: he suddenly transforms into a giant beast whom the survivors must then behead and destroy.

This example indicates the close link between creation, destruction and textual transformation in the bar. We witness a transformation in established modes of character and self: We will see at least two of many characters who have previously been one and this doppleganger effect is doubly suggestive of Sade's idea that without evil there can be no virtue. This appears again and again in the Tarantino camp as the equation: to be a professional or not to be a professional .

As Mr White says in **Reservoir Dogs**; "A psychopath is not a professional. You can't work with a psychopath, cause ya don't know what those stick assholes are gonna do next ." And as Seth Gecko says to his brother in **From Dusk Till Dawn**; "This is not me. I'm a professional fucking thief. I steal money . . . What you're doin' ain't how it's done. Do you understand?

The fact is, we don't want to work with these psychopaths, we don't want to be professional, we don't want to adhere to rules of how it's done . Their s is an ethos of play and this is what triggers the different modes of audience engagement.

So what do we know about vampires ? Multiple Pleasures and Points of Recognition.

One of the key triggers for the generic shift in **From Dusk Till Dawn** is the seductive dance routine performed by Satanico Pendemonium. Importantly, her performance is introduced by the club compare Razor Charlie as being For Your Viewing Pleasure , and in many respects the statement extends beyond her obvious coding as a site of erotic visual display. Rather, what the announcement echoes in is the transition of the narrative towards a mode where thrill, titillation and spectacle replace narrative drive.

In so doing, the self reflexive nature of the medium is also foregrounded, with an appeal not only to the viewing audience of The Titty Twister but also to the film's audience. Their's is a presence which is increasingly acknowledged by the text, both through direct address of characters to camera, as well as the focalization of mayhem and violence directly towards the camera lens.[18]

While the shift from realist to contemporary horror narrative is accomplished through an alternation in generic mode it is complicated by the playful and parodic incorporation of elements of slapstick, humour and gag routines into this transformation. Central to this textual alteration is the re-centring of the comedic and the obscene. In its conflation of the disturbing, and the erotic, the obscene and the absurd, **From Dusk Till Dawn**'s display mode becomes increasingly comic. The film s audience wait to see what transformations take place and cheer for grotesquery.

As a result, we also cheer for the dialogue between inside and outside which is not simply a dialogue between self-motivated individuals, but of phylogeneis- a developmental change of the species. We also cheer for the transformative human body which here is not closed down by death nor subject to the ambivalence of work. Here, monstrosity is a powerful way of organizing and understanding human experience, and of avoiding abstraction.

From Dusk Till Dawn seems at this point to be almost undercranked, to be unnatural, jerky, syncopated. In this comical stage we are never far away from self- or generic parody. In this film gangsters trade off not only with themselves but with the genre's generic history. The parody is outward looking, the audience is called to participate in the fun. What trade offs can we make in our love of spectacle, our love of the catalyst, our love of the Sadean ideal, our love of the humorous.

In films like **From Dusk Till Dawn** the Freudian thesis that joking serves as a safety valve, saving energy, sparing cognitive processing, and discharging hostile or sexual feelings is complicated. Here laughter and the forbidden go entirely hand-in-hand as displayed communicative and communal strategies. Here sexual safety valves are discharged from the hands of individual psychopaths into the hands of the audience whose own pleasures, motivations and interests are as diffuse as the Sadean hole through which these forms of gratification have emerged.

In this respect, it remains for film theory to finally reconsider the role of the audience of the contemporary horror film. Such group's function not as a homogenized mass whose pleasure is dependent on a single aspect of the text, but rather as a series of pleasure seekers able to take multiple forms of gratification from what they consume. Multigeneric texts such as **From Dusk Till Dawn** produce a heightened series of emotional engag ments which revolve around moments of laughter, titillation, disgust and recognition.

As viewer's, we shift in such comic, self-reflexive films from a position of superiority (in our expectations of the film s opening segment), to a recognition of incongruity (having those expectations upturned at The Titty Twister) and thus to a feeling of psychic release. But this shift is also a shift into the recognition that in aesthetic experience the emotions function cognitively: we learn from these overloaded, multi-generic engagements. We learn that cinema's collective experience is also the experience of the individual, a place where multiple pleasures separate and collide.

We might ask, finally then: what can this Sadean reading tell us about cinema and its relationship with the audience. We know that there are points of performance and play. That they involve a hyperstimulated, overloaded state. These are works that are impossible to contain, even referring to other texts outside the film .[19] In so doing they involve interaction, actions by human agents, challenges to established structures of communication, belief and knowledge. In this respect they open up both body, narrative and mind in ways that highlight human creativity and the profound schematic abilities of audience imagination.

A longer version of this feature is included in the Graeme Harper & Xavier Mendik edited collection ; Unruly Pleasures: The Cult Film and Its Critics **(London: FAB Press, 1999).**

NOTES

1.   Timo Airaksinen. *The philosophy of the Marquis de Sade* (London and New York: Routledge, 1995), p.129.
2.   The bold subsections which accompany this article are all elements of dialogue taken from Robert Rodriguez's film **From Dusk Till Dawn** (1996).
3.   Airaksinen, p.128.
4.   Paul A. Brown *King Pulp: The Wild World of Quentin Tarantino.* (London: Plexus Press, 1996), p.8.
5.   This massacre is itself another method of engaging in intertextual narration - specifically pointing to an identical blood bath featured in Rodriguez' first film **El Mariachi** (1992), of which **Desperado** is a partial remake. Indeed, **El Mariachi's**

plot involving a guitar player on the run from the mob after being mistaken for a hitman, points to the ease with which the narratives of disparate characters can become inextricably linked with negative and violent outcomes.

6. Airaksinen, p.13.

7. See James Donald, (ed) *Fantasy and the Cinema*. (London: British Film Institute, 1989).

8. In particular, see Barbara Creed 'Horror and the Monstrous Feminine: An Imaginary Abjection', pp. 63-91.

9. Vanessa R. Schwartz 'Cinematic Spectatorship Before the Apparatus: The Public Taste for Reality in *Fin-de-Siècle* Paris' in Leo Charney and Vanessa R. Schwartz ed's *Cinema and the Invention of Modern Life*. (Berkeley, Los Angeles, London: University of California Press, 1995), p. 297. One of the important features of Schwartz's analysis is her attempt to place the birth of cinematic spectatorship within a historical and cultural context, while pointing to the plurality of differing pleasures offered to the spectator by such apparatus. Importantly, she identifies sites such as the Paris Morgue as a crucial precursor to cinema. It was both a location frequented by differing audiences as well as a site of "morbid attraction" (p.302) which prefigures the drive of spectacle film that defined much silent cinema. This fascination in locations of death that the article details provides a good point of comparison with **From Dusk Till Dawn**. See also Ben Singer 'Modernity, Hyperstimulus and the Rise of Popular Sensationalism' in the same volume. Singer argues that geographical changes which mark modernism resulted in the construction of popular narratives marked by peril, impending doom and chaos. His conclusion that these examples of macabre thrill continue in certain cycles of contemporary film is replicated by Rodriguez's film. Here, narrative, order and logic and sacrificed to an increasing drive towards dismemberment anarchic spectacle and generic confusion.

10. The casting of Juliette Lewis in the role of the preacher's daughter Kate confirms the link to previous Tarantino productions. Her indicated instability in the text casts allusions to the character of Mallory Knox from the Tarantino scripted **Natural Born Killers**. It therefore appropriate that Kate is a figure to which Richard Gecko is instantly attracted.

11. Richie's role as Sadean libertine who gratifies the film's audience by orchestrating displays of violation and textual transformation it reciprocated in Wes Craven's recent film **Scream** (1997). Here, two killers stalk and taunt their victims with a series of references culled from established horror movies. The heroine unmasks the killers as her boyfriend Billy Loomis, the surname itself a reference to a character from John Carpenter's **Halloween** (1978) and his friend Randy. She derides the pair as having been desensitized by an excess of cinematic violence. However, Randy's reply that cinema "does not create psycho's it in fact makes psycho's more creative" references the Sadean ideal of knowledge and pleasure as occurring through the realization of suffering and terror. Indeed, the disturbing aspect to Randy's characterization is the absence of motive for his quest to terrorise the heroine Sydney. As he admits, in this respect he continues the tradition of seeking pleasure through the punishment of the innocent that marked horror film libertines such as Hannibal Lector of Jonathan Demme's **Silence of the Lambs** (1991).

12. Lizzy Francke 'From Dusk Till Dawn,' *Sight and Sound*, (June 1996), p.42.

13. Airaksinen, p.157.

14. Ibid., p.130.

15. A similarly perverse undermining of identity through the fictional role is given in Wes Craven's casting of Henry Winkler as the college principal Mr Hembry in **Scream**. At one point, Hembry cannot resist staring in the mirror and adopts the macho pose made famous by Winkler's role as Fonz in the 1970's television show *Happy Days*. However, his narcissistic self obsession in **Scream** fatally prevents him from seeing the killer waiting to attack from behind the mirror.

16. Airaksinen, p.70.

17. As **Desperado** features an identical weapon in the Mariachi's armoury, the inclusion of the device in **From Dusk Till Dawn** once again underscores the intertextuality occurring between these two films.

18. This latter feature confirms the close link between audience and victim that Sade defined. It also once again indicates the self reflexive understanding of the cinematic sources that the film is drawing upon. The presence of Savini points to the origin of p-o-v cinematic technique as Romero's **Dawn of the Dead**. See *The Living and the Undead* (Urbana and Chicago: University of Illinois Press, 1986), p.307. Here, Gregory A. Waller notes Romero's use of subjective camera to involve the audience at the point of the zombie's destruction. While the technique serves to generate suspense, it also functions to underscore the vulnerability of the viewer's position.

19. Michael A. Arnzen, Whose Laughing Now ? The Postmodern Splatter Film, *The Journal of Popular Film and Television* Vol.21 No.4 (winter 1994), p.179. In his analysis of contemporary horror cinema Arnzen's article considers not only the humour that underpins the genre. By identifying a duel process of physical and narrative destruction in Sam Raimi's film **The Evil Dead 2** (1987), Arnzen's comments clearly open themselves to a Sadean reading. For instance, in one scene, the hero finds his own hand possessed by a malevolent spirit, and is forced to sever the appendage with a chainsaw. At this point, the scene (which has been filmed in real time) suddenly alters: "...the camera is hyperactive, and the scene is destabalising, offering the viewer only fast glimpses of things in motion." (p.178).

Le Frisson Des Vampires

Vibrant colours and dazzling surrealism, plus a heady infusion of sex inform Jean Rollin's sanguinary vampires.

Andy Black

"The dead are present with us and that is not fanaticism. Those who don't know us accuse us of sacrilege and blasphemy. Our time is devoted to pursuing the memory of eternal darkness." (Vampire philosophy from **Le Frisson Des Vampires**).

Amongst the litany of emphemeral images French surrealist Jean Rollin elevates to the screen in **Le Frisson des Vampires/Shiver of the Vampire** (1970), both the twisting, contorting branches from a gnarled tree which snake around a master bedroom and the startling appearance of a beautiful vampire Isolde (Dominique) bursting out from within the confines of a grandfather clock, serve to illustrate the unfettered imagination and Hoffman-like atmosphere which the filmic *artiste* Rollin includes within his palette.

Not for him the mundane mechanics of the slasher film, the prosaic images of *cine-verite* or the artifice intrinsic within the "art" film. Instead, his canvas is awash with a myriad of colours, eccentric characters and exceptional locations - all adding a decidedly artistic grist to his most painterly mill as his visual elan shines through as his true *metier*.

Indeed, Rollin confesses that "It was a great pleasure constructing the images" for **Frisson**, in this, his third film. His seminal feature **Le Viol du Vampire** (1968) began his process of imbruing his particular oeuvre with dazzling imagery, only mediated somewhat by the monochrome stock the film is shot on, with his follow-up work, **La Vampire Nue** (1969) becoming his first colour feature and the kaleidoscopic splash of colour continues with ferocity in **Frisson**. As Rollin reveals of his camerman Jean-Jacques Renon, (his) "..co-operation was essential, he was entirely in tune with me, splashing colour in the castle tower as if it were a candy cane."

As is his want, Rollin quickly dispenses with such mundane

Le Frisson Des Vampires

niceities as "plot" - quickly introducing us to a honeymooning couple Ise (Sandra Julien) and Antoine (Jean-Marie Durand), arriving at a seemingly deserted castle, save for the two voluptuous servants (Marie-Pierre Castel and Kuelan Herce).

The couples' search for their cousins sees Ise gradually becoming initiated into the vampiric realm of Castel and Herce, together with the mesmerising Isolde, before being reunited with the effete duo of Michel Delahaye and Jacques Robiolles, who it transpires, are the the long-lost cousins as well as angst-ridden vampires content to philosophise at length about the existential nature of the vampire.

Antoine's anxious attempts to affect a speedy escape from the castle and the clutches of its' vampiric occupants, ultimately flounders on the "forbidden fruit" that Ise enjoys in her sapphic encounters with the female vampires and upon the cerebral fertilisation which Delahaye and Robiolles use to engage Ise's mind. Thus, the staking of an "innocent" female victim is explained in that; "There was no other way. This malediction whch is ours must not be passed onto others." Delahaye continues, "Because she would have been allowed to live like the dead, she would have shared our everlasting eternity and pursued forever our fatal destiny" he concludes.

Around the relative paucity of this threadbeare framework, Rollin embellishes events with his customary flair and in doing so, transcends the deliberately cliched horror genre elements - arcane castle; fog-shrouded cemetery complete with creaking gates; flaming torches; vampires and virgins.

His real skill however, is in utilising these visual accoutrements in the manner of his own favoured artists such as Trouille and Magritte in order to transcend the mere medium of film and breathe new life into them beyond. It is no surprise to see the wealth of Rollin-related features in numerous film publications in recent years, given the unique nature of rollin's illustrative materials. A Rollin film still isn't simply that - it is also a still-life, a fragment of the auteur's fevered imagination, captured, preserved and gloriously independent of its' filmic lineage.

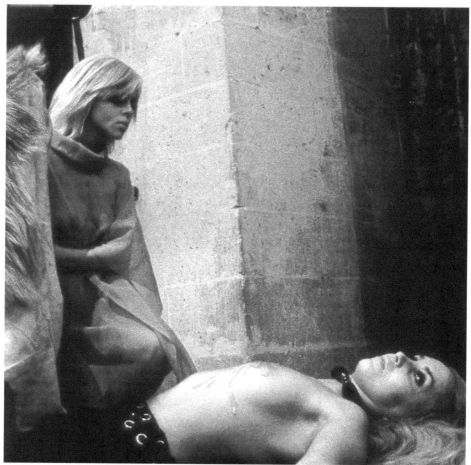

Le Frisson Des Vampires

In many respects, Rollin's love of utilising horror genre conventions in his images and then bombarding them with a collision of colours, echoes the style of Mario Bava, although any further similarity is dissipated with Rollin's favouring of more abrupt cutting and editing techniques which allows for none of the celebrated tracking shots which became a trademark for Bava's ever-prowling camera.

When Rollin is not drowning his interiors with incandescent red and blue hues, he's drowning castle walls with blood as he literally does draw blood from stone during the film's climax and his correlation between human characteristics and inanimate structures also fuels much of Rollin's vision.

As such, the castle also has an almost living and breathing library - when Antoine is trapped in the library, its' claustrophobic bookshelves seemingly encircle him, the books taking on a life of their own as they begin to hurl themselves off the shelves and engulfing him, juxtaposed with the sight elsewhere of vampires dying, so the library too bleeds like the castle walls which contain it, as the truly organic nature of the structure is revealed.

Likewise, Dominique's aforementioned entry from within a grandfather clock delineates that it too is alive. "I don't know where it came from, it's kind of a surrealistic vision" as Rollin appropriately describes the image, also stating his own filmic philosophy thus; "A grandfather clock is of no interest - a vampire woman getting out of this clock at midnight, that's me."

A bizarre concoction of eccentric, singular characters is also pure Rollin one could say when discussing his work and **Frisson** certainly doesn't disappoint on this score. Whether it's Dominique's sexual predator, Delahaye and Robiolles "hippie", kaftan-wearing vampires, the sexually provocative duo of Castel and Herce (the latter replacing Castel's twin-sister Catherine who was pregnant at the time !), or Julien's naive virgin - "...beautiful..and not too clever. She was a model" being Rollin's description of her, there's no shortage of outrageous characters here to compliment the eye-catching scenes.

It is Dominique however, who has the pivotal role here when, in the fatalistic denouement, she is reduced into drinking blood from her own veins in an act of self-perpetuation which also serves to expose the pernicious and ultimately futile nature of her vampirism.

The inherent symbolism here which correlates blood drinking/vampirism with oral sex, draining the bodies life-fluids as it were, reaches its logical conclusion on Rollin's favoured location, Dieppe beach, as Delahaye and Robiolles ravish Ise with wanton abandon as the sea crashes against the shore - only for their ecstasy to be supplanted by agony as the rapidly rising rays of the sun begins to sear their flesh, resulting in their abrupt demise. Their "petit mort" or dual "death orgasm" becoming their external death here - the figures vanishing from the screen, with the ensuing silence then crudely broken by the raucous seagull cries overhead.

Supremely aided by the crashing, flailing chords of the short-lived college rock band Acanthus (evoking the vibrant, theatrical music and images of Alice Cooper's "Welcome To My Nightmare" concert), **Frisson** remains a classic triumph of style over substance.

By concentrating solely on the vampires visual aspects, Rollin does jettison any opportunity to dissect or come to any real sense of understanding of the vampires' condition, merely relying on (in this case) Delahaye and Robiolles pretentious, improvised philosophical ramblings in order to put any flesh on the vampire bones.

As these self-appointed barometers of taste so acutely observe of vampirism; "It is a great honour. A very important privilege. You couldn't escape your destiny. cultured people often come to us. You can't elude your destiny."

In Rollin's case, his "destiny" is very much making vampire films for the more discerning (or cultured ?!) cognoscenti and amen to that in a film world dominated by commercialism before imagination and expediency before principles.

Wax Mask
A neo-gothic Italian Model?
Andy Black

"Very soon we'll open our doors to the public and my work will be revealed to the world." - Volkoff (Robert Hossein), the curator of the wax museum in **Wax Mask**.

Whilst the hysterical cries of "frying tonight" from Kenneth William's Dr. Watt in **Carry On Screaming** (1966) reverberate around my head whilst writing this, Sergio Stivaletti's directorial debut, **Wax Mask** (1997), jettisons the "mad doctor" mixing molten wax cariacature in favour of a more reverential and yet rejuvenating approach, with its' considered blend of gothic elements and futuristic conceits as the audacious climax shows.

In fact, it is these gothic trappings which led Stivaletti to these shores, not to plunder the inspired lunacy of the *Carry On* team (shame !), but to recreate the halcyon days of our most famous horror studio as he admits that he "wanted the film to have a Hammer look about it."

Borrowing liberally from Michael Curtiz' **The Mystery of the Wax Museum** (1933), Andre de Toth's remake **House of Wax** (1953), together with Gaston Leroux's famous novel, *The Phantom of the Opera* , Stivaletti composes a real hybrid of ancient beliefs and alchemy, fermenting with far more contemporary motifs.

Given this veritable pot-pourri of influences, plus the initial collaboration between both Dario Argento and Lucio Fulci, it is no surprise that **Wax Mask** endeavours to cover so many disparate bases.

The untimely death of Fulci, who was slated to direct the film only two months before filming was due to commence, deprived the maestro of his intended opportunity to rekindle the long-ailing Italian horror film industry, especially as he was workng alongside an equally vaunted luminary in Argento.

Fulci's death, together with the absence of first choice Robert

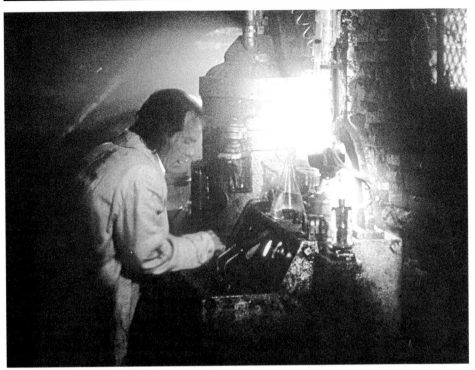

Wax Mask

Englund for the role of museum curator Volkoff, on the negative side, deprived the film of a star name and visceral impetus, but on the positive side, allowed Stivaletti to eschew his "sfx only" mantle (effectively showcased in the likes of **Demons**, **Creepers** and **Cemetery Man** to name but three), by also enabling him to handle the directorial reigns for the first time.

Stivaletti explains his evolution into director and sfx maestro - combining prosthetic make-up effects with modern CGI techniques in **Wax Mask** thus; "What I want to do is to put all these different types of effect into my new film and my next projects. **Wax Mask** is a project which was born for another director, so I cannot put everything I would like into it."

Continuing to outline his own ambitions for the film, Stivaletti reveals that "My personal goal for **Wax Mask** was to design the very best special effects and also direct the movie. For me, it was an ideal opportunity to control both artistic elements."

And it is most certainly these artistic elements which Stivaletti does concentrate on, unsurprisngly considering the somewhat heterogeneous script provided by Argento, Fulci and Daniele Stroppa.

Their handiwork begins in Paris circa 1900 on New Years Eve as cascading fireworks illuminate the night sky, silhouetting the Eiffel Tower, only to cut to a grisly murder scene as we see police officers pouring over two bloodied corpses - their hearts ripped out by a masked man using a metal claw as recounted by the sole survivor and witness to the heinous act, the victims' frightened young daughter , Sonia (Romina Mondello).

As the action then advances twelve years to Rome, we see Sonia, now an attractive young woman, gaining employment as a costume designer for a newly opened waxworks museum, run by the curator Volkoff (Robert Hossein).

That the main "attractions" in the museum are the life-like recreations of gruesome murder scenes, appears not to unduly phase our Sonia, but the spate of violent and suspicious deaths which ensue, raise her fears and those of an investigative journalist/photographer (yes, that old cliche !), Andrea (Riccardo Serventi Longhi), especially given the close correlation between the murders and the new exhibits that Volkoff proudly displays in his museum.

What's most refreshing here, is to see Stivaletti's concerted attempts at evoking a cogent gothic atmosphere, given the period milieu

Wax Mask

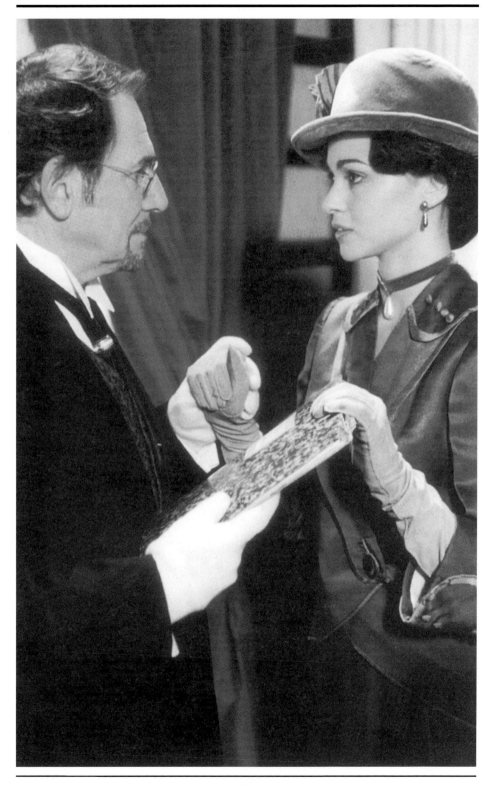

the film occupies - a welcome change from the usual gamut of teen-fodder gore films where creativity is measured, not in the artistry of the work but in the length of time the de riguer knife-blade spends embedded in the skin of the cherub-faced victims.

As such, we have the Bava-esque image of Volkoff entering the museum - a personnification of mystery clad in a black fedora and billowing cape; the disquieting wax figures - lifeless in appearance and yet silently watching or so our minds tell us, and Volkoff's underground laboratory cum torture chamber, where bubbling, smoking vials, coloured liquids and sparking instruments suggest a Frankenstein element.

Most bravura of all however, proves to be Sonia's ill-fated, night-time journey - walking the (almost) deserted Rome streets as the rain lashes down, thunder crackles overhead and the wind (or is it ?) rustles the trees and hedgerows, all under the eerie silhouette provided by the gas-lit street lights, before an ominous black hansom cab careers towards her and she is kidnapped by the unseen assailant.

The almost playful, naive charm of the local brothel also reinforces the period setting here as we see lingerie-clad sirens seducing their all-too willing clients in an atmosphere of unrestrained hedonism. The presence of the prostitutes here is also non-judgemental as we see Andrea visiting when he is not cultivating his burgeoning romance with Sonia, as well as Alex (Umberto Balli), Volkoff's (sorcerers) apprentice,

Wax Mask

Wax Mask

whose lively S&M sessions in the brothel are greedily devoured vicariously by his voyeuristic employer, who watches undetected via a bedroom peephole.

Just as Alex may be searching for his own sexual "perfection", so too is Volkoff searching for his own artistic "perfection" as in the wax figures he so lovingly covets and whose lifelike qualities represent not so much Volkoff's artistic skills, but his embalming ones - comprised of his victims' blood and flesh we later learn in a shocking moment where Sonia discovers fluid pipes draining from the wax bodies and fake eye-sockets concealing the ravaged flesh beneath.

In time-honoured tradition, the demented Volkoff does indeed see himself as an "artist" - creating new life and "perfection" from each new victim he kills (Sonia's own parents numbering amongst them it is revealed). To further this pursuit we see Volkoff lure the vivacious Georgina (Valery Valmond) with a "false" note into a secret rendezvous/trap. Having been abruptly knocked unconscious by Volkoff's well-aimed syringe to the neck, Georgina later awakens, only to find herself half-naked and strapped to a mechanical chair in Volkoff's laboratory. As the imposing image of the now masked Volkoff advances towards her, we then see Georgina drained of blood and her beauty, morphing into a hideously wrinkled old hag - her life taken in order to sustain Volkoff's waxen effigies above.

The denouement sees Andrea frantically descending into the bowels of the museum using a lantern to pierce the enveloping gloom, as he seeks the now similarly imprisoned Sonia. As we see the now helpless and naked Sonia, strapped to the same mechanical chair, Volkoff reveals the extent of his misguided fantasies; "..even then my art was touched by genius, but now it has a new dimension. The world refused to recognise me then, now it will be forced to do so. My gentle sensitivity was mocked, despised as if a true weakness. People wanted only violence and terror. Alright. I could give them that. No one has expressed pain and sorrow as I have done because I carried a vast store inside me. And sorrow, I bestow on the wax figures and so in their moment of death, I grant immortality. I honour those who like me were cast out by society, reviled by it."

The depth of Volkoff's hatred for society is now revealed, his attempts to play god are sumarily ended as Andrea aims to send Volkoff to meet his maker by blasting him with acidic vapours whereupon, Volkoff's face liquifies into a hideous, putrifying mess, allowing the duo to escape. As the curator's embittered assistant Alex then throws a lantern at him, shouting the epitaph "Burn in hell", we see the shrieking Volkoff engulfed by the flames, his life now appropriately ending (?) as simultaneously, his wax creations meltdown to reveal the true identities of their human victims.

The horrific skeletal figure with erubescent eyes that reaches out

Wax Mask

menacingly only to be arbitrarily decapitated by a swift sword strike, instantly evokes the similar endoskeleton image from **The Terminator** (1984) - a germane reference considering the extraordinary climax as we glimpse Alex, peeling off his face mask to reveal similar skeletal features beneath, before utilising his metal hand to pick up a Volkoff face mask from an array of masks in front of him.

The alarming sight of the "reborn" Volkoff attired in requisite top hat and suit, walking calmly into the night crowd and away from the burning museum, suggests not only Volkoff's embodiement of Freud's "self-preservative drive", but also a deliberate ambiguity and blurring of identites. Just as a certain physical appearance and characteristics can be stripped away like an artificial veneer, so too can we re-examine the mind and soul, teasing away the ptetences and aura of mystery which surrounds our inner-most recesses.

Though as regards the stated aim of re-igniting the stagnant Italian horror genre, **Wax Mask** may ultimately fail, it al least offers a more deserving case for support than say Argento's most recent, lacklustre works; **Trauma** (1993) and **The Stendhal Syndrome** (1996), with his

Wax Mask

Wax Mask

The Phantom of the Opera (1999) also running low on imagination and ingenuity.

The compelling atmosphere he creates, his effective use of both colour and shadows, coupled with some bravura camera moves, all suggest that Stivaletti, the director has a future - not least for his much-criticised stand against merely producing another blood-filled platter - "I'd like to think that the splatter scenes are quite elegant, since I approached the film with a classic touch. I really didn't want to have that much gore."

The characters may not all be fleshed-out to the extent one would wish, but the energy and craftmanship is there, together with a highly audacious, climactic frisson which suggests that although Stivaletti may not have instantly revived the corpse that is the Italian horror genre, he has at least restored the vital signs to it by ensuring that the crimson liquid is once again coursing through the veins, a feat which has proved to be beyond many of his more lauded contemporaries.

Plastic Surgery Disasters
Body Horror in Eyes Without A Face and Faceless

Andy Black

"It's an anguish film. It's a quieter mood than horror, more internal, more penetrating. It's horror in homeopathic doses." - Georges Franju, director of **Eyes Without A Face**.

"It's a horror film but with human beings instead of bizarre monsters. It's not a gore film." - Jess Franco, director of **Faceless**.

"Doctor said you need surgery now,
You're feeling good until the side-effects fuck up something else.."
"The magazine says your face don't look quite right,
Until you wear our brand new wonder cream tonight..."
(**Dead Kennedys** - *Plastic Surgery Disasters* - Alternative Tentacles CD)

Whilst Andy Warhol famously commented that members of contemporary society each demand their own fifteen minutes of fame, the populace in the western world require much greater longevity when it comes to the thorny issue of preserving their "beauty" in order to massage their vanity.

As civil wars, natural devastation and global conflict tears apart the fabric of the remote (and not so remote) world, many in the so-called "civilised" nations find themselves not preoccupied with survival but with the misguided quest for the ultimate body in order to hide the ravages of natural ageing.

So, out goes wrinkles and in comes skin grafts, out goes excess fat and in comes tummy tucks, out goes atrophying flesh and in comes

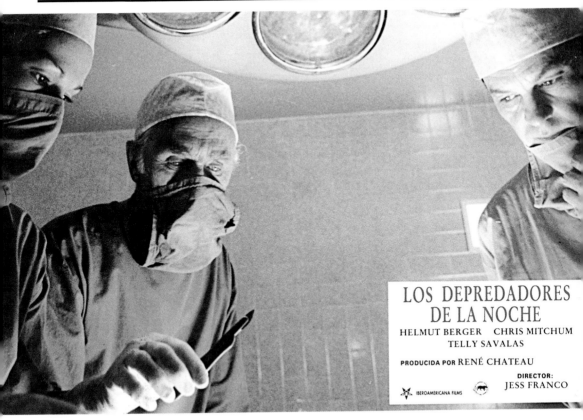

LOS DEPREDADORES
DE LA NOCHE
HELMUT BERGER   CHRIS MITCHUM
TELLY SAVALAS

PRODUCIDA POR RENÉ CHATEAU

DIRECTOR:
JESS FRANCO
IBEROAMERICANA FILMS

Faceless

donor flesh - ultimately out goes the natural and in comes the plastic, the artifice that plastic surgery provides. It may not be rooting out the blonde-haired and blue-eyed as special, but it *is* the rooting out of imperfection in favour of the egotistical pursuit of the vacuous concept that is vanity.

It is just these cosmetic concerns which informs both Georges Franju's masterly **Eyes Without A Face/Les Yeux Sans Visage** (1959) and Jess Franco's thinly-veiled homage, **Faceless/Les Predateurs De La Nuit** (1988) - though not a remake per se.

Whera's the traditional strain of mad doctors and even crazier experiments mined a rich seam in numerous horror and sci-fi genre films over the years, essentially borrowing much of their inspiration from Mary Shelley's *Frankenstein* (1818) with its' core theme of creating new life from a mosaic of donor body parts, both Franju and Franco's work strikes more at the heart of contemporary society.

In both films, the creation of life is not the driving *raison d'etre* behind the surgical experimentation which takes place, rather it is the

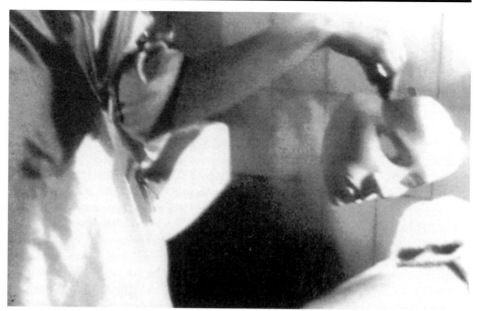

Eyes Without A Face

restoration of superficial "beauty" or "normality" which provides the defining impetus.

The surgeons in each film - Professor Genessier (Pierre Brasseur) in **Eyes** and Dr. Flamand (Helmut Berger) and Dr. Moser (Anton Diffring) in **Faceless**, are seen operating as much to satisfy their own medical egotism as the well-being of their patients, literally operating under the misguided view that by restoring a patina of perfection to their patients, they can somehow bypass the moral bankruptcy of the soul they embody. The goal for each surgeon is not the salvation of the spirit but the achievement in making beauty once again become (only) skin deep.

In both films it is (dysfunctional) family relationships which serve to instigate the nefarious activities of the respective surgeons as they spiral into the detritus of the human psyche with ever increasing urgency with each successive operating failure.

In **Eyes** it is Genessier's daughter Catherine (Edith Scob) who is the unwilling recipient of numerous facial skin grafts following her hideous disfigurement in a car accident (itself the result of her father's driving) - "He always has to dominate, even on the road he drove like a demon" she remarks, and so reveals her father's deep-rooted guilt complex for her condition, a burden he seeks to remove by restoring her former beauty.

Likewise in **Faceless**, Flamand's domed surgery is the result of

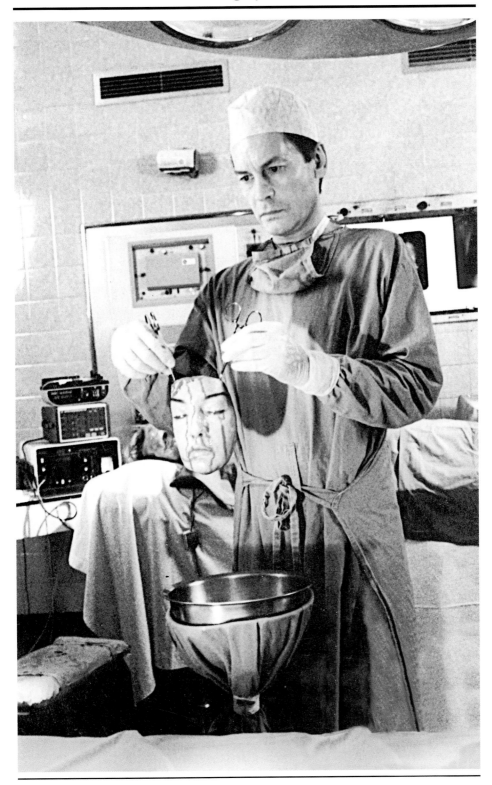

his beloved sister Ingrid (Christiane Jean) being disfigured with acid thrown into her face by one dissatisfied client of Flamand's expensive plastic surgery clinic and which was intended to hit the doctor instead. Unlike Catherine however, Ingrid proves a more enthusiastic recipient of the numerous attempted face grafts, perhaps a sign of the increasingly cosmetic-obsessed 80's - she must have her "beauty" returned at any (human) cost.

Although the acquisition of unwilling donor victims - all chosen for their facial attractiveness and pristine skin is instigated upon the instructions of Genessier in **Eyes** and Flamand in **Faceless**, it is the doctors' willing accomplices who carry out the subsequent kidnappngs and as such become equally guilty for their complicity in these crimes.

Whilst Genessier's loyal assistant Louise (Alida Valli) is content to trawl the streets looking for intended victims and later to callously dispose of their dissected bodies, Flamand's vivacious confidant Nathalie (Brigitte Lahaie) adds an extra dimension in her hedonistic pursuit of sexual pleasure with male and female partners, coupled with a sadean zeal

LES PREDATEURS DE LA NUIT
RENÉ CHATEAU PRÉSENTE
DISTRIBUTION: ATC 3000 - LES FILMS DE LA ROCHELLE

Faceless

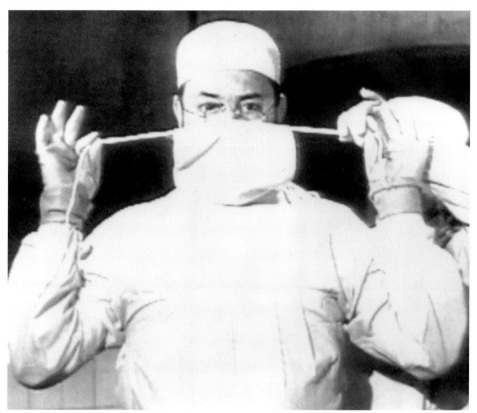

Eyes Without A Face

for inflicting pain upon her victims - "I believe in reincarnation, don't you ?" mocks the syringe-wielding Nathalie as she prepares one patient for her abrupt demise.

The most horrific aspect in all of this is the single-minded determination to pursue the surgical experimentation until "success" is achieved - no matter how many innocent victims are butchered in theprocess.

This paucity of respect for human life is most harowingly revealed in **Eyes** as Genessier cruelly and incorrectly identifies a disfigured corpse as that of his daughter (it is in reality a donor victim for Catherine), whereupon he meets the real victim's father, Tessot (Rene Genin) on his departure from the morgue. As the anguished Tessot pleads with Genessier as to his certainty that the body is Catherine's, Genessier coldly lies; "All too certain, unfortunately" as he maintains it is his daughter's body which has been found. He compounds the deceit by continuing to Tessot disingenuously that it is "Strange that I should have

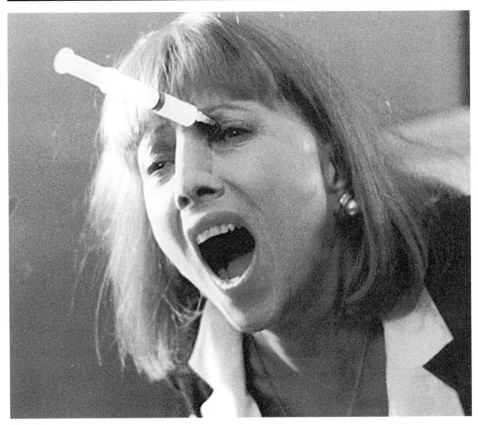

Faceless

to comfort you, for whom some hope yet remains."

When we later see Genessier continuing the deception at his daughter's "funeral", calmly laying a wreath on the grave, Louise threatens to crack urging, "Let's go, I can't take any more" only for Genessier to continue the deceit, replying simply that "I like things done properly."

Genessier continues this calculating, dispassionate approach, coolly chloroforming a new victim, Edna (Juliette Maywel) whom Louise has inveigled back to their spacious, isolated residence. When the ensuing operation on Edna ends in failure Genessier sighs to Louise; "Look after her, feed her; I'll let you know later" regarding her fate, whilst treating the unfortunate victim like one of the many barking dogs he has caged up adjacent to his operating theatre.

In one moment of emotional outpouring, Catherine opines the fact that her father treats her "like a dog" in effect, the numerous operations she undergoes condemning her to be no more than "A human

Faceless

guinea pig, what a godsend to him."

In a similar vein in **Faceless**, we see Flamand's soulless streak unmasked as having kidnapped the voluptuous model Barbara (Caroline Munro), Flamand observes that "She's still very beautiful, don't you think ?", suggesting that this will soon change in his hands. His cynical comments to one elderly patient who genuinely feels that his clinic "is like a paradise on earth", reveals his contempt for others as he chides; "The capsules i gave you contain hormones, glands and bone marrow from virgins sacrificed by me when the moon was is full." He finishes with great insincerity; "Don't forget, your body is a temple" - only for Flamand it becomes more a bloodied altar of vivisection.

When Flamand's oafish, salivating servant Gordon (Gerald Zalcberg) later attempts to rape the captive Barabara, her resultant injuries provoke not compassion from Flamand, only the selfish response that "The worst thing is that her skin is damaged."

With Flamand then confessing that he cannot operate on his own sister, he enlists the help of an exiled nazi war surgeon, the aforementioned Dr. Moser (Anton Diffring) - "If you offer him a lot of money and a new passport allowing him to return to Austria and last but not least, the possibility to experiment on human beings again, why not ?" Flamand is informed as he sounds out the possibility of hiring Moser.

Having met Ingrid, Moser reassures his new "employer"; "Don't be too sad my friend. I'll get her back all of her beauty" having also complimented Flamand on his taste in artists - "Greco, Degas, Hals. Very nice", suggesting the doctor's conscious attempts to surround himself with beauty, be it great works of art of the feminine beauty supplied so readily by Nathalie's vibrant form.

It is later during dinner when Moser perceptively cuts through the pretence and hypocrisy here, observing the irony that; "You French are strange people. you are very sentimental over trivial things. On the one hand, you protect the baby seals and on the other, France the country of human rights, has become the third largest arms dealer in the world behind

Faceless

Russia and the United States. This industry of death, earns your country, the land of refuge, four thousand billion dollars a year."

Having continually referred to the "victims" of the surgery in both **Eyes** and **Faceless**, it is also pertinent to understand the emotional as well as physical victims in both films, namely Catherine and Ingrid themselves. Neither asked or deserved their disfigurements and shattered lives but both remain the victims of the surgeons' scalpel as surely as the innocent girls plucked from the obscurity of the street - though here it is interesting to note Franco's ironic social satire in **Faceless** with Munro's cocaine-snorting model and glitzy read superficial actress, Florence Guerin starring as herself, numbering among the victims here.

If the "eye is the window of the soul" then truly Edith Scob's pathos-inducing performance as Catherine in **Eyes** proves the point. She is truly a tortured soul, her eyes staring out from behind the white death mask which enshrouds her face, a listless, heart-broken figure. When she is not wearing her mask, she is lying face down on a bed or sofa, crying, with all mirrors/reflective surfaces removed from her reach so she is spared the sight of her own reflection. "My face frightens me, my mask terrifies me even more" are her heart-felt words to her father, at once

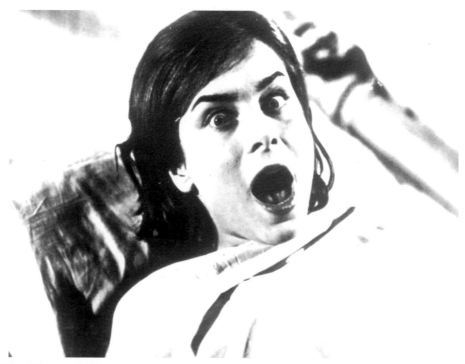

Eyes Without A Face

Faceless

distancing herself from his imperious "professionalism". For Catherine, her own disfigurement at least provides a natural, honest aspect, preferable to the artificial "beauty" her father seeks to create.

The vivid contrast between the smooth, doll-like mask and the dark, staring eyes within is further enhanced by her slow, studied movements as she navigates the labyrinth corridors and stairways of the house like an animated mannequin, an image reinforced by the carnival, circus-themed musical score.

Her baleful, emotive gaze at the vibrant painting of her mother which adorns one wall, whilst holding a white dove in her hands - a symbol of freedom and a precursor to the emancipating finale is memorable in the extreme, as her agonisingly silent phone calls to her fiance Jacques (Francois Guerin) - frightened to speak to him for fear of revealing to him that she is still alive and has inadvertently and cruelly deceived him, and yet longing to hear her loved one's voice again.

Her complicity in her father's deceit and murderous deeds is ultimately too much of a cross for Catherine to suffer as she confides to Louise; "I know the dead should be silent, then let me really die", continuing dispairingly that; "I can't bear it any more...afraid to look at one's face for fear of feeling the cracks and furrows."

Catherine's final flight of freedom sees her release the latest intended victim Paulette (Beatrice Altariba) - her use of a scalpel to untie the girl's bonds, eliciting a frightened reaction which serves to reinforce Catherine's belief that she is dangerously close to embracing her father's characteristics and (im)morality.

Her subsequently fatal scalpel wound to Louise's disfigured neck (a skin wound previously operated on by Genessier), allows Catherine to affect her escape, stopping only to let loose the baying dogs which then sumarily tear her father to pieces, blood symbolically splashing his surgical gown, and atoning for the years of mistreatment the dogs have suffered at his hands.

The final, poetic image is one of liberation as Catherine frees a dove from its' cage, walking into the woods in the distance, cradling the bird in her hand as its' companions fly overhead into the freedom of the night sky.

As Franju himself eulogised regarding Scob's qualities; "Fever,

Eyes Without A Face

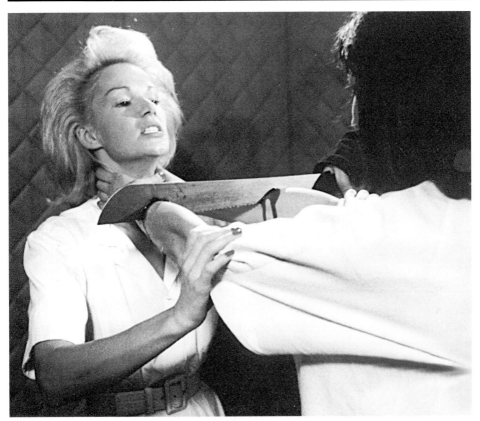

Faceless

yearning, fear, hope...I found all this in the beautiful eyes of Edith Scob. But I was always troubled by them. Troubled in the presence of this young, sweet girl. Because sweetness was an emotion which her face never expressed."

Christiane Jean's Ingrid doesn't do "sweetness" either in **Faceless**, somewhat lacking the innocence of Catherine in **Eyes**, being an equally forelorn but much more worldly-wise figure who elicits far less sympathy from the audience because of it. Whilst Catherine's every act is seen as selfless and caring, Ingrid is instantly portrayed as self-serving and selfish.

When Flamand's brutish assistant Gordon misbehaves he is sent to ingrid for punishment ! - flamand and Nathalie watching on CCTV screens as Gordon stoops to kiss the stocking-tops of Ingrid's fishnet-clad legs, before both parties simultenously disrobe. "Does Ingrid know we're watching ?" asks Flamand as he stares intently at the monitor with Nathalie replying; "Of course, that's what she gets off on."

Later we see Ingrid all alone in the dark, gazing at her tv screen full of beautiful girls - "I'm so alone...I need love, to be loved, to be touched" she laments, so for her, physical beauty represents the only road to personal happiness as opposed to Catherine's refutal of such superficiality in favour of keeping true to her honest emotions.

Ingrid's search for happiness through sexual fulfilment also turns sour, even when Nathalie brings her back a male prostitute to "enjoy". As Ingrid luxuriates on her bed in exquisite lingerie and a mettalic face mask (notably much more brazen than Catherine's porcelain-like face mask), the sexual coupling commences only for coitus interruptus to strike big time when her inquisitive "suitor" suddenly removes her mask, screaming at the horror beneath only to be silenced when Ingrid stabs him in the throat with a pair of scissors. Her night of passion now lies in ruins, surrounded by bloodied sheets instead of carnal pleasure.

More blood flows during the climactic operation scenes as Guerin's face is successfully transplanted onto ingrid's and we later see

Eyes Without A Face

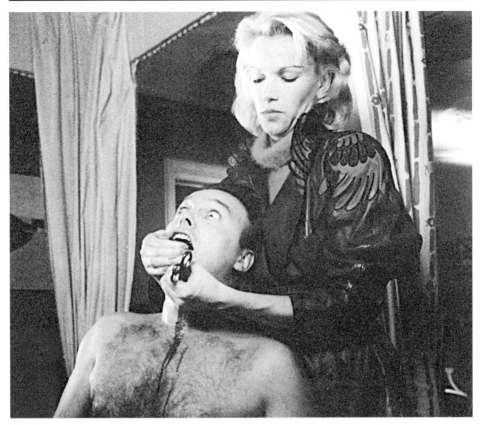

Faceless

her, resplendent in her new face, happily toasting in the New Year with Flamand, Nathalie and Moser - only for the ambiguous ending to suggest that flamand's scheming is about to be, ahem, unmmasked (!) by the authorities.

Ultimately, both **Eyes** and **Faceless** are each successful films to varying degres, but in different ways, mainly thanks to the individual interpretation of the salient themes here by the respective directors.

Franju's work is undoubtedly the more poetic and overtly haunting. Cruel and tender. Sadean and surrealistic in almost equal measures, Franju manages to complete the fine balancing act between delineating graphic horror; as evidenced in the truly harrowing surgery scene where Genessier's perspiring face presides over the skin graft operation - scalpel incisions and then scissors used to clamp all around the facial section, before the bloodied face mask is then levered off the victim's face - ugh!; and lyrical passages as evidenced in the stunning Cocteau-like images of Genessier's house - all elongated corridors and

Faceless

stained glass windows, lending an eerie, phantasmagorical atmosphere to it.

The stark, unflinching documentary-style shooting of this scene, has its anticident in Franju's early career as a documentarist, witness **La Sang des Betes** (1949), which focuses on an abbatoir; **Hotel du Invalides** (1951), his subversive film on a French military museum - "Legend has its heroes, war its victims" and **Cathedrale de Paris** (1957), where the familiar, *Notre Dame*, is shown from a seldom-seen rear prospect, "decorated" with the rubble of broken stone gargoyles.

Franju's unique style stems from his ability to initiate feelings of dysfunction and perversity and yet present them within a natural framework, in other words, fantasies emerge not from real life as such but are instead simply uncovering the hidden qualities of life. As Franju confesses; "For me, the fantastic is above all realism. I detest fiction...I love what is realistic because I think that it is more poetic. Life is much more poetic than anything you can imagine."

Faceless

He continues his personal ethos thus; "any screen image has an immediate presence. Whatever you do, a film is always in the present tense. The past is spontaneously reactualised by the spectator. That's why anything artificial ages quickly and badly. Dreams, poetry, the fantastic must emerge from reality itself. Every film is a documentary, even the most poetic."

Though some have picked fault with Franju for his cursory coverage of the police investigations into the murders and disappearances in **Eyes**, and for the lengthy takes which sometimes serve no purpose except inviting cries of ennui, Franju is far more concerned with investigating the diverse characters here, their motives, their foibles and their ambitions and how they interact with one another, together with the complexities of the surgical/moralistic can of worms which propels the film and underpins its' considerable dynamics.

He himself is inspired by masters, witness; "I was asked which.was the most intensely poetic film and I quoted Bunuel; which was the most beautiful horror film and I quoted Murnau; which was the most intensely graphic film and I quoted Lang." If you learn and are inspired by masters of this quality, then perhaps Franju's skill and vision should come as no surprise.

For the mercurial Franco, **Faceless** proved two things. One - that when given the time and budget (this was his largest to date), he can produce a coherent, action-packed film. Two - ironically all these factors also serve to negate his own improvisational skills and visual imagination ! Although **Faceless** fairly speeds along at a relentless pace, it leaves no room for Franco to imbrue it with the oneiric qualities found in his finest work such as **Venus In Furs** (1969) and **Succubus** (1969).

Instead, it allowed Franco to return to some of his earlier screen motifs, namely the ubiquitous Dr. Orlof from **The Awful Dr. Orlof** (1961) and **The Secret of Dr. Orlof** (1964), with Orlof himself (played by Howard Vernon), making a cameo appearance in **Faceless** as one of Franco's in-jokes, as well as Diffring's final screen appearance (almost reprising a similar role he essayed in 1967's **Circus of Horrors**).

Whilst Franco aims for the jugular with some startlingly graphic scenes as we see hands lopped off, heads punctured by power drill, cut off by chainsaw and some incredibly sanguinary surgical scenes - in close-up

The Awful Dr. Orlof

The Awful Dr Orlof

we see surgical pliers tease away the skin from a victim's face as their bloody facial mask is then held aloft in a restaging of Franju's scene from Eyes, only here, we also see the dissected tissue that remains beneath as white eyeballs stare up in anguish and white teeth gleam unnervingly at us. As Moser helpfully informs us; "The donor's fear and panic are the best muscular stimulants. The face remains stretched tight which is an additional guarantee of success."

Franco also invests his film with the voyeuristic and fetishistic motifs he enjoys so much - filling Flamand's clinic with banks of tv monitors a la **The Thousand Eyes of Dr. Mabuse** (1960), where he can observe all manner of sexual couplings if he wishes, whilst the ample displays of lingerie and hose adorning Lahaie, Guerin and Jean are influenced more by Franco's own prediliction for such imagery rather than any particular fashions.

Given that Lahaie was the (then) "squeeze" of **Faceless** producer Rene Chateau and who then curtailed Berger's sex scenes with her in the film (!) - "It was such a difficult movie for everyone involved" confessed Lahaie afterwards, and that Franco quarelled with the sfx man Jacques Castinau and Chateau himself, as the proposed low budget film transmogrified into a high budget affair with an all-star cast, Franco does

The Awful Dr Orlof

surprisingly well to hold things together. As he confided; "It was a compromise - it's not a real horror film, it's a thriller."

Whatever the case, it is certainly true to say that both **Eyes** and **Faceless** cover similar ground, with very different results and conclusions, providing much thought-provoking material along the way.

It is fitting to leave the last words to Franju however, who in expressing his embryonic yearnings for the surreal, provides a suitably stimulating insight into how the mind of a genuine creator actually works; " I remember one day when I was tiny, I found myself before a wardrobe with a mirror...I opened it and because the wardrobe was damp, the side was infested with mushrooms... The sight startled me and has probably established a certain mechanism in my sense of the bizarre."

The Wicker Man
A View To Pleasure
Ian Conrich

As a cult film, few British productions come close to **The Wicker Man**. Made in 1973, its much talked about non-release and drastic editing have helped to secure the film a seemingly legendary position within popular culture. As the respected fantasy film publication Cinefantastique declared in 1977, **The Wicker Man** is "the **Citizen Kane** of horror films." [1]

Much has been written of the performances of Edward Woodward (Sergeant Neil Howie), Christopher Lee (Lord Summerisle) and Britt Ekland (Willow) and of the quality of Anthony Shaffer's screenplay and the direction of Robin Hardy. Little analysis, however, has been presented in relation to the film's form and structure. Placing elements such as acting and direction aside, there exist within **The Wicker Man**, crucial factors as to why so many have reacted favourably to the production. An examination is required of how pleasure and satisfaction, or what J.P. Telotte has described as a "loving experience", have constantly been provided by this particular film. [2]

Of the Anglo-American prints in circulation there exists essentially three versions of **The Wicker Man**. The shortest version, running at 86 minutes is the print which has been most commonly available. A slightly longer version of approximately 89 minutes has occasionally been screened on British television.

What would appear to be the near complete print of the film, running at approximately 100 minutes and therefore two minutes shorter than the full version, has been available in America on Magnum video.

The 89 minute print is the only one that commences with a title informing "Sunday - The 29th of April 1973". The shortest version, at 86 minutes, reduces Howie's stay on the island of Summerisle to just one night; the longer prints present Howie on the island for two nights and three days. The shortest version bears the scars of this unfortunate reduction. The events of the first night, when Howie observes Lord Summerisle sexually initiate a young boy, are lost and replaced by the

The Wicker Man

events of the second night, when Willow performs her erotic ritual.

Scenes present in the longest version include Howie arriving on the Scottish mainland at the film's beginning, talking to a colleague, attending church and while at a West Highland police station, receiving a letter from Lord Summerisle.

All that remains from this lengthy sequence in the two shorter versions is Howie's church scene; the 89 minute print featuring it at the beginning and the 86 minute print featuring it in part as a flashback at the start of Willow's performance.

The longest version also includes Howie visiting Summerisle's doctor, prior to visiting the registry office and an extended search of the island by Howie on May Day, that includes an inspection of a hairdressers. Howie's second visit to Lord Summerisle's castle is also extended with an organ shown at the start of the scene.

Whatever the version, what is repeatedly established within the film is a point of authenticity. The start of the film, for instance, presents either the April 1973 date or a thank you for the fictitious Lord Summerisle's co-operation with the making of the film. Locals were employed as extras and considerable made of exterior locations; this realism and the use of contemporary situations helped to suggest that the events viewed have happened. Unlike the threats of the supernatural presented by some horror films, the seemingly veritable threats of **The Wicker Man** appear far more disturbing.

As Howie's seaplane flies from the mainland to Summerisle over the film's opening credits, a location is firmly established. Flying over an expanse of islands and water, isolation and remoteness are made

The Wicker Man

The Wicker Man

apparent. Summerisle is a "far away land" where the "other" can quite conceivably exist; a land into which viewers are invited to escape. With the story concentrated into the defined space of a small, isolated island and to a specific short period of time, the events on Summerisle are controlled and intensified. Anxiety and suspense are increased as the viewer's emotions are carefully channeled towards the film's dramatic conclusion.

The linear narrative of **The Wicker Man** presents a series of individual locations within the island that function episodically. Each situation is just one block in the film's overall construction to both develop and satisfy the viewer's curiosity. As David McGillivray wrote "every scene which at first seems too melodramatic...rebounds beautifully on the viewer when he realises that each has its individual purpose." [3]

The locations provide information and introduce characters, such as the gravedigger, the chemist and the confectioner, who become for that scene, a particular focus of narrative attention. The film is continuously fascinating as new and interesting characters and locations are introduced.

The Wicker Man has been described variously as a horror film, a terror film or a mystery thriller. In terms of its' narrative structure, it remains closest to the detective film, with Sergeant Howie, a policeman from the Scottish mainland, conducting an investigation into the disappearance of a young girl, Rowan Morrison. [4] David Bordwell in *Narration in the Fiction Film*, identifies the existence of two narrative properties, the fabula and syuzhet. [5] The fabula is the chronological ordering of the story as constructed by the viewer. It is as Bordwell writes;

a pattern which perceivers of narratives create through assumptions and inferences. It is the developing result of picking up narrative cues, applying schemata, framing and testing hypothesis. Ideally, the fabula can be embodied in a verbal synopsis, as general or as detailed as circumstances require. [6]

The syuzhet is the plot as it is presented in the film's development. It both distorts and hinders the arrangement of the fabula

The Wicker Man

and "is a more abstract construct, the patterning of the story as a blow-by-blow recounting of the film could render it." [7] With the detective film naturally following a process of investigation and requiring the elucidation of a story or event, the construction of the fabula is more notable. Here, elements of the "crime" are withheld by the syuzhet so as to sustain our interest and curiosity and to establish particular moments of surprise.

Gaps and retardation occur within **The Wicker Man** syuzhet. Through Howie's investigation, the syuzhet reveals elements of the fabula, but crucially the most important information remains concealed. A striking illustration is presented in the darkroom scene where it is learnt, with the developing of a photograph, that the previous year's harvest had failed. Such narrative information had been obscured, existing as a "negative"; as the photograph is understood, the fabula is "developed" and a clearer "image" of events acquired.

It is, however, in the film's climax, that the investigation becomes perverted, with the revelation that both Howie and the viewer have been fed incorrect information. Rowan Morrison was never missing, while the investigator turned victim is debilitated for having accepted the false knowledge. It is in the film's dramatic conclusion in which the hunter becomes the hunted, or the saviour the sacrifice, that audience participation and identification reaches a crisis point. A twisted form of pleasure is received as disorientated viewers are rapidly forced to analyse and reassess their position.

It could be argued that Howie is presented as the figure with which the viewer should identify. [8] He is perhaps the perfect protagonist. A senior policeman, he is the upholder of law and order and a representative of the Government; a fact that is reinforced by his uniform which is worn throughout.

An ethical and moral figure, he is righteous, forthright, non-corrupt, motivated and a devout Christian. Howie is a "correct" character, who allows the viewer to feel "safe" amongst many eccentric or aberrant figures. [9] More is learnt about Howie as the investigation proceeds and as his character develops our identification becomes stronger.

The viewer, like Howie, is isolated in a space in which they exist outside of the island's community. In identifying with Howie, the viewer is manipulated emotionally, enduring the tension and suspense present in the process of the investigation.

Dependent on Howie for information, we too experience frustration and anxiety as he desperately searches the island for possible

The Wicker Man

clues to Rowan Morrison's disappearance. This enables the viewer's curiosity to be managed as information is leaked only gradually by the investigation. It is here, that the position of the voyeur is created as the viewer desires to learn more and observe further examples of the "other" as represented by the islanders.

Pleasure is present as a privileged insight into the arcane is offered. As McGillivray writes; "the equally eerie confectioner's is a joy, a veritable Aladdin's cave of olde worlde sweetmeats with not a bar of Cadbury's to be seen." [10]

Whether the image discovered is that of a couple copulating on a gravestone, a woman breast-feeding in a desecrated church or the importance of the phallus being taught to young school children, the viewer's fascination and desire to see is constantly fed.

Observing the islanders to be irreverent and dissolute encourages the predominance of Howie and the viewer. From the beginning, Howie, as the officer of the law, imposes himself on the small community. Stuck in the water, in his seaplane, Howie hails across to the watching islanders to bring him a dinghy. A communication gap, or distance, is immediately constructed.

Crucially, Howie, who has to indicate that he is a Sergeant for the locals to respond, may believe that he is controlling the situation, but it is he who is requesting mercy. A situation that is to be cruelly mirrored at the end of the film, with Howie mistakenly assuming that he has managed to rescue Rowan Morrison. As Lord Summerisle states, Howie has been "a king for a day."

A common theme in the film is the leading of the fool. From the constant image of a ragdoll clown, observed during the frantic search of

The Wicker Man

the island, to the more emphatic May Day costume of Mr Punch, Howie is established as the fool, tricked and decieved.

With the viewer's knowledge restricted to that of the protagonist, it would appear that they too become the figure of the fool, but importantly, the fool being led by the fool. Like the beetle tied by a string to a nail, in a school desk, both Howie and the viewer have been controlled like puppets, their actions and emotions planned. The beetle going around and around in the same direction is helpless to avert its' fate.

It is in this revelation that power and pleasure exists. As the deceit is realised, the viewer would appear interestingly to analyse their own position rather than that of the islanders. For the locals are innocent, perhaps naive, but it is the viewer who has been folled and as Lord Summerisle says, come of their own free will.

The viewer's identification with Howie becomes problematic, as he is seen to have been weakened. Both Howie and the viewer felt safe in their superiority only for positions to be reversed with the islanders in the film's climactic twist. This establishes one of the two positions for the viewers. If, after the islanders' trickery is revealed, a strong identification remains between the viewer and Howie, then the two will die together. With the death of the protagonist, there is also the death of the viewer, who having been fed with information is now left abandoned and defenceless, without the security and assurances that Howie had provided. It is here, where safety is replaced by pain, that the viewer experiences a masochistic pleasure. If, however, Howie is critically regarded to have failed, the viewer could discontinue their association and distance themselves from this tragic figure.

Consequently, the viewer is saved and voyeuristically observing the death of the protagonist, experiences a sadistic pleasure. The martyr-like figure of Sergeant Howie, reciting the Lord's Prayer as the straw wicker man burns, dies with the viewer saved.

Most horror films, in a genre where narrative expectations cannot be more conventionalised, present the triumphing of Christianity over evil with the re-establishing of a new equilibrium in the film's conclusion. In **The Wicker Man,** however, the reverse would appear to be true, with the pleasure experienced from the alternative and unexpected ending. In the wake of 1968 and its' series of social and cultural revolts, pleasure could also be received through viewing the conquering of hegemony: law, the Government and Christianity as represented by Sergeant Howie.

The Wicker Man

The fiery wicker man, crammed with cows, geese and bleating lambs appears hellish and apocalyptic. This nihilism is explicitly portrayed in one complete shock image, with the burning Sergeant Howie screaming "Oh God, no!...Jesus Christ!". It can, however, also be read that chaos is averted, for as the burning head of the wicker man topples back, a setting sun is revealed. Paganism's bringer of life and creation is seen to disappear from the skyline. Perhaps it suggests that the next year's crops will also fail or even that a new dawn awaits law and Christianity. At a point where the viewer is still shocked and bewildered, involvement is total.

NOTES

1. *Cinefantastique*, (1977) vol.6 no.3, p27. For a detailed account of the production and distribution history of **The Wicker Man**, see this special issue of *Cinefantastique*, p 4-18 and 31-49. See also *Wicker Man - The Making of a Cult Classic* in Movie Collector, (1994), vol.1 no.8 and Danny Peary, *Cult Movies 2* (1984), Vermilion, London, p164-5.

2. J.P. Telotte, *The Cult Film Experience: Beyond All Reason*, (1991), University of Texas Press, Sustin, Texas, p.16.

3. David McGillivray, *Monthly Film Bulletin* (1974), vol.41 no.480, p.16.

4. The scriptwriter, Anthony Shaffer, had a law degree and foregrounded puzzles, conundrums and intellectual games in his work. He wrote **Sleuth** which was filmed in 1970.

5. David Bordwell, *Narration in the Fiction Film* (1985), Methuen, London.

6. Ibid, p.49

7. Ibid, p.50

8. Some viewers have felt that they should identify with the islanders. For them Howie is weak and arrogant, while the islanders offer a resistance to hegemony.

9. It is interesting that a senior figure on the island, the Doctor, who is a man of science, is removed from all but the longest version of **The Wicker Man**.

10. McGillivray, p.16.

I would also like to thank Steve Chibnall and Simon Davies for their comments and suggestions.

"I Think, Therefore You Are"

Or How I Lost Myself In the Mouth of Madness.

Xavier Mendik

> In psychosis, the rejection of the Other not only results in the transformation of the subject's sexuality, but also a distortion of the subject's relation to language and the social order... it is the rejection of the Symbolic Other of language and   law that results in... the subject's loss of sexual identity. [1]
> -Robert Samuels *Between Philosophy and Psychoanalysis: Lacan's Reconstruction of Freud*

Introduction

The title of this article references a line from John Carpenter's recent film **In the Mouth of Madness** (1994). It is dialogue spoken by the maverick horror novelist Sutter Cane (Jurgen   Prochnow) to the world weary and cynical insurance investigator John Trent (Sam Neill). The encounter occurs while Trent is on assignment in a New England town of Hobbs End, attempting to resolve the fate of the missing author. Here, Cane shatters Trent's perceptions of reality and identity by revealing that both the investigator and his surroundings are nothing more than a fictional creation from his new novel *In the Mouth of Madness*. This unsettling revelation occurs at a central moment in the narrative. Up until this point, Trent has remained convinced that Cane's disappearance (along with the reports of hysteria and violence that his works are reputed to evoke in "less stable readers") are a carefully constructed marketing ploy to promote his new book.

It is Trent's repeated encounters with the "bizarre" and the "irrational" while in Hobbs End which gradually alters his accepted vision of reality, speech and human identity. These disturbing encounters include interactions with deformed and devilish parent-torturing children, aged motel owners who transform into tentacled beasts and paintings which appear to merge and alter before the viewer's gaze. With Cane's final revelation that Trent is himself nothing more than a piece of fiction created by the author, the investigator's previously resolute and "logical' world view is replaced with violent mania and paranoid tendencies. This subversion of the mind's rational potential is even referenced in Cane's distortion of the Cartesian *cogito*. Within the deformed universe of **In the Mouth of Madness**, the certainty of the thinking subject is perverted from "I think therefore I am", to "I think therefore *you* are".

The film's displacement of Cartesian logic is significant because it robs John Trent's mind of any interiority, implying that his most inner thoughts are Cane's property. What is more important is that Trent's interaction with the author also renders hm inarticulate at the point where he is revealed as *being spoken for* (a fictional delegate of Cane's) *rather than speaking* (being controller of his own patterns of communication). His feelings of horror and disgust have to be verbalised by Linda Styles, Cane's former editor whose own personality has now altered under his control. The profound basis of the author's disclosure is underscored when he suddenly begins to tear at his own body, revealing nothing but printed pages of discourse behind his human appearance.

It is such shocking and disturbing scenes which indicate one possible way in which we can make sense of John Carpenter's film. In this narrative it is indeed possible to comment on both the text's literary influences (in writer's such as H.P. Lovecraft), as well as its cinematic references to a wide variety of horror film texts.[2] However, I wish to consider the film's preoccupation with the duel loss of speech and identity through the work of the French psychoanalyst Jacques Lacan. In particular, I shall follow Lacan's famed "return to Freud", by arguing that the stability of adult sexual identity results from not only the resolutions of the Oedipal drama, but also the extent to which such libidinal tensions become recoded and "contained" through language's operations.

Lacan termed this essentially alienating system of speech as the Symbolic. He argued that its usage points to the extent to which our adult sexuality, fantasies, desires and mental processes are dominated by forms of communication whose symbols are based on nothing more than

In The Mouth of Madness

arbitrary sets of linguistic, social and cultural distinctions. In response to the certainty of the Cartesian subject, several critics pointed to Lacan's formulation of the *cogito* as "I am not where I think".

Descartes clearly remains aligned to a belief in what Slavoj Zizek has termed as "the epistemological field regulated by the problematic of representations (ideas in the subject), their causal enchainment, their clarity and evidence, the connection between representation and represented content, etcetera".[3] At the other extreme, Lacan (like the fictional Cane) is more interested in exposing the splits, fissures as well as linguistic underpinnings of the mind and human identity.

As Robert Samuels opening quotation indicates, disorders such as psychosis are viewed by Lacan as an attempted "foreclosure" or negation of the structures of the Symbolic which limit us. Lacan refers to the notion of the "Real" as the domain where language's ability to define identity (and indeed the world) falters. The Real's effect as seen in psychosis, nightmares (and arguably the work of Sutter Cane) presents inexplicable, disturbing and radical spaces through which all that is repressed in the Symbolic can re-emerge. Indeed, the idea that infantile and repressed material is aroused by the author's work seems implicit in his reference to Trent that "when people begin to lose the ability to distinguish fantasy from reality, the old ones can begin their journey back".

It is thus possible to argue that by peeling back his body image to expose his linguistic underpinnings, as well as revealing a un-symbolised world in all its gooey glory, Cane enacts a form of "cine-psychosis" on the unity of text and its characters. Indeed, from its opening credit sequence, where a montage of images reveal the production and distribution of Cane's book *Hobbs End Horror*, the film makes clear its fascination with the articulation of patterns of speech and the verbal act. However, as the title of the film implies (and later references to Cane as a "madman of the printed page" underscore), the modes of communication contained herein very much take the form of defective discourse.

"Reality Isn't What It Used to Be": From Confused Characters To Fused Genres.

In the absence of any guiding or overarching system of language and discourse, **In the Mouth of Madness** remains a film which not only depicts scenes of psychosis and abnormality, but is also profoundly schizophrenic in its construction. Carpenter's film is one of several produced in recent years which feature protagonists forced to radically reassess the access to their own pasts and identity through language structures.[4] Importantly, these works are not only dominated by a thematic concentration on psychosis, but also feature a "confused" and overloaded generic state.[5] In particular, Slavoj Zizek has noted a curious class of film which conflates elements of the fantastic (such as horror and science fiction) within a detective/thriller milieu (as if underpinning the subject's obsession with "investigating" their own fragmented pasts).[6] As Carpenter himself confessed when quizzed about the film's cross generic construction:

Sam is basically playing Humphry Bogart in the **Big Sleep**. He starts off with a great deal of self confidence because he's a professional and is extremely charming with it. But he's faced with such unimaginable horror, he cracks up, and we then proceed to terrorise him for the next ninety minutes.[7]

Alongside the explicit references to private eye's such as Philip Marlowe, the depiction of John Trent as a cynical insurance investigator who is mislead by other characters also draws parallels with film noir's most famous and fatalistic insurance "detective": Walter Neff from **Double Indemnity** (1944). The connection to Billy Wilder's film is underscored by the nihilistic outlook that both characters share. For instance, Trent remains convinced that as everyone has a corrupt "angle" and a predisposition for "the con" and therefore contends that "the sooner we we're off the planet the better". When Linda Styles replies that "you sound like Cane", her reference can be taken to include not only the fictional author the pair are looking for, but also James M. Cain, the writer of **Double Indemnity** and several other pessimistic hard-boiled books of the era.

The link to films such as **Double Indemnity** is confirmed by Carpenter's use of flashback - the favoured noir technique which reveals the past events underpinning the hero's current predicament. In Wilder's film, the narrative opens with a dying Walter Neff disclosing his embroilment in activities such as murder and fraud into an office Dictaphone- an act which triggers the flashback structure. The opening to Carpenter's film reveals a similar structure. Here Trent (who has been incarcerated in a mental institution for attacking the readers of Cane's books) has to explain his decline from rational insurance investigator to psychotic madman to a therapist. His revelations thus initiate the flashback which dominates the rest of the movie.

However, while it is possible to argue that **In the Mouth of Madness** is indebted to noir by virtue of its thematic constructions and stylistic devices, Zizek is quick to differentiate original from contemporary noir. According to his analysis, a film such as Carpenter's is part of a recent "attempt to resuscitate the noir universe by combining it with another genre, as if film noir were today a vampire-like entity which, in order to be kept alive, needed an influx of fresh blood from other sources."[8] Zizek's point of distinction is significant, not because of any need to make aesthetic comparisons/judgements between the original noir and its recent cross-generic cousins. Rather, what it points to is the degree of insecurity and trauma which haunts constructions of the self in such contemporary horror/thrillers.

While the original noir universe featured fatalistic male protagonists plagued by the doubts over their pasts and their motives, the genre at least held out the hope that the truth remained "out there" in the

accepted domain of reality (even if its discovery entailed the death of hero's such as Walter Neff). As Zizek has noted:

> Classical films noirs remain within these confines: while the a bound with cases of amnesia - the hero "does not know who he is", what he did during his blackout this amnesia is here a deficiency measured against a standard of integration into the field of intersubjectivity, of Symbolic community. Successful recollection means that, by way of organising my life into a consistent narrative, I exorcise the dark demons of the past. [9]

However, in the confused, cross-generic narratives that make up movies such as **In the Mouth of Madness**, no such security or opportunity of reintegrating the alienated or "psychotic" self is evident. Not even death is an option through which John Trent can escape the contradictions which surround his past and identity. The narrative ends with him escaping from the asylum to be greeted by an external world littered with discarded pages from Cane's work. (The disorganisation of the written word once again underscoring the severity of language structures that have been subverted). A radio broadcast reveals that the readers of his literature have sparked a worldwide epidemic of violence and insanity, and in the chaotic events that follow Trent finds himself drawn towards a deserted cinema.

Sitting down before the screen he is horrified to discover that the film is projecting and re-rerunning his own fictional past through the experiences he endured in Hobb's End. Importantly, these images unwind without any hope of resolution to the questions of his own status in external reality. Indeed, the film abruptly ends while Trent remains transfixed at what he is viewing. What these closing scenes (and the film as a whole) point to, is the protagonist's shifting from reality to the Lacanian Real, whose features of identity loss can further be charted against the narrative's depictions.

"Trent Stood at the Edge of the Rip": The Features of Cine-Psychosis

According to Lacan's analysis, the Real disrupts every element of identity that language and the Symbolic grants us. In particular, it has profound ramifications for the individual's sense of external reality, use of speech and perceptions of self/body image. All of these features are in someway subverted by John Trent's experiences in Hobbs End.

For instance, his interactions with the town's inhabitants not only upset his established perceptions of the real, but also destabilize the depicted reality external to the town. Thus when he leaves the locale and heads back to the city, he becomes beset with a paranoid tendencies that result in him viewing people as plotting to unbalance his mind. These feelings are confirmed when Cane's publisher Jackson Harglow denies knowing Linda Styles, the editor whom Trent insists was sent by Harglow to assist in the search for the author. For Lacan, such feelings of persecution and the fear of being mislead frequently accompany the onset of psychosis.

What such experiences convey is the fact that a "rip" or "tear" has upset the sufferer's established relations with the external world. In this respect "the problem lies not in the reality that is lost but in that which takes its place".[10] Although it is still possible for some sense of the "normal" to occur, the psychotic finds that established patterns of the everyday life become distorted or overloaded with sinister or threatening potential. An example of such a subversion is indicated in Trent's obsession for the poster for *Hobbs End Horror* which he notices on a city wall. Repeated visits to the site of the billboard convince him that the otherwise innocent image is in fact masking a far more sinister representation which relates to his own fate. It is only on his return from Hobbs End that he is horrified to find that the image is concealing another advert: that of **In the Mouth of Madness** with his own image as the book cover's key "fictional" element.

While this ambivalent status as either fact or fiction undermines Trent's perceptions of reality, it also alters his use of language and the speech act. In its displacement of the Symbolic, Lacan argues that psychosis dislodges the link between discourse and identity. Here, the subject finds themselves both persecuted and driven by a series of disembodied voices which drive them. **In the Mouth of Madness** indicates the duel loss of language and identity by pointing to the fact that Trent's fictional status denies his ability to "author" his own discourse. As Cane tells him during his Hobbs End visit "You are what I write. This town wasn't here before I wrote it and neither were you".

Indeed, the destabilizing impact that the loss of speech has on the narrative can be seen in its undermining of both the film's thematic and stylistic concerns. To return to the distinction between film noir and recent emulations such as **In the Mouth of Madness**, it is interesting that the

In The Mouth of Madness

initiation of Trent's flashback structure is not accompanied by a voice over
-unlike   Walter Neff's in **Double Indemnity**. While Neff uses the
Dictaphone machine as a form of vocal "exoneration", it also underlines
what J.P. Telotte refers to as the crucial link "between the narrator and his
narrative, between discourse and its subjects".[11] By using the power of the
voice to clarify any ambiguity surrounding his past actions and identity,
Neff confirms that in such works:

Beyond all other motivation, then, the narrator's speech assumes a kind of causal posture, accounting for all that happens, and even for the speaker's existence. It serves as a point of demarcation, gesturing in one direction toward a consciousness that stands outside of the images we view, distanced from them by the flow of words, and in another direction towards a world those words vividly conjure up. [12]

As **In the Mouth of Madness** progresses, it becomes clear that the lack of voice over accompanying Trent's flashback results in an inability to analyse and anchor the true status of his past recollections. Equally, it also has another profound effect on his identity. The failure of the "voice" to accompany this crucial shift from present to past tense narration underscores the ambiguity of time which accompanies Trent's memories. **In the Mouth of Madness** remains a narrative which creates impossible spaces where past and present collide and where future event is mistaken for recollection. Once again, this inability to differentiate distinct timescales profoundly undermines the individual's sense of self. As Robert Samuels has argued:

In psychosis and the dream state, it is the lack of temporal difference which often contributes to states of confusion and disorientation... For it is time which provides the possibility for the spacing and the differentiating of ideas. Without this function of difference and deferment, the subject finds itself excluded from its own thoughts, the subject becomes spoken and thought of, instead of speaking and thinking.[13]

An example of the temporal ambiguity occurs in the film's opening scene, when Trent is visited in his asylum cell by Cane. Although this unsettling encounter forces the investigator to relive the events of Hobbs End (which are evidenced as a montage of flashback shots), the segment contains shots of the investigator in the cinema at the end of the film. Thus, the sequence effectively preempt events that have not yet occurred to Trent within the present tense space of the movie.[14]

Equally, Trent's "past" narration refers to publisher Jackson Harglow employing him to travel to Hobbs End to retrieve the master copy of Cane's new novel *In the Mouth of Madness*. However, upon his return from the town, Harglow reveals that Trent has already delivered the missing manuscript several months earlier when his services were first commissioned. What such examples make clear, is that the film's repeated conflation of differing temporal planes curse John Trent to endlessly relive the trauma of past experience in present tense, real time. (This point is underscored when he continually attempts to flee Cane's town only to find that each road leads him back to its unholy centre). In this respect, it is significant that Trent while reading a passage from *Hobbs End Horror* refers to the people who took over the town as a "race of creatures whose vile existence affected time itself".

If it can be argued that t he confusion of differing schemes of temporality is evidence of the cine-psychosis which haunts **In the Mouth of Madness**, then it is a disorder which also afflicts the capacities of language users in the movie. The film makes clear that Sutter Cane not only renders his victims inarticulate, but also unable to communicate using established patterns of grammar and syntax. Paradoxically, the effect that the author has over his readers is to reduce their ability to read - at least in the unified, logical ordered sense which the Symbolic demands. In this respect, Cane's work reduces language's operations to an infantile articulation, by robbing the reader of the rule bound use of language that governs "adult" communication. In particular his works attacks speech across the planes of "selection" and "combination" that Lacan identified as key mandates of communication. To give just one example, it is noticeable that when Linda Styles is forced to read into the author's latest manuscript, she is only able to utter the repeated (and ungrammatical) statement "I'm losing me" upon her return to Trent. Her expressions evidence the traits of "continuity disorder", which prevent the psychotic comprehending the relationship that exists between words. This results in their producing confused and illogical statements. [15]

Alongside these reductions in temporal and linguistic comprehension, it is worth finally considering the film's fragmentation of established perceptions of the self and body image. If it is language that binds identity together, then psychosis and the Real prevent the sufferer from retaining established definitions of their own corporeality. Here, it is important to note that this radical undermining has an effect on both the individual's body and control over the scopic field.

According to Lacan, the child's absorption into the linguistic field of the Symbolic is accompanied by a visual experience he defines as the "Mirror Stage". This concept relates to the child's recognition of its own body-image in real or imagined reflective structures. It is the ability to receive the unified appearance of the self, along with the ability to

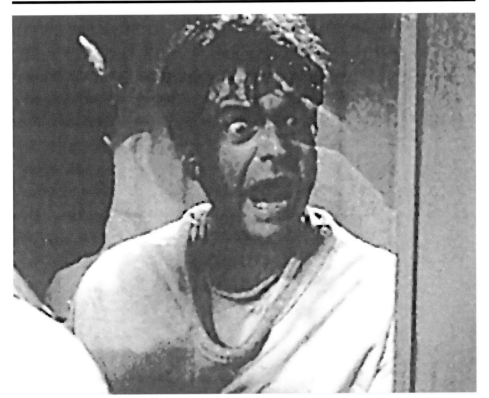

In The Mouth of Madness

verbalise this reflection as "I", "me" or "mine" that provide the cornerstones of identity. However, just as the Symbolic provides an essentially false view of communication, so the mirror stage is premised on a visual "con", giving the appearance of a unified and powerful image to the child's otherwise fragmented and underdeveloped body. It is this perceptual misconception which the subject then projects onto the visual field, presuming a mastery and control over all that is surveyed.

It is through disorders such as psychosis that these presumptions of power over the gaze are upturned. Here, the sufferer is presented with disturbing, double edged or constantly altering images which continually challenge the stability of visual control. It is this inability to control the perceptual which marks John Trent's decline into psychosis in Carpenter's film. At the beginning of his flashback narration, the investigator's visual powers are established via his brutal interrogation of a businessman suspected of an insurance fraud. These perceptual skills are intimated not only through his manipulation of photographic evidence of the client's crime, but also in his ability to detect subtle changes in the suspect's body language.

While it is these powers which give Trent "the edge" over other operatives working in his field, the detective finds the power of his gaze undercut by the psychotic environment that Cane creates in Hobbs End. Here, the consistency of vision is challenged by paintings which appear to shift and merge into bizarre configurations before Trent's very eyes. Just as the radical loss of language involves the shift from "speaking" to "being spoken", the loss of control over the scopic field involves an alteration from being the owner to the subject of the look. (This unsettling effect reaching its conclusion when Trent sits before the cinema screen to find his own image rather than the external world projected back to him).

What is significant about the horrific images that Hobbs End forces Trent to endure is not merely that they entail lost control over the visual field, but also that they present physiology in a grotesque state of flux and alteration. From the transformation of hotel owner Mrs Bickman into a tentacled sadistic murderer, to Cane's own bodily transmutation into broken, printed verse, the film renders the human form as an incomplete and unstable entity. Once again, the basis for these horrific depictions can be found in Lacan's account of psychosis. In particular, the unity of the body that language and the Mirror Stage construct are shattered. As a result, what is reproduced is the infant's experiences of its body "as fragmented, as a collection of uncoordinated parts and experiences".[16]

This reduction of identity to a series of unconnected or incomplete Êbits' is seen in Linda Styles' transformation as she and Trent attempt to leave Hobbs End. Her backbone cracks to accommodate a shift in her status from two to four legged creation while her head revolves in an unnatural three hundred and sixty-degree motion. Alongside a distinctly masculine display of strength which accompanies her transformation, Styles begins to taunt Trent with a vocal style more suited to male than female gender. (This alteration in her speech pattern once again indicating that psychosis splits the presumed unity between language and identity).

"Do You Read Sutter Cane?": Notes on the Ultimate Lacanian Novel!

In its undermining of every aspect of John Trent's identity it becomes apparent that **In the Mouth of Madness** upturns the Cartesian certainty surrounding the subject's ability to logically scrutinize the basis of its own existence. With the features of psychosis that the film depicts, Trent is recast from the subject who contemplates to what Zizek terms as "the thing that thinks". Here, unified identity is replaced by monstrous aberration: the individual so split that their existence can no longer be guaranteed. As Cane comments to an investigator struggling to comprehend his constantly shifting environment, any attempts to "rationalise" psychosis are futile. In its depiction of the subject's loss of external reality, speech and body image, the film underscores what can be defined as "the total loss of my Symbolic identity: I am forced to assume that which I am not what I thought myself to be, but somebody or something else entirely different." [17]

NOTES

1. Robert Samuels, *Between Philosophy and Psychoanalysis: Lacan's Reconstruction of Freud*. (London: Routledge, 1993), p.31.

2. The film's reference to horror writers such as Lovecraft can be see in its' use of "cosmic horror" or madness as a gateway between the rational and irrational and monstrous worlds. Equally, the location of Hobbs End in a New Hampshire environment redoubles the author's use of the location as a repeated source of terror. Beyond these novelistic reference points, the fact that **In The Mouth of Madness** depicts a deranged horror author allows Carpenter to point to, play up *and* poke fun at both fictional and film versions of the genre. At one point, Linda Styles claims that Cane's work is far more significant than Stephen King's, while Hobbs End contains many features clearly cribbed fro other notable U.S. horror films. (The repeated close-ups of a water tower identical to that in Tobe Hooper's 1974 movie **The Texas Chainsaw Massacre** provides just one example). Even the director's previous works are referenced in a narrative which owes more than a little to **The Thing** (1982) as an inspiration for its' tentacled transformations. **In The Mouth of Madness** even restages the multiple gun shot blasting of killer Michael Myers from **Halloween** (1978). This is seen in a sequence where Trent is attacked by one of Cane's "unbalanced" readers. (Later revealed as being his former literary agent).

3. Slavoj Zizek, *The Thing That Links: The Kantian Background of the Noir Subject*, in Joan Copjek (ed) *Shades of Noir* (London: Verso Books, 1996), p.203.

4. Other examples of this trend include Ridley Scott's **Blade Runner** (1982), Alan Parker's *Angel Heart* (1987), Adrian Lynne's **Jacob's Ladder** (1991) and Peter Medvak's **Romeo is Bleeding** (1995).

5. For an analysis of the "schizophrenic" construction of contemporary film see Fredric Jameson, *Postmodernism and Consumer Society*, in Ann Grey and Jim McGuigan (ed's), *Studying Culture: An Introductory Reader* (London: Edward Arnold, 1993), pp. 192-206.

6. For an analysis of how these psychotic constructions function in **Blade Runner** and **Angel Heart** see Zizek's article *The Thing That Thinks: The Kantian Background of the Noir Subject*, pp.199-226. In relation to other examples of this

trend mentioned above, these generic confusions can be seen as working in the following way:

In **Jacob's Ladder**, the "paranoia/conspiracy theme of a hero whose past has literally been poisoned by his exposure to chemical agents in Vietnam is juxtaposed with the possible indication that he is encountering shape-shifting demons from another world. In **Romeo is Bleeding**, crooked cop Jack Grimaldi's encounter with femme-fatale Mona pushes the narrative into the realms of horror as she is revealed as a phantasmagoric and indestructible figure. Although she is hacked at, shot and strangled, she continues to return (complete with artificial arm) and haunt Grimaldi throughout the narrative.

7. John Carpenter, cited in Alan Jones *Novel Horror*, *Shivers* (issue 12, May 1994), p.26.

8. Slavoj Zizek *The Thing That Links: The Kantian Background of the Noir Subject*, p.199.

9. Ibid., p.202.

10. Jacques Lacan, cited in Bice Benvinuto and Roger Kennedy, *The Works of Jacques Lacan: An Introduction*. (London: Free Association Press, 1986), p.145.

11. J.P. Telotte, Voices in the Dark. (Chicago, University of Illinois Press, 1989), p.40.

12. Ibid., p.41. Telotte notes that the studio system attempts to override some of the ambiguities in Cain's script for **Double Indemnity** which sees crooked investigator Walter Huff allowed to go free. Interestingly for the discussion at hand, Telotte concludes that such scripts reveal Cain's implicit interest in the doubleness of discourse. (p.45).

13. Robert Samuels, p.35.

14. For further readings on the "psychotic" dislocation of time and space as a contemporary phenomenon see Fredric Jameson, *Postmodernism, or the Cultural Logic of Late Capitalism*, *New Left Review*, p.146 (1984), pp.53-93.

15. My use of this concept is adapted from Ian Parker's discussion of Lacan's work on psychosis in the recent book *Psychoanalytic Culture*. (London:Sage, 1997), pp.186-206. Here, he adapts the term "continuity disorder" (p.196) employed by the linguist Roman Jakobson to consider the examples of language disruption occurring in psychosis via his analysis of Paul Verhoeven's film **Total Recall** (1990). He argues that the protagonist Quad (Arnold Schwarzeneggar) experiences a split from the Symbolic order when he discovers that his "memories" and experiences are actually artificial implants imposed to suppress the actual recollections of a more anti-social and radical past.

16. Ian Parker, Psychoanalytic Culture, p.216.

17. Slavoj Zizek, *The Thing That Links: The Kantian Background of the Noir Subject*, p.202.

CONTRIBUTORS

Take a bow please....

Daniel Bird was born in Staffordshire in 1978. He read Philosophy and Psychology at Keele University. Since 1998 he has curated several programmes for The National Museum of Photography, Film and Television and The Cine Lumiere, including retrospectives of Andrzej Zulawski and Vera Chytilova.
He is currently at Warwick University working towards an MA in Philosophy.

Laurence Rémila was born in Grenoble, France, in 1972, raised in Borehamwood, England and now lives in Paris. He earns money translating and spends time writing. His articles have appeared in a number of magazines, including *Zoo* and *Vertigo*. He also writes and publishes *Contraband*, a newspaper he distributes to undeserving Parisians.

Graeme Harper is the Director of the Development Centre for the Creative and Performing Arts at the University of Wales at Bangor. A writer and film producer, his awards include the NBC New Writer of the Year, the Premier's Award and the EU film producer s fellowship. He has just completed editing *Unruly Pleasures: The Cult Film and Its Critics* (with Xavier Mendik). His other publications include work in: ABR, New DLB, *Sight and Sound*, *CineAction*, *Outrider*, Penguin New Writers, Southerly, Ariel, Dalhousie Review, New Writing and books such as *Swallowing Film* (Q Books) and *Black Cat, Green Field* (Transworld). He is the general editor of the film Journal *Unscene Film: New Directions in Screen Criticism*.

Xavier Mendik is a lecturer in Media and Popular Culture at University College, Northampton and a freelance film consultant. Having completed Britain's first MA research degree on the films of Dario Argento he is currently completing a PhD on the death drive in the European exploitation cinema at Kent University. Since 1994 he has written extensively on the subject of psychoanalysis and cult/horror cinema for a wide range of books, journals and magazines. Xavier's book credits in this area include *Ethics and the Subject* (Rodopi), *The European Detective Since 1945* (Rodopi), *Necronomicon* Books 1, 2 and 3 (Creation/Noir Press), *The Modern Fantastic: The Cinema of David Cronenberg* (Flicks Books) and *Harvey Keitel: Movie Top Ten* (Creation). He has just completed editing *Unruly Pleasures: The Cult Film and Its Critics* (with Graeme Harper, FAB Press), a forthcoming Joe D'Amato book for Creation Books and is the general editor of the new film Journal *Unscene Film: New Directions in Screen Criticism*.

Michael Grant teaches at the University of Kent at Canterbury, where he is Senior Lecturer in Film Studies. He has published extensively on both literature and cinema. His writings include a collection of critical essays on the poetry of Anthony Barnett and a selection of the poetry of John Riley. On cinema, he has published a book on **Dead Ringers** with Flicks Books, and is about to publish, again with Flicks Books, a collection of new essays by various critics on the work of David Cronenberg more generally. Also forthcoming (from Macmillan), is a Reader featuring selections from the critical and philosophical work or Raymond Tallis. He co-edits, with Ian Christie, *Film Studies: an international review*.

Martin Jones was born in Torquay in 1970. He has contributed to *Headpress*, *Necronomicon*, *Penthouse UK*, *Samhain* and the *Amygdala* website. His book *Psychadelic Decadence: sex deugs low art in 60's and 70's Britain*, is published by Critical Vision in 2000.

Ian Conrich is a Lecturer in Media and Cultural Studies at Nottingham Trent University. He has contributed to *Sight and Sound*, the *Journal of Popular British Cinema* and *Anglofiles* and he is the author of *Yakov Protazanov's Aelita* (I.B. Tauris, forthcoming), and co-editor of *The Films of John Carpenter* (Flicks Books, forthcoming). He has contributed to the following recent publications: *The British Cinema Book* (BFI, 1997), *Trash Aesthetics: Popular Culture and its Audience* (Pluto, 1997), *A Handbook to Gothic Literature* (Macmillan, 1998), *British Science Fiction Cinema* (Routledge, 1999) and *The Modern Fantastic: The Films of David Cronenberg* (Flicks Books, 1999).

INDEX OF FILMS

Page Number in bold indicates an illustration

Noir Publishing
Mail Order Sales:
PO Box 28, Hereford HR1 1YT
E-mail: noir@appleonline.net

Noir books should be available from all proper bookstores; please ask your local retailer to order from:

UK & EUROPE:
Turnaround Publisher Services, Unit 3, Olympia Trading Estate, Coburg Road, Wood Green, London N22 6TZ
Tel: 0181 829 3000 Fax: 0181 881 5088

USA:
Last Gasp, 777 Florida Street, San Francisco, CA 94110-0682
Tel: 415-824-6636 Fax: 415-8241836

Canada:
Marginal, Unit 102, 277 George Street, N. Peterborough, Ontario K9J 3G9
Tel/Fax: 705-745-2326

Please note :-
Necronomicon Books One & Two are still available from the publisher:-
Creation Books, 4th Floor, City House, 72-80 Leather Lane, London EC1N 7TR
Tel: 0171 430 9878 Fax: 0171 242 5527
www.pussycat.demon.co.uk
E-mail: creation@pussycat.demon.co.uk

NECRONOM

BOOK ONE

CREATION BOOKS

INTERNATIONAL

Necronomicon
Book One
Edited by:
Andy Black
ISBN 1 871592 37 2
© Andy Black and all contributors 1996, all rights reserved.
First published 1996 by:
Creation Books
83, Clerkenwell Road, London EC1, UK
Tel: 0171-430-9878
Fax: 0171-242-5527
E-mail: creation@pussycat.demon.co.uk
Necronomicon – a periodical publication.
Copyright © Creation Books 1996
Design/layout/typesetting:
PCP International, Bradley Davis
Photos by courtesy of the distributors; all additional visual material taken from the Jack Hunter Collection.
Special thanks to Redemption Films
Cover photo:
Le Frisson Des Vampires, Jean Rollin
By courtesy of Redemption Films/Jean Rollin

The Other Face Of Death by Carol Jenks first appeared in *Popular European Cinema*, edited by Richard Dyer & Ginette Vincendeau and published by Routledge.
A brief extract from Andy Black's Jean Rollin interview was previously published in *SFX* magazine.
Xavier Mendik's *Detection And Transgression* is adapted from the MA thesis "Reclaiming The Gaze Structure And Sexuality In The Films Of Dario Argento". Xavier Mendik is a lecturer in media with cultural studies at Southampton Institute of Higher Education.
Adèle Olivia Gladwell's essay on **Last Tango In Paris** first appeared in *Bridal Gown Shroud* (Creation Books, 1992).

Editor's Acknowledgements
Special thanks to: Jean Rollin, Michael Donovan, Richard Kalman, James Williamson, Laurence and Peter at Creation for their support and assistance, not forgetting the love and support of my wife Caroline and son Aaron.

British Library Cataloguing in Publication Data:
A catalogue record for this book is available from the British Library

CONTENTS

CONTENTS

FOREWORD

Okay, okay, so it's not exactly the February '96 publication date I faithfully promised in the last issue of *Necronomicon* magazine all the way back in February '95 now, but heck, better late than never eh?!

I hope you share my conviction that the hiatus has been worth the wait with the new re-vamped book format and the especially eclectic selection of articles herein.

My aim of combining more traditional film critique with avowedly academic theory has certainly been fully realised in this seminal tome. Too often, the accent in genre writing relies solely on the thematically empty gore genre, or the pseudo-intelligence of protracted film theorising, failings I sincerely hope this book transcends.

This approach has allowed *Necronomicon* to pay its dues to the inspirational (at times!) cinema derived from H P Lovecraft, and the unchartered film universe of Marco Ferreri, and to broaden the horizons beyond the dominant European film into such "mainstream" works as **Last Tango In Paris**, which Adèle Gladwell dissects with stunning imagination.

In an equally impressive style, Mikita Brottman combines psychoanalytic readings of the fairytale (using Freud, Jung and Bettelheim), with film criticism (Sharrett, Wood and Telotte), together with anthropological material (Bloch and Parry, Strathern and Briggs) to re-interpret Tobe Hooper's **The Texas Chainsaw Massacre**.

Julian Hoxter explores the interpolation of sfx and film technique into narrative in the **Evil Dead** series – a unique phenomenon to this film genre – whilst also coining the phrase "splatshtick", whereas Xavier Mendik applies the work of Slavov Zizek (Europe's leading cultural thinker) to argue that the sexual ambiguity prevalent in the detective "heroes" of the *giallo* renders them unable to "read" the various clues laid before them in order to solve the case.

So, if diversity, imagination, controversy and visionary excess appeals to you, this edition of *Necronomicon* should deliver in spades.

And whilst it's vital to look forward, the continuing mediocrity of the genre scene necessitates rediscovering neglected gems and redefining classics from horror's halcyon days, which *Necronomicon* will continue to do.

Over the past year I can only recall viewing two standout genre films – David Fincher's nihilistic, serial thriller **Seven** with its expertly drawn characters and valedictory conclusion, and Ole Bornedal's cogent chiller **Nightwatch** which more than makes the most of its eerie morgue milieu.

Let us hope for more such treasures to emerge over the coming months.

Also over the next year, as always, your thoughts, comments, even criticisms (!) regarding *Necronomicon* are welcomed (care of the publishers), and all that remains is for me to bid you farewell until the second volume.

—**Andy Black** (May 1996)

ONCE UPON A TIME IN TEXAS

The Texas Chainsaw Massacre As Inverted Fairytale

Mikita Brottman

Based on the premise that film genres serve the same function as myths within an institutionalised, mass-mediated popular culture, this paper explores Tobe Hooper's 1974 *succès de scandale* as a myth which, through a sustained inversion of the symbolic rituals and motifs of the fairytale, creates an apocalyptic narrative of negativity and destruction. Whereas the majority of horror films, by affording their audience uncanny glimpses of the fairytale's animistic universe, lead them through the dangers of the adolescent sexual predicament, reinforcing the culture's taboos in a ritual display of rule-breaking, **The Texas Chainsaw Massacre** instead serves to mislead, misdirect and confuse its audience in a bewildering nightmare of suggested bloodshed and violence.

Using psychoanalytic readings of the fairytale (Freud, Jung, Bettelheim), critical writings on the film (Sharrett, Wood, Telotte) and an amount of anthropological material (Bloch and Parry, Strathern, Briggs), the essay looks closely at some of the ways Hooper inverts the traditional mythic order of the fairytale, and inverts the ritual narrative script (and on a cosmic level) through the use of several groups of images and fairytale motifs (the forest, the broomstick, the farm, the woodcutter's axe, lost children, the grandparents, the escape back into the "real" world at sunrise, and so on). Narrative stability evaporates right from the film's outset, when the lost children are diverted from whatever trip they *were* planning to take and are led instead onto the *Other* film, the cinematic unconscious of the traditional horror film narrative.

The essay goes on to analyse a series of archetypal elements within the fairytale which Hooper's film proceeds to invert, one by one. The Wise Old Man has his counterpart in the mute, hammer-wielding Leatherface; the gingerbread house is replaced by the charnel house; the transition of power and authority through generations is negated by monstrous parent figures that destroy children; acts of cannibalism are emptied of any kind of cultural or pragmatic signification in the sense usually associated with collective violence and other acts of ritual aggression.

The film's narrative disorder, illogical sequences of action and apocalyptic sense of destruction are ritualistic, but without the regenerative or collective functions generally associated with ritualised violence. Most fairytales teach us about the possibility of mastering life's difficulties. A fairytale which misleads, bewilders, confuses and ultimately delivers the expectation of defeat is a dangerous story indeed.

ONCE UPON A TIME IN TEXAS

"The Texas Chainsaw Massacre is a vile little piece of sick crap... It is a film with literally nothing to recommend it: nothing but a hysterically paced slapdash, imbecile concoction of cannibalism, voodoo, astrology, sundry hippie-esque cults, and unrelenting sadistic violence as extreme and hideous as a complete lack of imagination can possibly make it".
—Stephen Koch, *Harper's*, November 1976

Film genres have sometimes been described as serving the same function as myths within an institutionalised, mass-mediated popular culture. Based on an anthropological definition of myth, this function involves a ritual and systematic exploration of a culture's founding values. According to anthropology, a culture is compelled to repeat, through its mythic narratives, the symbolic tale of its origins. These stories generally deal with the particular series of semiotic and iconographic elements that represent a culture's value systems, rituals, ethical conflicts and moral inconsistencies. Within this narrative framework, different film genres could be said to provide a number of variations on the classical mythic structure. The western, for example, has much in common with the epic; the horror film relies for its innate symbolic resonance on the structure of the fairytale.

The many functions of the fairytale within modern society have been explored in depth, by Bettelheim and others. It is generally agreed that fairytales have much to teach their readers about the conditions of human consciousness, about the inner problems of human beings, and about the right solutions to their predicaments. More specifically, according to Bettelheim, the fairytale helps its young reader to master the psychological problems of growing up; problems which involve "overcoming narcissistic disappointments, oedipal dilemmas, sibling rivalries; becoming able to relinquish childhood dependencies; gaining a feeling of self-worth, and a sense of moral obligation".[1]

Through its unambivalent plots and archetypal polarisation of human characteristics, the fairytale both entertains the child, enlightens him about himself, and fosters his personality in development. In its narrative and allegorical capacities, the fairytale, it has been claimed, enriches the child's existence in a multitude of diverse ways.

In Freudian terms, the importance of the fairytale relates to the fact that such stories unfold within an animistic universe, governed by the belief that spirits, good and bad, inhabit all things and that thoughts and wishes are all-powerful over physical reality. Animism is the force that forges the mind of the child, and also the neurotic, and the primitive incarnations of all cultures. Freud argues that none of us has passed through this animistic stage of development without unconsciously retaining certain residues and traces of it which are still capable of manifesting themselves in those feelings of fear and terror Freud refers to as versions of the *uncanny*. "...everything that now strikes us as *uncanny* fulfils the condition of touching those residues of animistic mental activity within us and bringing them to expression."[2] This is the symbolic structure linking the fairytale with the horror film. The fairytale takes place in a primitive, animistic universe ruled by spirits and magic; the horror film also gives us glimpses of this animistic state of mind but in a repressed, unconscious form and thus recognisable only as terrifying, bewildering, and often malefic.

Most traditional horror films share the functions of the fairytale in that they serve to teach their mainly teenaged audiences of the dangerous consequences of inappropriate sexual (and other) behaviour, thereby serving as a ritual process of acculturation for the modern adolescent, just as the fairytale helps the child to come to terms with many of the psychological problems of growing up. Most horror films, by affording their audience uncanny glimpses of the fairytale's animistic universe, lead them through the dangers of the adolescent sexual predicament, reinforcing the culture's taboos in a ritual display of rulebreaking.

THE TEXAS CHAINSAW MASSACRE

Occasionally, and often accidentally, films are made which transgress the structures and traditions of a genre, sometimes with notorious consequences. Such a film is Tobe

Hooper's **The Texas Chainsaw Massacre** (1973), in which a sustained inversion of the symbolic rituals and motifs of the fairytale creates an apocalyptic narrative of negativity and destruction, wholly unredeemed by any single element of plot, mood or characterisation. Through its systematic inversion of the fairytale structure, **The Texas Chainsaw Massacre** functions not, as most horror films, to acculturate its adolescent audience into the difficulties of adulthood and the inconsistencies of human consciousness, but serves instead to mislead, misdirect and confuse its audience in a bewildering nightmare of violence and bloodshed.

The film begins with a fairytale warning:

> The film which you are about to see is an account of the tragedy which befell a group of five youths, in particular Sally Hardesty and her invalid brother Franklin. It is all the more tragic in that they were young. But had they lived very, very long lives, they could not have expected, nor would they have wished to see as much of the mad and macabre as they were to see that day. For them, an idyllic summer afternoon drive became a nightmare. The events of that day were to lead to the discovery of one of the most bizarre crimes in the annals of American history. The Texas Chainsaw Massacre.

A group of teenaged friends are enjoying a day out in their camper van: Sally Hardesty, her wheelchair-bound brother Franklin, her boyfriend Jerry, and their friends Kirk and Pam. During the trip, the radio reports a series of bizarre graverobbings in local cemeteries; the friends, worried about Sally's grandfather, stop at one of the cemeteries but Sally is unable to locate her grandfather's grave. Moving on, the friends pick up a "weird-looking" hitchhiker with a huge birthmark and twisted face, who proceeds to disgust them with tales of the local slaughterhouse (where Sally and Franklin's uncle also works), then takes Franklin's knife, slits open the palm of his hand and turns the knife on Franklin. Thrown out into the road, he smears the van with blood, laughing and cursing.

Pulling into an isolated garage, Kirk discovers that they are short on fuel and there will be no petrol delivery until the next morning. The friends drive a short distance to a dilapidated house by a creek, owned by Sally and Franklin's father. Sally and Jerry explore the old house, leaving Franklin downstairs, while Pam and Kirk set off for a swim. Discovering the creek has dried up, however, they decide instead to investigate a neighbouring house they believe may have a gas pump. Pam remains in the garden while Kirk goes inside. Here, he is attacked and killed with a hammer wielded by a huge masked figure in a leather apron. Pam, looking in the house for Kirk, discovers a room full of bizarre artifacts and human remains; she too is attacked by the masked man, dragged into a back room and impaled on a meat hook. Pam is followed by Jerry, who, exploring the house, discovers Pam's dead body in a meat freezer, then is killed himself by a hammer-blow to the head.

Meanwhile, back at the van, the sun has set and Sally and Franklin decide to go in search of the others together. Sally pushes Franklin up the hill in his wheelchair, but on the way the pair are attacked by Leatherface wielding a buzzing chainsaw, and Franklin is killed. Sally, chased into the house, runs into the attic where she discovers what appear to be the decomposing bodies of two people and a dog. She escapes by hurling herself through the window and runs to the garage for help. Here however, instead of

helping her, the garage owner attacks her with a broomstick, puts her in a sack and drives her back to the house where she is tied to a chair at the dinner table and tortured and tormented by the whole family of slaughterers, including the hitchhiker, until she once again manages to escape through the window. In the light of dawn she limps, blood-splattered, to the highway, pursued by Leatherface with his buzzing chainsaw, where she flags down a truck (which runs over the hitchhiker on the way), whose driver, in an attempt to rescue her, is killed by Leatherface, but not before a brief fight during which Leatherface is injured by his own chainsaw. Moments later, Sally flags down a second truck and climbs in the back, leaving Leatherface swinging his chainsaw through the air in rage and frustration.

SATURN IN RETROGRADE: AN INVERTED FAIRYTALE

Like many horror films, the basic narrative structure of **The Texas Chainsaw Massacre** has elements in common with a number of popular fairytales. It is not difficult to spot structural parallels with Jack and the Beanstalk (the ascent into a secret world, ruled by an ogre; the descent back into the "real" world, given chase by an axe-wielding giant); "Goldilocks" (the golden-haired girl encountering a bestial family sitting round their table at dinner[3]), "Beauty And The Beast" (the beautiful daughter "stolen" by the ugly beast and dragged off into his own world); Bluebeard (the "dreadful room" with its terrible secret); Little Red Riding Hood (the girl lured into the house by a monster in disguise): and, perhaps most of all, "Hansel And Gretel" (children lost in the woods, stumbling across an attractive house owned by a cannibalistic fiend who kidnaps them and attempts to use them for food).

Other elements of the film's structure incorporate a number of random fairytale symbols and motifs: the forest, the broomstick, the woodcutter's axe, lost children, the child in a sack, the bucket, the dinner table, the farm, cows, chickens and pigs, the giant, grandparents, the disguise, the "escape" back into the "real" world at sunrise. And just as the lost children comprise one family group – two young couples and a brother and sister – the fairytale family is paralleled by the wizened and macabre family of men: Granpa (virtually a corpse), Grandma (actually a corpse), their dog (mummified), Father (the garage owner), Leatherface (the eldest son) and the young Hitchhiker. The clan construction of the chainsaw family reminds us, as Christopher Sharrett points out, that the story takes place in Texas, "a state brimming with folklore and key signifiers of frontier experience: the Alamo, Davy Crockett, cattle drives, frontier justice, Indian wars...", but in the pathological inversions of this perverse folktale, Leatherface's mask is made not of buckskin, but of human flesh.

From the very opening of the film, there are hints of anarchy and disorder; Sally tries to restore a sense of stability, but she cannot even locate her grandfather's grave. By the time of her capture, the narrative has descended into a dark carnival of chaos and hysteria. Order has been abandoned; the potential violence of the dinner party recurrently relapses into absurdity as Grandpa, too weak to grasp the hammer, is unable to deliver his famous killing blow. All dialogue is drowned out by Sally's uncontrolled screaming, which does not abate as the film ends but transforms into hysterical laughter. Narrative stability evaporates from the film's outset, when the radio report about the grave robbings diverts Sally and her friends from whatever they *were* planning to take on that "idyllic summer afternoon" and leads them instead into the *Other* film, the unconscious of the traditional horror film narrative.

The fairytale is controlled by a mythic order and a ritual narrative script. The story of Hansel and Gretel, for example, gives body to the child's anxieties about abandonment, separation anxiety, being deserted or devoured, suffering from starvation or being punished for oral greediness. But the children are victorious in the end, when Gretel achieves freedom and independence for both, and the witch is utterly defeated. By bodying forth the child's anxieties, fairytales help him to understand and overcome these difficulties, as well as come to terms with Oedipal tensions within the family by separating and projecting various aspects of his own personality and those of, for example, his parents, into different characters in the story.

Since fairytales begin from an animistic standpoint, they lack the aspect of involuntary repetition characteristic of adult manifestations of the animistic – in the uncanny images of the traditional horror film, for example. Most horror films share the positive, pragmatic functions of the fairytale in that – when they *do* allow unconscious material to come to awareness and work itself through in our imaginations – its potential for causing harm is greatly reduced. As with the fairytale, the traditional horror film generally works to serve positive acculturating purposes[5].

Tobe Hooper's film inverts this mythic order and upsets the ritual narrative script – and on a cosmic level. The inverted fairytale narrative is not simply a tale of personal tragedy, but – like all fairytales – works to universal dimensions. This apocalyptic sentiment is suggested first by the film's "documentary" aspect. On one level at least, the film is meant to be approached as a "true story", and has many of the stylistics of the documentary, such as the opening "explanation" and the specification of an exact date printed on the screen ("August 18, 1973"). In fact, the story is based very loosely on the murderous exploits of Ed Gein, a mild-mannered and retiring grave-robber from Plainfield, Wisconsin who also provided some of the inspiration for the character of Norman Bates in Robert Bloch's story *Psycho*. **The Texas Chainsaw Massacre** is compelled to repeat a fixation on a non-regenerative apocalypse, an end to history, a cosmic destruction ultimately denied by the film's ending. Sally's escape however, is not a forestalling of the apocalypse, but simply a postponement of the end of the ritual violence. Her escape signifies a return to the cycle of horror, never to be redeemed by any sense of an ending. As Christopher Sharrett points out:

> The denial of causality and emphasis on ritual structures suggest an atmosphere that is both primitive and modernist in spirit. The "primitive" aspect refers to the ritual atmosphere surrounding the film's horrors and the way characters interact in a situation of chaos; the "modernist" aspect denies the primitive belief in a cyclical view of history and asserts instead an absolute dead end without possibility of renewal or even resolution.[6]

The mythic dimensions of Hooper's film are constituted by four separate groups of images. Firstly, elemental images of solar fire during the opening credits are counterbalanced by visions of a huge moon, then again, at dawn, further images of a gigantic, blazing sun. These elemental images are complemented by the lunar symbol smeared in blood on the side of the van by Hitchhiker, which starts to make Franklin anxious. Secondly, the uses of totemism as an iconographic emblem brings a cosmic element to the narrative in the opening shots of the exhumed corpses, propped into a bizarre tableaux. Leatherface's mask of human skin, and the symbolic resonance provided by the recurrence of bones, teeth, skulls and other human offal. Thirdly, a prescient chorus to the drama takes the form of an old laughing drunk in the cemetery. "Things happen hereabouts", he tells the teenagers. "I see things. You think it's just an old man talking. Them that laughs at an old man knows better". This choric warning is echoed by a macabre series of images (a dead armadillo lies on its back in the road, a huge hornet's nest has been built in the corner of the room in the old house where Sally used to stay, before her grandmother died) and an apocalyptic series of disasters reported on the radio news, which includes, apart from exhumations and grave-robbery, references to an "18 month old daughter kept chained up in the attic". Finally, Pam spends the journey reading horoscopes aloud from an astrological magazine – and the forecast, as she warns her friends, is far from auspicious. Saturn is in retrograde, its powers of malefluence increased. Franklin's horoscope forecasts " a disturbing and unpredictable day". Sally's is even worse: "There are moments when you can't believe what's happening to you is really true. Pinch yourself and you might find out that it is".

THE WISE OLD MAN AND THE LORDS OF DARKNESS
The traditional fairytale is based on a narrative structure composed of symbolic and iconographic archetypes which are, according to Jung, fundamentally universal, since the basic essentials of human consciousness are held in common by all mankind. Every child is born of a mother, has to grow up, attain independence, and win a mate, and yet details of such a progress will vary from culture to culture. In a similar way, variations will be found in the manifestation within each culture, and even within each genre, of archetypal elements: elements which **The Texas Chainsaw Massacre** ritually inverts, one by one. Perhaps the best known and most important fairytale archetype is the Wise Old Man, the benevolent Father in "Hansel and Gretel" and "Beauty and the Beast", who in other fairytales takes the form of the good Grandfather, the Wizard or the Wise King, giver of judgement and knowledge, sharer of wisdom. According to Jung, the figure of the Wise Old Man represents "the factor of intelligence and knowledge" or "superior insight".[7]

The counterpart to this pillar of wisdom in **The Texas Chainsaw Massacre** is the mute, hammer-wielding Leatherface, the Wise Old Man's devilish shadow. With his huge, bloated body, his tangled curly hair, his leather apron and his mask made from pieces of human skin, Leatherface communicates through a series of grunts. After the murder of Jerry, he runs off swinging his hammer and squealing like a pig. In the history of anthropology, Leatherface bears a number of similarities to a set of abject Hindu ascetics known as the Aghori. Polluted and contaminating Wise Old Men, the Aghori are filthy mystics who dress sometimes in the skins of beasts, sometimes in human flesh, many of whom are simply insane, in the medical sense. The Aghori perform atrocities at, and live on, the cremation ground or cemetery, sometimes in a mud shack, into the walls of which are set human skulls. They may go naked or clothe themselves in shrouds or skin taken from a corpse, wear necklaces of bones around their necks and their hair in matted locks. Their eyes are conventionally described as "burning red" and, like Leatherface, their demeanour is awesome. Another "inverse" Wise Old Man, the true Aghori is entirely indifferent to what he consumes, drinks not only liquor but urine, and eats not only meat but excrement, vomit and – like Leatherface – the putrid flesh of corpses. According to anthropological sources, the Aghori:

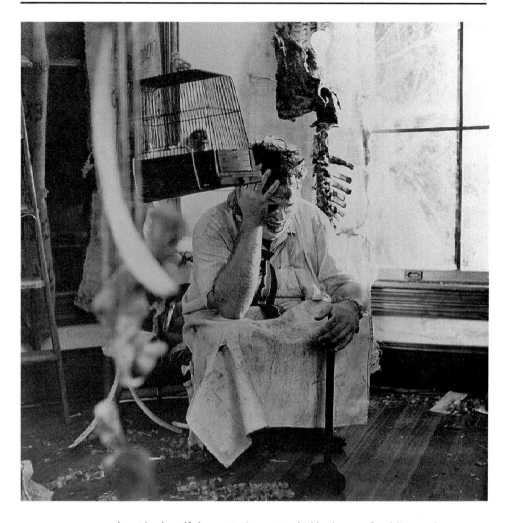

...roams about in dreadful cemeteries, attended by hosts of goblins and spirits, like a mad man, naked, with dishevelled hair, laughing, weeping, bathed in ashes of funeral piles, wearing a garland of skulls and ornaments of human bones, insane, beloved of the insane, the lords of beings whose nature is essentially darkness...[8]

A second recurrent archetypal element of the fairytale is the house, the rooms inside the house, and their internal decorations. Houses – either the family house or an isolated house discovered in the middle of a forest – play a significant part in many of the best-known fairytales, including "Little Red Riding Hood", "Jack And The Beanstalk", "Beauty And The Beast", "Goldilocks", "Bluebeard", "The Three Little Pigs" and "Hansel And Gretel", where the house is made of gingerbread. Rooms within the house figure prominently in "Little Red Riding Hood", "Goldilocks", "Beauty And The Beast", "Hansel And Gretel" and "Bluebeard", where the virgin entrusts the girl with the keys to thirteen rooms, twelve of which she may open, but not the thirteenth. The internal decoration of rooms plays a significant part in "Hansel And Gretel", "Goldilocks" and, again, "Beauty And The Beast", where inanimate objects, including items of furniture, turn out to have human properties, and comfort Beauty in her loneliness.

Two houses are featured in **The Texas Chainsaw Massacre** – the dilapidated cottage owned by Sally and Franklin's grandparents, and the house inhabited by the family of slaughterers. The latter, like most fairytale houses, is attractive and welcoming from the outside, with brightly-lit porch, swing chair, and the possibility of a petrol supply. Inside however, things are a different matter. The house is almost totally in shadow. Downstairs, it has been divided into two sections; a thick steel door separates the front room and hallway from the slaughterhouse at the back. The front room is decorated with a gruesome selection of human offal; the floor is scattered with bones; skulls and more bones hang suspended from the ceiling; feathers and human teeth lie on the ground; sculptures made from skulls and jawbones are mounted at the windows; the corners of the room are covered in cobwebs and, hanging from the middle of the ceiling, a huge chicken is stuffed into a tiny cage. Outside in the yard, tin cans, cups and pieces of metal are strung from the bushes and trees. Elsewhere, a pig squeals constantly.

Upstairs in the attic (which is also used as the dining room), the main decoration consists of the mummified corpses of Grandma and Grandpa (who revives upon tasting fresh blood sucked from Sally's slit finger, in a grotesque echo of Hitchhiker's gleeful self-mutilation in the van), and the stuffed corpse of their dog. This is the room in which the armchairs, quite literally, have human arms. During the dinner party scene, the dinner table is festooned with bones, skulls, scalps and other graveyard detritus, around which buzz a number of flies. During this parody of the fairytale feast – the film's most protracted and frightening sequence – the food about to be consumed is Sally herself. Leatherface is smartened up for the occasion in evening dress and black tie, and keeps leaning over to peer at Sally through his mask. The rest of the family all sit round in their allotted, neatly-laid places and whoop, cry and gibber in a grotesque parody of Sally's terrified screams. Eventually Grandpa, "the best" killer, is brought out to deal the blow: Sally is undone from her chair and led to kneel at his feet with her head over a bucket.

According to Jung, the motif of the house in fairytales stands for the unavoidable entrapment of our minds in archetypal relationships and modes of thought. Sometimes the house is replaced by the symbol of the maze hiding its secret, the minotaur, symbol of man's duality and mortality, the half-man half-beast to whom young people are sacrificed. As Bettelheim notes, the house is the central image of the "residues and traces" of a previous animistic world-view, with the motif of the forbidden room connoting sexual knowledge. The mysterious house in **The Texas Chainsaw Massacre** is not a house of life and knowledge but a house of death whose counterpart may be found – again – in anthropological sources. Its diversion into living space and slaughterhouse recalls the Tikopian house in Polynesia, one half of which is not actually lived because underneath the mats which cover the floor are buried the former occupants of the house.[10]

Human remains are also frequently used decoratively within such cultures, but generally with some regenerative symbolic significance. In the Melpa of the West New Guinea Highlands, for example, the jawbones of pigs are hung up on fences in commemoration of sacrifice, and at death – prior to the influence of Christian missions – the skull of an important man and some of his limb-bones might also be taken as relics and established in a *peng manga* ("head house").[11] And for the Doubans of Melanesia, all creation is the result of the metamorphosis of one thing into another. Yams, for example, are metamorphosised people, and they still retain many of their human characteristics. They have ears and hear, are susceptible to magic charms, walk about at night and give birth to children.[12] In such societies, as in the fairytale, human relics are associated with the regenerative properties of the corpse, and other inanimate objects are given life by spirits and magic, as is usual in the animate universe. Bettelheim points out that the fairytale hero proceeds for a time in isolation, just as the child often feels isolated. He is helped by being in touch with primitive things – a tree, an animal, nature – as the child feels more in touch with these things than most adults do.[13] In "Beauty and the Beast", the human element attributed to inanimate objects allows Beauty to befriend them, and they comfort her while she is away from her sisters and her father.

This symbolic process is again inverted in **The Texas Chainsaw Massacre**. Here, rather than inanimate objects having special, magical powers of life, even living things are reduced to mere objects or superficies, as in the armchair made out of human arms, and the table ornaments composed of human remains. Instead of imagining a world animated by spiritual magic as in childhood and primitive cultures, **The Texas Chainsaw Massacre** presents a world not only antipathetic to "normality", but forged from an antipathy finally to life itself, showing life drained of all value: an ultimate, apocalyptic threat to the vital principle.

THE FAMILY, GENERATIONS, AND DEGENERATION

Most fairytales deal in one way or another with family relationships and the transition of power and authority through generations. For example, many fairy stories centre around a family where one of the parents is either an "evil" substitute, or else missing completely (as in "Snow White", "Hansel and Gretel" and "Jack and the Beanstalk"). Others, such as "Beauty and the Beast", begin with the death of a mother or father which creates a number of ongoing problems, just as it does in real life. Yet other fairy stories, as Bruno Bettelheim notes, tell about an ageing parent who decides that the time has come to let the new generation take over. But before this can happen, the successor has to prove himself capable and worthy.[14] Fairytales which deal with orphaned children or animals (such as "The Ugly Duckling") represent, according to Freud, a displacement of the child's fantasy in which both his parents are replaced by others of better birth. Freud claims that this exaltation of the parents is a reminder of the time when the child believed his parents to be supreme, noble and strong.[15]

The Texas Chainsaw Massacre presents us with two separate families: the "good" family of the children, and their evil counterparts. The children are closely interlinked: Kirk and Pam are a couple, Sally and Jerry are a couple, and Franklin is Sally's brother. There are also references to Sally and Franklin's father – the owner of the old house by the creek – their grandparents, and their uncle. It is not clear quite to what extent the family of slaughterers are related to one another, since there are no female members of the family (with the exception of Grandma, now a corpse). Basically, the males of the family are all retired – but still practising – slaughterhouse workers, made redundant by the mechanisation of the local slaughterhouse, who have decided to use their talents on human prey ("a whole family of Draculas!", exclaims Franklin in the van). Hitchhiker, the youth of the family, seems to be the grave robber, responsible for the macabre series of exhumations reported on the local radio. Leatherface, his older brother,

follows in the steps of his grandfather as the family butcher of carcasses, and Father, the garage owner, is "nothing but the cook", who sells human barbecue at his roadside store. "I can't get no pleasure in killing", he tells Hitchhiker during the dinner party. "It's just something you gotta do. Don't mean you gotta like it".

Anthropologists have drawn attention to some of the ways in which those who bear the responsibility of disposing of corpses serve an important and practical function as cultural scapegoats. Lowest in the hierarchy of Cantonese society, for example, are those menial labourers employed to handle the corpse and dispose of clothing, bedding and other materials most directly associated with death. The corpse-handlers, apparently, are considered "so contaminated by their work that villagers will not even speak to them; their very glance is thought to bring misfortune".[16] The same pragmatic scapegoating is seen in the Hindu attitude towards the Aghori, whose fascination with decomposition is sometimes regarded as a spasmodic reaction against the excessive sensuality of their culture, particularly its younger generation.[17] By systematically embracing death and pollution in life, the Aghori aims to suspend time, to enter an eternal state of *samadhi* in which death has no menace.[18]

Similarly, the death of the parent or the displacement of their power in the fairytale not only helps the child come to terms with death, especially the anticipated future death of the parent, but also dramatises the natural transition of power and authority from generation to generation, thereby exploring the eventual takeover of the new age. In **The Texas Chainsaw Massacre**, this transition is blocked and inverted: traditional values are refuted and negated by monstrous parent figures that destroy children. Robin Wood has noted how the "terrible house" of the chainsaw family signifies "the dead weight of the past crushing the light of the younger generation",[19] an obliteration that has no redeeming or regenerative qualities whatsoever. There is a Hindu expression *alp mrityu* (meaning "death in life") which is used as a synonym to mean an "untimely death", such a death being always *ipso facto* degenerative, in any narrative or culture.[20]

Whilst on the one hand the monstrousness of the chainsaw family suggests a parallel with the stultifying bonds and tensions of the "normal" family most of the film's adolescent viewers are currently dealing with, on the other hand, critics have drawn attention to the alienation and breakdown within the Hardesty family itself. There are two scenes of crisis: the first when Franklin, unable to climb the stairs to join the others in his father's old house, is left outside spitting, crying and imitating his sister's laughter, the second when Sally's frustration with Franklin leads to a violent argument and scuffle over the possession of the flashlight. D. N. Rodowick argues that in scenes such as these, the bourgeois family "manifests a degree of violence which equals or exceeds that of its 'monstrous' aggressors, effectively implicating the family in the monstrosity it is trying to combat".[21]

SACRED AND GRATUITOUS CANNIBALISM

The final fairytale motif mocked and inverted by **The Texas Chainsaw Massacre**'s apocalyptic economy is that of cannibalism. In fairytales like "Little Red Riding Hood" and "Goldilocks And The Three Bears", the threat of cannibalism is modified into a threat of being devoured by humanesque characters in animal form. In stories like "Jack And The Beanstalk" and "Hansel And Gretel", cannibalism is threatened directly – though the threat is never carried out – at least, never upon the tale's protagonists. Like many forms of death and violence in the fairytale, cannibalism seems to be generally associated with regenerative functions. In this form, the threat of cannibalism helps the child come to terms with his fear of punishment for oral greediness and – correspondingly – his own fear of being devoured or "swallowed up" by the parent. The same is true of cannibalism in its anthropological manifestations. On a symbolic level at least, the consumption of sacred flesh during the Eucharist involves "replenishing the spiritual aspect of a culture and reminding society of its sense of communion".[22] This regenerative notion is also the basis of scalping and tribal headhunting, where the killer takes the substance of his enemies in order to re-charge his own strength and power, or where the very act of killing gives the killer the power of his victim.[23]

In **The Texas Chainsaw Massacre**, however, the cannibalism is gratuitous and functionless. Hitchhiker's graphic description in the teenagers' van of the making of head cheese (boiling cows' heads, scraping out their flesh, muscles, eyes, ligaments and so on) leads to an act of self-mutilation that parodies this family's means of sustaining and nourishing itself[24] by slaughtering people and robbing graves, then either consuming the bodies themselves, or selling them off as barbecue. Pam's body is strung up on a meat hook then transferred to the freezer; Jerry and Kirk are both killed with a sledge hammer. The sacrifice of these children inverts the regenerative ritual of cannibalism: it is empty of any kind of cultural or pragmatic signification in the sense usually associated with collective violence and other acts of ritual aggression.[25]

COSMIC APOCALYPSE

In fairytales, this kind of terrible punishment is not a deterrent to crime so much as a means of persuading the child that crime does not pay. Morality is promoted not through the fact that virtue always wins out at the end of the story, but because the bad person always loses, and, as Bettelheim has noted, because the hero is most attractive to the child, who identifies with the hero in all his struggles.[26] In **The Texas Chainsaw Massacre**, however, humanity is completely powerless, and the annihilation is complete. There are no heroes or heroines, only victims and villains. Sally Hardesty *would* be a heroine if there were anything rational or calculated she could do to escape her situation, but there is nothing, and, when she does escape, it is by pure accident. In this fairytale there are no clues, no magic passwords, no treasures to rescue or battles to fight because this is not a narrative governed by any logical order. Neither victims nor slaughterers have any kind of control over themselves or each other, and this lack of control is cosmic and universal. Malevolent predictions come true; not one of the young victims has any control over their destiny, suggesting that our defence against horror is finally subject to the forces of an arbitrary fate. Robin Wood has described **The Texas Chainsaw Massacre** as a "collective lust for destruction, that seems to lie not far below the surface of the modern collective consciousness".[27] Christopher Sharrett agrees:

> The idea of "redemption" that occidental man has assigned to the spirit of art, underlined by the "great works" continuing the concepts of sacrifice and the revivification of society, is parodied here, even if the parodic process is itself unconscious... Tobe Hooper's film is one of cinema's strongest statements of the general paucity of myth and communal belief in the contemporary world.[28]

The Texas Chainsaw Massacre is perhaps one of the only stories of true horror that our culture has produced. The film's narrative disorder, illogical sequences of action and apocalyptic sense of destruction are ritualistic, but without the regenerative or collective functions generally associated with ritualised violence. In the fairytale, virtue is as omnipresent as evil; good and evil are both given body in the form of some figure and

19

their actions. But in this fairytale there is only one evil: the good that exists is either defeated, annihilated or driven away. The morality of the fairytale is inherent in its potential for assurance of success. Most fairytales teach us about the possibility of mastering life's difficulties. A fairytale which misleads, bewilders, confuses and ultimately delivers the expectation of defeat is a dangerous story indeed.

NOTES

1. Bettelheim, *The Uses Of Enchantment: The Meaning And Importance Of Fairytales*, p6, London: Thames & Hudson 1976. Reprinted Peregrine 1982.

2 Freud, "The Uncanny", in *The Standard Edition Of The Complete Psychological Works Of Sigmund Freud*, p240–1, translated by James Strachey, London: Hogarth Press.

3. "Young Lady, we'll fetch you some supper", says Father to Sally in a macabre parody of Daddy Bear. When Sally later regains consciousness, still tied to the chair, a plate with a knife and fork beside it have been placed in front of her.

4. Sharrett, "The Idea Of Apocalypse In *The Texas Chainsaw Massacre*", p270, in Barry Keith Grant, ed., *Planks Of Reason*, Metuchen, NJ: Scarecrow Press 1984.

5. Bettelheim, p7.

6. Sharrett, p262.

7. Storr, Jung, p59, London: Fontana 1973.

8. Briggs, *Goraknath And The Kanphata Yogis*, p153, Calcutta: YMCA Publishing House 1938.

9. Frith, *We, The Tikopia: A Sociological Study Of Kinship In Primitive Polynesia*, p33, London: George Allan and Unwin Ltd 1936.

10. Strathern, "Witchcraft, Greed, Cannibalism And Death", in Maurice Bloch and Jonathan Parry, eds., *Death And The Regeneration Of Life*, Cambridge University Press 1982. According to the Melpa, bone comes from the father and flesh from the mother. Similarly, for the Bara tribe of

Madagascar, it has been observed that life is a precarious balance between the sterile forces of "order" associated with bone derived from the father, and the chaotic forces of "vitality" associated with the flesh derived from the mother. In death, the balance is upset: the corpse is reduced to bone, order and sterility (see Huntington, R. "Death And The Social Order: Bara Funeral Customs (Madagascar)", in *African Studies* 32(2):65–84 (1973). Such traditions may help to explain the connection between the preponderance of bone imagery in **The Texas Chainsaw Massacre** and the sterile, wizened family of men, lacking a female principle.

11. Bloch and Parry, p28.
12. Bettelheim, p11.
13. Telotte, "Faith And Idolatry In The Horror Film", p25, in *Planks Of Reason*.
14. Bettelheim, p8.
15. Freud, *On Sexuality*, Collected Papers Vol.7, p3, 1923.
16. Watson, "Of Flesh And Bones: The Management Of Death Pollution In Cantonese Society", in Maurice Bloch and Jonathan Parry, eds., *Death And The Regeneration Of Life*, p157, Cambridge University Press.
17. Huizinga, *The Waning Of The Middle Ages*, p65, London: Harmondsworth, Penguin. 1974.
18. Briggs.
19. Wood, "An Introduction To The American Horror Film" in *Planks Of Reason*.
20. Parry, "Sacrificial Death And The Necrophagus Ascetic" in *Death And The Regeneration Of Life*.
21. Rodowick, "The Enemy Within – The Economy Of Violence In *The Hills Have Eyes*", in *Planks Of Reason*.
22. Sharrett, p265.
23. Horner, "Jivaro Souls", in *American Anthropologist* 64, p258–272, 1962.
24. Wood, p182.
25. Sharrett, p266.
26. Bettelheim, p9.
27. Wood, p191.
28. Sharrett, p272–3.

DAUGHTERS OF DARKNESS

A Lesbian Vampire Art Film

Carol Jenks

Daughters Of Darkness occupies a privileged position among lesbian vampire films – in addition to being an exploitation movie and a genre piece, it is very consciously an art-film, made by a mysterious figure, Harry Kumel, who is also an academic and was a friend of both Josef Von Sternberg and Orson Welles, the two supreme mythic constructs in cinema history of the alienated artist against the commercial system. (Kumel dedicated his first film to Von Sternberg and directed Welles in his third, **Malpertuis**, which is so knowing in its turning of certain key theoretical concepts into the narrative of the film itself that it gives the impression it should have "For Students Only" stamped on to the celluloid.)

This infusion of art into the horror genre, both via the film's director and its star (Delphine Seyrig, trailing connotations of **Last Year In Marienbad**, still the ultimate art movie, behind her) has enabled it to acquire status as an "erotic" film, as opposed to vulgar sex-exploiters like **The Vampire Lovers**, and as a progressive text in its erotic attitudes, so progressive, according to both Parker Tyler and Bonnie Zimmerman, that it depicts heterosexuality as abnormal and is violently "anti-male". (The sheer oddity of the latter point, if taken at face value, in regard to a film made by a man, never seems to strike the film's enthusiastic partisans, nor do they ever question what the determinants of such a fantasy might be).

It is true that the two major conventions of the lesbian vampire film (an entire sub-genre of the horror movie in itself) are missing from **Daughters Of Darkness** – the power of the gaze and the enigmatic masculine control-figure. These are both fully present in the very first of the films, **Dracula's Daughter**, made in 1936. In Gloria Holden's first appearance in the film, she is heavily veiled, and all that is visible of her face are her enormous, black, glowing eyes, which have hypnotic powers. The Countess, moreover, is a painter – a producer of images – and, in the studio sequence, the young woman who has been enticed to pose for a head and shoulders portrait exclaims "Why are you looking at me that way?", as Holden begins to advance on her. Just as the very title of the film connotes father-fixation, the Countess is continually reminded by the displaced father-figure, her pallid, "vampiric" looking manservant, of her supposed destiny, from which she cannot escape, and from which she desperately hoped her father's death would set her free.

In the much later **The Vampire Lovers** (1970), the issue of Carmilla's gaze and its direction forms the material of her entry into the film at an engagement ball. All the unattached men in the room immediately flock to the scarlet-clad figure who emerges from under a black cloak – she chooses one as a partner with the utmost indifference and joins the dancers. The engaged couple discuss the mysterious stranger, and the young woman comments that she knows her fiancé loves her because he is the only man to ignore the new arrival, especially, she adds, in view of the fact that the beautiful woman is looking at him with interest. No, comes the reply, after a glance in Carmilla's direction – she's looking at *you*. The whole sequence is played on the move, as the camera keeps pace with the dancers, making the assertion of the fixity of this unwavering gaze, which

Dracula's Daughter

we observe for ourselves, all the more emphatic.

But the apparent desire communicated by this ardent look is displaced in exactly the same way as in **Dracula's Daughter**. Every one of Carmilla's sexual encounters/ attacks is followed by a shot of an unknown man (obviously a vampire, connoted by his appearance) usually laughing satanically. He plays no apparent part in the narrative and the images of him have the quality of insert shots. Therefore his symbolic function (particularly as he survives the vampire hunters and the film, which Carmilla of course does not) requires explanation. We see Carmilla slip away from the ball in the first sequence, out into the forest, clearly for a rendezvous with this figure. It is as if she were receiving instructions – or, rather, receiving her desire from him, being granted permission to enact a transferred desire.

Given that the power to gaze, to fix women as objects, is the defining prerogative of the male in mainstream cinematic narrative, the two conventions begin to weld together into a whole. Lesbianism is not only violent, "draining", destructive and power-based (the vampire manifestation as metaphor) but the product of a transferred masculinity or masculine identification. The specifics of female desire are, as always, unimaginable and unrepresentable. (Although there is an interesting submerged paradox here – if this violent model of sexuality is undesirable in itself, how does this reflect upon traditionally "masculine" attributes of aggression and power? The answer is no doubt intended to be that it is only undesirable when it is appropriated by the female, but the question remains, tantalisingly).

By the removal altogether of the male control and by de-emphasising Bathory's power to gaze, it is true that **Daughters Of Darkness** seems to want to enter into the realm, the regime of feminine, signified by touch, all-encompassing sensuality, the tactility of furs and feathers and, more specifically, the maternal. But what this feminine regime, this maternal kingdom, consists of and how it is represented is crucial in any consideration of the film as a proto-feminist progressive example of a notorious genre.

The idea of the mother-figure is introduced into the film almost as its first narrative element, certainly as its first narrative area of conflict or enigma. The married couple we are introduced to have, it quickly becomes apparent, nothing in common but sex, and even the act we are allowed to witness in the opening shots, with a mixture of complicity and accusation (Isn't this what you want to see when you watch a movie? Very well, here it is), has an aura of desperation about it, particularly characterised by Stefan's frantic attentions to Valerie's breasts. The icy, frigid blue aura that tinges everything (flesh, hair, the white flowers) only enhances the violence. After this frenzy, to be suddenly confronted by the issue of the bridegroom's mother and her supposed snobbery, dislocates the tone abruptly – the marriage is forced to enter the arena of the social, "For years she's been telling me we are different, that is God's gift to us, we must never debase it". When we discover the truth about "Mother" later, only then do these words acquire their full retrospective meaning in conformity with the textual workings of the art movie. They have nothing to do with Valerie's social status, but are concerned with her gender (or perhaps both). The equation of gayness with aristocracy, as something reserved for superior people, is consistent throughout the film, after all, and Stefan's mother becomes not only the dialectical opposite of the Countess but also a very suggestive parallel.

The way the film manipulates the different modes of access to meaning in the art movie and the genre-piece becomes a two-way stretch – the backward infusion of understanding in the art film and the anticipatory signifiers of genre. The first of these is the close-up of Valerie's pallid, slightly parted lips in her compact mirror, which, in a vampire movie, lets us in on her eventual destiny, and is of a piece with Stefan's regulation cutting of himself while shaving (which anticipates, in no uncertain terms, *his* fate) and, of course, the entry of the Countess, showing her scarlet lips and white, white teeth underneath a black net veil. She erupts into the film at the point where, having been married one day, Stefan and Valerie have agreed to separate so that he can travel alone to see his mother and break the news. His family name, Chiltern, is surely an in-joke – it's probably intended as a nod to the wealthy politician with a secret in Wilde's sardonically titled "An Ideal Husband".

Stefan isn't one either. In the dining room he ignores everything Valerie says, changing the subject and clearly regarding her feelings of uneasiness as mere sulks. "I'm just a little bit sad because you don't even try to understand", she remarks, raising the question of whether men and women have anything, ever, to say to one another in a shared language. Shortly before, Stefan carried her over the threshold, the gesture of arriving "home", but home is a deserted, cavernous, "rather dead" (as the concierge observes) hotel, in which Valerie is shut out from the conspiratorial bonds between men, a foretaste, should she ever reach it, of Chiltern Manor. We witness money and a note, "Say there is no reply" (*à propos* of phoning Mother), change hands between Stefan and the concierge, and their hands clasp on the bargain in close-up. Since Valerie, like most women, has been trained not to know about the fraternal conspiracy of men, any moves she wishes to make are shown to be checkmated from the outset, but this hidden

Last Year In Marienbad

freemasonry is what the Countess is about to break in on.

Valerie is instantly fascinated by the beautiful figure she glimpses from a distance in the lobby, "Who is that lady who has just arrived? An actress or something?". The answer, of course, is yes – the enigma represented by the Countess is very much a matter of play with the image to which the name Delphine Seyrig is attached. The discussion with the concierge about whether Madame has or has not stayed at the hotel before immediately lets us know that we are in **Marienbad** territory. Only this time it is not a question of where the frozen and impenetrable icon who must be investigated and controlled was a year ago, but forty years ago, unchanged and still got up as Dietrich on the Shanghai Express one presumes. The Countess initially deflects the concierge with the telling suggestion that it was not her he saw but "my mother perhaps?". Also, her position in the game has changed (the husband-master-father figure in **Marienbad** compulsively demonstrates his absolute authority through the match-game, which "I could lose, but I never do") – she now controls the rules, although that is revealed only gradually, her revenge both on men and, possibly, the film that made her famous.

We first see her in private in a more or less exact replica of her woman-bird **Marienbad** costume, in colour this time, deep purple, with the approximately three million feathers, from behind which her face emerges, that Susan Sontag once included among the hallmarks of Camp. She is with her "assistant", Ilona, and it is here that the nature of her function begins to be defined – the all-indulgent but all-powerful mother of Oedipal fantasy, a seducer. She exercises complete control over Ilona's desire: "I won't

be able to wait another night", "Yes you will because I want you to"; and reads her feelings with an instinctive all-knowing insight, "You're jealous". But Ilona's frustration and rivalry give way when Elizabeth whispers "Come here", her feathered arms beckoning in a fusion of the erotic and the maternal, to which Ilona responds by kneeling at her side and putting her head in Elizabeth's lap like a tired child. Elizabeth's movements during this sequence, her constant gesture of caressing herself, her facial skin, with her feathery halo, suggests not narcissism but a dispersed sensuality, sexual but not located in the so-called sexual organs, the body of the mother, which is entirely eroticised. But the maternal body, in the pre-Oedipal phase, is not yet fixed within the realm of difference – it is bi-sexual, hermaphrodite, phallic.

This is revealed when the Countess' maternal authority is raised to an absolute value as Ilona makes an attempt to leave. Elizabeth, in a very overdetermined image, is seen wool-working. The long, thick needles are the first symbols of the awesome list later attributed to her of phallic being and authority. She is weaving a black and white rope, which echoes the colour scheme she, Valerie and Stefan revolve in and also marks her as someone who can create patterns, make (in several senses) designs. The twisting of the thread also recalls the female Fates of Greek mythology, who controlled life and death – death being the moment at which the thread was cut. (These beings make a very literal appearance in Kumel's **Malpertuis**). In response to Ilona's pleas, Elizabeth is inflexible. "But you need me – without me you'd have no life". When Ilona explodes, "You call this a life? Let me go!", she replies with quiet unruffled confidence, "I never would and you never could", and it is clear that their quarrel is an old, repeated one ("Not again? Don't be ridiculous"), which always has the same ending.

Elizabeth's daughter/lover is denied any autonomy – if she separates from the maternal body she will die. It nurtures, but it also consumes.

This demonstration of Elizabeth's power is followed immediately by her taking possession (Valerie's phrase) of Stefan and Valerie, using an imperious maternal concern when they come into the hotel soaked. "If you have the slightest hint of a cold, I'd never forgive myself" (thus is guilt instilled in children and their compliance assured). The bravura sequence that follows, apart from containing the film's most deathlessly camp line ("Diet, and lots of sleep", the Countess' explanation for her beauty), reveals Elizabeth, literally, in her true colours for the first time, although the enigma of what and who she is is often predicated upon paradoxical negation. "I am not a sorceress", she purrs mockingly. But she is. Valerie and Stefan now know from the concierge of the forty-year-old mystery surrounding Madame's appearance to which Stefan suggested the answer "This must be the daughter", the "match" of the Countess' own solution. This confusion of the two figures, the duplication, one becoming the other is crucial to the end of the film. When Stefan tests her out to her face, "He also told us you had stayed here forty years ago, which is absurd, of course", her offhand reply "of course" has the frozen aristocratic chic which suddenly becomes very marked in her. Her equally glacial dismissal of the policeman, "I find your conversation almost distasteful", when he is in reality talking about her own activities, is both a put-down and a put-on, considering the much more hideous and explicit description she is soon to participate in. Plebeians, evidently, have no right to express opinions about her.

The policeman, it should be noted, is "retired". Earlier he had confessed, about the Bruges murders, "No one understands them, not even the police". He hovers on the fringes of the action, a fascinated voyeur, and although he knows the truth this does not empower him. The exchanged look of male conspiracy he gives to the concierge is, ultimately, an empty look. The sole representation of the Law in the film, he proves as helpless and ineffectual as all the other men. The Countess' empire is not only outside, but above the Law.

She combines the marks of blood (lips, nails, the flowing chiffon), the signifier of femininity – only women bleed – with her now unveiled phallic attributes, the cigar she makes Stefan light for her and the hideous inventory of torture devices Stefan enumerates ecstatically as she leans over him – pincers, whips, needles, rusty nails, shears, white-hot pokers. This speech and the couple's mounting excitement must have some claim to being one of the most horrible sequences in the whole of cinema, partly because an historical reality erupts into a camp fantasy, and partly because it does so verbally, in a film which has very little direct visual violence, which would usually be its generic hallmark. Instead, in a genre notorious for impoverished dialogue, it gives the power of horror back to language.

What Stefan fails to notice in his orgasmic identification with the "scarlet Countess" is that he is actually placed in the position of a "feminised" victim – as he described how Bathory attacked the nipples of her victims with pincers, Elizabeth murmurs "Yes, yes, that's it" while rubbing her hands over his chest, digging her nails in. This replies to his assault on Valerie's breasts during the earlier lovemaking and forecasts his end, drained and "limp", under the Countess' hand.

But as the actual scene takes place, we are led into believing that Stefan and the Countess will eventually form the final couple among these figures on a chessboard – the fact that, when he first heard her name from the concierge, he recognised and reacted with curiosity to "Bathory", marks him out, surely, as her partner in cruelty and

decadence. Valerie is presumably to be their victim, placed as she is as only a terrified outsider, whose mounting hysteria at what they describe keeps pace with their sexual arousal. She reacts so violently that her previous fascination appears to vanish completely and she rejects Elizabeth with seeming finality. "I don't need anything from you, I need to be alone with Stefan", she screams, clinging to him back in their own bedroom. Her behaviour from this point until the Countess' final victory is an almost comically speeded-up oscillation that Freud saw as characterising female sexuality as a whole, due to the original attachment to the mother, which never dies, thus giving woman her greater capacity for bi-sexuality.

Ilona, having failed in her unauthorised attack on Valerie, must beg the Countess' forgiveness for having desired without her permission ("You couldn't wait, could you?"), but then they obviously make love. We infer, but do not see, this, as a shot of the naked Ilona waiting expectantly inside their suite is followed by the door being closed very slowly in our faces by Elizabeth. The teasing nature of this shot is difficult to interpret – it undermines any easy ideas that the camera is being respectfully non-voyeuristic where two women making love are concerned, as opposed to the extreme explicitness (for a film made in 1970 with at least some chance of mainstream distribution) over heterosexual encounters. It is rather as if the absolute unrepresentability of lesbianism, this time not desire but its fulfilment is being evoked again. It is an absence, a blank, beyond the reach of the film-maker's camera and imagination.

The fact that we then immediately spy again on Valerie and Stefan seems to confirm this, although this time, without apparent reason, Stefan pulls away when Valerie becomes passionate. An implied explanation for this is offered when the camera tracks back to the window – outside Ilona and the Countess are staring fixedly in. The power of the female gaze here seems to have an obvious castratory function. This literal pulling apart of the couple already indicates that their new plan of "going home" together to escape Elizabeth will never be accomplished.

The abrupt transition to a long shot of what turns out to be Chiltern Manor, in a wintry morning light, is at first so deceptive that it merely appears to be yet another punctuation shot of the hotel, thus emphasising even more the parallel between the Countess and Mother, who at least makes "her" appearance. The butler who answers the phone does so in front of a portrait of a young and beautiful woman, which is another tease – we naturally assume this to be her ladyship in younger days, or her mother perhaps. In fact, like Elizabeth, Mother is frozen in time. The telephone is in the style of ones used circa 1900, as is everything else about the milieu. Mother is having breakfast, in the conservatory, a space which became drenched with erotic connotations in the *fin-de-siècle*. The "hot-house" forcing of "natural" vegetation also ensured that the meanings were always of perverse or excessive sexuality, the most extended use of the location probably being in Zola's *La Curée* (1872), where it becomes the setting for the "unnatural" encounters of a dominant woman and her effeminate stepson, who has also had sexual relations with men. This configuration of incest and homosexuality is here re-duplicated in Stefan's relationship with the symbolically titled "Mother". The reference to the new lily, a *"cathleya valencia"*, can't help but recall the slang between Swann and Odette in Proust – "doing a cathleya" as a code for sex.

This signification overload of "poisonous" eroticism has a dialectical undertow of economics – we get a very clear view of Stefan's relations with his lover. Like Ilona, he has obviously tried to escape before, for when he remarks with relief that Mother is taking the news of his marriage well, the dry response is "As always". Stefan is caught between wanting to get away and a complete inability to leave, mostly owing to his incapacity to assume the correct social and economic position proper to masculinity. Mother speaks very clearly about his inability to support his wife, "When I think of you working – at whatever it is you can do". Stefan's ignorance of and unpreparedness for the labour market and his consequent complete subjection to someone of superior economic status is a parodic mirror-image of male-female relations – he has been feminised and castrated by Mother. The lack of perturbation Mother feels about his other sexual escapades also reflects his complete control over Stefan's desire, another parallel with the Countess and Ilona.

In fact, it now becomes clear that Stefan's true complementary figure is Ilona – the two players who are to be dispensed with as redundant so that a new couple can be formed. Valerie decides to leave after Stefan beats her horribly with his belt – instead of being an involved participant, the camera retains a static distance, outside the window of their room, just as it did earlier when they arrived on their honeymoon and were unpacking. This duplication of shot implies a direct causal link between the two scenes – the violence is inherent in, the inevitable outcome of, the power base of marriage. When we see them from the inside, naked in bed, it is to be presumed that only through the beating could Stefan regain his potency (taken away by talking to Mother): the suggestion is that he then raped Valerie.

The submission he demands is enacted by Ilona, there on the Countess' orders ("Do as I told you") to replace Valerie when he wakes up. She seduces him with a parody of feminine helplessness, an appeal to him for protection, "I'm frightened, I'm so unhappy, I don't know what's going to happen to any of us", by making a feint of leaving so that he will force her to stay, and finally initiates lovemaking by going down on him – an ambiguous act in a vampire, making an analogy between sucking a man dry of blood/semen. Later, in an extraordinary image, as she is on top of him, he reaches out supplicatingly for her breasts, but she denies him the nourishment they represent by crossing her arms over them, barring his access. Stefan has been dispossessed of relation (in any shape or form) to the maternal, and has undergone a complete reversal from violence and aggression, as in our initial view of him having sex with Valerie, to passivity. When he accidentally causes Ilona's death, through her falling on the razor he had left lying open after he cut himself shaving, the two of them become sutured as one even more emphatically by this object of destruction. It's obvious his fate will follow hers.

The Countess' intention, in fact, had only been that Stefan and Ilona would form a sexual spectacle for Valerie to recoil from, as she is still alternating violently between attraction and repulsion towards Elizabeth, telling her "You disgust me", and, in spite of the beating, returning to Stefan when Elizabeth comes too close. Valerie has reverted to the all-white outfit of her honeymoon/virginity, while the Countess is now dressed in boots, trousers and a "Slavic" tunic, in "masculine" fashion, a convention to maintain an artificial difference between two members of the same sex. The palm-reading scene, with its rosy rather than black humour ("I won't bite"), tender, delicate sensuality, the finger-by-finger removal of Valerie's white glove, Elizabeth's kissing of and enfolding Valerie's hand between both of hers, echoes but outdoes the handclasp between two men as a token of understood conspiracy in the early part of the film. A new type of bond has been formed, one that now excludes men. The residual fear and apprehension this creates in Valerie are only finally resolved when she sees Ilona lying in a pool underneath Stefan.

The images of the burial are very disturbing – wrapped in a sheet, her white arm flopping down, Ilona becomes identical with the vampirised victim in Bruges, whose dead body so excited Stefan (now, displaced, it punishes him for his pleasure), and whose killing Ilona had evidently participated in. She is first shut up in the car boot and then flung into the hollow of clayish soil that Stefan digs in the shore-dunes. Ilona's inability to sever the umbilical cord here becomes very literal, she could only escape by going forward into death or backward into the womb, swallowed up altogether. The two movements fuse together in these images.

The Countess takes alarm only once, at the sense that "The day, the day is coming. Time is running out. Deep in my bones I feel it". She sees not only the faint streaks of dawn, but, by their light, the figure of the policeman. Although she disposes of him easily enough a few moments later, she experiences him as a warning – the sunlight, the realm of the masculine, the law, the day itself all come together as her enemies. The English title of the film suddenly acquires its full meaning: the daughters of darkness are, in the old phrase, creatures of the night, ruled by the moon (so omnipresent in the film), the female planet/goddess, both virginal and witchlike, who presides over all the feminine mysteries and cycles and controls the tides of blood and the sea. The whole of the last part of the film takes place within sight or, particularly, the sound of the sea, the oceanic, unbounded, fluid symbol of the mother (*le mer/la mère*). Valerie looks out to it longingly as she whispers "I'm so cold", and is duly enfolded in the Countess' all-encompassing black bat cloak. The sun, the day, is under the command of a male god, Apollo, destructive to the Countess' role as Queen of the Night, her empire of darkness and desire – "So many nights, tumbling and tumbling away into the abyss of time, eternally," she promises to Valerie later.

(Intriguingly, as a parallel, in Walerian Borowcyzk's **Contes Immoraux**, made in 1974, the third of four episodes is about the Bloody Countess, and in this one of the captive virgins draws a graffito of an erect phallus on the bath-house wall. When the

Countess, sweeping past, glimpses it, she demands "What is that?, to receive the answer "The rising sun". Furious, she erases the cartoon.)

When they return to the hotel, Valerie instinctively goes to the Countess' suite, and she waits in an exact repetition of Ilona's posture, only for the door to close in our faces again. But this time we do see a little: Valerie, lying naked on the bed, glimpsed through a suffused red filter (the warm reply to the frozen blue of the opening sequence), obliterated by the Countess, back in her feathers again, leaning over her to kiss/bite. This cuts away to Stefan, tossing and turning and finally waking up with a yell – an image that suggests wittily that two women together are a man's nightmare, although it also has the ambiguous effect of reducing what we see to being the product of male subjectivity.

Valerie then appears in a long, absolutely plain, spotless white dress, obviously her new bridal gown. The Countess binds up the drawstrings of the bodice, an image that has clear connotations of literal bondage, as does the later fastening, in Stefan's presence, of a jet neck collar. When, obeying orders like Ilona, Valerie goes to Stefan, she walks looks and speaks like a blanked-out zombie. In answer to Stefan's arguments, she replies robotically, "She told me you would accuse her" and admits in confusion, "When she's near me I become someone else". She seems to still have regrets, suddenly asking "What happened to us, Stefan? Why did she cross our path?", staring at nothing. This nostalgia for her charade of a marriage, combined with her emptied-out gaze, is deeply disturbing; it suggests that whoever Valerie is with, she is only a vessel for others' desire. Her desire is a terminal absence – in the ensuing fight between the Countess and Stefan for their rights in her, she literally never speaks, expressing physically only revulsion, not positive passion, turning in the end for help to the stronger. Perhaps the early close-up of her pale lips was meant to tell us that Valerie is the real vampire, a characterless parasite.

Elizabeth's triumph enables her to reveal herself fully at least, the black candles at her dinner table recalling the policeman's reference to "Satan's ritual under a full moon". So she is, as we always knew, a witch and a sorceress. The silver/black metallic dress encases her like armour and throws off a million blinding points of light – she dazzles sight, puts out eyes as she moves, a walking emblem of castratory power. She caresses her hair, her body, and her postures are more swan-like than ever, back arched, arms flung out. This is femininity as the masquerade, the excess that hides the lack. Finally, she mocks Stefan's supposed knowledge of her on the basis of the name "Bathory", offering up an alternative version of herself: "Oh no, my dear, I'm just an outmoded character, nothing more. You know, the beautiful stranger, slightly sad, slightly mysterious, that haunts one place after another". "Death seems to follow in your wake from one place to another". "Perhaps it's looking for me."

Here, her function as image is laid bare – if she cannot die, if she is eternal, it is because of a fusion of two things. She owns the name of a real woman whose abominations rendered her "immortal" in history, but, far more important, she is nothing *but* an image, that a real figure can be used to take the stamp of. And that image is the eternal feminine itself in its Fatal Woman manifestation, whose attributes never change, nor, in the cinema, does her appearance. She is love, cruelty and death, the promise of exquisite destruction. ("I alone survive. I am love and I am death. Look into my eyes," says Eurylae, the immortal Gorgon in **Malpertuis**. Of all the pagan gods, she is the only one still living, i.e. the only one still imbued with a mythological signification where desire and the cinema can meet). Elizabeth is the Vampire as Vamp, wandering in a hall of mirrors where she can never (of course) truly see herself, but will keep coming face to face with other versions of herself, in **Marienbad** or on the Shanghai Express, other male constructions of the being who seems to have the power of life and death, the mother.

Elizabeth's absolute position of knowledge gives her the power to ever-so-delicately blackmail Stefan, "Believe me, you'll find it greatly to your advantage to be nice to me", but it is clear that what she desires most is the appearance of freely given homage, "I want everybody to love me" – her voice is full of vague wonder at the perversity of those who don't and who could wish to leave her. Her apparent plan for a tranquil regime in which all three of them could leave together as a family breaks down over Stefan's disregard for her admonition "Be soft" when she sends Valerie to kiss him, and Valerie's subsequent physical disgust. This incites him, as a response, to his final attempted assertion of power through violence, as he drags her away, hitting her about the face and evidently intending to rape her. The crude physical eruption into the calm and ceremonious order with which Elizabeth veils everything only ensures his own death. No insurrection will be tolerated. With wicked irony, the instrument is a glassbowl sent flying from the heaped-up food trolley overturned in the chaos – two of the three people present couldn't have touched the food. Instead, as the glass shatters in half, severing both Stefan's wrists in a final castration image, Elizabeth and Valerie take one each avidly, and we see, in displaced fashion, what we did not see when Ilona made love to Stefan, the undertones present then now realised to their limits. As Parker Tyler puts it, "le monsieur est fini". He actually ends in a winding sheet, like Ilona, tossed from the getaway car into a watery ditch, an even more overemphasised womb symbol than her burial place.

Admittedly, Valerie now displays desire for the first time, but there is no one else left but Elizabeth to turn to, and it is her pleadings of "Your hand, your hand", as she looks away from the wheel of the car (she is re-duplicating Ilona's position in everything), that inadvertently causes the fatal crash. The sun, rising, blinds the two women unawares, as they turn to each other. As the car goes out of control, Elizabeth, in an ascending series of bodily violations, is flung through the window, impaled on a tree branch and

Malpertuis

catches fire as the car explodes in flames. She is a witch, and a witch shall be consumed to ashes, through the agency of the male principle, the sun, she so much dreaded. Where mortal men failed, nature reasserts its power over the unnatural. Elizabeth had been urging Valerie to go faster so that they might reach "the border, the other side" in safety, before sunrise. What this other side consisted of may be guessed at – it was the realm outside the borders of patriarchy, of the dark – feminine, formless, unimaginable, a territory of limitless desire. Elizabeth and Valerie are not allowed to reach it, because it is unrepresentable.

This seemingly massive, terminal erasure of Elizabeth is recouped in the coda of the film, after the literally explosive violence of the images. When the deadpan banality of "A Few Months Later" appears on the screen, it is surely a tip-off that one possible response to whatever we are about to see is to regard it as a joke. But perhaps not. When we see Valerie, dressed in the Countess' "masculine" attire, complete with the bat cape she wore when she acquired definitive control of Valerie, making up to a new, all-in-white, anyone-for-tennis couple, in another deserted hotel and, as a final touch, speaking earlier words of Elizabeth's and in Elizabeth's voice, it is impossible, in the last resort, to tell whether Valerie has vampirised Elizabeth or the other way about – the film's final image of fusion and symbiosis.

But Valerie seems a shell, into which is projected a posthumous existence. So, far from appearing powerful and immortal, she seems desolate and bereft. When Elizabeth explained how she despised provincial hotels, especially out of season "when there's no-one", the meaning of the words was social, they referred to the lack of sympathetic members of her own class, instead of the "terrible vulgar people" who overrun modern resorts and among whom she could find no place. When Valerie, as a ventriloquist's dummy, utters the words, staring blankly into vacancy, they clearly refer to her own isolation. Her look that does not see is the signifier of the loss of any object to which desire can attach itself, of desire itself. She has lost Elizabeth, as we have. As she runs, in extreme long shot, towards the couple, stretching out her bat cloak, the camera moves in the opposite direction until it leaves us outside the bars of the hotel grounds. Apart from being an obvious reference to **Citizen Kane**, the shot replies, in the negative, to the opening of the film: then, we spied on lovemaking, now our vision is literally barred. We are dismissed, we can go home. The object of the camera's fascination, the icon Elizabeth, is no more and there is nothing left for us to see.

We are separated at one and the same time from the text and the mother, from the text that literally embodies the mother, a text concerned with the maternal. But what is this maternal, in the film's terms? It is a vision of an absolute, primal monarchy that turns tyrannical if disobedience threatens, and that wishes to feminise the entire external objective world – it dispenses with the father by pre-existing him. (The being who should stand in for the father is metamorphosised into a second mother, and the nominal representative of the Law is killed). This in no way implies that the text is anti-male or justifies the elimination of men. Instead, it is a fantasy composed of equal fascination and fear, about re-fusion with this primal being, for which the price would be loss of self, but if the desired union were possible this would be offered up ecstatically enough. But ambivalence creeps in – it is a woman, Valerie, who seemingly achieves what men cannot, because of woman's greater closeness to the pre-Oedipal, due to her re-duplication of the maternal body, but the effect is not joyous but bleak. It also brings the text to a halt.

The film's fantasy breaks down – having attempted (sufficiently remarkably) to reverse the order of the fall into difference, it can find no signifiers to represent what might come into being. The film extinguishes itself. The opposite of this might be considered **Fellini-Satyricon** (1970), which actually does succeed in bodying forth a pre-patriarchal, pre-difference imaginary world, but then inscribes a particularly over-determined fall into difference as a means of narrative closure – without this the film would be without limits, infinite.

The one male figure who survives **Daughters Of Darkness** without loss is the concierge, the outsider who watches and knows everything ("If one wants to know something, one asks Pierre"), but never intervenes in the action. He remembers the Countess from when he was a young bell-boy – he is the eternal spectator, whose own life is in abeyance as he watches the dramas that unfold in front of him, inscribed into the text, a male spectator, contemplating a male fantasy.

Detection And Transgression

The Investigative Drive Of The Giallo

Xavier Mendik

INTRODUCTION

"I love Sherlock Holmes very much. People think he's all rationality, but his methods aren't rational at all. They're like hyper-realism in paintings... beyond rationality, almost magic"[1].

Dario Argento has openly acknowledged a debt to the classical methods of detection; in particular, the works of Agatha Christie and Sir Arthur Conan Doyle have influenced the construction of the investigative drives of his narratives. Yet these influences frequently seem at odds with the *giallo*'s obsession with displacing the actual logic and mode of detection.

What this article seeks to do is to analyze the problematic that surrounds detection in both Argento's cinema and the *giallo* in general. It will be argued that this inability to successfully detect indicates the fundamental insecurity that surrounds identity in these texts. This in turn will be analyzed using advances in both psychoanalysis and linguistics.

In terms of the *giallo*'s narrative construction, identity and detection seem to be fractured through three interdependent plot situations which this article will explore:

1. As McDonagh identifies in relation to Argento texts such as **The Bird With The Crystal Plumage** (1970) and **Profondo Rosso** (1976), the process of investigation reveals not one apparent suspect, but a second more transgressive accomplice.

2. Often related to the above is the strategy whereby the process of detection reveals a murderer who transgresses the norms of gender expectation. This device is clearly fore-grounded in Argento's cinema which is premised on the exploration of displaced female aggression. Other texts in this category include the female killer from Sergio Pastore's **Crimes Of The Black Cat** (1972). An interesting example of this strategy is also seen in Lucio Fulci's **A Woman In A Lizard's Skin** (1971). Here key suspect Carol Hammond manipulates existing gender values that equate femininity with neurosis and paranoia in order to detract a "male" police investigation away from a series of sexual murders that she has committed.

3. The process of detection as revealing or implicating the detective in the source of transgression. A key example of this is Argento's **Tenebrae** (1982), discussed below. Even when not directly revealed to be a murderer, it is marked that the *giallo* detective is often revealed as transgressive through an act of complicity. A key example here is provided in Roberto Montero's **The Slasher Is A Sex Maniac** (1972). Here Inspector Capuana allows the text's murderer to kill his own wife before arresting her after discovering her marital infidelities.

Using Lacanian psychoanalysis, it can be argued that the *giallo*'s inability to attribute transgression to individuality embodies the "real". This is the place (marked by disorders such as psychosis) that Lacan defines as replicating an infantile collapse of identity, mastery and the self.

As such, the genre provides a radical counterpoint to the "symbolic". This is the phase which displaces the infant's ambivalent perception of its own gender and identity, providing a personality that is profoundly mediated through discourse.

Defining language as "the murderer of the thing", Lacan argued that the identity that is provided through language is essentially alienating. In particular he points to its organising and regulating of sexual difference through a series of discourses which privilege the masculine. Thus Lacan's account sees the real as a radical interspace where the oppressive hold of language falters, dislocating identity in a way which replicates the repressed infantile experience.

According to Zizek's recent work, both the phases of the symbolic and the real are evidenced in narrative forms such as detective fiction which he argues either work to confirm or deny the link between discourse and gendered identity. To posit the *giallo* as evidence of the real is to acknowledge why texts such as **Tenebrae** are so frequently seen as overriding what Franco Moretti defines as the "good rules" of detective fiction[2]. This is because Argento's film fails by containing not just one killer but two or more, which produces:

> ...the nightmare of detective fiction...the featureless, de-individualised crime that anyone could have committed because at this point everyone is the same[3].

In many respects Moretti's comments prove pertinent, because the displacement of any stable notion identity and of subjectivity is fundamental to the *giallo*'s operation. Although **Tenebrae**'s Peter Neal is victimised by the Rome killer, he uses the principles of detective narration to discover his identity as that of Christiano Berti, a conservative television critic.

However, Neal's motives have little connection with legitimacy or the reintegration of law and logic. His proximity to the murders has awakened his own psychosis, and after killing Berti, Neal assumes his identity in order to continue his murderous quest.

Although Sherlock Holmes, defined by Moretti as incarnate of "a scientific ideal" is foregrounded as an influence on the detectives in the narrative, what the film reveals beneath this appeal to the principles of logic and rationality is a world governed by chaos, psychosis and gender ambivalence.

"READING" THE REAL.

If **Tenebrae** is concerned with the problematic definition of identity, then this world can be evidenced by the repetition of a particular flashback sequence in which a seductive woman strips and is then assaulted in a beach location.

The scenario conflates images of sexuality and gendered violence that forms the core of Argento's imagery. Here the woman strips before a group of partially clad youths before the erotic encounter is fragmented by the arrival of another (unidentified) male. When this male is refused entry to this coupling he assaults the girl before being chased and assaulted by her assembled male lovers. The sequence ends with her forcing the spike of her heeled shoe into his mouth.

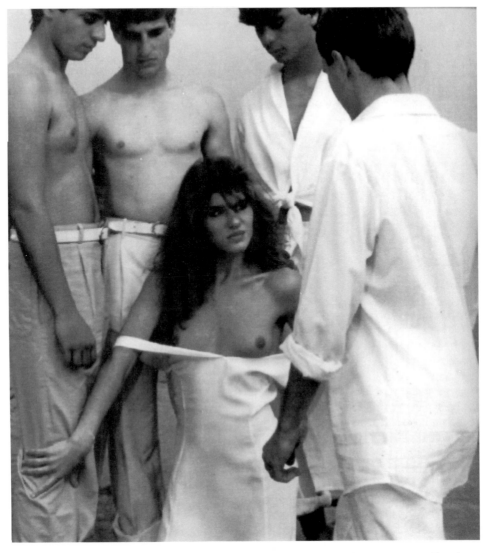

Tenebrae

For critics of the film, this sequence seemed to confirm the text's sadistic conflation of sexuality and violence directed against the "feminine"[4]. The flashback is attributed to the killer's subjective vision[5] through two further elaborations of the sequence.

Firstly, the killer, represented by point of view camera concealed in some bushes, watches the woman courted by an officer, and after he leaves stabs her to death. When after the death of Christiano Berti the flashback is repeated, this scene of violence is elaborated, as it is revealed that the killer then steals the girl's red shoes.

Rather than being seen as exemplifying the symbolic's regulation and punishment

Tenebrae

of the woman as a sign of difference, it can be argued that the scene embodies key characteristics of the real, a psychosis which works in Argento's film[6] to wreck the link between social logic and sexual location.

In terms of the subject's relationship to reality Lacan argues that a "rent" appears in the signifying structures that have kept the subject's identity in place. This gap often reveals repressed childhood traumas such as the primal scene with the infant witnessing or imagining the act of parental coitus, and the ramifications for his discovery of the logic of sexual difference.

Importantly, as with the case study of the "Wolf Man", the scene of sexuality, and the trauma that it induces often becomes recodified as a site of sexual violence, with the mother being forced to submit to the father's sexual will. This "screen memory" often involves a conflation or recodification of the actual sites of genital difference. In the case of the Wolf Man's recollection, the childhood memory that had haunted him was recast as that of anal coitus with its implications of violent intent.

If, as the case study indicates, this basis of the Oedipal trauma is not repressed, it continually afflicts the subject through a series of scenes (such as dreams, hallucinations), which constantly disturb the individual's identity. In the case of the Wolf Man, his inability to accept paternal law was codified through a "perceptual recurrence"[7].

For instance, his dreams reordered the sexual act as one of violence, through a scenario where he believed a pack of wolves were about to savage him. As Benvinuto and Kennedy have indicated, evidence of the real also occurred for the patient through consistent fantasies and hallucinations which conflated images of castration and loss of established body image.[8]

As they note in *The Works Of Jacques Lacan – An Introduction*, one fantasy occurring when the child was carving the bark of a tree with his penknife, and was momentarily traumatised by the fear that he had partially severed a finger with the implement. Importantly, the real is not only evidenced by the imagery of castration, but by the *"unspeakable"* terror"[9] that accompanies the event. As Benvinuto and Kennedy indicate, the emergence of the real shatters the subject's use of the strategies of language classification and distinction:

> The altered structure of the psychotic subject coincides with his using of language in various ways: the symbolic moorings of speech may be dislocated and he may speak in a roundabout, fragmented or confused way, or else in an excessively stylized way in which he is "spoken" rather than speaking.[10]

The emergence of the real, the fragmentation of identity, gendered body image and discourse that it produces are key in comprehending **Tenebrae**'s fragmented mode of detective narration and its preoccupation with sexual ambivalence.

The opening sequence of the film depicts the unidentified killer hurling a copy of Neal's book into an open fire, while the first murder in the film involves a shoplifter who is choked with pages from **Tenebrae**. Both actions indicate that this is a film in which language, words, grammar, syntax and logic are cut up, burned, destroyed. What these acts reveal is a fundamental instability in its core aim to attribute transgression to secure sexual identity.

As McDonagh indicates, the applicability of definition and clarity of sexual identity are replaced in **Tenebrae**'s ambivalent terrain by Neal's reviling in the realms of the "flesh". While not explicating the use of the term in a Lacanian sense, the references to the primal scene as a denial of discourse and established body image are implicit through the casting of the transsexual actor Eva Robbins/Roberto Coati as the seductive girl in the flashback.[11]

According to Francette Pacteau, androgynous cultural representations draw on the fascinations that both artists and audiences have for that which places existing and totalising categories under stress. As a result, she concludes that the androgyne is seen as a threat to symbolic structures and its stress on differentiation of gender through language.

She notes the construction of the hermaphrodite as a figure that carries with it the symbolic signs of castration, (marked by the frequent equation of acts of violence or forced bodily transformation that accompanies such scenarios), as well as the desire to transcend gendered distinctions. This factor seems marked not only in the construction of physical pain that marks Neal's recollection, but also the sexual construction of violence that marks many examples of the *giallo*.

For instance, Monica Ranieri's psychotic reconstruction of herself beyond the limits of female lack in **The Bird With The Crystal Plumage** is accompanied by the sexual nature of the attacks on her victims, who suffer penetration with a knife. This element of female sadism is a recurrent trait in both the *giallo* and Italian horror cinema in general and can also be seen Pastore's **Crimes Of The Black Cat**. Here blind detective Peter Oliver discovers the killer of a group of fashion models is boutique owner Françoise Balli, not her male lover as suspected.

Importantly in relation to Pacteau's thesis, the motivation for Françoise's actions is premised on her "damaged" female body which she exposes to Oliver before falling to her death. She reveals that her breasts were destroyed through a car crash, thus allowing her to feel distanced from her attacks on "feminine" figures desiring her lover Victor.

In the case of **Tenebrae**, the use of Coatti (an actor whose other screen appearances stressed even more fully than Argento's film his possession of both phallus and breasts) can also be tied to the idea of gender ambivalence that Pacteau explores. The virtual suppression of hermaphroditic imagery which features the vagina as a site of difference not only encapsulates the symbolic's equation of genital difference with "lack". It also points to the ambivalent conflation of both phallus and breasts that the infant identifies as a site of physiological power. As Pacteau notes, it relates not only to the infant's equation of the phallic mother as a powerful and often threatening figure, but also to the oral gratification experienced via breast feeding:

> In this light the hermaphrodite becomes a figure of excessive powers, endowed with both female and male signifiers of fertility – breast and power[12].

Indeed, the ability of the androgynous figure to disrupt the power of difference is marked by the basis of the dream which fragments the security of Neal's identity. Just before she is assaulted, the "girl" sinks to her knees and gestures with a downward thumb movement that the (unidentified) killer does not belong in this sexual coupling.

Although critics of the film took the beach scene as further evidence of the overt (and regressive) sexualisation of women, it has another meaning within the ambivalence of identity relating to the primal scene. Rather than being degraded, her gesture can be read as a possible sign that Neal also descend to his knees and accept the reciprocity that exists between them.

Indeed, in the sequence of his humiliation that follows this shot, the denial of difference is further evidenced by Coatti's forcing of the heel of his shoe into Neal's mouth. The act (which prefigures his later fatal "penetration" by a steel monument at the end of the film) functions to link a type of circularity or series of connections between the two bodies, which are based around:

> ...the restoration of a less differentiated, less organised, virtually inorganic state[13].

To return to Argento's confessed affinity with the classical detective, theorists such as Zizek have argued that all forms of cultural representation carry with them the capacity to slide over into the troubling lack of distinction that embodies the real. It is how these elements are recuperated that decides whether they work to confirm or upturn the symbolic's drive for sexual regulation. This factor can be analyzed by discussing how the real figures in relation to the detection process of the *giallo*.

THE SURPLUS OF THE REAL IN THE GIALLO: THE DETECTIVE AS ANALYST

Returning to the study of the "Wolf Man", Zizek has noted the patient's fondness for detective fiction. This he argues informed many of the defence mechanisms that Freud had to circumvent in order to discover the root of the subject's psychosis. Freud's effective adoption of the role of detective is pertinent. As Zizek argues, the processes of deduction in works of detective fiction are analogous to those of the analyst, forced to piece together the truth from a series of fragments or clues.

As with the analyst involved in dream analysis, the fictional detective deals with acts of transgression which foreground "the impossibility of telling a story in a linear consistent way"[14]. Zizek argues that these detection processes threaten to expose the infantile trauma of the primal scene, with its focus on sexual ambivalence and loss of identity:

> At the beginning, there is thus a murder – a traumatic shock, an event that cannot be integrated into symbolic reality because it appears to interrupt the "normal" causal chain... This radical opening... bears witness to an encounter with the "impossible" real, resisting symbolization.[15]

As with the psychoanalytic experience, the source of transgression in detective fiction replicates destructive infantile drives through its frequent equation of acts of sexuality and death. However if these contradictory elements are present in the classical detective tales that Argento discussed they are also clearly countered and restrained through the detective who functions to reinstate the realm of language and symbolic order.

FROM THE AGENT OF THE SYMBOLIC...

According to Zizek, this is the role of Poe's Dupin, and the "classic" detectives such as Holmes who replace him. They function to relocate and label "identity" to the evidence at scene of violent and sexual excess. For example, their success in this task is confirmed in their ability to read the "fragment" within a scene of transgression. In particular they retain the ability to isolate apparently insignificant details at the scene of crime which later proves central to the text's resolution: "Quite an interesting study that maiden," notes Holmes in *A Case Of Identity*[16], referring to Miss Mary Sutherland who has come for assistance in finding her missing fiancé. "You appeared to read a good deal upon her which was quite invisible to me," replies Watson. "Not invisible, just unnoticed, Watson. You did not know where to look, and so you missed all that was important." As Holmes continues:

> I can never bring you to realise the importance of sleeves, the suggestiveness of thumb nails, or the great issues that may hang from a bootlace... Never trust general impressions, my boy, but concentrate yourself upon details[17].

As Holmes explains, his quest to uncover the particular within the visual scene even takes on gender ramifications. For instance, he confesses that he pays particular attention to the trouser leg of a male and the sleeve of a female for "traces"[18] of gender activity during an investigation.

For detectives such as Holmes, this vital clue is usually figured in the form of a "visual fragment", that which Zizek sees as an excess, an "uncanny" surplus which upturns "the scene's totality and meaning". Importantly, what the detective has to do is re-articulate that which draws his attention, the visual, the absent, the un-symbolizable[19], and bring them back into the realm of discourse.

In *A Case Of Identity*, Holmes' reconstitution of the elements of signification is seen not only in his ability to deduce the resolution from the typeface of a letter sent to Mary by her fiancé, but also his proficiency in reading the mystery as a series of visual fragments relating to her appearance. Not only are the traces of activity Holmes seeks on Sutherland's sleeve proven to be much more than insignificant detail[20], but other deductions that he reads into her appearance such as indentations on her nose as a sign of her being short sighted also prove central to the resolution of Miss Sutherland's missing fiancé.[21]

Behind Mary's inability to see properly lies her scheming stepfather, who fearful of the loss of financial control of her earnings, did his best to shelter her from would be suitors by imposing on her a strict moral code.

When her emerging sexuality threatened this ploy, he transformed his identity into Mr Hosmer Angel, a would-be suitor for the girl. Using her poor eyesight as a means to assist his disguise, Mary recalls how they only used to meet in dimly lit night locations, where his appearance was further obscured by "tinted glasses".

By getting Mary to swear eternal loyalty to him as a precursor to their marriage, Windibank ensures that following the mysterious disappearance of Hosmer, Mary will remain unavailable to other suitors.

In *A Case Of Identity*, the indication of a coupling between a woman and someone who occupies a paternal role is clearly libidinally charged[22]. More importantly, it charts the transgression from a linguistic as well as a social position. As Holmes deduces when he reads letters that were sent to Mary by Hosmer, the wear on the typeface matches that of a communiqué that Windibank has sent to Holmes:

> "It's a curious thing," remarked Holmes, "That a typewriter has really quite as much individuality as a man's handwriting. Now you remark in this note of yours, Mr Windibank, that in every case there is some little slurring over the "e", and a slight defect in the tail of the "r".[23]

Although no direct punishment is attributed to Windibank, Holmes task being rather to highlight this actual transgression, the resolution seeks the reintegration of language and law. If this paternal agent possesses a speaking position, it is one which is defective, as is the typeface that reveals his hand. Indeed, Mary's comment that Hosmer seemed troubled by "infirmity of speech"[24] carries inferences of the imaginary's denial of discourse beyond Windibank's attempts to disguise his voice.

Yet it is not only Windibank who is punished, Mary does not figure in the narrative again, her fate and desire being left unresolved following Holmes' decision not to inform of her of the truth of his findings. According to Catherine Belsey, the marginalisation of the feminine via such methods forms a repeated method of resolution to the Holmes narratives.

In a universe ordered by a quest for logic, rationality and discourse, the feminine represents the threatening body, the other that must be restricted to the limits of the fictional world. As Belsey indicates, the Holmes narratives reproduce the symbolic's desire for both scientific logic and "total explicitness, total verisimilitude", through the reduction of woman as a signifier of sexual difference to a position of marginality and silence.

Indeed, it is not merely their desires that are thwarted, but often their actual ability to communicate. This is indicated in her example of *The Case Of The Dancing Men*, where the female under investigation remains either silent or unconscious for the majority of the narrative. This leads to Holmes having to crack a cypher that will not only explain the motive behind her behaviour (the desire to protect a criminal lover), but will also bring such a troublesome body back within the realm of the law.

In terms of the Lacanian construction of sexuality, Holmes remains very much the unified subject of the symbolic, who is able integrate visual[25] and verbal registers and thus provide the narrative with both coherency and mastery. Despite the difficulty of translating the iconic back into language, he "possesses the stable code, at the root of every mysterious message"[26].

If, as Zizek suggests, the format of detective fiction embodies the drives and compulsions of the primal scene, then Holmes like Dupin before him "forestalls the curse"[27] of these endless repetitions. He is able to reconstitute "the un-narrated"[28] back into discourse.

However, if the Classical Detective functions as an "armchair rationalist"[29], marked by stability both in sexual identity and access to the law, then the *giallo* provides a transgressive counterpoint to this position. It details the activities of amateur detectives, whose own identity, sexuality and subjectivity is as compromised as the murderers they seek to expose.

The classic detective such as Holmes manages to isolate himself from the source of transgression under investigation, by remaining absent from the scene of the crime when the actual transgression takes place.

However the *giallo* detective is never furnished with the same degree of security. Argento's detectives are consistently trapped by a desire to gaze in on the crime that they uncover, while the blind Peter Oliver is drawn to a whispered conversation of death and blackmail he overhears. In all cases the *giallo* detective's position is marked by a fundamental inability to distance themselves from the site of the real's excess.

To this extent the position of the *giallo* detective is comparable to a second type of investigative role that Zizek identifies. Unlike the classic, logical distanced process of deduction that defined Holmes, he defines this "hard boiled" mode of detection the "Phillip Marlowe" Way.

This references a universe where Chandler's Philip Marlowe is prevented from extricating himself from the site of sexual and violent excess because of his debt to a compromised protagonist; it is also universe where Spillaine's Mike Hammer works through a series of vendettas. Equally, recalling Todd French's reference to the "paranoid alienated seeker" of Argento's *giallo*, this is the universe where the protagonist, unable to comprehend his own gender biases, struggles in a sphere where subjectivity is itself under stress.

Unlike the classic detective, the *giallo* hero's inability to extricate himself from the site of the real is reiterated at the level of the narrative's structure. Specifically it is indicated by the failure to close off the act of crime from that of its investigation.

If, as Zizek indicates, this results in an inability to close off the tensions of the primal scene, its affects are seen not only in the psychosis which grips Peter Neal, but in the structuring of a series of sexual scenes which populate other *giallo* narratives. For instance, an example of this is seen in the construction of the amateur detective Sam Dalmas from Argento's earlier **The Bird With The Crystal Plumage**.

Although Dalmas attempts to pose in the fashion of the classical detective, he lacks the crucial ability to re-articulate this visual "symptom" within a linguistic

The Bird With The Crystal Plumage

framework. As with all Argento heroes there remains another excess, one more visual fragment beyond the reach of the comprehension of these male protagonists.

According to both Belsey and Moretti, the classical detective confirms his ability to distinguish and categorise crime by successfully integrating his investigation within the existing power structures of authority. In the case of Holmes, the narrative's drive towards mastery and control emphases the use of emerging methods of communication, transportation and forensics in the arrest of the villain. As Moretti notes:

> Holmes's culture... will reach you anywhere. This culture knows, orders and defines all the significant data of individual existence as part of social existence[30].

...TO THE DETECTIVE OF THE REAL

Although such methods of deduction are frequently employed in the *giallo*, they fail precisely because they are directed at transgressions which do not fit easily with the symbolizable.

The Bird With The Crystal Plumage employs the use of a wide range of forensic equipment from voice enhancement machines, infra red photography, microscopic analysis and identity parades all in an effort to trap the "man" Dalmas believes he has seen in the gallery.

From this constant attempt to categorise and classify, the police believe they have pinpointed accurate details of the killer's identity, such as what type of cigars he smokes, his height, taste in dress and which hand he uses to writes with. However, these processes of categorisation and distinction are proved to be futile. As Dalmas discovers, the visual fragment that forms the vital clue to investigation is based on a misrecognition that fails because it equates femininity with passivity.

As with **Tenebrae**, the film deals with the impossibility of locating transgression to identity, specifically within the processes of discourse. If the processes of speech are foregrounded in Argento's first film, they function not to shore up the symbolic but draw attention to the fact that the voice as an enunciative apparatus can no longer retain the threatening surplus of the real. As the processes of voice enhancement used by Morrisini's men indicate, the text is governed by an impossibility of locating the "voice" within the specifics of identity.

This is indicated in the taped recording of a phone call from the killer to Morrisini, which forms the basis for the police investigation as to the type of man they are looking for. It is revealed to be separate from the recording of a phone call to Dalmas which forensic equipment discovers differs in its "vocal harmonic intensity".

Importantly, the voice that Morrisini and his men study (that of Monica's husband attempting to throw police off her trail) establishes the parameters of sexual difference the detectives attempt to scrutinize, in their belief that the killer is male. Although their equipment is able to distinguish the alternation in the "grain" of the voice between the two recorded messages, it seems unable to identify Monica disguising her voice as a male in the message sent to Dalmas.

According to McDonagh, Argento's first three films are governed by a pattern of "weird science", whereby amateur sleuths attempt to solve a series of murders using scientific and criminological processes of classification and deduction.

However, their failure to integrate these findings back into any legitimate process of symbolization is confirmed by Roberto Tobias's use of optical technology in **Four Flies On Grey Velvet**. Tobias, is blackmailed and stalked by an unknown assailant who claims to have evidence of Roberto killing a man in an abandoned theatre. After members of his household and family are slain, Roberto uses scientific advances in optical technology to visualise the last image on the retina of a dead victim, which he too hopes will lead to the identity of the killer.

What the resultant image reveals, an amulet with the painting of a fly imprinted on it, leads to the discovery that the killer is in fact his wife, who only married Roberto with the idea of later victimising him.

To return to Todd French's, definition of the "paranoid alienated seeker" it seems that these (characteristically male) detectives are plunged into danger in an attempt to confirm their intellectual vanities. Although presuming mastery over these situations, a sense of their social dislocation is evidenced through the ease with which they misread elements, or visual fragments of the enigma they seek to resolve.

From Dalmas' misreading of the gender of the attacker he views in the gallery, Tobias' inability to link the medical representation he captures to the fly painted amulet that his wife wears. Even Marcus Dailey's misreading of a murder scene in **Profondo Rosso**, foregrounds the fact that Argento's heroes are unable to master either the visual or the textual elements under investigation.

In forcing "his tortured protagonists, to look back and reassess what they have seen"[31], Argento draws attention to the ease with which masculine perceptions of sexuality and gendered behaviour can be unhinged. As with Dalmas, Marcus Dailey (another "artistic" foreigner living in Rome) becomes unwilling witness to the brutal murder of a psychic Helga Ullman, and similarly has to extricate himself in the eyes of the law after being found at the scene of the crime.

As with Dalmas, Marcus remains convinced that something is lacking in his recollection of Helga's scene of death, a painting which he believes has disappeared. It is only by his returning to the scene of the crime that Dailey recalls that what he actually saw in Helga's apartment was in fact not a painting but the mirror reflection of the killer. As McDonagh notes, in both films the discovery of the truth, leads to mutilation, near death and a "displacement of the protagonist's sense of harmony with the world"[32].

Importantly, in reducing the vital clue or element that his male protagonists have to reconstruct, what Argento's narratives introduce is a duel process of criminal deduction and solution, whereby the paranoid alienated seekers' deductions are displaced by something far more threatening.

In the case of **The Bird With The Crystal Plumage**, the scientific "evidence" pointing to Monica's husband as the killer is displaced by Monica's final assault on Dalmas when he returns to the Gallery at the end of the film. In **Profondo Rosso**, Marcus' belief that he has found evidence which incriminates his associate Carlo to the murders, is proven equally miscast when the true killer, Carlo's mother, attempts to kill Dailey following her son's death.[33]

To return to Zizek's formulation that the hard-boiled detective is unable to extricate himself from the site of transgression, it seems pertinent that this feature is often overcoded in the *giallo*. Peter Oliver of **The Crimes Of The Black Cat** is personally implicated in Françoise's violations, having lost two girlfriends to her murderous quest. Indeed, his profession as composer of the soundtracks to *gialli* which feature similar images of sexuality and death indicate an inability to establish an identity beyond these transgressive concerns.

Equally, from the very opening of **The Bird With The Crystal Plumage**, Sam Dalmas' link to the symbolic remains tenuous. If Ranieri's psychosis renders her obsessed with the image rather than discourse (she not only stalks her victims but meticulously photographs them prior to an attack), then Dalmas becomes similarly equated with the iconic.

This is implicit from the film's opening sequence, which unexpectedly fragments diegetic time and space with stop motion photography which charts the killer tracking another victim. Importantly, the subsequent murder is only referenced via an ellipsis, as the screen cuts to a black-framed diegetic insert and the victim's scream is heard on the soundtrack.

The disruption of the unity of the sound and image band reiterates the function of the sequence to fragment the spectator's alignment to the text. Importantly, it is through this disjuncture of discourse and image that Dalmas is introduced to the text, when his associate Carlo lowers a newspaper photograph of one of the murders which reveals Dalmas in frame behind it.

Importantly, the sequence functions to establish a syntagmatic relation between the photographic preoccupations of the killer and Dalmas' problematic relation to discourse. As he reveals to Carlo in this scene, he only came to Italy to try and cure a writer's "block", but had been unable to find any work until Carlo had approached him.

Carlo hires Dalmas to produce the text for guides that accompany photographs of birds. Dalmas' link to the iconic is thus established before his encounter at the gallery. Indeed, the sequence where he and Carlo walk through the museum even prefigures it with Mussante literally coded as the "split" subject being dissected within the frame by a series of mirrored display cabinets they are walking past.

Importantly, the struggle that Dalmas views in the gallery replicates key features identified by Freud's analysis of the primal scene and its resultant compulsion repetitions. As with the "Wolf Man", the scene conflates images of sexuality and violence. This is particularly marked after the event, when Dalmas' recollections of the event constantly intervene on his love making with his girlfriend Julia.[34]

Indeed, the gallery sequence is a "scene" that not only positions Dalmas as viewer, by trapping him in the set of glass doors it also concurrently cuts him off from the processes of speech. This is indicated in his inability to communicate via discourse with either the injured Ranieri inside the gallery or the passer-by who cannot hear the protagonist's pleas from the street outside.

Equally, its relation to the fragmentation of established body image is indicated via the reduction of the figure with which Monica struggles to a black clad figure who lacks a definable identity. This placement replicates the primal scenes recodification of the paternal agent, whom "though usually present is represented as an absence"[35].

Similarly, the gallery is populated with figures which underscore the locale as a site of both voyeurism and gendered ambivalence. For instance, during her crawl around the gallery space Ranieri positions herself beneath a statuette of an obese woman whose signs of genital difference are marked by the enormity of her breasts. Equally, the figure foregrounds the functioning of vision through as it is constructed with distended eyes which seemed focused on Monica's body.

Other prominent iconography in the gallery includes an androgynous statuette. This embodies the fusion of masculine and feminine anatomical features of breasts and phallic shaped beak instead of the head that Pacteau confirms as subverting the symbolic's drive for classification of difference. This is the site where:

> ...desire is unobstructed, gender identity is that of the symbolic, the law, it is the nodal point where the symbolic and the imaginary meet and resistance occurs. The androgynous looking figure presents ...an impossibility, that of the erasure of difference, which constructed me as subject[36].

Although Dalmas enthuses to Julia that the mystery has managed to cure his "writing block", this reference to the articulation of discourse fails to re-establish his link to the symbolic. Arguably his proximity to the primal scene as a site of transgression functions to orientate his subsequent detection around the unsymbolizable.

Thus it seems pertinent that one of the first questions that Morrisini asks Dalmas when he finds him slumped at the scene of Monica's assault is if he is English. Dalmas' reply that he is in fact American contains resonances beyond the diegetic motivation of establishing characters information. Rather it functions to further delineate the distinction between the detective of the symbolic and that of the real.

Morrisini is linked to classical English processes of detection, indicated by his power in the realm of statistics, forensics and modes of classification and a pseudo-scientific base which keeps him structurally separate from the investigation. Contrastingly the greatest clue that Dalmas uncovers once more links him to the same "iconic" compulsion repetition as Monica.

This is the painting that artist Berto Consalti constructs as a record of Monica"s original assault, and initiates her subsequent killing spree after she sees a copy in a Rome art gallery. The picture itself redoubles the primal scene motif, depicting a sexual attack on a young girl, with her assailant's knife entering her flesh around the site of her genital area. (As with Dalmas' "scene" the assailant's identity remains ambivalent).

While Monica erects a copy of the painting in her secret shrine where she also develops the photographs of her victims, Dalmas also constructs a photomontage of clues that he hopes will resolve the case. Argento underscores the reciprocity between the pair in one sequence by cutting from a shot of Dalmas examining a carbon copy of the painting to Monica analysing the original prior to a murder.

Importantly, the clues that lead to the revelation of Monica's true status confirm Dalmas' status within the real. For instance, his meeting with the artist Berto Consalti, who lives in filthy apartment, feasts on live cats and concentrates his paintings (such as the one of Moncia's assault) on the slicing open of the human body, indicates his location in the realm of ambivalent flesh.

If this artist's preoccupation with filth can be traced back to the source material that Argento adopted from Frederic Brown's novel *The Screaming Mimi*, the use of this figure functions to equate the paranoid alienated hero in an infantile universe divided through both the flesh and waste matter. As McDonagh notes, although Argento extracted the character of "God" from Brown's novel, he features as Roberto's sidekick in **Four Flies On Grey Velvet**, and as a vagrant is also equated with the filth and physiology.

Thus it can be argued that the *giallo* replicates the real via this inability to locate identity to transgression, or even contain and isolate violent and sexual excess from the position of the detective. If this process of detection operates beyond the legitimacy of the symbolic (and its "classic" fictional delegates such as Holmes) then it is also marked by a recurrence of a "phallic" fatalism or masochistic acceptance of the inability to dominate the flow of the investigative drive.

In terms of the construction of Peter Oliver in **Crimes Of The Black Cat**, this is translated into a dependence on peripheral characters to either assist him or rescue him when endangered by his proximity to Françoise's actions. This masochistic intent is also seen in the recodification of Dalmas from investigator to potential victim in the closing scenes of **The Bird With The Crystal Plumage**. It is also present in the construction of male amateur detectives such as Franco Arno and Carlo Giordani from Argento's **Cat O' Nine Tails** (1971).

Here, the diegesis is once again split between the systematic examination of the modes of scientific and criminological forms of detection and their incompatibility to the *giallo*'s concentration on terrains of abjection, death and decay. The film centres on a group of scientists conducting research into the XYY chromosome which they link to a human predisposition towards violence.

However, when the group begin to fall victim to an unidentified killer the culprit is revealed to be Casoni, one of the group who has the defective gene. As with Argento's other detectives, Giordani and Arno are unable to reconstitute the fragmented clues they uncover, as they literally represent a split between the mastery of both image and discourse that represents the classical detective. For instance, Arno is blind and dependant on his young niece Laurie for visual information, while Giordani's link to the symbolic via his status as journalist is compromised by his involvement with the daughter of a scientist involved in the murders.

Cat O'Nine Tails

Giordani even confesses the impossibility of solving the crime they are investigating commenting that it has so many leads that resembles "a cat with nine tails". However, Arno corrects his statement arguing that its resembles "a cat *of* nine tails, like the old naval whip!"

This alteration of Giordani's statement is important as it recasts the site of the investigation through a metaphor equated with punishment of the male body. Once more, this can be seen as reflecting the lack of symbolic mastery of the codes of investigation implying the crime as a site that involves the detective "ethically and often painfully. The deceitful game of which he has become a part poses a threat to his very identity as a subject"[37].

Thus it can be seen that in the *giallo*, the emphasis is not on the restriction and recuperation of the real, but its facilitation through the dislocation of identity within a diegetic space. Whereas the detective of the symbolic deals with quests such as *A Case Of Identity*, the detective of the real is prevented from even defining the parameters of such singularity.

If, as Zizek argues, detective fiction deals with elements of desire and primal sexuality which must be contained, then the foreclosure at the heart of the *giallo* threatens the annihilation of the very borders of subjectivity. These tensions are present from the pre-credit scene of **Tenebrae** where the camera pans across a page of written text of Neal's book, which links elements of suffering and humiliation with acts of "annihilation: murder".

This preoccupation with the decomposition of the human form and the identity that it encompasses, reveals the desire for death that marks the inability to contain the *jouissance* of the real. Rather than talk of the relocation of masculine identity and sexual difference, as the reviews of the film suggested, **Tenebrae** (along with other *gialli*) proclaims the destruction of the symbolic's system of self and gendered classification.

When playing the two systems of detection to the captive Giermani at the scene of Christiano Berti, Neal admits that the mystery has him stumped. As he claims: "...I've made charts. I've tried building a plot the same way you have."[38] The breakdown of the modes of structure, classification and detection that Neal admits, results from the psychosis that his latest book has unleashed. Continuing to discuss his "block" with the case, Neal concludes that the murders do not add up because someone "who is dead should be alive and someone who is alive should be *dead*".

The latter part of his statement refers not to any continued quest to destroy the female "other" as critics of the film would suggest, but to his own death, the desire for annihilation that emanates from his recollections of the primal scene. Indeed Freud's interpretation of the "fort/da" game as an example of compulsion repetition proves important in linking Neal's flashback to a notion of the death drive.

As his account of *Beyond The Pleasure Principle*[39] indicated, the child's "active" attempts to master the maternal absence via language and symbolisation often belie a fatalism which can be linked to the death drive. Freud notes the initial "passive" position of the child's feelings of helplessness and loss were often "staged as a game in itself[40]", and only later recorded as a process of mastery and control. Applying this process of visualised "recodification" to the flashback in **Tenebrae**, it is noticeable that Coatti's punishment only occurs as a *revision* of the original scene of Neal's humiliation[41].

This recodification of the primal scene, takes account of the symbolic positioning of woman as a site of "lack", but is still premised on the male subject's inability to extricate themselves from the humiliated, degraded body.

For instance, in his study of "Mr M" Michel De Musan has noted how the patient both attempted to efface the genital distinctions that differentiate sexuality, while still retaining the symbolic's definition of the woman as a site of castration. As De Musan's account indicates, the whole of "M"'s torso was covered in tattoos which defined the feminine in derogatory and sexual terms. However, by being printed on his own flesh, these statements were not distinct from his desire to incorporate those degraded physiological traits.

Thus in a series of controlled experiments "M" actually altered key areas of his external body image (such as the remoulding of his flesh into a mock vagina) to produce fusion with this female form. While still constructed as the "other", the account of "Mr M" indicates the lack of distance and mastery from the female form that embodies the real. As the patient stated "I am not a man nor a woman. But a bitch. A slut. Flesh to be fucked"[42].

It is the purpose of **Tenebrae** to position both Neal and the spectator at the site of the original flashback, the point of the writer's experience with "the pleasurable counterpart of death"[43]. If "M" experienced psychosis and sexual dislocation via the recodification of his body as an ambivalent site of flesh, then the end sequence of **Tenebrae** provides a similar pattern. Here, Neal is found wallowing in pity while Giermani verbalises the rationale for his crimes.

Tenebrae

Linking this to the death of a girl in Rhode island during his youth, McDonagh argues that the text gives the appearance of resolving the narrative enigmas it raises. This is particularly as his statement is followed by a diegetic insert of Robbins, who appears to be addressing the audience directly.

However, regarding the text's preoccupation with the ambivalent location of identity, he notes that Giermani qualifies his statement by stating if this was Peter Neal's crime:

"If" is the key word here. For even if Peter Neal did not commit this crime, if the scenes on the beach represent something other than Neal's haunted memories of a youthful transgression... then they still dominate the fictive space setting the tone of perverse dreamy menace[44].

As with Argento's other *gialli*, the statement followed by the diegetic insert do little to re-establish the clarity and security of the symbolic. If as McDonagh argues, these flashbacks are the "embodiment of **Tenebrae**'s driving imagination"[45], then they indicate the *giallo* to be an interspace of the real where identity and the classification of sexuality are rendered void.

NOTES

1. Argento, cited in McDonagh, p238.
2. For instance, in his review of **Tenebrae** Phillip Strick argued that the text displayed an explicit disregard for elements of investigative plotting and the processes of logical deduction.
3. Moretti, *Clues*, p239.
4. This perception of sadism in the film was a consistent feature of reviews of the film. For instance in the journal *Films And Filming* Mark Le Fanu argued: "Argento's preoccupation... seems to be with devising novel and increasingly nasty ways of killing his characters, especially when they are women. Each murder scene occasions a dazzling assemblage of cinematic effects – the camera tracks its victims who gaze back in erotic appreciation of their own vulnerability." (p36)
5. As with the vision of Casoni, the killer from **Cat O'Nine Tails**, the assailant's perspective is represented through the close-up of an iris that sub-segments the shots by opening and closing the sequence.
6. Adapted from Benvinuto and Kennedy's section on psychosis in *The Works Of Jacques Lacan – An Introduction*.
7. Freud, "Beyond The Pleasure Principle" in *On Metapsychology*, p923.
8. In her work on "Primal Scene And Sexual Perversion", Joyce McDougall has also noted "episodes of depersonalisation, bizarre body states" (p372), which accompany the traumatic re-emergence of the primal scene in patients.
9. Opcit, p153.
10. Ibid, p146.
11. The inability of Anglo-American critics to recognise this reflexive use of casting once more confirmed the negative criteria under which the film was judged. Coatti, a recognisable icon to Italian audiences, has appeared in a number of productions which have exploited his ambivalent sexuality. For example he starred with fellow transsexual Ajita Wilson in Antonio D'Agostino's sex film **Eva Man** (1980), released in France under the title **Ambi-Sex**.
12. Pacteau, p76.
13. Ibid, p82.
14. In his *Two Ways To Avoid The Real Of Desire*, p49.
15. Zizek, p58.
16. Conan Doyle, *The Adventures Of Sherlock Holmes*, p152.
17. Ibid, p153.
18. Ibid, p153.
19. Or in the case of Mary Sutherland, re-configure not only the visual clue, but also her appropriation of discourse, which Watson defines as "a rambling and inconsequential narrative" (p149).
20. In fact Holmes argues that they indicate her genuine concern for Angel, indicating that she was working on letters to publicise his absence prior to her visit.
21. Holmes reveals in the resolution to the narrative: "You see all these isolated facts together with many minor ones, all pointed in the same direction." (p158)

22. As Holmes notes, Windibank: "...appears as Mr Hosmer Angel and keeps lovers at bay by making love himself." (p156) Commenting upon this aspect of the narrative, Moretti notes that it foregrounds the role of paternity through transgression of the Step Father. This provides a counterpoint structure to the legitimacy of lineage and a point of comparison to the actions of natural fathers. (Who as Moretti notes, along with the upstart and the noble form a recurrent criminal type in the Holmes narratives). However, he argues the tale still carries incestuous resonances: "That is the poor Stepfather is a bit like the well-known uncle enlisted by early psychoanalysis as a mask for the father." (p245).

23. Conan Doyle, *A Case Of Identity* p155. As Moretti comments on the narrative, Holmes' capacity to locate guilt via the power of discourse clearly indicates that it is language and access to the power of communication that defines individuality. Indeed, what the resolution to the narrative confirms is that Holmes is not merely a user of such codes, but a proficient analyst able to decode mystery in terms of grammatical and syntactical structures: "I am thinking of writing another little monograph some of these days on the typewriter and its relation to crime. It is a subject to which I have given some little attention." (p155)

24. Ibid, p153.

25. Even Holmes' reference that he will "glance into the case" for Sutherland (p152) reiterates the importance of integrating vision into his investigative drive.

26. Moretti, p248.

27. Zizek, p61.

28. Ibid, p58.

29. Copjec, *Read My Desire*, p165.

30. Moretti, p246. In her book *Read My Desire*, Joan Copjec has also drawn Foucauldian interpretations to the basis of the classical detective, using Roger Hacking's research on "the avalanche of numbers" (in the form of governmental statistics) which divided citizens into numbers, classifying them along an axis such as gender, class and nationality. As Copjec notes, the period of this numerical initiation (1830 to 1848) coincides with the birth of the "classical" detective novel, and thus shares its concern with the ultimate ability to deduce with crime and murder.

31. John Martin, "What You See Is What You Don't Get", p1.

32. Opcit, p101.

33. This dual pattern of investigation and revelation is also present in Argento's **Trauma** (1993). Here the paranoid alienated seeker is represented by the film's central protagonist David Parsons, who wrongly assumes the psychiatrist of his anorexic girlfriend Aura to be the "head hunter" killer. When the analyst is killed trying to escape from the scene of one of the murders, the real killer is revealed to be Aura's mother who proceeds to torture Parsons for his stupidity.

34. Importantly, these recollections occur via an identical pattern of stop-motion photography indicating Dalmas' inability to extricate himself from the close proximity he shares with Ranieri. The link between them seems confirmed when Dalmas begins to collect information about the killer's victims. These clues (adapted from press clippings) take the form of non-diegetic inserts of black and white still photographs of the victims' bodies, once more linking Dalmas to the violent site of representation.

35. McDougall, p379.

36. Pacteau, p63.

37. Zizek, p62–63.

38. Cited in McDonagh, p179.

39. In *On Metapsychology*.

40. Ibid, p285.

41. Importantly, this recodification involves an increasing narrativisation and control of the scenario. Arguably the original trauma of the beach scene was marked by an absence of the camera as signifying subjective vision. However, the use of point of view positioning is present in the revised scenes where Neal's presence is indicated by a point of view surveillance of Coatti from the bushes. This process of visual recodification is also central to a scene that haunts Roberto in **Four Flies On**

Grey Velvet. As McDonagh notes, this takes the form of a dream (repeated four times with increasing narrativisation) that deals with a man about to be beheaded in a Middle Eastern location. As she notes, the basis of the dream begins with a long shot establishing both location and the casting of the victim's body as a site of public spectacle before the crowds. Only in later revisions does it take a more distinct form of enunciation with increasing close-ups of the proximity of the executioner and the victim. As McDonagh notes, the final dream occurs just before Nina is revealed to be the killer. Rather than reveal his mastery over his investigation, the scenario (which prefigures Nina's own decapitation in a car at the end of the film) functions to underscore Roberto's masochism.

42. De Musan, p169.
43. Ibid, p169.
44. Ibid, p184.
45. Ibid, p184.

BIBLIOGRAPHY.

Ashworth, Mark: "**The Crimes Of The Black Cat**", in Stephen Thrower (Ed) *Eyeball – The European Sex And Horror Review*, Issue 1, Autumn 1989.

Belsey, Catherine: 'Deconstructing The Text: Sherlock Holmes" in Bennett, Tony (Ed) *Popular Fiction, Technology, Ideology, Production, Reading*. Routledge, London 1990. Benvinuto, Bice & Kennedy, Roger: *The Works Of Jacques Lacan*. Free Association Books, London 1986.

Copjec, Joan: *Read My Desire – Lacan Against The Historicists*. October, London 1994.

De Muzan, Michel: "M", in *Semiotext(e)* 10, edition on "Polysexuality".

Doyle, Arthur Conan: *The Adventures Of Sherlock Holmes*. Wordsworth Press, Hertfordshire 1993.

French, Todd: "Dario Argento Myth And Murder" in Chas. Balun (Ed) *The Deep Red Horror Handbook*. Fantaco Enterprises Inc, Albany 1989.

Freud, Sigmund: *On Metapsychology*. London: Penguin 1991.

Hunt, Leon: "A (Sadistic) Night At The Opera – Notes On The Italian Horror Film". *The Velvet Light Trap* No.30, 1992.

Jones, Alan: "**Opera**" in *Cinefantastique* Vol 18, No 2–3 March 1988.

Le Fanu, Mark: "**Tenebrae**" in *Films And Filming*, September 1983.

Martin, John: "What You See Is What You Don't Get", in Pierre Jouis (Ed) *Fantasy Film Memory* No.4–5: Directed By Dario Argento. Gothic, Paris 1991.

McDonagh, Maitland: *Broken Mirrors Broken Minds, The Dark Dreams Of Dario Argento*. Sun Tavern Fields, London 1991.

McDougall, Joyce: "Primal Scene And Sexual Perversion" in *The International Journal Of Psychoanalysis* Vol 53 (1972).

Moretti, Franco: "Clues" in Tony Bennett (Ed) *Popular Fiction, Technology, Ideology, Production, Reading*.

Pacteau, Francette: "The Impossible Referent: Representations Of The Androgyne" in Burgin Victor, Donald James, Kaplan Cora, (Eds) *Formations Of Fantasy*. London: Routledge, 1986.

Palmer, Jerry: *Potboilers*. Routledge Press, London 1991.

Poe, Edgar Allan: *Tales Of Mystery And Imagination*. Wordsworth Editions, Hertfordshire 1995.

Strick, Philip: "**Tenebrae**" in *Monthly Film Bulletin*, May 1993.

Williams, Linda Ruth: *Critical Desire – Psychoanalysis And The Literary Subject*. Edward Arnold, London 1995.

Zizek, Slavoj: *Looking Awry*. October Press, Massachusetts, 1991.

Marco Ferreri

Sadean Cinema Of Excess

Andy Black

"To do a dangerous thing with style is what I call art."
—Ben Gazzara's character Charles Serking in **Tales Of Ordinary Madness**.

Antonioni, Bertolucci, Fellini. All celebrated, much vaunted, greatly revered figures in the annals of Italian cinema history and rightly so. To a lesser degree, albeit because of a lesser numerical audience, we also have such luminaries as Mario Bava, Riccardo Freda, Antonio Margheriti, whose gothic horror ancestry has now been assimilated into contemporary cinema on the shoulders of Lamberto Bava, Dario Argento and Michele Soavi.

But the name Marco Ferreri? Relatively unknown in the UK, America and Europe, Ferreri is only accorded the acclaim his unique oeuvre deserves in his native Italy, whilst in France he barely cuts the mustard as a cult figure.

Born in Milan in 1928, Ferreri first came to any kind of critical attention with **The Wheelchair** (1959) – a wicked black comedy in which a vindictive old man murders his caring family because they refuse to buy him an electric wheelchair (!), despite the fact that the "invalid" is perfectly capable of walking unaided.

Since then, he has courted controversy with great frequency with his fiercely individual brand of salutary satirical comedy – not the style of humour to earn huge guffaws, more of a cerebral experience, aligned with an outrageous visual style – which is equally flirtatious with sexuality and social mores and being all the more enticing to the awe-struck viewer because of it. One by one Ferreri selects his targets with consummate zeal, be they age, sexual relationships, masculinity, new femininity or family life.

As befits any genius the customary "accusation" that he is "ahead of his time" should in reality be seen as "complimentary" to his undoubted vision and ideas. Unfortunately, the narrow confines of the UK's "moral guardians", objected to such vision with the result that arguably Ferreri's finest work **La Grande Bouffe (Blow Out)**, was originally banned in Britain from general release during the 1970's. It's limited exposure to London audiences was in fact prefaced with the cautionary notice, that the film is "A black comedy about four world-weary pleasure seekers who decide to eat themselves to death in an orgy of high cuisine and sexual indulgence".

Despite such a clear warning some spectators felt the need to walk out of screenings either in protest or sickness – one such walk-out engineered by the "crusading" Mary Whitehouse, reputedly condemning the film thus: "It is totally disgusting... the most revolting film I have ever seen".

From modern-day puritan to latter-day pornographer, we may take the Marquis de Sade's words (spoken through Saint Fond in *Juliette*) "...who cares about the poverty of the people if it is the means to satisfy one's perversions", as a starting point to discuss Ferreri's varied body of work.

Not for him the elitist, decadent perversions of the Marquis, even when his films such as **La Grande Bouffe** betray such hedonistic pursuits as food and sex orgies – "Why do you eat if you're not hungry. Disgusting", one character questions in the same film,

La Grande Bouffe

at once pinpointing the "sin of gluttony" in rather less graphic terms than the recent **Seven** (1995).

Ferreri *is* concerned with human nature, why we behave how we do. Like the Marquis, he does spotlight the evils of human nature, but unlike him, he also searches for the good in society, albeit with a bizarre cadre from which his venomous humour arises to add such germane observations on life, lust, living, society and sexual (im)morality.

To this end, many of his films adopt a typically 1970's approach of post-fordist, post-modernistic delineation of the collapse of the family against a background of a rigid society which is simply *too* inflexible to accommodate the eccentric characters within Ferreri's diverse universe.

To complement the aforementioned bizarre characters we have a divergent range of films to absorb, from the almost "normal" (for him) western **La Cagna** (1971), human deformity in **La Donna Scimmia (The Ape Woman)** (1963), the oneiric **Dillinger Is Dead** (1968), the gastronomic pornography of **La Grande Bouffe** (1973), the modern-day western **Touche Pas La Femme Blanche! (Don't Touch The White Woman)** (1973), a man's atavistic regression to ape-like characteristics in **Ciao Maschio (Bye Bye Monkey)** (1977), a theme continued in **Chiedo Asilo** (1979), emotional detachment in **Tales Of Ordinary Madness** (1981), fetishistic attachment to musical key-rings in **I Love You** (1986), self-mutilation and sexual conflict in **La Dernière Femme** (1976), infidelity in **Il Futuro E Donna** (1984) and explicit sex comedy in **La Carne (The Flesh)** (1991).

An equally impressive range of actors have populated Ferreri's films, including Fellini star Marcello Mastroianni, the sultry Catherine Deneuve, Ben Gazzara, Gerard Depardieu, Anita Pallenberg, Carroll Baker and **Highlander** star Christopher Lambert.

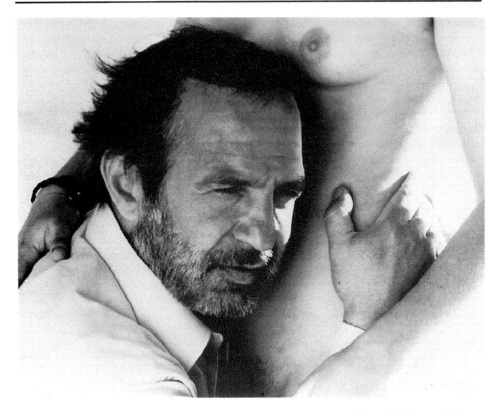

Tales Of Ordinary Madness

Investigating the deep-rooted societal explorations in Ferreri's work one need look no further than the appropriately-named **Tales Of Ordinary Madness**, with Ben Gazzara's character of Charles Serking being a compelling study into one mans' gradual descent into madness and detachment, mirrored by that of his new-love, a prostitute named Cass (Ornella Muti).

Gazzara's perpetual downwards spiral, stumbling from one vacuous sexual encounter to another finally ends in his acquaintance with Muti – herself, an alter-ego combining sophisticated sensuality with a child-like innocent quality, her propensity for self-mutilation a physical expression of her emotional angst.

Gazzara's violent, rapturous erotic encounters – cavorting on the floor, pressed up against the wall, encapsulated in his throwaway one-liner; "She was that rare kind who gives you an instant hard-on", describing one of his conquests, "Vera", although "I wasn't about to embrace the American wet dream... I'd rather get drunk", more incisively expounds his personal philosophy as well as pouring scorn (and semen!) upon the American "ideal".

Whilst Cass' character is busy piercing first her cheeks with wire in a wince-inducing scene, and later moving down to her genitalia, we are left to reflect upon her physical scars and Gazzara's mental ones. Despite this intense chaos the film's message seems to be relatively uplifting, in that even the lowest of low-lifes can still believe in the value of love.

(Gazzara's character was actually based upon 1960's sub-culture writer-poet, Charles Bukowski, whom Ferreri considered as a kindred spirit; and the film is based on Bukowski's book *Erections, Ejaculations And Other Tales Of Ordinary Madness*).

Not content with championing (?) the underprivileged of L.A. here, Ferreri turned his attentions to racial injustice and discrimination in the surreal **Touche Pas La Femme Blanche!**. Reuniting his cast from **La Grande Bouffe**, this satirical slant on the western finds the (ill) treatment of the native American Indians put under the microscope, together with the (over) idolisation of Wild West Heroes.

As such, we see General Custer (Marcello Mastroianni no less!) portrayed as a weak and vain coward, attempting to fight off the advances of both Sitting Bull (Alain Cuny) and Marie-Helene (Catherine Deneuve), whilst Buffalo Bill (Michel Piccoli) preens himself prior to a bloody re-staging of the Battle of Little Big Horn.

The incongruous sight of Custer riding on horseback through modern Paris and of the Indians owning modern clothes boutiques lends a bizarre edge to the proceedings to say the least.

The rotting underbelly of a (dysfunctional) society again forms the basis for **Bye Bye Monkey** where a plague of rats symbolically engulfs New York City (akin to the albino rats who proliferate in Werner Herzog's oneiric **Nosferatu** remake).

Lafayette (Depardieu) lives in the city working at the New York Wax Museum and with an aggressive feminist theatre group. Lafayette and his friends (mainly outcasts themselves), make a strange discovery on the banks of the Hudson River – namely, the body of a forty foot ape cradling a newly-born chimpanzee in its arms.

Lafayette adopts the monkey and gradually becomes less human as his attachment to the ape increases. This apocalyptic dissection of society and human relationships poses many provoking questions. Have Lafayette's "new woman" friends alienated him so much that he prefers the company of a monkey? Are animals indeed more humane than humans? Is the Waxworks Museum a symbol of an unfeeling, android-like society, devoid of compassion, proliferated by cold and unappealing concrete towers? (The image of the giant ape lying prone in front of the New York City skyline also recalls a certain other giant ape, scaling the Empire State Building in **King Kong**, and indeed the ape model is actually the same as was used in Dino de Laurentis' ill-judged **King Kong** remake with Jessica Lange.)

The all-consuming greed of society, our general lack of altruism and show of fraternal feelings to one another also informs Ferreri's most infamous work, **La Grande Bouffe**. "Do you know how to cook?" one character in the film asks – "No, I'd rather eat," is the ironic reply. So, greed, sloth, lust, selfishness, many foibles of the human psyche are exhibited here. Even the main protagonists – a quartet of middle-aged men (Marcello Mastroianni, Philippe Noiret, Ugo Tognazzi and Michel Piccoli) – are un-named, merely referred to by numbers as if to reinforce the feeling that numbers not people matter in modern society.

All four are sick of their dull lives, bored and in need of one last fling – an orgy of food, wine and women in a millionaire's mansion. As expected, the *Daily Mail*'s critical reaction that the film "Makes **Last Tango In Paris** look like kindergarten stuff" is somewhat ill-judged and overactive, but it became the viewpoint of many others too.

Crude imagery and crude manners abound – we see the chef packing a case with an obscene number of carving knives in it, or Michel cradling a cow's head in his hands

La Grande Bouffe

and shouting, "To be or not to be" in literary sacrilege.

From one piece of "meat" to another as a duo of ingenues arrive to provide the men with their sexual sustenance – resplendent in tiny g-strings and leather boots. Unfortunately for them, Mastroianni has a severe car fetish and is usually to be found lying under four wheels rather than two legs, even to the extent of "pumping" a phallic manifold into one girl's groin!

Noiret's character isn't much of an improvement, his Oedipal/oral stage fixation leaving him gasping for air between the cavernous cleavage of a schoolteacher (Andrea Ferreol).

The gastronomic orgy then moves into overdrive in Python-esque style ("Another wafer sir?!") as Piccoli unsurprisingly falls ill with flatulence – "you don't chew enough!" he is rebuked, one girl vomits (a heinous crime here as she doesn't *love* food), Mastroianni has an accident in the toilet only to be engulfed in a tidal wave of faeces (a comment on what his character is indeed wallowing in), culminating with Tognazzi being fellated by Ferreol as Noiret feeds him a grotesque paté binge, leaving Tognazzi to expire on the dual point of orgasm/full stomach!

Noiret himself then dies gorging himself on breast-shaped desserts. The moral appears to be that you most certainly can have too much of a good thing – be it food or sex or both. Overindulgence, lust, greed – all lead to untimely ends here.

The continual sexual innuendo, banqueting and feasting certainly appear to have informed the likes of **The Cook, The Thief, His Wife And Her Lover**, presenting us with

La Grande Bouffe

an orgy of gastronomy and sexuality upon the screen.

The obsession of the characters in **La Grande Bouffe** is mirrored, though admittedly to a lesser degree in **I Love You** – a most unorthodox love story as Michel (Christopher Lambert) finds all his numerous female companions lacking in one area – unfaltering devotion and loyalty. His search for such a sincere companion leads him too... an electronic key-ring (!!), which answers his whistle with the three magic titular words.

Even now however, Michel is not contented as his "new-love" also answers to other people's whistles in the same manner – so, complete devotion is unobtainable, especially if you betray such obsessive, fetishistic character traits.

Similarly, obsessive behaviour rears its ugly head in Ferreri's **La Carne (The Flesh)** also. Here it afflicts Paolo – a divorcee struggling to make ends meet. His night-time stints as a cabaret pianist in a local bar bring him into contact with Francesca Dellera – so, voluptuous siren meets pot-bellied pianist, united in one common goal – love. Or so we think, until Paolo's obsessive behaviour spirals dangerously – "I want to stay inside you. I'll die if I'm not there" he pants as they make love.

As always with Ferreri however, the intensity of the eroticism is paralleled with the intrinsic comedy of human sexual relations – hence Paolo's love for his dog (Giovanni!), is satirised as he penetrates Francesca "doggy-style" whilst her pendulous breasts have other uses besides mesmerising Paolo, as she helps a young mother breastfeed her baby(!) near their beachhouse.

"I'll be the lascivious virgin," gushes Francesca at one stage during the film – a

La Donna Scimmia

more perfect microcosm of Ferreri's contradictory universe would be hard to find.

Ferreri's film work for others has been equally contradictory in a way, ranging from an acting role in Pasolini's **Il Porcile (Pigsty)**, to being productions manager for Federico Fellini's affectionate comedy **Il Voce Della Luna (The Voice Of The Moon)** (1990).

His working relationships with such exalted figures seem appropriate given the accolades bestowed by numerous critics upon his films – "Ferreri is the equal of Antonioni" (*Time Out*) and "Ferreri is fit to be compared to Buñuel" (*The Times*) – this latter eulogy perhaps the most meaningful as far as Ferreri is concerned, for if anyone can match the social vitriol, voracious sexuality – if not quite the religious satire – of Buñuel, then it is Ferreri for sure. High praise indeed.

FASCINATION

Jean Rollin: Cinematic Poet

Daniel Bird

"To attract and delight by arousing interest or curiosity."
"To render motionless, as with a fixed stare or by arousing terror or awe."
"To put under a spell."

—Definitions of "fascinate".

For a quarter of a century English cinephiles have tended to resist Jean Rollin's work, his descents into hermetically sealed worlds of desolate châteaus, solitary vampires and violent seduction, and above all the bizarre genius and poetic imagery with which he weaves his morbid fascinations.

My claim is then a minority one; however, I feel Rollin's burgeoning renaissance is far from its zenith, and whilst the majority of the sexual interpretations of the vampire myth of the last quarter of a century now seem little more than kitsch anachronisms, his work remains raw and ripe for reappraisal.

Unlike many filmmakers, Rollin's lineage is one of writers, poets, painters, serialists, and comic strip artists as well as filmmakers. The vampire, the (pair of) virgin(s) and the castle form the cardinal points of Rollin's art.

The vampire is often portrayed as the embodiment of both sex and death, so it seems natural that Rollin's perception lies confined to more salacious variations of the "exploitation filmmaker" legend. However, despite these "low art" connotations, his nocturnal fantasies perhaps dwell more readily in the company of those belonging to Tristan Corbière, Gaston Leroux and Jean Ray rather than those of, say, Jess Franco. Although Leroux's *Phantom Of The Opera* is widely acknowledged as one of the great horror novels, not only does it remain little read, but it eclipses the rest of his body of work. Although *The Perfume Of The Woman In Black* (magnificently interpreted by both Maurice Tourneur and Francesco Barelli) and *The Mystery Of The Yellow Room* (one of the first locked room detective stories) have been filmed, his extraordinary and rather horrific Grand Guignol pulp shorts remain trapped in obscurity. These are pulp novels which have undoubtedly made a huge impression on Rollin. Several of these stories, notably *The Woman With The Velvet Collar*, are prefaced with a maritime scenario of sailors reciting weird tales at coastal taverns, which is perhaps why this location has such resonance in Rollin's films, particularly **Démoniaques**. The element of organised crime present in Leroux's novels proliferates into almost every Rollin opus, from bandits in **Le Viol Du Vampire**, **Fascination** and **Démoniaques** to the runaways in **Requiem Pour Un Vampire**, **Nuit Des Traquées** and **The Escapees**.

Tristan Corbière's poetry has a romantic preoccupation with memories. Perhaps it is this one vein which runs consistently through Rollin's films, lending them a unique ambience of mystery. **Lèvres De Sang** is perhaps the conclusion of this preoccupation, which has haunted both **Le Viol Du Vampire** and **La Vampire Nue**. Corbière and Leroux wrote around the circle of French Decadent writers, among which was Jean Lorrain, the author of this passage from the short story "The Glass Of Blood":

"...It is the governess who has the task of conducting the girl [Rosaria] into the

depths; every morning they go down, at five or six o'clock, to the devil's kitchen beneath the rue de Flandre, to an enclosure where the blood is drained from the living calves, to make the white and tender meat.

And while the young girl makes her descent into that place... La Barina stays here... perfectly tragic in her velvet and lace, mirroring in her mode of dress the snow-whiteness of the narcissi, the frost-whiteness of the tulips and the nacreous whiteness of the irises; here, striking a pose with just a hint of theatricality, she watches.

...and her anguish reaches into the uttermost depths of her soul while she anticipates the first kiss which the child will place upon her lips, as soon as she returns: a kiss which always carries an insipid trace of the taste of blood and a faint hint of that odour which perpetually defiles the rue de Flandre, but which, strangely enough, she does not detest at all – quite the contrary – when it is upon the lips of her beloved Rosaria."

The lurid tale documents how a wealthy aristocratic marquise (La Barina) cures a consumptive young girl's (Rosaria) wax-like pallor, by leading her down to an abattoir to drink blood. The arresting image of a beautiful girl standing in an abattoir germinated into a truly evil flower, a masterpiece of *amour fou*, **Fascination**. It also serves as an ideal preface to Rollin's artistic output, that of allure and its fatal consequences. Lorrain was perhaps the most decadent of all French writers; his nemesis, like that of Aubrey Beardsley and so many Decadent writers, was tuberculosis. The writer enlisted the help of alternative medicine to prevent the worsening of his illness, using such remedies as ox blood; others, like ether, had hallucinogenic side effects and fuelled, as with Poe and opium, his extravagant literary descents into perversion and sin more profoundly than with any other writer of his day. The above passage is written with an almost fetishistic attention to detail, and the detached sense of timelessness is reminiscent of a Rollin film.

It is not just the aesthetics of a decadent genre that have inspired Rollin, but even more so their philosophy. Rollin's philosophy is essentially Sadean, the same philosophy that cornerstones both the Decadent and Surrealist movements, which have both made a profound impression on Rollin. Baudelaire felt, as did Sade, that sin was a "natural state of human nature" and that "in the act of love there is a great resemblance to torture or a surgical operation", concluding that "one must always come back to Sade, that is to say to natural man, to explain evil". Baudelaire cultivated poetry in themes of the most appalling taste, which is often remarked about Rollin. The ubiquitous *Aurum Film Encyclopedia* notes **Requiem Pour Un Vampire**'s "stylised Sadean sex scenes" and goes onto say that "..the sex scenes look as if they were inserted as autonomous fragments, probably to ensure box office successes". Indeed they were, as Rollin has explained in many interviews, but despite his insistence of his dislike for these scenes, they are filmed with a dubious relish and intensity to rival some of Franco's earlier sado-masochistic chronicles. However, they are not without redeeming features, as the *Aurum* continues: "But within these terms, they are beautifully achieved comic strip nightmares." Even *Video Watchdog*'s Tim Lucas admits that "It's nasty and out of character with the surrounding footage, but it also has a ferociously tactile, undeniably sexual appeal, and the culminative image of a bat nestling in female pubic hair is quintessentially Rollin." (Perhaps to be more accurate, it's Rollin paying homage to a quintessential image of Clovis Trouille).

Returning to the abattoir scene in **Fascination**, the sequence is shot in an almost identical manner to one in the first part of Walerian Borowczyk's **Contes Immoraux/Immoral Tales**, based on a story by André Pyere De Mandiargues entitled

La Vampire Nue

Fascination

"The Tide". The sequence in question is where a sixteen-year-old girl anticipates fellating her older cousin on a beach, where long shots are cut with extreme close-ups of the ajar mouth of the girl whilst she runs her finger over her lips. Even if Borowczyk had not filmed the scene six years before, Rollin surely would have invented it. In fact Rollin, in some ways, is rather similar to Borowczyk. They both have their own equally distinctive idiosyncratic style; Borowczyk's seems to have arisen from his background as a brilliant painter and animator, like Rollin having few, if any, cinematic influences whatsoever. Rollin's canvas is often motionless, characters walk in and out of frame, appearing as dots on the horizon, ending in tight unfocused encounters with the audience. The effect is claustrophobic and forms an air of unease between the audience and characters. Rollin utilises the full potential of the medium by synchronising the visuals with an equally extravagant soundtrack, comprising a vast range of musical accompaniments, from the fragmented, disjointed jazz of **Viol** to the angelic wails of **Fascination**. The soundtrack to **Fascination** is very similar to Popol Vuh's in Werner Herzog's somnambulistic **Nosferatu**, despite both of them being released in the same year – "great minds" as they say...

Interestingly, the fleshed-out "Immoral Tale" **La Bête** features the same château as in **Fascination**, and the scenario of the aforementioned film, that of a thief who hides in a château, but no matter how hard he tries cannot bring himself to leave, was a theme similarly explored in Borowczyk's truly amazing **Dr Jekyll Et Les Femmes**.

The locus of these dark fantasies remains a singular poetic image. The lithe female vampire whose coming ruptures the chimes of midnight as she slithers out of a

Le Frisson Des Vampires

clock in the bridal chamber of a lone virtuous virginal bride, whom she proceeds to seduce, in **Le Frisson Des Vampires**. The scene embodies the archetypes of the sexual sub-conscious; the vampire's lesbianism prises apart the newly weds, her spectre sways the girl to sleep alone on her wedding night, where she can be corrupted. Likewise the girl playing the graveyard-bound piano in **Requiem Pour Un Vampire**, the afore-mentioned scene in **Fascination** and final scene in Rollin's most overtly Oedipal piece, **Lèvres De Sang**, where the protagonist is vampirised by a sister figure in a coffin as it floats off to sea – the image justifying the incestuous relationship between the lovers, as does the Surrealist preoccupation of *amour fou*, that of being loved to death. In a similar vein, the opening sequence to Borowczyk's live-action companion piece to his animated **Les Jeux Des Anges**, **Blanche**, in the words of Philip Strick "spells out the story of **Blanche** for us in just... three cyphers; the fairytale fortress which could easily be the ogre's lair, the white dove fluttering in panic behind wooden bars like innocence over-protected, and the defencelessly nude Blanche herself, an instant target for unpermitted lusts".

Georges Franju, even more so than Luis Buñuel, must be Rollin's primary influence. Rollin met Franju and Buñuel whilst filming his very first shorts; he admired the political anarchism of Buñuel and the poetry of Franju's documentaries. Franju, like Rollin, was deeply influenced by a cinematic style of the past, especially the serials of Feuillade which he lovingly parodied in his **Judex**. Rollin has acknowledged **Judex** as the source for the animal-masked cult in **La Vampire Nue**. Franju and Rollin have also been influenced by German Expressionism, particularly the work of Fritz Lang, which Rollin has paid homage to by referring to **Moonfleet** in several of his films. Franju also shared the

Judex

classical cinematic urban poetry of Carne, a style which was revolted against during the emergence of the New Wave when Rollin was starting to make films. Franju and Rollin are always "black and white", never grey. There are virgins and there are vampires. In **Judex** there is the masked, black-garbed villainess, Diana, and Edith Schob's innocent, even celestial, figure. These contrasts are reflected in the expressionist approach to

Living Dead Girl

lighting in both of their films. From these images grow films constructed in an inimitably anarchistic, almost improvisational manner, taking a cue from the early crime serials of Feuillade. Feuillade was in fact the sort of commercial filmmaker that was opposed by the avant-garde, as was Rollin, and he fell under similar criticism. Witness Louis Delluc: "**Judex** and **The New Mission Of Judex**, are more serious crimes than those condemned by court martial." Harsher words have been spoken about Rollin for precisely the same reasons. However, Feuillade was – and Rollin probably would have been – favoured by the Surrealists.

Rollin's penchant for his expressionist style, which perhaps climaxes in **Démoniaques**, began whilst working with French psychedelic comic strip artists Phillipe Druillet and Caza. The trilogy of **La Vampire Nue, Le Frisson Des Vampires** and **Requiem Pour Un Vampire**, have the look of a comic strip, their interiors drowned in colourful spotlights, integrating them into his flat mosaic of cobalt blue and scarlet akin to that of the criminally ignored Mario Bava. Whilst the chaotic collages of Max Ernst and Yves Troille have made an indelible stamp on the younger Rollin opuses, the languid approach of Paul Delvaux's paintings has suffused the Rollin tableaux after **La Rose De Fèr** and **Lèvres De Sang**. While the allusive girl in the abattoir appears to gaze at us infinitesimally, like the girl in the cinema in **Lèvres De Sang**, she appears obtainable only at a price, for sex is equated with death. The ambience in **Lèvres De Sang** and **Fascination** is no longer one of pulp gothic, rather a landscape of silence and emptiness. Rollin's brand of eroticism is generated by combining opposites, the ideal and the obscene. The juxtaposition of religious iconography and blasphemous perversion is a much dwelt-upon theme, from the black mass in **Viol** to the congregation of hooded skeletons at the altar in **Requiem**.

The third character in Rollin's films, a castle or château (a notion consolidated by Rollin when he described how the castle in **Le Frisson Des Vampires** was originally intended to "bleed" when the vampires were killed), is repeatedly crammed with antiquarian objects from the past, giving rise to a long-forgotten memory. The most memorable sequence in **The Living Dead Girl** is where the long-deceased Françoise Blanchard phones Marina Piero amidst sentiments of her childhood.

An aesthetic which has constantly plagued Rollin's work is that of women dressed in brilliant white. This can be perceived as either a wedding gown (**Frisson**) or a death shroud (**The Living Dead Girl**); naturally, like Buñuel in **Abismos De Pasión** – his take on *Wuthering Heights* – Rollin unites the two perceptions. In his first film **Viol**, the vampire is wedded in a theatre and then nailed into a coffin with her lover.

As with Surrealists and their literary predecessors, Rollin is fascinated with the *femme fatale*. The Rollin female distinctly conforms to one of the two characters found in vampire literature, whether they be virginal or a Lamia – beautiful, full of ambiguities and paradoxes which make her all the more alluring. She is told to "stop playing games" at the beginning of **Fascination**, but instead she continues. She's passionate but her love is inaccessible; the final part of **Fascination** elaborates this idea, where a string of female vampires are lined against a wall as if in some amateur wedding photograph, enticing their victim. Lust triumphs over love in the Rollin film. When Elizabeth in **Fascination** reveals her love for Mark, we later learn she desires his blood above anything else, and once she's taken that blood she returns beneath the sapphic gaze of her vampire cult's leader.

Rollin's relationship with his *femme fatales* is as intense as, and comparable to, that of Baudelaire. This philosophy goads accusations of misogyny, but is more a result of sexual unease felt by an artist overwhelmed by desire. Reducing women merely to objects is, after all, a typical Surrealist preoccupation. The sadism in Rollin's films has more in common with the subversion and defiling of dolls in the photographs of Hans Bellmer, than perhaps anyone else working in the genre. But what Rollin has done, for all of his failings, is to have created some of the most arresting images to be captured on film. He is a genuine poet composing in the cinematic medium.

THE EVIL DEAD

Die And Chase[1]: From Slapstick To Splatshtick

Julian Hoxter

"All is disjointed for the sake of shock in a splatter film, and the spectacle of violence replaces any pretensions to narrative structure, because gore is the only part of the film that is reliably consistent."
—Michael A Arnzen, Who's Laughing Now? The Postmodern Splatter Film[2]

"Rather than providing knowledge, slapstick misdirects the viewer's attention, and obfuscates the linearity of cause-effect relations. Gags provide the opposite of epistemological comprehension by the spectator. They are atemporal bursts of violence and/or hedonism that are as ephemeral and as gratifying as the sight of someone's pie-smitten face."
—Donald Crafton, Pie And Chase: Gag, Spectacle And Narrative In Slapstick Comedy[3]

In his paper *Who's Laughing Now? The Postmodern Splatter Film*, Michael Arnzen proposes a generic definition of the "splatter film" as: "...a filmic text that promotes itself in the marketplace as one of "horror", and self-consciously revels in the special effects of gore as an artform".[4] In doing so, he specifies a generic corpus [sic] that would include films such as **Halloween, Slumber Party Massacre** and **Prom Night** alongside the **Evil Dead** films and the **Nightmare On Elm Street** cycle. Arnzen goes on to argue that the "splatter film" is, in part by virtue of this self-conscious process of signification, a postmodern phenomenon and, moreover, that it functions in such a way as to "...portray the postmodern condition as an optimistic vehicle for cultural transformation".[5] My purpose in writing this paper is to attempt to historicise, and thus call into question, Arnzen's generic definition through an exploration of the function of visual humour in recent American horror films.

Specifically, I will argue against the centring of gore as the primary mechanism for generating affect in many of these texts and propose that the display of bodily dismemberment functions, rather, as a means of camouflaging the parallel process of narrativising the disruptive attraction of the gag. Certainly Arnzen is aware of the structural function of gore in **Evil Dead 2**: "Splatter films are gore for stability's sake..." but he makes the mistake of assuming that if gore has a stabilising (even a regulatory) function in these films it is because "...such stability resides in a consistency of genre expectations, not of text".[6] On the contrary, what sets the **Evil Dead** cycle and to a lesser extent the **Nightmare On Elm Street** cycle apart from the rest of Arnzen's splatter texts is in the fact that they confound generic expectations through the *attractive* mechanisms of slapstick and the gag. This is not to claim that visual humour is absent from other horror films of the last ten years, but it is certainly not present to the extent that it overrides the functions of both fear and disgust. I would argue that it is not possible to watch these films with the same expectation of being frightened or disgusted as one would before watching the **Prom Night, Friday The Thirteenth** or **Halloween** cycles, for example. Structural, narrational and aesthetic changes in groups of texts within a certain genre must, by definition, change genre expectations to some extent and fans of

Ash (Raimi?) and/or Freddie come to expect specific pleasures which the other cycles cannot provide.

In foregrounding the gag and, thus, slapstick as legitimate objects of inquiry in horror film analysis I will be drawing upon the pioneering work of scholars of early cinema. The considerable debt this paper owes to Tom Gunning, Donald Crafton, Peter Kramer and Henry Jenkins amongst others will be clear to those readers familiar with their work.[7]

Arnzen initially focuses our attention on the sequence in **Evil Dead 2** in which Ash's (Bruce Campbell's) hand becomes possessed and "rebels" – first knocking him unconscious and then attempting to reach a meat cleaver, an act of murder clearly on its, er, mind. The battle which ensues, entailing acts of self-mutilation (Ash is driven to cutting his own hand off with a chainsaw while screaming "Who's laughing now?" – hence the title of Arnzen's paper) and providing moments of outrageous gallows humour (Ash traps the hand under a bucket weighted down with books, the top title being – what else – *A Farewell To Arms*) understandably causes Arnzen some unease...

> There's more going on in this scene than the typical "slice and dice" gore and droll horror associated with exploitative films of this ilk. There is a disturbing feel about it – an uneasiness that is not caused by a fear of demonic possession... nor terror from the gore of dismemberment (the camera focuses only on the man's face, laughing as his own blood drenches him), nor the insanity of the soundtrack and dialogue (a cacophony of gangling chainsaw engines and screaming combined with the hand's Gremlin-like chattering), but there exists in all this horror an unsettling and sublime hilarity about the scene that refuses to be ignored. It is nearly impossible not to chuckle at the outrageousness of the hero's self-mutilation. And when the character cries "Who's laughing now?" the moment is too hyperreal to be cast aside as frivolous coincidence. This scene from **Evil Dead 2** is the postmodern turn "in the flesh".[8]

I would argue, however, that the source of Arnzen's disquiet has less to do with an ahistorical (periodising but, significantly, not overtly periodised) theorisation of postmodernism than it does with a (historical) shift in the position of humour – and specifically the gag – within horror cinema certainly, but also more broadly within visual culture. Arnzen is unquestionably correct in his assertion that the film's use of humour can hardly be put down to "...frivolous coincidence..." – the director Raimi, Campbell and producer Tapert not only list the Three Stooges as a major inspiration but acknowledge the centrality of slapstick to their design – however his ground is less solid when he proposes that the presence of humour in this context should, in itself, provide grounds for surprise.

This is not to say that **Evil Dead 2** cannot be described as postmodern under certain definitions, on the contrary it could be seen, alongside the **Nightmare On Elm Street** cycle and others, as being indicative of a significant development (closure?) from many of the films Arnzen proposes in support of his initial definition. However, to claim the film ahistorically for postmodernism – that it is postmodern because of the transgressive potential of narrative fragmentation, for example – betrays both a reluctance

Evil Dead 2

to analyse the function of visual horror in these films and an unwillingness to consider the broader significance of the gag and slapstick not only through cinema history but also as increasingly central tropes of contemporary, or what has been called "post-classical", cinema.[9]

In order better to understand both the aesthetic and structural functions of the gag and slapstick, historically and in terms of their contemporary significance, we need to return to the period of filmmaking before Hollywood hegemony – to what might hesitantly be called the period of pre-classical cinema. In his article "The Cinema of Attractions: Early Film, Its Spectator And The Avant Garde", Tom Gunning argues against teleological readings of film history which imply a necessary and/or unproblematic development of film form from Lumière through Griffith to Hollywood melodrama.[10] In its place, Gunning puts forward an account which allows for a reading of early film, at least before 1906, as being both unprivileged as an "art form" and as offering its first audiences pleasures based in large part upon the new and unique properties of its apparatus rather than upon the narrative content of the films themselves.

For Gunning, then, early film was offered initially as a technological attraction – it was presented and sold, as many nineteenth century technologies (such as the telephone) were before it, as an extraordinary scientific advance and the first films were mobilised simply as examples or proofs of its capacity to produce moving images. For early audiences the attraction of the cinema lay in part in a very modernist fascination with the investigation and reification of the working of machines – an interest in what has been called (by Neil Harris and later by Charles Musser) the "operational aesthetic".[11] Also in this period film rarely has its own exhibition space. Films are shown as one item (attraction) on a vaudeville bill, for example, and initially there is neither an explicit nor an implicit assumption either from filmmakers or audiences that the new medium has, or should have, higher artistic pretensions based on film content. Indeed, where specific content issues are foregrounded for an audience, by advertisement or by a narrator and so forth, it tends to be either because what the film shows is unavailable to its public on a regular basis – for example, actuality films depicting events and/or locations at which the spectators could not have been present – or, conversely, because it presents the commonplace as estranged – seeing ourselves through the mediation of cinema. In neither case is narrative foregrounded – *what can be shown* is the attraction, not what can be told. It is to this spectacular arena, then, to the space of the attraction, that we shall return in our discussion of horror. "What can be shown", both in the above sense and in others (technological and political as well as in relation to shifts in cultural "standards" and changes in patterns of censorship), has always been an issue central to any discussion of the presentation of horror and the fantastic in film. Intersecting with this discussion are, of course, questions of film form and genre and here again, Gunning's account of early film has much to offer.

Early film style reveals both its technological and vaudeville roots. Subjects are typically positioned frontally to the camera and no attempt is made pro-filmically to disguise the relational chain of the apparatus from subject through technology to spectator. Early films, then, emphasise the presentational over the representational – they organise their subjects openly for display and usually engage in, and indeed require, direct address. In this way, it could be argued that the positioning of the early film audience is negotiated primarily through an exhibitionistic rather than a voyeuristic mechanism (and here, perhaps, we can also begin to see the significance of this historical digression for post-classical horror). Even in early erotic narratives (and Gunning uses the example of **The Bride Retires**), the audience is often privileged in its position in relation to specifically voyeuristic characters in the film. In this example, the undressing bride openly acknowledges audience location and communicates directly with the camera while her husband tries to peep from a less advantaged position.

While narrative is less important than spectacle in this early period, generic markers can immediately be discerned. Although, with the notable exception of the gag film **L'Arroseur Arrose** the first Lumière films are primarily actualities, from 1895 onwards gag and trick films begin to appear in Europe and America with increasing regularity. Working from an analysis of the abovementioned gag film – in which a gardener is tricked by a small boy who steps on the gardener's hose to cut off the water supply and then releases it, drenching the gardener when he points the nozzle towards his face – Gunning proposes a classification of the "mischief film" – what might be referred to as a proto-slapstick form.[12]

Gunning argues that the mischief film is constructed around the playing of a simple prank or "mischief gag". The mischief gag operates in two stages, or phases, linked by the mechanism of the gag – the "mischief device". The first stage sets up the premise and foregrounds the victim of the prank (the gardener waters the plants and the small boy steps on the hose), often implying an outcome around the anticipation of which audience pleasure can cohere. The second stage presents the result of the prank (the gardener looks down the nozzle of his hose and is drenched when the boy removes his foot). The linking function between the first and second stages of the gag is performed by the mischief device – in this case the hose – as Gunning describes:

> Although the human actants of rascal and victim are certainly essential to the gag, a detour is taken through an inanimate object, or an arrangement of objects. As a mediatory visual element which takes some time to operate, the device possesses its own fascination, one which brings us back in an unexpected way to the operational aesthetic. Although some mischief gag films are very simple, most of them make use of the possibilities such devices offered. The enjoyment of the gag lay at least partly in watching the device work.[13]

Having presented one approach to understanding the basic operation of the mischief gag, it is now possible to position the gag within wider theories of slapstick and visual humour, and it is here that the debate between early film scholars becomes a little more complex. However, understanding the subtle relationship between the individual gag, visual humour and narrative progression in the context of developments in film form and genre after the period of the Cinema of Attractions will allow a second historical move, this time from past to present, from early film back to our initial discussion of contemporary horror. This is the move from slapstick to what might productively be termed "splatshtick" – the interface between narrative progression and non-narrative interruption found in films like **Evil Dead 2**. "Splatshtick" is a mediation between the technology of special effects (pro-filmic and cinematic); the active interpolation of technique (cinematography, sound and picture editing) into narrative and the effect of a particular aesthetic of actorly performance through the figure of the central protagonist (combining, in Bruce Campbell's work, elements of clowning, pastiched naturalism and melodramatic gesture).

If slapstick is interruptive, this begs the question whether or not narrative has the capacity to contain that interruption. Donald Crafton argues that it does not. In doing so, he defines the function of visual humour in terms of *non*-narrative intrusion. Under Crafton's grid, slapstick is the generic term and the gag one specific form of such intrusion. Further, he argues that the purpose of the gag is precisely to intrude so radically that it produces an unbridgeable gap which the structures of conventional film causation cannot re-absorb:

> I contend that it was never the aim of comic filmmakers to "integrate" the gag elements of their movies. I also doubt that viewers subordinated gags to narrative. In fact, the separation between the vertical domain of slapstick (the arena of spectacle I will represent by the metaphor of the thrown pie) and the horizontal domain of the story (the arena of the chase) was a calculated rupture, designed to keep the two elements antagonistically apart.[14]

Conversely Tom Gunning, in critiquing Crafton's analysis, argues for the regulatory power of narrative – non-narrative intrusions are instances of "necessary excess" that can be absorbed and contained.[15] Their debate is conducted around comedy films from the 1920's, films structured in a significantly different manner from those of the period of Gunning's Cinema of Attractions. The films in question, including those of Chaplin and Keaton, combine elements of slapstick and of linear narrative – hence Crafton's irreconcilable opposition of "pie" and "chase". Indeed for Gunning it is also around the

issue of this combination of elements that his position on narrative is formed, only he conceives of its significance as evidence of a process of *the narrative integration of attractions*.[16] Gunning argues that this process causes the attraction to go "underground" after 1906, appearing thereafter in a variety of filmic contexts (from the avant garde to special effects) but never re-establishing a position of pre-eminence.

I would argue that in the **Evil Dead** films, at least, the attractions of slapstick are once again centred as primary mechanisms for generating effect. Although in conventional terms splatshtick could be seen to be interruptive, in the **Evil Dead** films the mechanisms which centre visual humour do so by wrenching audience expectation so far that splatshtick becomes normalised. Indeed this process is so successful that more conventional narrative sequences come to take over the interruptive function. It is important, however, to emphasise the broader significance of this position. Arnzen mobilises arguments from postmodern theory in an attempt to expose and explain the "problems" of narrative in the **Evil Dead** cycle. He views these "problems" both in terms of a lack of story coherence within the films themselves and in terms of the issue of duplication between the first and second films of the cycle. He argues with some justice that **Evil Dead 2** is in many ways nothing more than a copy of the first film with a larger effects budget. This argument assumes a broadly "presentist" position in relation to film history and, following on variously from the work of Fredric Jameson and Jean Baudrillard amongst others, implies the impossibility of constructing an historical reading that treats with the past as having any more than (at best) an etiolated relationship with contemporary culture :

> Splatter films incorporate a culture that recognises that it must violently cut itself free from its own past by chainsaw, butcher's knife, or cleaver, while at the same time understanding the dangers involved with such a revolutionary act. These films are not merely a re-animation or dissection of contemporary culture. Splatter films are an audience-centred participation in the spiritual transcendence from Baudrillard's "dead body" of contemporary reality, which we can only understand through our own present-tense reactions to films like **Evil Dead 2** [sic].[17]

Leaving the specifics of Baudrillard's arguments aside, what is tacitly being denied by this presentist argument is the possibility that the films may, in fact, be other than what they seem to be on the surface level of plot and through their marketing: horror or "splatter". I propose that if anything is to be cut away by and from these texts it is the bindings of Arnzen's earlier splatter film cycles. The importance of the **Evil Dead** cycle lies in its re-acquisition of film history and its active, even analytical, participation in that history. The cycle represents simultaneously the end of a phase in genre history – that of the "classic" stalker film – and the beginning of another – that of the return of the horror film to vaudeville. In other words, the function of slapstick/splatshtick in these films is not merely to displace narrative from its (assumed) position of dominance, but to override generic coding in many ways as well. After all, what do the filmmakers do with the larger budget of **Evil Dead 2**? They make the same film again, only *funnier*.[18] Within these films, familiar tropes of horror cinema are being reconfigured, much in the way Brophy argues in his important paper on *horrality*.[19] In this context, however, horror is not only reorganised as a mode and deployed self-referentially, it is deployed "in the service" of visual humour. The fact that fear itself, alongside gore and the special effects mechanisms of "death gags", becomes little more than a mischief device in this process is telling. The **Evil Dead** films are organised around a hyperbolised approach to all aspects of filmmaking and, thus, pose the question "What can be shown?" in a much broader and more fundamental sense than is the case in other splatter cycles. Hyperbole also characterises the structure of the gag in these films. Donald Crafton reminds us that one of the characteristic features of the sight gag is a manipulation of the rules of causality to allow a simple action to produce excessive reactions.[20] The **Evil Dead** films are full of examples of this "causal hyperbole", but they tend to follow the structure of the moment in **Evil Dead 2** when Ash finally manages to shoot and "kill" his disembodied hand. His joy is short-lived as, rather than a trickle of blood marking the demise of his current nemesis, he is deluged by a fountain of gore which pours out of the wall as if sprayed from a high pressure hose (which is, of course, quite probably what is really happening).

Unlike the slapstick of the mischief film, however, splatshtick does not simply cohere audience pleasure around specific anticipatory structures set up by the deployment of a mechanical mischief device. Mischief devices (and here we are generally talking about sharp implements of one kind or another) are used in these films in quite traditional gag structures, but the slapstick mechanisms particular to these films operate on the level of the *routine*. The films are structured as a series of set-piece performances that tend to set up, and offer resolutions to, a particular (and usually physical) problem through complex sequences of visual humour. In these routines audience pleasure rests not in the anticipation of the resolution of the individual gag, but in a general awareness of the

Army Of Darkness

imminence of individual instances in the continuing sequence of micro resolutions that form an ongoing "pay-off cycle". Examples of these routines would include the battle between Ash and his hand; the battle with his girlfriend's head ("you're going down") which precedes it; the problem of destroying the book in **Army Of Darkness** and various conflicts with mirror images throughout the cycle.

This is not to say that splatshtick routines just serve narrative. Visual humour replaces linear narrative in these sequences having first alerted us that it will do so through specific structuring devices. The routines are typically introduced either by "shakycam" sequences rushing through the woods and towards the cabin, announcing the approach of the demon entity or by sound effects indicating ruptures in diegetic "normality" linked to acts of demonic possession.[21] The "shakycam" sequences in particular (and the frantic pursuits they sometimes initiate) cannot be dismissed unproblematically as "chase" sequences to splatshtick's "pie"; they have become the signature moments of "Evil Deadness" in the cycle and thus operate distinctly as attractions.

Special effects sequences in contemporary cinema are typically prefigured by moments given over to the explicit, and simultaneous, introduction and retention of those very special effects – it's coming but not quite yet. In these moments, characters perform (display) the audience's assumed response to the upcoming effects attraction within the diegesis. This response is typically an awed or horrified reaction, depending in general upon whether the effect occurs in science fiction or horror narratives respectively, and is prefigured precisely in order to prepare the audience for the narrative rupture that the special effects will produce.[22] The "shakycam" sequences from the **Evil Dead** films perform a broadly similar function except that, because they are attractions in their own

right, and because they have come to represent and encapsulate the "project" of the whole cycle, they signify not just the imminent return of pleasure but also in a curious way the return of normality in these films. The splatshtick routines are so much what the films are "about" that their absence, and particularly their replacement with awkward dialogue scenes, signifies excess rather than the other way around. Indeed, so central are the routines to audience pleasure and understanding (this is why we are here) that it is possible to argue that the films offer pleasures that have more to do with the cyclical experience of vaudeville or a variety bill than they do with received notions of the unfolding experience of cinema.

The **Nightmare On Elm Street** cycle uses the routine in a slightly different way. These films expend more effort (money) in setting up character so that their comically engineered death sequences can be played out fully – in other words both "in" and "to" character. Unlike other splatter villains, Freddy needs to understand his victims to a somewhat greater extent in order both to find their dream weaknesses and to fully engage his sadism. The doomed characters *embody* the mischief devices of their own death gags which are then made concrete through Freddy's control of the dreamscape – hence the drug habit of Jennifer Rubin's character in **Dream Warriors** for example. In the **Nightmare** films, the set pieces are usually implied through character exposition early on and may even be "rehearsed", often several times, as Freddy's early attempts are sometimes thwarted. The knowing audience has the pleasure of waiting for the inevitable playing out of these gag lines. Jeffrey Sconce has explored the function of spectacle and self-reflexive narration in the **Nightmare** cycle in a recent paper published in the collection *Film Theory Goes To The Movies* and suggests that:

Fans of Freddie certainly do not attend these films expecting or hoping for a compelling narrative. There is no mystery as to what is going to happen in these films, nor is suspense really at issue. Romantic subplots among the doomed teens, frenetic last-minute rescues, and even Freddy's perfunctory "death" at the end of each film are just so much window dressing to surround the core attraction of these films – episodes of intense visual excitement. Conventional notions of narrative, such as they exist, function only to link the five or six ingeniously staged kill sequences, "set pieces" that became increasingly elaborate as the series progressed through the 1980's.[23]

In relation to the **Evil Dead** cycle however, it is not enough to say that spectacular sequences foreground self-reflexivity or, for that matter, visual humour. Technology and technique operate intrusively on the level on both "splat" and "shtick" – hyperbolising the horror-gag (splat) by taking on a *performance* function in relation to the routine (shtick). Camera plotting, editing strategies and soundtrack elements operate alternately in combination and opposition, not so much deprivileging or problematising the spectator's position as removing any possibility of secure purchase other than in the appreciation of the gag or routine. In this way a character looks one way while the camera consciously "looks" another, panning as if it were a point-of-view shot, through 360 degrees and finally gazing on the character once more as it finishes its scan. Sound effects shift from coherent diegetic positions and become personalities – gimmicks of the films' recurring demon antagonist which is itself somehow both omnipresent and distinctly located by "shakycam" point-of-view structures.

Performance, both of actors and technology, is also central to the operation of humour in these films. It functions variously as an estrangement device and as an aid to interpretation. In the first context, gags often involve the animation and/or reanimation of inanimate or supposedly dead objects as persecutory entities for Ash or the others to deal with. An example from **Evil Dead 2** occurs after the severed hand sequence when all the objects in the front room of the cabin begin to make fun of Ash – laughing maniacally and performing a peculiar, synchronised dance in which Ash is drawn to participate. In the second context, performance style works to naturalise excessive events. Bruce Campbell's acting style is put on prominent display during the major splatshtick sequences as a key for the audience in decoding the problem of gauging appropriate response – if we can't take *him* seriously then perhaps this really is a kind of comedy after all.

As a mediatory mechanism, then, performance also signifies a change in the function of the hero. Ash is well named, simultaneously the ghost of countless hero-functions from the past (melodramatic gesture); the residue of the human driven half mad by the horrific events that have overtaken him in the present (pastiched naturalism) and the tattered phoenix, presaging what is increasingly becoming the only possible refuge for the splatter hero of the future (clowning). He is simultaneously meta-hero and meta-victim, playing straight man to the maniac entities which surround him and wise-guy to the anodyne caricatures of humanity with whom he is lumbered and whose function is only to be, as we have known all along, what Joe Bob Briggs would call "spam in a cabin".[24] In taking on the functions of both an Abbott and a Costello (not to say a Larry, a Moe and a Curly) Ash becomes not so much a postmodern cypher for the end of

Army Of Darkness

history, he is – as is Freddy in his own way – an embodiment of actively intersecting histories. He is both a gag in himself and a reconfigured mischief device, a fetishised master of ceremonies and interpreter, for the **Evil Dead**'s vaudevillian cinema.

NOTES

1. With apologies to Donald Crafton.
2. Michael A. Arnzen, "Who's Laughing Now? The Postmodern Splatter Film", in *Journal Of Popular Film And Television* Vol.21 No.4 (Winter 1994).
3. Donald Crafton, "Pie And Chase: Gag, Spectacle And Narrative In Slapstick Comedy", in *Classical Hollywood Comedy* eds. Kristine Brunovska Karnick and Henry Jenkins, London: Routledge, 1995 p106–119.
4. Arnzen, p177.
5. Ibid. p177
6. Ibid. p178
7. Peter Kramer's detailed analysis of the subordination of visual humour to character and plot in Buster Keaton's films can be found in his paper "Derailing The Honeymoon Express: Comicality And Narrative Closure In Buster Keaton's **The Blacksmith**", in *Velvet Light Trap* No.23 (Spring 1989) p101–116.
8. Arnzen, p177.
9. A full account of the concept of film classicism can be found in David Bordwell, Janet Staiger and Kristin Thompson, *The Classical Hollywood Cinema: Film Style And Mode Of Production To 1960*, New York: Columbia University Press, 1985.
10. Tom Gunning, "The Cinema Of Attractions: Early Film, Its Spectator And The Avant Garde", in *Early Film: Space, Frame, Narrative*, ed. Thomas Elsaesser with Adam Barker, London: BFI, 1990

p56–62.

11. Neil Harris, *Humbug, The Art Of P.T. Barnum*, Chicago: University of Chicago Press, 1973; and Charles Musser, *High Class Moving Pictures: Lyman H. Howe And The Forgotten Era Of Travelling Exhibition, 1880–1920*, Princeton University Press, 1991.

12. Tom Gunning, "Crazy Machines In The Garden Of Forking Paths: Mischief Gags And The Origins Of American Film Comedy", in *Classical Hollywood Comedy* eds. Kristine Brunovska Karnick and Henry Jenkins, London: Routledge, 1995 p87–105.

13. Ibid. p90–91.

14. Crafton, p107.

15. The description is from Kristine Brunovska Karnick and Henry Jenkins, "Funny Stories", in *Classical Hollywood Comedy*, p82.

16. Outlined in Gunning, "The Cinema Of Attractions".

17. Arnzen, p180.

18. Incidentally, I am not claiming that the resultant change in genre expectation has yet been manifested in fundamental changes in the economic or institutional context of the genre, rather I am suggesting that there may now be evidence of slippage of meaning between horror and its marketing.

19. Philip Brophy, "Horrality – The Textuality Of Contemporary Horror Films" *Screen* Vol.27 No.1 (January–February 1986) p2–13.

20. Crafton, p110.

21. The term "shakycam" is used by Sam Raimi to refer to a mechanism that was improvised on set (involving the attachment of a camera to a plank of wood) and was used to perform a broadly similar function to a Steadycam or Panaglide but giving a rough, dynamic "feel" to the movements so facilitated.

22. A science fictional example occurs in **Jurassic Park** just before the visitors in their jeeps see the first dinosaur. This particular sequence operates in distinct stages, each stage introducing new characters to the upcoming attraction and reinforcing the denial of vision that the audience is experiencing. The play with audience frustration performs the double function of indicating the characters' awed response and ensuring that the audience is uncaringly complicit in the process of narrative interruption. Perhaps the ultimate example from recent horror cinema occurs just before the first transformation scene in **An American Werewolf In London**. On the day of the full moon, David, the survivor of an attack by a supposed werewolf, paces around the flat waiting for something to happen. This extended and overtly dull sequence (despite the ironic soundtrack) is played out far longer than the narrative can readily sustain and then, finally, when we are sure the transformation must take place the film cuts to a brief scene in the hospital. On returning to the space of the flat, the transformation is upon us almost immediately. The sequence is so knowing, so transparently obtuse in its excess that it signifies and prepares us for the equally hyperbolic transformation scene to come.

23. Jeffrey Sconce, "Spectacles Of Death: Identification, Reflexivity And Contemporary Horror" in *Film Theory Goes To The Movies*, eds. Jim Collins, Hilary Radner and Ava Preacher Collins, London: Routledge, 1993 p103–119.

24. Joe Bob Briggs, *Joe Bob Goes To The Drive-In*, London: Penguin 1987.

PSYCHO/THE BIRDS

Hitchcock Revisited

Mikita Brottman

When considered alongside the latest gut-spilling sequences and special effects of the modern horror film, do Hitchcock's classics pale in comparison, or is there still a place in the world of splatter for the master of suspense?

Lumière's current release of Lewis Gilbert's **Haunted** – an adaptation of James Herbert's contemporary reading of the classic haunted house saga – raises a number of interesting questions about the horror film. The audience reception of **Haunted** should let us know whether or not there is still a place, amidst the gore-hounds' favourite epics of blood-flow, gut-spillage and open wound sequences, for horror films which, whilst still packing the punches, are set in the more subtle realms of mystery, suspense and gentle disquietude. For a horror film to make an impact today, it seems that the director has to include at least one token visit to the land of the lowest common denominator – that of bodily taboo, just as a porn film is never "hard" enough unless it involves at least one "split beaver shot": a similarly satisfying glimpse into the secret recesses of the human body. The commercial success of Brian Yuzna and Stuart Gordon's **Re-Animator** and Romero's zombie epics gives testimony to this fact, whereas equally exciting films which do *not* include the requisite graphics – Norton's **Gargoyles**, for instance, or Hellman's **Beyond The Door** – disappear without trace.

Two films often revered as classics of the horror genre and models of suspense (which countless subsequent directors, most notably Brian de Palma in **Dressed To Kill** and **Body Double**, have set to emulate) are Hitchcock's **Psycho** (1960) and **The Birds** (1963). Neither of these are particularly graphic pictures. The celebrated "shower scene" in **Psycho** includes not one shot of the knife entering, or even touching, the body, and the most vivid sequence in **The Birds** is a static and momentary glimpse, albeit close-up, of a body whose eyes have been pecked out by the birds. Made before the arrival of high-tech SFX gurus to the mainstream cinema scene, and pretty tame in comparison with something like Tarantino's **Reservoir Dogs**, can Hitchcock still cut the mustard? And if so, just how sharp is his knife?

Ghouls and gore-hounds might disagree, but most cineastes would argue that Hitchcock is a better director than, say, Yuzna or Romero because of his ability to convey psychological suspense and trauma through characterisation, narrative impetus, suggestion, implication and empathy. Or else they would argue that the question incorporates a category mistake. Hitchcock may be the master of suspense, but Romero is the master of guts and gore. Two different crowns, two different kingdoms.

Or are they? In **Psycho**, Hitchcock explores the horrifying outcome of sexual repression. Victim of an Oedipal rage so tormenting and powerful that it topples him over the edge into a psychopathic complex of schizophrenia, transvestitism and mass murder, Norman Bates is an abject character caught between cultural boundaries: both man and woman, both mother and son, both victim and tormentor, both "normal" and totally insane. As anthropology has established, that which fails to fit into established cultural categories is always regarded by a people as abject and contaminating. The pathological

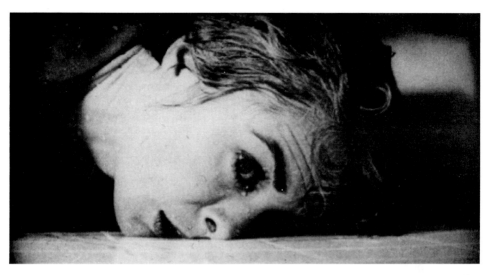

Psycho

dimensions of Norman's repression are symbolically embodied in the architectonics of his house, with its front façade, its secret attic symbolising Norman's unconscious, and – most terrifying of all – the fruit cellar, representing the dark nether regions of the human body, sexuality and repression.

The Birds is structured according to a similar governing principle. Something is "in the air" at Bodega Bay. The tension brought by Melanie into the Brenner household – between Mitch and his mother, between Mitch and Annie, between Cathy and Lydia – is symbolically manifested by the bird attacks, which always occur at moments of

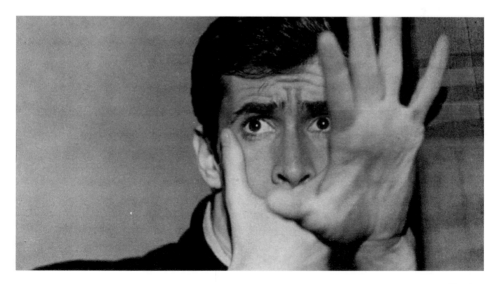

Psycho

The Birds

mounting familial tension in the narrative. Surplus repression reveals itself in the form of avian excess, and family traumas and conflicts manifest themselves in the form of inexplicable paranormal mayhem. The birds are out there alright, but they're also *in here*, in the head, pecking furiously at the temporary makeshift barricades we build to separate conscious thought from unconscious neurosis, to defend our unstable egos against the return of the repressed.

And this, if you think about it, is exactly what's going on in those gut-spilling, open wound sequences of a film by Yuzna or Romero. Why else would the sight of blood and guts provoke such horror when we can sit with perfect ease before an undercooked steak, a bowl of hot tripe or some nice chopped liver? The open wound sequence in the horror film is a vivid illustration of something out of place, out of context, neither inside the body nor outside, neither quite living nor yet dead, neither human nor animal, and therefore, according to our system of cultural classification, dirty, contaminating and horrific. But why horrific? Horrific because it is a symbolic representation of that which we, as human beings, fear the most: mental breakdown, neurotic collapse, or the process of becoming caught, like Norman Bates, in the liminal, terminal no-man's land between the conscious of logic and stability, and the unconscious of unreason, repression and neurosis.

Some film critics might want to argue that directors like Yuzna and Romero do exactly what Hitchcock does, but more graphically, more explicitly and more truthfully. In

Psycho

effect, it's the other way round. The vividness of the contemporary horror film might provide more of a shock and a shudder, but horror films like Hitchcock's are ultimately more frightening, more disruptive and more disturbing. By vivifying in the form of a crafted narrative the abject terror of the broken mind, Hitchcock does everything that Romero does, but more graphically, more explicitly, and with a greater and more horrifying truth.

THE OTHER FACE OF DEATH

Barbara Steele And La Maschera Del Demonio

Carol Jenks

It's not me they're seeing. They're casting some projection of themselves, some aspect that I somehow symbolise. It can't possibly be me.

(Barbara Steele, quoted in Warren 1991:68)

Angela Carter (1982:120) named the three surrealist love goddesses as being Louise Brooks first and foremost, followed by Dietrich and Barbara Steele. With regard to Steele, however, not all the following descriptions emanate from surrealists caught in the grip of *amour fou*:

The very symbol of Woman as vengeful, alien and "other".

(Nicholls 1984:52)

Her sculpted features and wildness of eye quickly typecast her as the dark goddess who can dole out pleasure and pain in equal measure.

(Hogan 1986:168)

All at the same time, a fairy with claws like the drawings of Charles Addams and the Vera of the Count of Villiers.

(Jean-Andre Fieschi, quoted in Beck 1978:296)

She glides about with the elegance and eroticism of a black patent-leather high heel.

(*Cinema*, quoted in Beck 1978:308)

Her image, more than any other, is the emblem and fetish of the [horror] genre.

(Hardy 1985:149)

It is the last statement that demands attention. How can such a claim be made for a woman who appeared in only eleven horror films between 1960 and 1968, nine of them Italian, which were released haphazardly outside Italy through exploitation companies in cut, dubbed versions and of which she herself remarked that they were "hardly worth creating a cult around" (quoted in Crawley 1983:42)? And beyond that, what can explain such ambiguous ecstasies, such a mixture of fear and desire as a response to an image?

The key term, of course, is fetish, since supposedly only a woman can constitute a fetish object, although in the context of the horror movie Roger Dadoun disputes this when he sees the male vampire figure, Count Dracula himself, as being the maternal phallus incarnate, the visible fetishistic substitute for the absent, non-visible archaic mother[1] (Dadoun 1989:41). The latter is a mythical being of crucial importance in trying to account for the textual workings of Steele's films, which constitute a distinct and specific subgroup of their own amidst the overall explosion of Italian horror in the first half of the 1960's.

At the time, they were the films on which attention focused, due to her star

Sie Donne Per L'Assassino

presence, but the later developments of horror in Italy evolved from quite other strands. The type of narrative where a nominal framework is provided by an investigation into a series of murders but in which any actual coherence or resolution is completely overwhelmed by the excessive violence of the murders themselves as spectacle could hardly be better summed up than by the stark title of Mario Bava's **Sie Donne Per L'Assassino (Blood And Black Lace**[2], 1964), which anticipated the work of Dario Argento. A complacent, non-gender-specific description of the film, "the murders are photographed to appear gorgeous and titillating, forcing the audience to feel an accomplice's share of the assassin's pleasure" (Lucas 1985:30), gives a clue to the drives fuelling the narrative and the answering emotions it expects to evoke in the (male) spectator.

The very different concerns of the films starring Steele suggest how hermetically sealed is the body of work dedicated to, and celebratory of, her image. The cultural fantasies embodied by the films, and the lure they hold, have perhaps ultimately more to do with the figure of the all-devouring *femme fatale* than with any crucial stage in the development of the horror genre. Their very cultishness, even by horror film standards, places them outside the mainstream, as does the purely practical problem of their extreme difficulty of access. This latter factor, of course, is often an important one in the very existence of a cult, but here it seems to have the added resonance of creating a particularly intense and ardent desire to see a mysterious and inaccessible being whose rare manifestations are thus extremely precious.

The question remains, however, why such an anachronistic figure was enabled to reappear in the form and in the country she did at the beginning of the decade of Cool, the 1960's, whose affectless heroines represented a notion of sexuality as liberation (however false), not as the promise of a sadomasochistic dance of death.

To discuss the provenance of the killer *femme fatale* (and the veiled figure of the archaic mother in the shadows behind her) is entirely outside the scope of this chapter. Her death throes as a European cultural icon took place with the advent of the First World War. Immediately prior to that, she had found the new medium of cinema a fitting place for a final incarnation. It was the Italian cinema's extravagances in the areas of fantasy and spectacle, using the words in their widest sense, that accounted for its early international predominance and influence. In the late 1950's, popular cinema harked back to its roots by reviving the various male and female figures who had inhabited historical epics and peplum fantasies, taking what had once been regarded as the art of the film and turning it into genre material.

However, as the only outright horror film of the Italian silent period was a version of the archetypal dyadic fantasy dependent on the expulsion of woman altogether, namely **Il Mostro Di Frankenstein (Frankenstein's Monster**, 1920), it is clear that this recreation of scenarios from the early national cinema cannot have led in some simple or direct fashion to the first wave of Italian horror.

A figure not normally considered even remotely in relation to horror and who dominated the terrain of early Italian films could provide the missing link – the diva. Francesca Bertini, Lydia Borelli and others were arguably the first women in world cinema to fulfil the role of star, and that to the utmost. Their grandiloquent, hieratic acting had to take the place of the missing voice, and the emotions it created, of the opera singers from whom they took their title.

The melodramas created to display them, actually called *divismo* films, were usually contemporary in setting and dress but dealt in archaic fantasies, formerly pinned on historical figures: "The woman as predator, as the dominating figure, the man in subjugation: this is a situation virtually unprecedented outside the Delilahs, Shebas and Cleopatras, outside tales of princes in thrall to courtesans" (Shipman 1985:17).

It is the invocation of Cleopatra that is particularly interesting here. Lucy Hughes-Hallett, in her study of Cleopatra through all her historical changes as a cultural icon, identifies what she calls the killer-Cleopatra as a romantic archetype of insatiate lust and cruelty, a phallic figure of "equivocal gender" in "splendid but transparent drag", a projection of male masochist drives, "or at least a part of the male psyche" (Hughes-Hallett 1990:229), who bears no relation whatever to any real woman. The very last manifestation of the killer-Cleopatra, as Hughes-Hallett notes, was in the person of Theda Bara in 1917.

Bara had been consciously created as the American cinema's answer to and incorporation of the Italian diva and she was remembered as the woman who put the vamp in vampire when the divas had become the concern solely of professional film historians. Remembered to the extent that in 1964, *Cinema* magazine could evoke her in relation to Steele, whom it described as going "on her own high-heeled, porcelain-skinned, vamp-eyed way to stardom as a modern Theda Bara" (quoted in Beck 1978:308). The idea of anybody in 1964 being a modern Theda Bara on screens ruled by Monica Vitti and Julie Christie bespeaks the depth of cultural dislocation and anachronism involved, a revival of fantasies grounded historically elsewhere, re-emerging from out of the past.

The key figure in the return from the repressed of Italian neo-realism of various mythic/historical female figures was Riccardo Freda, whose career as a director began in 1942 and who had kept up the tradition of melodramatic spectacle. In 1953 he had cast his wife, Gianna-Maria Canale, as the Empress Theodora and he revived the archetypal victim, Beatrice Cenci, in 1956, the same year he made **I Vampiri (The Vampires**[3]), a film

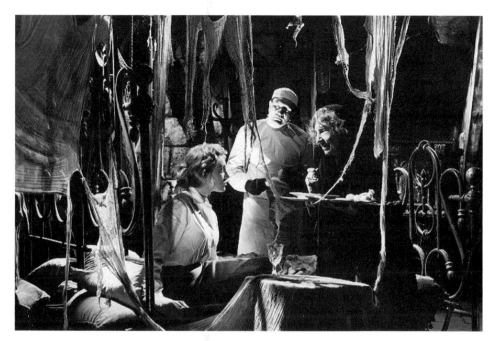

I Vampiri

so entirely isolated generically, with no national tradition to back it up and predating the Anglo-American horror revival, that it can only be accounted for as a final step from melodrama into overt Gothic, for the purpose of enabling a new female figure to be added to the cinematic repertoire.

Freda once declared, "I am not in the least interested in banal humanity, everyday humanity" (quoted in Lephrohon 1972:179), and it is possible that he wanted to extend the imaginative field of operations of the literally imperious woman, by turns either actively suffering and imperilled or personifying what has been designated as "the promise of cinema – the beautiful, cruel woman" (White 1987:80). This hypothesis is supported by the fact that **I Vampiri** was inspired by the female standby of horror film makers, the Bloody Countess, Elizabeth Bathory, and that having cast her as his Theodora, Freda again used Canale in the lead role. Also, the plot, concerning an older woman whose lover brings her young women whom she can drain in order to rejuvenate herself, clearly foreshadows the fascination with a symbolic "monstrous" mother figure. When rejuvenated she passes herself off in society as her own niece, an enactment of the fantasies of incorporation and loss of identity that are particularly supposed to haunt dyadic relations between women.

It was the film's very isolation, however, that ensured its utter failure both in Italy and on the export market, and it appeared at the time to be an experiment that would lead nowhere. It was the immense success of the Hammer **Dracula** (1958) in Italy that changed the reception climate. When Mario Bava was offered the chance to direct a film of his own choosing as a reward for taking over, uncredited, from Jacques Tourneur on **La Battaglia Di Maratona (The Giant Of Marathon,**[4] 1959), his request to be allowed

La Maschera Del Demonio

to base a scenario on Gogol's *Viy* was granted by the producers, Galatea Film, something very unlikely to have happened pre-**Dracula**. He used the popularity of the British film to argue that Italian audiences were now ready to accept a "new wave" of horror.

When the finished product, **La Maschera Del Demonio (The Mask Of The Devil**,[5] 1960), was discovered by international critics, who turned it into a cult movie, they praised it for its ability to create atmosphere, "brilliant intuitions of the spectral" (*Time*, quoted in McGee 1984:139), through visually poetic black and white photography, thus linking it to the classical tradition of the horror genre. But they also commented on its power to shock by the introduction of a new element, overt images of sadism and bodily corruption, which almost overwhelmed narrative drive and coherence. The success of the film ensured that Bava became the only Italian director of the period to work almost exclusively in the horror genre for the rest of his career, apart from the occasional excursion into spoof spaghetti westerns or the exploits of Viking marauders. The allegations, which became habitual, that he sacrificed narrative to image were conventional in the case of someone who had had a long and distinguished career as a cameraman prior to his directorial debut.

In **Maschera** the images which arrest his fluidly mobile camera in contemplation are of the face and body of his star, Steele, formerly a small-part actress in British films whose services he had gone to great lengths to acquire and who was transformed into something undreamt of by the J. Arthur Rank Charm School, whose last contract starlet she had been. She came into the studio system immediately prior to its disintegration and as the available 1950's range of female types was going into bankruptcy, but the accident of her looks would have debarred her from the coming "realism".

La Maschera Del Demonio

Raymond Durgnat, lamenting that British directors failed to explore the possibilities of certain actors who didn't "fit", credits Bava, conventional auteurist-style, with having recreated Steele Pygmalion-like. Her British films, he claimed, revealed only "a weakly pretty face", not the "spiky, whiplash strength" unleashed by **Maschera**, which rendered her "mesmeric" (Durgnat 1970:184). The tell-tale imagery here gives away the nature of the projection involved: the male critic praising the male auteur for having brought an image into being that is determined by their own need to see it and from which the actual woman is entirely absent. Her weakly pretty face – as the face is traditionally the mirror of the soul, the words cunningly suggest a trivial or vacuous personality – becomes a mere *tabula rasa* to be sculpted by the intense play of light and shade.

It follows logically that in her career in Italian horror, Steele was removed from the arena of language, literally reduced to silence by the process of redubbing. She disliked the absence of psychological realism in horror movies, the fact that there were no characters, only situations, and that they were directors', not actors', films. As a compensation, she brought a mimetic style of acting into play, diva-like, becoming a figure in a landscape, an essence, a mimed emotion. Two extraordinary examples are the scenes in Antonio Margheriti's **I Lunghi Capelli Della Morte (The Long Hair Of Death**, 1964), in which she lets her mother's ashes run through her hand, while her knee-length hair and the long velvet sleeves of her dress are whipped up by the wind, and her protracted death scene in Massimo Pupillo's **Cinque Tombe Per Un Medium (Terror Creatures From The Grave**,[6] 1966), a series of jerky, flailing gestures across the length and breadth of a room, as angular and contorted in relation to the actual lines of the

I Lunghi Capelli Della Morte

body as anything to be found in Expressionist acting.

This concentration on the body of the woman raises further questions: the same writer who found Steele to be "the emblem and fetish of the horror genre", also thought that her face "is probably how Norman Bates remembers his mother in **Psycho**" (Hardy 1985:149). Leaving aside the absurdity of the writing, this is a very overt invocation of the primal mother, archaic, phallic, all-consuming. Instead of Dadoun's male fetish-figure, who stands in for this hidden being, **Maschera** attempts to realise the implications of actually making her present and visible.

The film's textual sadism is marked out from the beginning by an extreme violence towards the audience, an aggressive desire to wound the very site of vision, the eye. The unspoken agreement of the cinematic contract is broken: the spiked mask of Satan is carried forward into the camera to pierce the gaze of the spectator. There are then two further shots of the mask, but these are marked as being from the witch Asa's point-of-view and punctuated by a reverse close-up of her huge-eyed terror.

Asa is thus presented as the owner of a violated gaze, one which she shares with the spectator. This immediately introduces issues of gender and identification, because it is a profoundly held tenet of film distributors that the spectator of a horror movie will almost inevitably be male, no matter what empirical evidence can be brought to refute this. It is unquestionably true that many women do avoid horror films, and not only on the grounds of aversion to their overt violence. They are a disreputable, marginal cultural form, second only in that respect to pornography, which in certain manifestations – the work of the French Jean Rollin and the Spanish Jess Franco – they actually fuse with. Horror has been perceived as functioning for men as melodrama does for women, that is as a cathartic working through of the impossible contradictions between desire and the social dictates appropriate to gender.

If, then, a film whose own hypothetical constructed spectators are male, places a woman about to have her eyes put out as the figure to whom they are sutured in the text, there is an obvious point of crisis, an almost literal ravishment. The conventional interpretation would be that it is raising the spectre of castration, which would easily fit a view of horror as concerned with specifically male anxieties.

Another way of looking might reveal a fantasy not necessarily predicated upon the axis of castration, because predating the Oedipal scenario and its ensuing positions – a refusion with the primal mother, a merging of identity with her, thus a "becoming feminine". However, the resultant loss of gendered subjectivity, the dissolving of the self's boundaries in the return to an imaginary undifferentiated state, albeit one of plentitude, inextricably threads desire with fear.

This means that the figure who embodies the prospect of refusion will be represented negatively, as a threat, as the other face of death. What is so unexpectedly fascinating about the narrative proper of **Maschera**, which starts after the prologue, is that it seemingly leaves direct anxieties about male subjectivity by the wayside, deflecting the threat towards another female figure, Katia. Katia is the descendant and double of Asa, who desires literally to "fuse" with Katia in order to "regain her life completely", as the priest, who wishes to prevent such a thing ever happening, expresses it.

A title tells us that we are now two centuries on, fixing Asa all the more as that being who is always in the past, mother. The image-trace of her prehistoric existence is her portrait, which affects Katia strangely. "There's something alive about it, something different about the eyes, the hands, as if it were hiding something. Sometimes I'm afraid to go near it." The prince, her father, is obsessed by the history of an earlier descendant of Asa's, the princess Masha, who died as she reached the age of maturity, 21, and who was "the very image" of Asa. He believes Asa will try to take Katia in turn, who is also just 21 and "her living image".

What is being presented here is a version of the construction of female subjectivity as something demonic. Whereas the male subject is constituted precisely by leaving mother behind, the female must "become" her own mother through the process of identification, in order to attain access to subjectivity, albeit precisely, a subjectivity characterised according to orthodoxy as perpetually incomplete and in the grip of regression. Mary Ann Doane has gone so far as to claim that the loss of subjectivity in the paranoid state, the place where meaning collapses, "characterised by the foreclosure of the paternal signifier" (Doane 1988:144), while identified as "perversion" in the male, and a residue of unresolved feminine identification, is therefore in essence the very condition of the female, who can only endlessly erase herself.

To confine consideration of the problematic nature of such a claim to the text of **Maschera**, why does this version of mother-daughter relations cause such fear in the male that it has to be represented as something monstrous? And how might an actual female spectator respond to the spectacle of such a dyadic relation, particularly when it is placed in the context of witchcraft? If, as has been claimed, the climactic encounter in the classic horror text is always between the heroine and the monster, patriarchy's two freaks mirroring one another (Williams 1984:87), then what can such a confrontation mean when the figure designated as the monstrous is the heroine's double, her other self, her-self?

Hélène Cixous provides a witty answer to the last question by asking rhetorically, "who, surprised and horrified by the fantastic tumult of her drives (for she was made to believe that a well-adjusted woman has a... divine composure), hasn't accused herself of being a monster?" (Cixous 1981:246)

The political/erotic celebration of witches and witchcraft by certain women writers, Cixous among them, in terms of the potentially explosive consequences that the return of patriarchy's ultimate repressed outlaw could have, points a way to read Asa and what she represents differently, to read from what Teresa de Laurentis calls "an elsewhere of vision" (de Laurentis 1984:83).

For Asa is literally an explosive force: in the self-propelled blowing open of her tomb she gives birth to herself. She is also a deflecting force, reducing reason and scientific knowledge to ineffectuality. The symbolic father-son pair of doctors, an all-male substitution for the more usual heterosexual couple, never reach their destination. The staple of the horror movie, the broken axle-wheel/projector that halts one narrative and begins another, initiates a complete turning away for them.

They leave the road that keeps them in the world of men and are drawn towards the being whom the prehistoric narrative of the prologue supposedly repressed for ever, as they are lured into the space of the feminine, the internal labyrinth of the castle, in which all hidden passageways lead ultimately to only one destination, Asa's tomb. The castle is the House of Incest that Raymond Durgnat perceived as the key locale of Italian horror, the decaying Gothic halls in which a return to archaic states preceding the Oedipal can be acted out (Durgnat 1968:28).

One of the chief attributes of witches, the power to "call", is linked to the even greater power of the primal, parthenogenic mother, when Asa summons her dead lover back to life, "Rise, Javutich. Javutich, Rise!" The answering scene, in which he fights his way out of the erupting earth, his hands appearing covered with a web of mucus, is an obvious mimesis of birth. The fact that he is thus symbolically placed as her son as well as her lover, and exists only to serve her and carry out all her wishes, ensures that he does not fulfil the safeguard role common to witch and female vampire films, the male control from whom the supposed protagonist actually receives her desires and the permission to enact them. (This is entirely consistent with the general disempowering of the male figures in the film, with the exception of the priest, the one untainted by desire.)

It is this dual son/lover position that represents and exposes even more within the film the threat of incest and its alliance with death for the male. When he speaks rapturously to Asa of how they will live again, there is an immediate cut to a close-up of Dr Kruvajan, who, having "known" Asa, has now become, as she proclaimed he would, "dead to man". As incest is entirely constructed by the film as desire for the maternal, the text has to go to the most extraordinary lengths to disavow the symbolically very obvious threat to Katia from her risen father. When she addresses him by that name, he responds, "I am no longer your father. The spirits of evil have rent that tie between us for ever". This seems so manipulatively unconvincing that only the narrative as a whole can explain it; his attack on her is prevented and she is immediately abducted to the tomb where Asa is awaiting her. What Katia has to be saved from is being transfixed for ever as a daughter of the mother, not the father.

What is striking about **Maschera** is how completely it inhabits the realm of the uncanny. The text deploys virtually all the signifiers that Freud identifies as hallmarks of that ambiguous area, at once linguistically "homely" and "unhomely". The threat of violence to the eye is central to the text, as is its converse, Asa's burning, penetrating gaze, the stare that petrifies. Uncertainty as to whether a body is animate or inanimate is exemplified both by Asa's half-revived state and by the question of whether her portrait is "alive" and has altered or not. Moreover, the entire narrative is predicated on the phenomenon of the double, in the form of Asa/Katia's dual being.

The eeriness of the uncanny has to do with that which "ought to have remained secret and hidden but has come to light" (Freud 1985:345). Its apogee is the return of the sexualised body of the mother from repression, in the spectre of the female genitals, the point of entry to where the subject was before, the womb, the first home. Even outside the regime of neurosis, the gaping genitals are therefore always seen as uncanny to some extent, always taboo, the signifier of danger of castration and death.

But why should this need exist to render the revealed mother as the other face of death? The petrifying gaze in the list of uncanny attributes recalls something else that Freud mused over – Medusa's head, which men cannot look upon and live. Yet he turns to stone, becomes "stiff" (Freud 1964:273). What threatens castration and death also arouses. Of this, Cixous mocks, "Men say that there are two unrepresentable things: death and the feminine sex. That's because they need femininity to be associated with death: it's the jitters that give them a hard-on!" (Cixous 1981:255).

There is no doubt that Steele was constructed as a Medusa by her devotees: the favoured French adjective for her hair was *vivante*, evoking the snakes. The American

I Lunghi Capelli Della Morte

poster for **Maschera** consisted of her face, from which her hair undulates out in non-naturalistic "serpentine" ripples, and the publicity slogan first invites the audience to "Stare into these eyes", and then promises that the film will *"paralyse you with fright!"* (my emphasis). The extreme close-ups of the landscape of her face, the slant of her cheekbones, her eyes, sometimes looking into the camera, her parted mouth and teeth in **Maschera**, turn it into an abstraction. The camera seems to go in so close because it wants to become an X-ray, to reach the skull beneath the skin. In later films her long thick hair was increasingly styled so that it fell over her cheekbones and cut out, as it were, the shape of a living skull from the planes of her face. In the two films she made for Antonio Margheriti, **I Lunghi Capelli Della Morte** and **La Danza Macabra (Castle Of Blood,**[7] 1964), she plays a woman who is dead. This is revealed to the male protagonist after he has had sexual relations with her. In **Lunghi Capelli** the man is trapped between her materialised image as a ghost which is flawlessly beautiful, dressed in white brocade and her hair threaded with pearls, and her actual mouldering, worm-ridden corpse in its tomb.

It is very clear in such scenarios that if the desire for refusion with the primal mother is a nostalgic longing for "home" in the uncanny sense, a place the (male) subject has by definition irretrievably left behind, then it can only be represented as a drive journeying forward to the sole other undifferentiated state – death. (The central paradox of the vampire myth depends on this – to have conquered death, the ultimate affront to subjectivity, to have re-entered a state of pure, absolute desire, signified by primal orality, one must actually be dead.) The only adequate explanation for the necrophiliac responses to Steele's image, and the construction of that image itself as it developed, is contained

La Danza Macabra

in this syndrome. The following rhapsody could hardly be clearer: "Beneath the flowing robe of this young woman with so beautiful a countenance there appear, distinctly, the tatters of a skeleton. Is she any the less desirable?" (Jean-Paul Torok quoted in Durgnat 1967:148). (That such a profoundly masochistic response is summoned up by an image embedded in horror texts is suggestive, for the entire body of such texts is always an invitation to masochistic conversion: from the spectacle of the unpleasing, the frightening, comes pleasure. The taboo nature of the desires involved in this form of spectatorship makes it a limit case and may be a partial explanation of the marginalisation of the genre.)

However, suppose the female viewer left the main road of male Oedipal subjectivity and found wandering off into the labyrinthine byways of female desire more interesting? What would she discover about the desire of the woman, who, according to Mary Ann Doane, is permanently endangered by the regressive pull of the maternal and whose subjectivity is literally in the dark? Asa's great triumphant speech over the unconscious Katia is certainly intended as the climactic point of the "monstrous" in the text, as it gives expression to this pull:

> "You did not know that you were born for this moment... But you sensed it, didn't you? That's why my portrait was a constant temptation to you. You felt that your life and your body were mine. You felt like me because you were destined to *become* me. The love that young man had for you could have saved you, do you know that? You might have been happy together, but *I* was stronger."

Regression, narcissism and lesbianism all merge together here. The priest's description of how Asa's resurrection can only come about through "possessing and entering the body of another young woman" does not leave the sexuality in doubt and **Maschera** is listed by Bonnie Zimmerman, along with **I Vampiri** and **La Danza Macabra**, as an early example of the lesbian vampire movie in her article on the subject (Zimmerman 1981:23). From this threat Katia is saved only by the father's mark, the cross, which will protect and reclaim her and prevent her from being arrested for ever as a victim of maternal incorporation, the fate she must be rescued from and wrenched instead into heterosexual subjectivity. Katia felt herself forbidden to respond to Andrei's very obvious feelings by "a sense of terror, a presentiment of death, of being destroyed by something that's inside me".

Yet this demonic maternal figure, however constructed by male cultural fantasies as the monstrous, something vengeful and rapacious, still signifies the disruptive possibilities of autonomous female desire and a desire between women. Even Katia felt it: Asa's portrait was after all a "temptation". And, more specifically, she signifies the desire of the mother herself in all her original power and completeness. When Asa and Katia do finally fuse, enabling Asa, however temporarily, to regain her life completely, a transformation takes place. Asa's "marks" heal, close up, her face no longer bears visible wounds but becomes whole. The insignia of castration have vanished away.

For the mask that pierced and wounded her was literally put on by men, the figures of the Inquisition. At one point in the text their mask functions as an actual fetish; found in the graveyard, it becomes the part that stands in for the whole, but the whole is the body of Javutich, who tore it off, but whose wounds never heal. However unwittingly, this betrays that castration is a term circulated entirely between men, that "woman" is absolutely outside its regime but forcibly marked by it through patriarchal institutions as a defence against the knowledge that in her original plentitude she constitutes both a lost paradise and a threat to the myth that it is the male who is the "whole" subject, a myth shored up precisely by fetishism and the construction of sexual difference after the inevitable entry into the Oedipal order, with all the losses that gendered subjectivity entails.

For the horrible – the truly horrible – fact of sexual difference is the repressed knowledge that the mother is the uncastrated, not the site of lack but of too much body. The primal mother, for women, need not at all be the shadow that threatens annihilation but Cixous's mother, "who makes everything alright, who nourishes, and who stands up against separation; a force that will not be cut off but will knock the wind out of the codes" (Cixous 1981:252). And as for castration: "Let others toy with it. What's a desire originating from a lack? A pretty meagre desire" (ibid.:262).

Asa had so much desire, so much body, that the Inquisition ordered its complete disintegration, that it should be consumed to ashes. When this finally takes place, she consumes the text along with her, bringing it to an end as the screen becomes a wall of flame – this body, which should have remained hidden but insisted on becoming visible, is, in more than one sense, burning up.

NOTES

1. The archaic mother is a transposition of the pre-Oedipal mother to the status of a mythic, archetypal force, but an ambivalent force with the power to consume as well as to nourish. The dyadic relation of the pre-Oedipal, where subject boundaries have not yet been established and are instead literally characterised by fluidity and absorption, in the form of primal orality, is crucial to the

vampire myth. For a brilliant discussion of the deployment of these fantasies in horror fiction see Hodges and Doane (1991).

2. Literally, "Six women for the killer".

3. Also known as **The Devil's Commandment** (US), **Lust Of The Vampire** (GB).

4. Literally, "The battle of Marathon".

5. Also known as **Black Sunday** (US), **Revenge Of The Vampire** (GB).

6. Literally, "Five graves for a medium".

7. Literally, "Dance macabre".

BIBLIOGRAPHY

Beck, Calvin Thomas (1978) *Scream Queens: Heroines Of The Horrors*; New York: Collier Books.

Carter, Angela (1982) *Nothing Sacred: Selected Writings*; London: Virago.

Cixous, Helene (1981) "The Laugh Of The Medusa", in Elaine Marks and Isabelle de Courtivron (eds) (1981) *New French Feminisms*; Massachusetts: Harvester.

Crawley, Tony (1983) "Interview With Barbara Steele", in *Halls Of Horror* 3(2):40–4.

Dadoun, Roger (1989) "Fetishism In The Horror Film" in James Donald (ed.) *Fantasy And The Cinema*, London: BFI.

de Laurentis, Teresa (1984) *Alice Doesn't: Feminism, Semiotics, Cinema*; London: Macmillan.

Doane, Mary Ann (1988) *The Desire To Desire: The Woman's Film Of The 1940s*; London: Macmillan.

Durgnat, Raymond (1967) *Films And Feelings*; London: Faber & Faber; (1968) "The Long Hair Of Death", in *Films And Filming* 14(7):28; (1970) *A Mirror For England*; London: Faber & Faber.

Freud, Sigmund (1964) "Medusa's Head", *Complete Psychological Works*, vol. XVIII; London: Hogarth Press; (1985) "The Uncanny", in Albert Dickson (ed.) *The Pelican Freud Library*, vol.14; Harmondsworth: Penguin.

Hardy, Phil (ed.) (1985) *The Aurum Film Encyclopedia*, Vol.3, "Horror"; London: Aurum Press.

Hodges, Devon and Doane, Janice L. (1991) "Undoing Feminism In Anne Rice's *Vampire Chronicles*", in James Naremore and Patrick Branlinger (eds), Bloomington: Indiana University Press.

Hogan, Davis J. (1986) *Dark Romance: Sex And Death In The Horror Film*; Jefferson, NC: McFarland & Co.

Hughes-Hallett; Lucy (1990) *Cleopatra; Histories, Dreams And Distortions*; London: Bloomsbury.

Lephrohon, Pierre (1972) *The Italian Cinema*; London: Secker & Warburg.

Lucas, Tim (1985) "Bava's Terrors", in *Fangoria* 43:30–4, 64.

McGee, Mark Thomas (1984) *Fast And Furious; The Story Of American International Pictures*, Jefferson NC: McFarland & Co.

Nicholls, Peter (1984) *Fantastic Cinema; An Illustrated Survey*; London: Ebury Press.

Shipman, David (1985) *Caught In The Act; Sex And Eroticism In The movies*; London: Elm Tree Books/Hamish Hamilton Ltd.

Warren, Bill (1991) "Princess Of Darkness", *Fangoria*, 102:15–19, 68.

White, Patricia (1987) "Madame X Of The China Seas", *Screen* 28(4):80–95.

Williams, Linda (1984) "When The Woman Looks", in Mary Ann Doane, Patricia Mellencamp and Linda Williams (eds) (1984), *Re-vision*; Los Angeles: American Film Institute.

Zimmerman, Bonnie (1981) "Daughters Of Darkness: Lesbian Vampires", *Jump Cut*, 24/25:23–4.

FROM "TRICK" TO "PRICK"

Porn's Primitive Pleasures

Xavier Mendik

"The rule seems to be this: narratives that are already rudimentary become truly primitive during their hardcore sequences."
Linda Williams, *Hardcore: Power, Pleasure And The Frenzy Of The Visible*

"An aspect of early cinema which... is emblematic of this different relationship the cinema of attractions constructs with its spectator: the recurring look at the camera by the actors... From comedians smirking at the camera, to the constant bowing and gesturing of the conjurers in magic films, this is a cinema that displays its visibility, willing to rupture a self-enclosed fictional world for a chance to solicit the attention of the spectator."
Tom Gunning, *The Cinema Of Attractions: Early Film, Its Spectator And The Avant-Garde*

FROM NARRATIVE DRIVE TO VISUAL SPECTACLE

To suggest a similarity between hardcore pornography and early silent film may appear an odd comparison to make. Yet the nature of this article seeks to link the two in order to begin to question assumptions about the nature of such representations as tools of patriarchal oppression.

While not wishing to deny the essentially exploitative and misogynistic nature of many pornographic images, Linda Williams' account of films such as **Deep Throat** and the Marilyn Chambers vehicle **Behind The Green Door**, has pointed to the way that such texts concentrate on the expression of women's desires, thus creating a "female" space that is lacking in most mainstream films.

One of the important ways in which hardcore differs from mainstream "legitimate" productions is in the way it addresses its audience. The way films such as **Deep Throat** transgress continuity rules and established stylistic conventions in order to reveal scenes of genital activity to its viewer link it to the era of silent film that Tom Gunning defines as "The Cinema of Attractions". This is the period from the beginning of film until 1908 when Gunning argues that cinema was governed by an "exhibitionist" drive, evidenced by the constant need to produce spectacles or "thrills" to please an audience.

Importantly, in these "primitive" stages of cinema, the desire to create visual thrills and spectacle took precedence over the creation of narrative realism, characterisation or plot, which Gunning argues only develops after 1908 when cinema begins to develop rules of narrative, continuity and style. In this primitive period of film viewing, the narrative of any film was itself of secondary importance as images were consumed in Vaudeville, theatrical or fairground settings where cinema received the same billing as "attractions" such as circus acts and comic performers.

Thus the first films ever made often centred on acts that were derived from popular theatre: "exotic" dancers, magic tricks, strong man acts and animal "marvels". It is in this environment I wish to argue that pornography flourished as a cinema of exhibition rather than exposition, a cinema concerned with showing rather than telling.

Marilyn Chambers

Both Williams and Gunning date the first pornographic or "stag" films to this silent period, with titles such as **Wonders Of The Unseen World** (1927), claiming to show the normally concealed regions of the body for "educational" purposes. This pretence of instruction which is also seen in the use of medical machinery such as X-ray equipment to produce images of the bodies interior before audiences is also arguably complimented by another of the forerunners of Pornography: the travelogue.

Under the guise of an educational context, companies such as the Lumières' exposed audiences to "exotic" views of regions of the non-western world, thrilling them with the camera's ability to travel and capture images from other parts of the world. Although the overt aim of such attractions was, as Gunning notes, to place "the world within one's reach", their exposition of Eastern and African rites allowed the viewer visual access to parts of the female body normally concealed in Industrialised society.

Arguably the pseudo educational context feeds through to cycles specifically associated with exploitation and sexuality, particularly the Italian Mondo tradition as well as the **Black Emanuelle** films of Joe D'Amato. For instance, a film such as **New Black Emanuelle Goes East** (1976) exhibits a similar disregard of narrative drive, as Emanuelle's investigations of the Bangkok elite are fragmented, not only by the sex scenes, but by the constant "travelogue" sequences whose only function is to reveal to the viewer the actuality of the Eastern locations.

A similar example of this cycle's basis in primitive narration comes from Bruno Mattei's **Mondo Erotico** (1976), which, narrated by Laura Gemser, is a travelogue which reveals the "swinging" sex locations of the world. In one segment the camera investigates the "exotic" dance of a coloured dancer named Lollipop, who ends her act by seducing members of the audience. However, as she begins to undress a female spectator, the film pans away to an unidentified muscleman, who adopting a classic pose of virility before the camera resembles a popular Vaudeville or circus act rather than extra from a sex film![1]

The importance of Gunning's analysis of early silent film lies in the distinctions it makes between the cinema of attractions, and the later dominant traditions of commercial film making such as that of Hollywood. Particularly with the introduction of film sound, continuity and style techniques cinema shifts from being spectacle, to being goal directed and more importantly, being directed from the perspective of a characteristically male protagonist.

Laura Mulvey argued that Hollywood cinema was governed by a "male gaze" which constantly seeks to investigate and scrutinise the female body for the purposes of patriarchal pleasure. This voyeurism is secured through stylistic devices such as shot framing, which confirm the male protagonist's importance to a narrative by giving him power over devices such as point of view cinema, whilst reducing the importance of female characters to the object of male vision.

Mulvey's thesis (presented in the important article "Visual Pleasure And Narrative Cinema") was crucial in establishing a feminist agenda around the ideology of certain gender images. Its influence informed much of the work around pornography, which has historically been seen as the domain of a male gaze exercised against the female form. Yet what this application overlooks, is that in reducing all imagery to a series of "attractions" pornography speaks less of its ability to show its images from a privileged male perspective, and more of its necessity to reduce the body (both male and female) to a site of visual spectacle.

Although a production such as Gerry Damiano's **Deep Throat** is organised to

Deep Throat

allow the viewer visual access to scenes of oral sex and ejaculation, as Williams notes it renders both the male and female bodies as a site of visual display, and in so doing actually begins to question the potency of male desire in such depictions.

The narrative, (which deals with Linda Lovelace's discovery that her clitoris is located in her throat) displays the relation between "education" and titillation that defined examples of primitive film such as the travelogue. Hence a pre-credit intertitle which figures the ensuing action as the medical "record" of how the Doctor helped a female patient fixated at a primary phase of sexual development overcome her neurosis. Despite these references, **Deep Throat**'s recodification of the body as a site of spectacle is confirmed by a number of scenes where Linda and her flatmate Helen attempt to cure Lovelace's inability to experience "earth-shattering" orgasms by pairing themselves with groups of different men.

In one "orgy" encounter, Damiano juxtaposes Linda's enactment of fellatio with Helen's sexual coupling with two muscular men. Although the sequence is lengthy in time, it allows the viewer visual access to both the male and female genitals, and ends abruptly after Helen's partners climax, and admit they no longer have the energy to comply with her continual sexual requests. At the entry of a neighbour who, clearly coded as gay, beckons the male guests away from the party, Helen replies to his entry: "some days nothing seems to go right," casting a disconcerting reflection on the performance of the male characters in the encounter. Indeed, the statement seems confirmed in

Helen's conversation with Linda after the orgy when the latter confesses that the encounter failed to produce the orgasm she has hoped for.

Although Linda's later liaison with Doctor Young produces the "responses" desired when he reveals the misplaced site of her sexual organs, it does little to recuperate any notion of masculine control in the film. In one later comic encounter, the Doctor played by Harry Reems, is himself rendered hospitalised with a bandaged penis after Linda has repeatedly forced her attentions on him. This ability to actually question masculine potency through the reduction of the male body to a site of spectacle is not limited to Damiano's film but informs many porn narratives. The films of Russ Meyer for example, are marked by male characters (such as Lemar Shed from **Beneath The Valley Of The Ultra Vixens**) being unable to adopt a virile stance in relation to the desiring women who populate these narratives.

FROM SILENT FILM TO SILENT "THRILL"

If as Laura Mulvey argued, the voyeuristic power of the male gaze is demonstrated by the male protagonist's control over stylistic features such as point of view camera, a film such as **Deep Throat** demonstrates its placement in an earlier tradition of silent cinema.[2] As with the cinema of attractions defined by Gunning, the film reduces all levels of plot, characterisation and use of features such as point of view camera to a minimum. Indeed, it is possible to argue that **Deep Throat** contains only two types of camera operation: the panning camera that accompanies Linda's travels and musings in exterior locations, and the static frontal placement that accompanies the scenes of sexual activity.

This static depiction of the human body demonstrates once more with the type of staging that accompanied turn of the century silent cinema, as well as the organisation of this type of event beyond the control of any of the characters depicted. If the cinema that Mulvey defines as an ideological enemy is dependant on features such as characterisation, point of view vision and spectator identification then directors such as Russ Meyer and films such as **Deep Throat** reduce the optimum clarity given to the identity of the actor and replace it with a concentration on often unidentifiable "body bits".

For example during the orgy scene in **Deep Throat**, Damiano shoots the sequence via a series of statically framed close-ups of male and female sexual organs in close proximity with each other. As a result, it often becomes difficult for the viewer to identify *whose* body is being depicted. For instance, although Linda and Helen's sexual liaisons take place in different locations in their apartment, he cuts between the two characters when their bodies are framed in similar gestures, only later including re-establishing shots which identify the actresses by including their facial features.[3]

This concentration on body bits as a site of spectacle can be traced from the silent stag film through to 1970's porno shorts as distributed by Tabu, Swedish Erotica and *Colour Climax* as well as to compilation films such as the recent **Splashing**, which features a series of the most inventive ejaculation shots from 1970's and 1980's shorts. In its attempts to thrill and titillate the film exhibits several of the features of "primitive" film. The concentration on body bits is almost paradoxically played on, as although the cast list claims the film to contain sequences featuring the most prominent of pornographic performers, the scenes actually rarely reveal the identity of the performers, concentrating instead on statically framed close-ups of penises ejaculating over different parts of the female anatomy.

Deep Throat

Importantly, when the identity of the performers is revealed, their visual construction differs in several respects from the presentation of narrative in mainstream productions. For instance, in one segment a photographer has an erotic encounter with his two models in a mud bath. After he manages to hit a dartboard on a nearby wall with a stream of his ejaculate, the photographer turns directly to the camera and appeals to the audience to applaud his prowess. This direct address to the film's spectator, a feature which instantly breaks the ideological "fiction" affect that Mulvey argues governs mainstream cinema, is again a feature that Gunning argues defines the spectacle of early film.

For instance, Gunning refers to the cycle of "facial expression films", where in the absence of a narrative drive assorted comedians, performers, showmen and magicians would look directly at the camera to display their skill at facial distortion for the audience. This tradition finds continuation in the ranks of "body" performers such as Lovelace in **Deep Throat** who frequently gazes directly into the camera and grins to the audience with pleasure during the sexual sequences. Even closer to this silent tradition is the response of actors such as Reems who insists on "clowning" distorted comic facial gestures directly to the audience when being pleasured by Linda.

It seems pertinent that the closest that Damiano's film comes to Mulvey's thesis of male protagonists exerting power over depicted females through voyeurism occurs in the film's closing sequences when a masked raider enters Linda's flat and watches her whilst she is undressed in the bathroom. Any potency or threat that this may offer to the female is immediately dissipated by two narrative features. Firstly, Linda recognises the intruder as Wilbour Wayne, one of Dr Young's patients, whose masculinity is instantly upturned by Linda's revelation that his raider's guise does not scare her.

More importantly the image track denies him any voyeuristic power, instead framing both their bodies as a site of display in a series of doorway interiors. (Indeed, Wilbour is even seen to back away from the door where he has been spying on Linda in order to give the camera greater access to her naked body.) The recodification of both the male and female bodies as a site of spectacle is confirmed by the final sex scene in the film where both Linda's and Wilbour's bodies are literally cut up into a series of "bits" by a series of statically mounted frames. The finale of the film is a close-up of Linda as she gazes directly at the audience, a series of filmic inserts of bells ringing and fireworks exploding indicating that she is finally gratified.

Gunning derived the term "Cinema of Attractions" from the Soviet director Sergei Eisenstein, who felt that the reduction of cinema to a series of static frames or "spectacles" allowed the audience to think creatively about what they had viewed, rather than being tied down with narrative concerns. Arguably pornography shares that tradition, by reducing both the male and female form to a series of body spectacles. Rather than acting as a guarantor of male power, these films employ the features of early film to ask their audience to question the masculine fear of female sexuality.

NOTES:
1. Another feature which links this and the Mondo cycle to early silent film is re-ordering and recycling of images for different films and versions of any one product. As Gunning concludes the "showmen" and exhibitors of early films often re-edited or presented additional effects and commentaries to fit the differing audiences and fairground venues that these images were displayed in. A film such as **Mondo Erotico** draws on this tradition of thrill and spectacle, with Gemser providing the commentaries over scenes clearly strung together from other exploitation productions.
2. Importantly, whereas the rest of **Deep Throat** is shot with direct sound, the sexual sequences, literally are silent with dialogue and direct sound being abruptly replaced by (often incongruous) songs that swell the soundtrack. According to Williams, this shift from dialogue and direct sound to the "exquisite embarrassment of silence" that accompanies sexual activity reveals the basis of films such as Damiano's in the silent tradition of "primitive" film.
3. Williams dates this pornographic concentration of "body bits" back to silent stag films such as **A Free Ride** (1915). She argues that the film displays its disregard for rules of narrative continuity by abruptly cutting between the coupling of a man and two women in a woodland setting, a man and a woman in an indeterminate setting and finally a close-up of a foot stroking a penis to orgasm. What remains unexplained are the important narrative cues that a mainstream Hollywood production would seek to clarify: what if any are the relations between the protagonists in the two locations depicted, and whose genitals are being pleasured before the film ends.

BIBLIOGRAPHY
Thomas Elsaesser (Ed); *Early Cinema, Space, Frame, Narrative* (BFI, London 1992).
Tom Gunning; *The Cinema Of Attractions: Early Film, Its Spectator And The Avant-Garde.*
Tom Gunning; *Primitive Cinema: A Frame Up? Or The Trick's On Us.*
Constance Penley (Ed); *Feminism And Film Theory* (BFI & Routledge, London 1988).
Laura Mulvey; *Visual Pleasure And Narrative Cinema.*
Linda Williams; *Hardcore: Power, Pleasure And The Frenzy Of The Visible* (University of California Press, California 1989).

CRAWLING CELLULOID CHAOS

H P Lovecraft In Cinema

Andy Black

"Remote, in the deserts of Araby lies the nameless city, crumbling and inarticulate, its low walls nearly hidden by the sands of uncounted ages. It must have been thus before the first stones of Memphis were laid, and while the bricks of Babylon were yet unbaked. There is no legend so old as to give it a name, or to recall that it was ever alive; but it is told of in whispers around campfires and muttered about by grandams in the tents of sheiks so that all the tribes shun it without wholly knowing why. It was of this place that Abdul Alhazred the mad poet dreamed on the night before he sang his unexplainable couplet:

'That is not dead which can eternal lie,
And with strange aeons death may die.'"

—H P Lovecraft, *The Nameless City*

Howard Phillips Lovecraft. A name synonymous with experimental tales of awe-inspiring terror, imagination and above all, an ethereal aura. It is this last, most vital quality amongst his diverse work which perhaps explains the cinema's relative lack of success (to date) in adopting his visionary output to the big screen.

It also partly explains why the body of films based upon his writings adhere to such a strict dichotomy, comprising on one hand the superficial "based upon" or "renascent" variety and on the other the more intriguing "inspired by" or "totemic" category, as I'll refer to them.

My own appreciation of Lovecraft stems from his continued ability to combine both arcane religions and locales with futuristic ideas and explorations. I can recall no other writer able to master such divergent themes, never mind the small matter of Lovecraft's ability to dovetail these strands into a cogent framework.

Stoker, Poe, Conan Doyle – all masters at creating a convincing gothic milieu, whilst similarly H G Wells, Jules Verne, Edgar Rice Burroughs have all created futurescapes of extraordinary vision; but Lovecraft, well – his command of both genres exceeds all others with only such luminaries as Shelley's audacious *Frankenstein* coming anywhere near close to being as effective.

So, in Lovecraft's *The Rats In The Walls*, prehistoric ancestry, skeletal remains and the suspicion of cannibalism prevail; alien visitations to the homely surroundings of Vermont occur in *The Whisperer In Darkness*; a meteorite crashes into a rural locale in *The Colour Out Of Space*; whilst a "lost race" mythos combines with a cosmic ethos alluding to extra-terrestrials in *At The Mountains Of Madness*.

His salient themes of aliens, of other races being considered more important and more significant than the human race is prominent in many of his finest works, and detailed "histories" of these races can be found in *The Shadow Out Of Time*, *At The Mountains Of Madness* and *The Call Of Cthulhu* to name but three.

Cthulhu, one of his greatest works, encapsulates Lovecraft's philosophy thus: "We live on a placid island of ignorance in the midst of black seas of infinity", thereby concisely challenging the notion that the human race is the master race, whilst also

The Creature From The Black Lagoon

extending the imagination to worlds (and beings) beyond.

As such, it is Lovecraft's pre-human gods, "The Great Old Ones", such as the tentacular beast in *Cthulhu*, which try to rule the earth. This same story also defines another salient Lovecraftian trait, his merging of not just gothic horror and sci-fi but of sci-fi and his own unique "invented" occultism in order to accentuate the heightened sense of dread inherent as the tale unfolds.

Considering the originality and audacity of Lovecraft's imagery and concepts, it's perhaps unsurprising that it took film makers over two decades to begin to decipher his work for the cinema screen (Lovecraft died of intestinal cancer in 1937 and yet the first "authentic" Lovecraftian films only appeared in the mid to late 1950's).

Given that this was a period recovering from post-World War 2 trauma, and the majority of the horror/sci-fi releases were escapist nonsense with giant ants (**Them!**, 1954), arachnids (**Tarantula**, 1955), and leading ladies (**Attack Of The 50 Foot Woman**, 1958) scenery-chewing cinema screens at an alarming rate, it is no surprise that any remotely Lovecraftian works merely followed the renascent category referred to earlier.

Jack Arnold's **The Creature From The Black Lagoon** (1953) seems to draw some inspiration for its titular monster from Lovecraft's early work *Dagon* (1917) where an underwater beast appears – the movie's aquatic predator complete with gills, scales, claws and salivating jaws (and a definite fascination for the female form). Equally dramatic is the fish-shaped alien in Irvin Berwick's rather less well known **The Monster Of Piedras Blancas** (1959) – both antecedents of the more recent underwater monster epics with Sean Cunningham's **Deep Star 6** (1989) and George P. Cosmatos' **Leviathan** (1989) being the most prominent examples. It took two of Italian cinema's most venerated figures however, to visualise one of the earliest and most effective Lovecraftian incarnations – take a bow director Riccardo Freda and cameraman Mario Bava, combining beautifully for **Caltiki, The Immortal Monster** (1959), where the creature emerging from

Die, Monster, Die

a Mexican lake recalls the *shoggoths* – the hideous servants of Lovecraft's "Old Ones".

Appropriately enough, when considering Lovecraft's status as one of the most revered authors of the horror genre, some of the genre's most celebrated performers have chosen his vehicles in which to display their talents, albeit with varying degrees of success.

The prolific and successful Roger Corman-directed, Vincent Price-starred AIP film cycle of the 1960's, mainly based on Edgar Allan Poe's work, also included Lovecraft's *The Case Of Charles Dexter Ward*, albeit retitled for the screen as **The Haunted Palace** (1963). Price's performance – more minimalist here than his customary flamboyance – is excellent in portraying both the sinned against Charles and the sinner, Joseph Curwen, and his eventual revenge on the descendants of a small town where he had been burned alive as a sorcerer. Any merit at selecting Lovecraft as a source is however negated by AIP's supplanting of his material with Poe-inspired necrophilia. (Price also starred in Jacques Tourneur's **City Under The Sea** [1965], reigning over a horde of gill-men smugglers). *Charles Dexter Ward* had been earlier quoted in John Moxey's **City Of The Dead** (1960), with Christopher Lee as a modern warlock in the New England town where the local inn proprietress is a centuries-old witch.

Horror icons don't come much greater than Price, but Boris Karloff can claim some parity at this point – yet his appearance in **Die, Monster, Die** (1965) can't redeem the rather prosaic sci-fi plotting as he experiments with a radioactive meteorite. By dispensing with the cosmic nuances of Lovecraft's source novella *The Colour Out Of Space*, the film degenerates into routine film-fodder. (A later version, David Keith's **The Curse** [aka **The Farm**, 1987] is even worse!)

The Shuttered Room (1967) was directed by David Greene and based on a novella started by Lovecraft and posthumously completed by August Derleth. Oliver Reed stars as the local New England thug terrorising a couple whose aunt hides a terrible secret

The Curse Of The Crimson Altar

– a human monster – in her locked attic. This theme was later reprised in such efforts as Tigon's **The Beast In The Cellar** (1971) and Stuart Gordon's **Castle Freak** (1995).

Boris Karloff continued his mini-Lovecraft revival unabated, and with greater success, in Vernon Sewell's 1968 potboiler **The Curse Of The Crimson Altar** – no doubt helped by the presence of two fellow horror icons. Barbara Steele appears as the 300 year-old witch Lavinia Marsh, burned at the stake and reincarnated in the guise of... Christopher Lee, who else? The film was loosely based on Lovecraft's remarkable *Dreams In The Witch House*.

There's rather more tension and furtive occultism here than in most of the previous Lovecraft films, but the zenith of the 1960's entries is undoubtedly Daniel Haller's ambitious failure **The Dunwich Horror** (1969). Here a young university student, and more importantly, a *virgin* (Sandra Dee) is kidnapped by Wilbur Whately (Dean Stockwell) in order that he and his crazed disciples may prepare for the coming of Yog-Sothoth, as he uses his stolen copy of the ancient tome *The Necronomicon* (the best known of Lovecraft's forbidden books and translated as "An Image of the Law of the Dead"), to release the "Great Old Ones". Psychedelic, hallucinatory, in fact typically 60's in approach, its vibrant, occultist themes actually complement rather than detract from its spiritual inspiration.

The Necronomicon also informs Javier Aguirre's **The Hunchback Of The Morgue** (1972), where a mad scientist (is there any other kind?), uses the arcane tome to create his own polymorphous beings, and even more curiously, occurs merely as the title in Jess Franco's excellent **Necronomicon** (aka **Succubus**) in 1970.

Amongst this veritable flotsam and jetsam of renascent Lovecraftian films are also

Texas Chainsaw Massacre 2

a slew of similarly superficial TV films and episodes, including Rod Serling's **Night Gallery** – *Pickman's Model*, *Cool Air* and more intriguingly *Professor Peabody's Last Lecture*, where the seasoned academic elucidates the "Cthulhu" and indeed entire Lovecraftian mythos, whilst reading from a paperback copy of *The Necronomicon*.

Kolchak: The Night Stalker's *Horror In The Heights* is also relevant here as Darren McGavin's likeable rogue reporter investigates an ancient monster who lures victims by imitating the appearance of someone they trust; likewise the inveigling miscarriage of Lovecraftian ideas **Artemis 81** (1981), a unique UK/Denmark production concerning the theft of a pagan statue from a Danish museum, bringing death to all those who come into contact with it, with bubbling sub-plots prophesising the devastation of the earth and a race of troglodyte human clones. Otherwise, titles such as **The Unnameable** (1988), **The Unnameable Returns** (1992) and **Cthulhu Mansion** (1994) continue to surface, sadly bearing only the most perfunctory resemblance to their inspiration.

Conversely, many of the more interesting, totemic Lovecraftian films remain less overtly Lovecraftian in their approach than their lesser renascent companions, yet more intrinsically aligned to the master due to their style, atmosphere and tone.

For example, few would bestow Lovecraftian virtues on Tobe Hooper's **The Texas Chainsaw Massacre** (1974) upon first appearances, but consider the rural Texas landscape, remote and with insular communities, depressed religions, whilst the "arm"-chairs and skeletal "trophies" within the 'saw family home echo the cannibalistic "history" of *The Rats In The Walls*, whilst the lugubrious, labyrinth tunnels of the desolate

City Of The Living Dead

amusement park in **The Texas Chainsaw Massacre 2** (1986) mirror the dark, dank caves and subterranean passageways of the fertile Lovecraftian mind as revealed in such tales as *The Outsider* and *The Festival*.

In a similar fashion, the gothic, ethereal atmosphere of the late Lucio Fulci's tension-filled gore classics, **City Of The Living Dead** (1980), **The Beyond** (1981) and **The House By The Cemetery** (1981) all betray telling Lovecraft influences. In **City** ancient tomes appear, sacred proclamations are espoused, deserted streets shadowed by night become instantly sinister and uninviting, whilst the enigmatic denouement finds the protagonists battling decomposing zombies within the confines of typically eerie, torch-lit Lovecraftian caverns. In the even more inspired **The Beyond** the *Book Of Eibon* is featured, another of the tomes in the Cthulhu mythos which is closely associated with *The Necronomicon*, and an executed sorcerer is the source of evil as in *Charles Dexter Ward*. Here, an underground netherworld exists, again populated by almost "timeless" (Old Ones?) zombies and where the audacious climax sees the lead players David Warbeck and Catriona MacColl "blinded" as they enter a mystery world previously depicted in a painting – the kind of imaginative and artistic conceit a certain H P Lovecraft would have been delighted by.

To complete an impressive trio **The House By The Cemetery** is arguably the most effective of all, as the sinister title house has its own "monster" beneath its rooms in the grotesque guise of Dr. Freudstein – perfectly-named and embodying both Frankenstein's propensity for spare-limb surgery and Freud's self-preservative drive, only over-zealously administered here! Freudstein has gone beyond the human dimension (as in Lovecraft's *From Beyond*), transforming not only his appearance – "a myriad of corpses" – but also his attitude to his (once) fellow humans above.

Similar genetic mutations pervade such entries as Gary A Sherman's notorious

The House By The Cemetery

Dead And Buried (1981), where a Herbert West-type mortician produces zombies in a New England town, and Willard Huyck's **Messiah Of Evil** (1974), which tells a similar story transposed to California. In Sergio Martino's **The Screamers** (1979) the curvaceous Barbara Bach is introduced to "Dagon"'s Italian descendants, and in Andrzej Zulawski's

Inferno

Possession (1981) Isabelle Adjani is raped by an obscene, tentacular creature, whilst Dario Argento's **Inferno** (1980) concentrates on Lovecraftian sorcery, doors to other realms and veiled references to perhaps "other worldly" figures. Argento's earlier **Suspiria** is a dark evocation of *Dreams In The Witch House*, where a deathless sorceress holds murderous dominion.

Argento collaborator Michele Soavi accentuates the other dimensional occultism alluded to in Lovecraft's work in his superior chiller **The Sect** (1991), where the labyrinth pipework which circumvents an isolated woodland cabin symbolises not only the complex Freudian sub-text but the mysterious satanic sect to which the pipe ultimately leads.

The majority of films discussed thus far have been firmly rooted on planet earth, but there have been moments of inspired inter-planetary travel merged with archaic references combining elements of Lovecraft's diverse thoughts. A monstrous being from another world crashlands at an arctic research station in John Carpenter's wondrous re-make of **The Thing** (1982) (itself virtually reprised in the **X-Files** episode *Ice*).

There's also the unforgettable sequence in Mario Bava's enthralling **Planet Of The Vampires** (1965) where a group of astronauts investigate SOS signals emanating from a mystery planet. Upon reaching its barren wastes, they trace the signal to a spacestation where prehistoric relics adorn a control room – ancient and futuristic segue for one special moment, a configuration not neglected by Ridley Scott's **Alien** (1979) where H R Giger's Lovecraft-inspired "industrial-flesh" and phallic creations dominate proceedings, the alien evoking the creature which haunts *At The Mountains Of Madness*, while the inhospitable planet reminds us of the wretched Yuggoth. Giger's creations have also reached prominence in the recent release **Species** (1995), while David Fincher's mordant **Alien 3** (1993) recaptures some of the original film's Lovecraftian traits, including

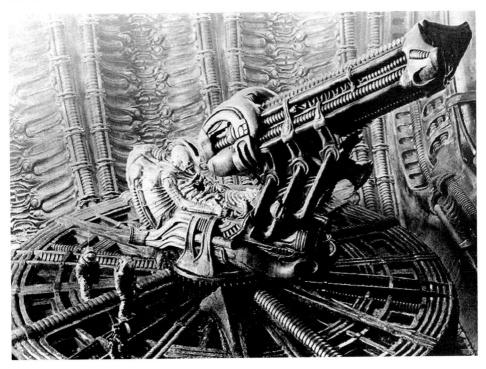

Alien

the hostile, howling winds of the remote penal colony setting, whilst Ripley's (Sigourney Weaver) reconnoitre of the spaceship's remains is equally unnerving. Giger has of course also published his own illustrated version of *The Necronomicon*.

There's also a measure of sci-fi interest via the time-portal contained in Sam Raimi's exhilarating **Evil Dead** series, especially the second and third instalments as the yellowing pages of the *Necronomicon* herald forth ancient demons and skeletal armies.

The seminal first film however probably most captures the nerve-stretching nuances of pure Lovecraft as antediluvian incantations summon forth the "old" demons into a dark and foreboding atmosphere. Although the 80's style humour and special effects don't always complement their source as much as one would like, the vertiginous camera is breathtaking to experience, reinforcing the age-old power of the adversaries.

Also typical of the 80's trend for gore above all are a varied trio of related films – the surreal sight of forty-feet of intestinal tract wrapped around the protagonist's throat doesn't exactly scream typical Lovecraft at you, but **Re-Animator** (1985), **From Beyond** (1986) and **Bride Of Re-Animator** (1991) are after all based directly on two of Lovecraft's more visceral pulp stories – *Herbert West, Reanimator* and *From Beyond*.

In **Re-Animator**, director Stuart Gordon intensifies Lovecraft's original with the above-mentioned grotesqueries. Jeffrey Combs plays Herbert West, a cold, calculating scientist utilising Frankenstein-esque experiments to prolong life by reanimating the dead. Black humour, Grand Guignol and, most perversely, a decapitated David Gale's head attempting to propagate oral sex with the delectable Barbara Crampton who is tied to a

Re-Animator

From Beyond

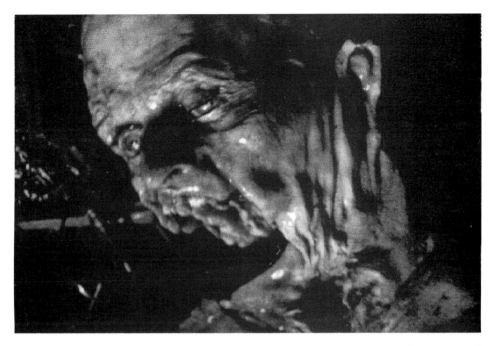

The Resurrected

table, add to the potent mix of "unnatural" acts and necrophilia that permeates the film.

The same director.promptly initiated in some ways an even better film in **From Beyond**, as the almost Sadean Dr. Pretorious employs a detector machine to explore other-dimensional entities, even to the extent of suggesting something even Lovecraft had stopped short of doing – a carnal union with creatures from a fourth dimension.

This transcendental aspect certainly raises the film above many of its ilk, whilst the visualisation of the assorted laboratory monstrosities is impressive, reinforced with liberal quotations from Lovecraft's work, plus the lascivious charms of Ms. Crampton on hand again to satiate and accentuate the more perverse fantasy aspects of the source material!

Continuing the Frankenstein themes, a belated sequel, **Bride Of Re-Animator**, directed by Brian Yuzna, squirmed forth – effects- laden it may have been, but certainly not effective. Earlier material is reprised, albeit stitched together and presented slightly differently in the manner of the good Baron himself and yet, like the self-same figure, the film is literally too disjointed to have the required impact.

Ulli Lommel's sadistic **The Devonsville Terror** (1983), was a modern version of *The Case Of Charles Dexter Ward*, as is **The Resurrected** (1991), directed by **Dead And Buried** scriptwriter Dan O'Bannon, also renowned for its excessive gore but ultimately disappointing.

Only one other current *auteur* appears to be mining the rich seam of Lovecraftian creativity – our own Clive Barker, with his expanding **Hellraiser** series featuring the now familiar "other dimensional" Cenobites, grotesque monsters and labyrinth corridors/caves – the protagonists lured by the omnipotent Cenobites who wield both punishment and power upon their victims, together with, surprisingly, universal enlightenment.

In Barker's ambitious **Nightbreed** (1990), the subterranean kingdom of Midian with its flame-lit passageways and myriad of monsters recalls the visions of *Pickman's Model* and *The Statement Of Randolph Carter*.

The latter tale was also the base inspiration for Jean-Paul Ouellette's **The Unnameable Returns** (1992). A scholar at Miskatonic University unwittingly unleashes a demon from a centuried graveyard. The demon combines with the living form of a virgin student who must be exorcised in the climactic battle. The film was a sequel to Ouellette's earlier and inferior **The Unnameable** (1988), a more prosaic effort with a plot reminiscent of *The Shuttered Room*. *The Necronomicon* is glimpsed, but the story is basically a teen slaughter movie set in Miskatonic.

As if to lend credence to the view that Lovecraft is steadily exerting more influence posthumously than his writing ever did when he was alive, a triumvirate of totemic titles have surfaced recently with more than a passing interest in the "Old Ones".

Brian Yuzna's **Necronomicon** (1993) is one of the few anthology takes on the master, presenting three tales. *The Cold* is a rather routine offering with David Warner as the sanguinary Dr. Madden, experimenting in crypto-biosis – the only "chills" here however, are provided by the sub-zero temperatures his body requires to survive. *Whispers* includes ancient catacombs, decaying human remains, walls which ooze green blood and outré bat creatures with human souls, but suffers from an interminable dream/real-time conclusion.

Best of all is *The Drowned*, directed by Christophe Ganz, which centres on a gossamer-coated hotel perched precariously upon a cliff-top, hollow honeycombed caves beneath which house a hideous sea-monster, and the protagonist's "back from the dead" lover whose tender kisses in fact reveal her sea-creature genesis as tentacles erupt from her skin and worm-like tendrils burst from her eyes – impressively imaginative enough to warrant being mentioned in the same breath as Lovecraft. Jeffrey **Re-Animator** Combs essays the great man himself in the framing story.

John Carpenter's intriguing **In The Mouth Of Madness** (1995), pays more overt homage to Stephen King than H P Lovecraft as a celebrated horror author, Sutter Cane (Jurgen Prochnow) disappears half-way through completing his next "subliminal" classic horror novel – but the meandering tunnels, time-portals and grotesque creatures Sam Neill's investigative insurance agent discovers upon locating Cane – "All those horrible slimy things trying to get back in, they are true" – betrays a quite blatant Lovecraftian influence. (The near Lovecraftian title is also a give-away!).

Lastly, but perhaps most importantly, Mariano Baino's seminal full-length feature, **Dark Waters** (1993) creates the most compelling, mesmerising Lovecraft aura on film to date. The genuinely spectral milieu, realised by the Ukraine locations, aligned with Baino's fledgling artistry and poise, makes for compulsive viewing.

A Lovecraftian demon has secreted itself in a remote and hostile island, populated only by a handful of locals and mysterious (and decidedly un-Christian) holy order of nuns. Into their clandestine world of arcane rituals enters the youthful Elizabeth (Louise Salter) – visiting the convent to discover how her late father's continuing gratuity to the order is being used.

It doesn't take too long for her to realise that there are far more than religious ceremonies taking place here – a notion singularly amplified given the bloody demise of her friend Theresa (Anna Rose Phipps), who is discovered observing rituals not designed

Dark Waters

for her prying eyes. Theresa's protracted stabbing – sepia blood ebbing away in rivulets – is audaciously juxtaposed with the surreal image of a monk before a canvas, painting her death, using blood-red paint for each brushstroke. This is not the last of the painterly images on show, nor is it the last of the viscera....

A triumph of style over content? Yes. Baino has not only assimilated the works of Bava and Argento, but, more importantly, used their *oeuvres* and Lovecraft's themes of esoteric occultism, alchemy and ancient demonology as a canvas for his own creativity and feral imagination, unlike so many of his peers who merely degenerate into second rate plagiarists.

There are mesmeric set-pieces here, including the unseen presence which crashes through the church doors, smashing the windows and collapsing its walls; a kinetic **Evil Dead**-style steadicam which circumvents a mountainside and careers over the top to catapult a startled nun into a watery grave, and an especially haunting dream sequence in which the young Elizabeth is dwarfed by the ethereal vision of a nun nailed to a cross which floats eerily above her, shrouded by mist and whose mouth forms a Munchian silent scream.

The final chapters of weird tales and repulsive nightmares have already been written by H P Lovecraft, but let us hope that there are many more cinematic pages to unfold, not least the much-anticipated but as yet unrealised *Gone With The Wind* of horror films, Stuart Gordon's oft-mentioned adaptation of *The Shadow Over Innsmouth*. Scriptwriter Dennis Paoli even penned a treatment incorporating another Lovecraft story, *The Thing On The Doorstep*, but as yet the project remains in production limbo. (Fritz Lang incidentally also harboured an interest in this same Lovecraft tale in the 1930's, but to no avail). Veteran producer Harry Alan Towers is also currently investigating possibilities for a TV series entirely adapted from Lovecraft.

So, thus far, those of us who crave "the ethereal, the remote, the shadowy and the doubtful" must wait, wait and heed Lovecraft's cautionary horror ethos:

> Searchers after horror haunt strange, far places. For them are the catacombs of Ptolemais, and the carven mausolea of the nightmare countries. They climb to the moonlit towers of ruined Rhine castles, and falter down black cobwebbed steps beneath the scattered stones of forgotten cities in Asia. The haunted wood and desolate mountain are their shrines and they linger around the sinister monoliths on uninhabited islands. But the true epicure in the terrible, to whom a new thrill of unutterable ghastliness is the chief end and justification of existence, esteems most of all the ancient, lonely farmhouses of backwoods New England; for there the dark elements of strength, solitude, grotesqueness and ignorance combine to form the perfection of the hideous.

> —H P Lovecraft, *The Picture In The House*

WITCHFINDER GENERAL

Michael Reeves' Visceral Classic

Leon Hunt

With the exception of **Peeping Tom**, no British horror film carries more critical baggage with it than **Witchfinder General**. Both have usually been seen in Britain in truncated versions – Redemption have rectified that now with their recent release, but will we ever see a print of **Peeping Tom** which draws even closer attention to Powell's fascination with Harrison Marks? Both films followed the same romantic path from critical damnation to an elevation which no Hammer film has ever enjoyed.

Alan Bennett described **Witchfinder**, at the time of its release, as "the most persistently sadistic and morally rotten film I have seen", while the *Aurum Horror Encyclopedia* follows director Michael Reeves' original defence of the film in asserting that "rarely has violence been used so legitimately". Both films have been largely decontextualised in "serious" critical accounts, so that in the former case, **Horrors Of The Black Museum** and **Circus Of Horrors** are little more than idiot cousins to a unique masterwork.

Witchfinder General was co-produced by Tigon, British Exploitation's most endearingly downmarket film company, and AIP, who simply sold it as a Poe film, **The Conqueror Worm**. Their ambitions for the film perhaps come more into focus when one looks at their respective follow-ups, **Blood On Satan's Claw** (Piers Haggard, 1970) and **Cry Of The Banshee** (Gordon Hessler, 1970).

Banshee virtually has Vincent Price reprise Matthew Hopkins in all but name, but it's a trifle undecided about its coven of witches, oppressed New Age Flower Children one minute and demon-summoning sub-Mansonites the next.

Blood On Satan's Claw, Tigon's most gloriously lurid horror film, marks a shift in the correlation between the 16th/17th century and '60s/'70s Europe that the Witchfinder genre seems to make – polymorphously perverse revolution on the one side, the repressive state on the other, and an undecided (and unrepresented) *bourgeois* dilemma in the middle. This is the same generational conflict initiated by Reeves' films, but more ambivalent in its positioning of the viewer. On the one side, Linda Hayden's Lolita-from-Hell, Angel(!), leads a Satanic cult so hormonally charged up – Horny = Hairy, in this film – that the signs of puberty are spreading alarmingly across the body, most memorably to Hayden's eyebrows. The film's most graphic scene depicts the surgical removal of this "monstrous" sign of sexual development, the "devil's skin".

On the other side, Patrick Wymark's "The Judge" (as the credits bluntly call him) reprises elements of Price's Hopkins, Rupert Davies' John Lowes and Wymark's own Cromwell – what are we to make of him? "I shall use undreamed of measures," he promises ominously, and is true to his word. In the final scene, he wields the most phallic sword one could imagine – it *stands to attention* as it penetrates the hairy demon who stirs up all these unholy passions. Even Hammer, by the time of **Twins Of Evil** (1971), has latched onto the puritanical Witchfinder, a particularly ruthless Peter Cushing; not that the film invites much sympathy for those incorrigible Karnsteins either.

But it's Michael Armstrong's **Mark Of The Devil** (1969) which most of all suggests the development of a sadistic witch-torturing sub-genre – the same rural cruelty,

Mark Of The Devil

often expressed through visual contrasts between Nature and Violence, the same archives-of-pain narrative-of-attractions (whose earliest predecessor would be **Hāxan/Witchcraft Through The Ages**), the opposition between localised, arbitrary power (Hopkins, **Satan's Claw**'s repressed priest, Reggie Nalder's illiterate Albino) and a centralised state power which usually turns out to be just as ghastly (Cromwell, implicitly, "The Judge" if you choose to read him so, and Herbert Lom's Lord Cumberland).

Armstrong's film is no less harrowing than Reeves', and its relative crudeness makes it all the more so. But its most intriguing element is the relationship between Cumberland and Udo Kier's appropriately named Christian. Unlike Ian Ogilvy's Richard, Christian is implicated in the torturing that takes place, and spends some two thirds of the film calmly watching its execution. He looks to Cumberland for a sense of certainty, a conception of the Law with explicitly Oedipal overtones, but learns that "there is no safety anywhere". This loss of faith in the Father, in the Law, and, it seems, in his own identity has consequences for the body, the site on which the film's political machinations are marked out. Cumberland escapes, and Christian is tortured to death in his place. There's a visible struggle going on between Armstrong's earnest ambitions and Adrian Hoven's lascivious torture show, but there's more going on in **Mark Of The Devil** than is generally acknowledged.

At the centre of **Witchfinder General**'s reputation is the seemingly irresistible mythology of Michael Reeves. In an industry notoriously short of traditional *auteurs*, Reeves fits the bill almost too perfectly, as that onetime pseudonym "Michael Byron" indicates – young, gifted and neurotic, the proverbial premature, good-looking corpse, with a recognisable authorial *oeuvre* established in just three films and part of another. Not for him the embarrassing drivel people like Sasdy and Hessler were forced to turn out as their careers failed to develop.

Peter Hutchings describes the popular critical representation of Reeves as follows; "The artist is in despair, a despair which is existential, outside history, ungendered, beyond analysis." And check out those exploitation credentials for genre fans – Reeves cut his teeth in Italy during the '60s Gothic boom, worked with Barbara Steele, Christopher Lee (at least indirectly), Boris Karloff and, more problematically, Vincent Price. I say "problematically" because Price was a very different kind of star from the others in that list, and brought a lot of baggage of his own to the film.

Steele was used iconographically by Bava, Freda, Margheriti and Corman – thus the fact that everyone likes her films more than she does. Lee and Karloff were "character actors" who found a niche in a genre which allowed them to lose themselves, willingly or otherwise, in different make-ups, sub-cycles or generic developments. But Price was arguably the biggest horror star of the early '60s, and the one who functioned most like a conventional movie star – that sense of familiarity, repetition, the pleasure of a larger-than-life known quantity. He was also the one major success within another tradition of horror stardom (Atwill, Rathbone and Gough come to mind) – the classically trained actor slumming it (and, in Price's case, thoroughly enjoying doing so), while using those "unclassical" qualities to suggest a decadent, slightly "fruity" and very un-American aestheticism.

Price, by 1968, was inseparable from the carnival-host persona of the Castle films and the Freudian-camp he has made so uniquely his own in Corman's magnificent Poe films. David Thomson didn't mean it as a compliment, but hit on something when he observed that "He surveyed the Horror genre as if it were a tray of eclairs." **Witchfinder General**, however, is rarely discussed as a Vincent Price film, except by default – it is a Vincent Price vehicle which strives not to be a Vincent Price vehicle.

To say that angry young Michael and camp old Vincent didn't quite hit it off would be something of an understatement if the stories are true – and we all know the story of *that* withering put-down. "I've made eighty-seven films," Price is alleged to have said, "What have you done?" Reeves replied, "I've made three good ones." Apocryphal or not, several horror histories have taken great delight in re-telling the story to put the old ham in his place. One publicity photo taken on the set of the film shows these two antagonists together. Price is in full Matthew Hopkins costume, clad in black, hunched over and solemn, barely recognisable. Reeves, in white polo-neck and black velvet jacket, very much the young turk with camera lens hanging around his neck, is facing in the opposite direction. The impression is of two figures worlds apart, the old and the new, the trivial and the serious, and the film seems to be at least partly about that conflict.

The critical consensus has been that **Witchfinder General** contains Price's most "restrained" performance, and that this restraint had to be aggressively imposed by Reeves. Robin Wood, who singles Reeves out as an oasis of talent in what he sees as the desert of British cinema, adheres to this view while also finding Price's casting unsatisfactory (Reeves apparently wanted Donald Pleasence, scarcely a model of restraint

House Of Usher

himself and one who was later to take on downwardly-mobile horror connotations of his own). S.S. Prawer, meanwhile, in *Caligari's Children*, makes an interesting distinction between serious and trivial uses of the actor:

> Even when an actor has come, at a certain stage in his career, to specialise in "horror" roles, different directors can bring out different facets of his personality and different techniques of perfecting them. One need think only of Vincent Price's performances for Roger Corman (neurasthenia and dandified sadism that are clearly *acted*, with occasional signals that seem to say: "don't be frightened, it's only me!"), for Robert Fuest (Price enjoying himself, camping it up, keeping his tongue visibly in cheek), and for Michael Reeves (what we are watching in **Witchfinder General** has the aura of real evil, and Price conveys this with subtlety and complete seriousness).

This could suggest no more than that different films require different styles of performance – several of Price's later roles foreground acting and performance thematically – except that phrases like "subtlety" and "seriousness" have a way of stacking the deck. In any case, Price's performances for Corman are more varied than is often acknowledged – **Tomb Of Ligeia** showcases a more low-key Price, for example, than in **House Of Usher** or the excesses of, say, **Pit And The Pendulum**, which has no room in it for restraint of any kind. He's got bigtime torture paraphernalia *and* Babs Steele to compete with – nothing less than full-throttle will do.

It isn't difficult to see why AIP, if not Tigon, thought they could sell **Witchfinder** as both a "Price" and a "Poe" film. In Lew Landers' **The Raven** (1935), there's a scene in which one of Bela Lugosi's victims is harnessed beneath a descending pendulum. Lugosi

is in control of this device, if not his performance, but rises to the film's most triumphant non-sequitur: "Poe, you are avenged!" Given that the author's poem has lent so little to the film, the implications are clear – Poe equals torture. By 1968, I think it would be fair to say that Poe equalled Price equalled torture (**Mark Of The Devil** suggests other directions for the torture movie only implicit in **Witchfinder** – the Women-in-Prison movie, the Nazi Death Camp movie). Matthew Hopkins presides over plenty of torture, but not with the sadistic glee with which Price extols the agonies of the blade to John Kerr in **Pit And The Pendulum**.

Hopkins is unshakeably matter-of-fact as he hangs, drowns, burns and has needles pushed into his victims – his face and voice betray comparatively little, even the sexual subtext implied by his interest in Sara (at least *before* she is raped by Stearne) or his pathological hatred of the desire he sees as being contained within the female body.

Price's performance isn't restrained, it's cold – stone cold, as befits the model of masculinity he embodies in the film. It's always intriguing to see such an against-the-grain performance, and not difficult to see what Price's critics were grudgingly impressed by – his tendency to generate solidarity with an audience would be problematic here. But the film goes further than holding flamboyance in check. It mounts an aggression towards "Price", as opposed to, say, "subverting" his meaning in some way (although how do you subvert what is already a little subversive?). What is taking place here?

The film's much-discussed opening depicts the hanging of a presumably innocent woman – unlike **Banshee** and **Satan's Claw**, the film doesn't cloud the issue by introducing supernatural elements – set against the countryside of Norfolk. There is no real dialogue, except for the monotonous incantations of a priest. Each sound is distinctive – the hammering of the gallows, the woman's screams, the swinging of her body on a rope, the wind in the trees as the villagers watch in silence. The camera performs a

circular movement around the gallows, then dissolves to a reverse angle. In the distance, we see another figure for the first time; a zoom confirms that it is Price, but a freeze keeps him in extreme long shot as the credits roll. Their wording and order is telling: "Matthew Hopkins" (then underneath) "Witchfinder General" (then fade to:) "Vincent Price". If one can isolate Price's appearance from this overpowering sequence, several projects reveal themselves.

1. Anticlimax. The first two Corman-Poe films reveal Price for the first time as a figure thrust from a doorway, into full close-up; he immediately speaks and barely stops for the rest of the film. Here, we are denied Price as a spectacle; instead, he is presented as a tiny, silent figure, strangely removed from the action. This image, one of two climaxes – the hanging is the other – simply cannot compete with what we have just seen.

2. "Real" Horror versus stylised, generic "horror". In some ways, **Witchfinder General** is tangential to the horror genre – it's a violent historical drama, concerned to a degree with (not necessarily factual) authenticity and "period". However, it offers sadistic violence as a spectacle – presumably what Tigon were after, judging by all their other films – and features one of Horror's central icons. An opposition is set up, therefore, between reconstructed historical atrocity and a star who represents horror as mass entertainment. The film cannot and will not contain Price's stylised presence.

3. "Matthew Hopkins" versus "Vincent Price" (Kim Newman argues that the proper title of the film is **Matthew Hopkins – Witchfinder General**, but the idea has never really caught on). The battle is already being fought during the credits, with Hopkins recast as the star of the film. It's appropriate that the film culminates with Ian Ogilvy, in the film's

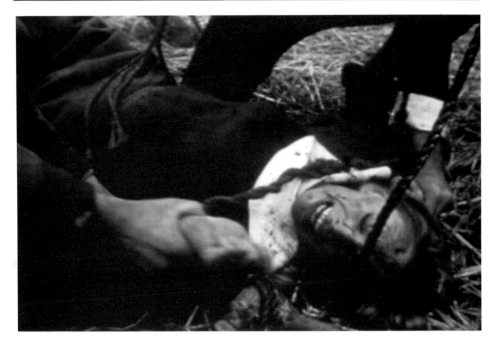

most energetic performance (the extraordinary Hilary Dwyer isn't far behind), setting about Hopkins with an axe – this is what the film has done to "Vincent Price".

Where Reeves' film scores over **Mark Of The Devil**, or any of the later Witchfinder films, is in its foregrounding and treatment of misogyny. Armstrong's film falls back on one of the most frequent representations of the sadistic torturer as sexually "dysfunctional" – it's a popular image of the Nazi, for example, to be either impotent or latently homosexual. In fact, this idea informs the characterisation of Hopkins in Ronald Bassett's novel.

Hopkins' pathology, in Reeves' film, is closer to the view of women Klaus Theweleit found in the fantasies of the German Freikorps, the proto-Nazi private army which set out to "clean up" Germany after the First World War. The Freikorps exhibited a recurring dread of a terrifying, unstoppable flood – "floods of papers, political, literary, intellectual currents, influences".

Given that this identity-threatening torrent was "threatening, but attractive", one of its most frequent manifestations was the female body – "the man holds himself together as an entity, a body with fixed boundaries. Contact with erotic women would make him cease to exist in that form." Hence the violence the Freikorps committed against those women who did not conform to the idealised image of the mother or the sister – the whore, the "Red" woman, the castrating revolutionary. Exterminating them – as Hopkins wants to remove "the foul iniquities of womankind" – was one way of damming up that flood. Hopkins and Stearne function like a private army, imposing some sense of masculine order, some sense of certainty, on the political, religious and social turmoil through this ritualised violence. Hopkins' one display of emotion – those terrifying, ego-threatening tears – is linked to his compromising feelings for Sara. But once she is no longer "pure", those feelings can and must be blocked – the needles inflicted on her during the final scene will open her up, reveal the formless, "bloody mass" underlying this conception of the female body.

But, of course, it's Hopkins whose body is dissolved into a bloody mass, on the point that, as for Christian in **Mark Of The Devil**, this symbolic power begins to fall apart. Richard, on the other hand, equally obsessive, equally prepared to sacrifice Sara in the maintaining of his own masculine identity (Honour, Revenge), submits to a "flood" of his own and the narrative gives way to hysteria. Hutchings sees Sara's endless scream as a "reinstatement of certainty in gender definition" after a "violence which seeks to preserve a certain masculine stability and power." The success, or otherwise, of this displacement can perhaps be gauged by the way that the film's most famous line links the male body both to the needs of another man and to a sense of loss – "You took him away from me," indeed.

LAST TANGO IN PARIS

Circles Of Sex And Death

Adèle Olivia Gladwell

For this investigation – which intends to explore the use of sex and death within the film **Last Tango In Paris** – I wish to go back to Freud and Jung, for their definitions of the social behaviour, instinct and psychology concerning sex and death. The assimilation of these two experiences and what symbolically, philosophically and psychologically they can mean when used in the context of **Last Tango In Paris**. Moreover I wish to move on from these ideas to those writers and theorists who believe in a wide range of consciousness and sensibility, which incorporates myriad human phenomena, as a reality. How the structure of individual narrative can be contextualized and/or at odds with mass social structure.

Bernardo Bertolucci wrote and directed **Last Tango In Paris** in 1972. Marlon Brando and the then unknown Maria Schneider were the leading actors in a film which caused outrage and was indeed banned in several places on its release. Bertolucci was, by all accounts, suffering from mental and emotional instability at the time of the film's production. The film was slated for its pretentiousness and acclaimed for being notable for its infamy. But few critiques or reviews delved into the psychology of the assimilation of sex and death. In my opinion **Last Tango In Paris** is one of the most profound portrayals of sex/death assimilation in film history. Its structure is a perfect vehicle; a veritable metaphor of personal life narrative in itself, and its motifs and symbols subtly obsessive. Its language is multi-faceted, operating on a linear dialogue level – Brando (Paul) and Schneider (Jeanne) participate in seemingly innocuous lovers' verbal sparring – but also on a darkly minatory and psychologically meaningful level (where their conversations communicate their true and sub/unconscious or anti-social self natures).

To fully understand this assimilation of sex/death one must look back to not only Freud and Jung (who did much to investigate the sensibilities and perspectives that pleasure and also pain depend on) but to two writers in particular prior to this psychological era. Both the Marquis de Sade and Leopold von Sacher-Masoch (from whom of course we derive sadism and masochism respectively) are in effect the forerunners to understanding what makes us view sex/death as such an apposite or inappropriate, fascinating or frightening proposition.

That desire is dependent on perspective and/or mediation – is an initial concept to the notion of extremes and ideals of human experience being seen in a similar light. Birth, sex (most importantly orgasm or *petit mort*) and death. Three phenomena that few would disagree are the three most extreme experiences known to humankind. They are interwoven. Three experiences so extreme we lose control of the ego, we touch archetypal elements. And that the aim of all life is death, is undeniable. Of course some may argue that from death comes life also. Sade and Masoch were very aware of the fact that unrestrained sexual activity of an obscene or anti-social nature was in fact a pertaining to the death instinct within us. Whether one was embracing, as a lover, the inevitability of the consummation with death, or warding it off by projecting death onto someone else (i.e. masochism and sadism). It is towards death that sexual activity tends; towards and

beyond is what we strive for. Here the life instinct meets the death instinct to battle or co-exist. And so often the instinct for death can be wholly erotic. The most dangerous, enticing and exciting love affair. A yearning for the ultimate copulation – where everything that holds, bonds and drags us down to society is lost – as it partially is with orgasm. Open to pleasure and death. A horror which excites and repulses desire. The one lover who knows no half measures. The gasp of climax; the gasp of death. And then the void. Or the heaven. The personal metaphysical space. A need to return to an inorganic state or a new narrative.

The film depicts events over a very short space of time. Literally a few days. At the beginning of the film, in the opening scene, we see Brando's character Paul, an American expatriate, standing on the pavement under a bridge. He covers his ears and screams a violent blasphemy against the cacophonous din of the overhead trains. We can clearly see from the tears on his face and his agonized expression that he is in great emotional pain.

A young Parisian girl passes by him, giving him a curious glance as she continues on her way. This is our first sighting of the characters. They both go to view an empty apartment. In a quietly menacing scenario Brando questions the young woman on whether or not she wishes to rent the flat. He has in fact decided and expressed the decision to take on the flat himself. The question he puts to her is significantly deeper than its surface intention. He is asking whether or not she wants him. She has but a split second in which to make a decision. The pre-text to this point is somehow full of innuendo and expectancy and it is almost a foregone conclusion that they will suddenly indulge in sexual intercourse. This "un-premeditated" coupling is quite unleashed and extremely passionate. The structure of this scene, with its tension-filled build-up and its air of menace or of danger in an erotic fashion, is heightened by the anonymity of the characters, as well as Brando's enigmatic, unsettling quality. This scene sets the precept for the entire film. We know that we have jumped several social stages and are directly involved with a relationship that has little to do with everyday social restraints. Already we are involved with a sexual relationship that has to and will stretch both characters to their utmost. We realize that the contractual obligation of sexual relationships in some way (if not conventionally) has to be played out – maybe broken or fulfilled. Within this relationship they will encounter all facets of their self and their collective unconscious or "dark" side. They will both encounter, in one way or another, their life and death instincts.

Within this essay I shall consider sex, orgasm and death as O's. The O of orgasm; of orifices and of pursed lips. O as in gender other. The O as the opposite of the social self; the collective unconscious; the alter-ego. O as an entirety of sensibility or emotion; ideal or god. The complete infinite shape; the eternal matrix; the chaos beyond conscious understanding. Existentialism, nature and nurture. The social ego and the unconscious. Reality and dream. When we view these experiences so – it is easier then to consider them as equatable within this film.

Death as the final punctuation of the individual text: a concept inspired by the French philosopher and theorist Jacques Lacan.

We begin **Last Tango In Paris** with, we later learn, a death. The suicide of Brando's wife Rose. She is a woman who is always unknown to us. We learn of her through the other characters. She is, in effect, the key to the film, but she is cryptographic. In the same way she apparently confused those who knew her during her lifetime (not in the present mode of the film), she is unknown and beyond us, as viewer.

Brando, as he stands, wrenched by pain, under the bridge at the inception of the film's narrative, is grieving for his dead wife. So the previous narrative ending in Rose's demise is the beginning of the narrative of Paul and Jeanne. Born of death. Indeed we get the feeling this film/event should never have gone on from there; existing as it does in the wake of such a significant death. Especially in the context of Brando's character, who is "existing" in his wife's death. He exists within a death context. We then ask ourselves what is it that Paul is aiming to do with, and for, himself in the film. Is he hoping to surpass death, to reconcile himself with it or possess death; or to stave off his own death instinct?

It's worth remembering that Brando came to this film already an established star, in comparison to the unknown Maria Schneider. He later claimed his role was one of the most unnerving, draining and frightening he had ever played. He said, "...it felt like my children were wrenched from me..."

In fact the role became not just Paul, but very much Marlon Brando. The two psyches interchangeable. Brando is constantly addressing his own persona within the character role and it is worth taking into account Brando's personality and legendary sex appeal – for this adds to the film's content.

In some ways there is a very clear structure to the film. If we consider concepts of structuralism it appears to be a sentence terminating with a full stop. But, if we consider more carefully the context of the film – starting with death (Rose's) and culminating with Brando in a foetal position – we see it's a crucial symbol in the film's imagery and also a reversal of structure. Or maybe a post-structure to the first structure of which we only know the end.

Paul's wife, as stated before, is for me a mysterious key or "macguffin" in the film. We can assume reasonably that she and Brando together are part of the other narrative. We can only guess her part in it. She gives birth to a question mark – which leaves all preceding texts/scenes very hard to imagine. We can ask if hers was another language or a differing narrative – but we cannot be certain. We, like Brando, can only guess as to why Rose is removed from this current sequence of events. But we cannot make judgements because Rose is not there. She is the catalyst of the ensuing action. The instigator of extremes like violent sex, death and abjection – in her wake. We do know that Rose had many lovers. And that she also had hotel residents who paid for her favours. She lied to her husband Paul and was adulterous. But how by her violent actions, adultery and lastly horrific suicide did she evoke a spiral effect to the point of the big O of death? Paul's death. Living death.

Was her death a "way-out" for her? Its effect is to trap Paul in a death context until death itself. Is it a resolution and a reprieve to which he wishes to journey?

In the middle of the film – after several encounters with Jeanne over a period of a day or two – Paul/Brando goes to see his dead wife, as she lies in her open casket in a death parlour surrounded by numerous flowers. The lighting, as almost always, is yellow. A strong and invading yellow resonant of gold (treasure), alchemy, the passing of time or insanity. This scene is one of the most important in the whole film, for me – it uncovers the crux of the situation. Up until this point we have little idea of the strength of Brando's ability to love. We know him as an enigmatic, sexual and menacing man – obsessed with his encounters with Schneider.

"I might be able to comprehend the universe – but I'll never be able to discover the truth about you," Brando says to his dead wife.

He laughs as he looks at her heavily made-up face – calling her a whore; remarking on the fact that her mother has really dressed her up.

"You're your mother's masterpiece."

Rose apparently never wore heavy make-up or lipstick. After contemplating the mystery of his wife he goes on to harangue her for lying to him. In the middle of a ranting dissertation of abuse, where he calls her foul and lowly names, he breaks down.

The abusive hollering turns to sobbing and imploring. He asks, begs her to lie to him. He no longer cares about her deceitful nature; he would be happy to receive a smile, and a lie. Suddenly it is just him and her. Half the enigma vanishes. He loses face; loses any sense of false pride or self-consciousness. He accuses her of leaving him to inherit himself. His double; a reference to Rose's lover who even received from her an identical bathrobe to the one she gave to Brando. As he sobs against his wife's corpse he cries that:

"I'd do the same thing too, if I could."

And then, before the scene is interrupted by a voice calling in the distance:

"I have to find a way."

He is, at this point in the film, at his most wretched. A man who no longer has much life left inside. And because of his verbal affirmation of his state he realizes that if he is going to die, in his mortality, he must be alive now. Not physically dead alongside Rose.

I think that from this point in the film we have few doubts about the destiny of the characters. Paul will and does die a secondary death. A death reliant upon the first death of Rose. The abject puzzle.

We can also probably guess that his "undoing" will be performed by Jeanne, and for various intertwining reasons. Jeanne is slowly revealed to us too. Both sides of her nature become exposed. Through a parallel narrative, wherein her fiancé Tom, a young filmmaker, in an exploratory fashion, films her childhood through physical and emotional reminiscences. We become aware of her past, her culture, her family and roots, as Tom delves further. We can therefore make guesses and judgements about her actions.

That both characters start off unknown to each other is integral to the feelings, during the film, of both parties. An unselfconscious, "free" sexual relationship where both can forget time and wallow in space, amputated from the excess baggage of past history,

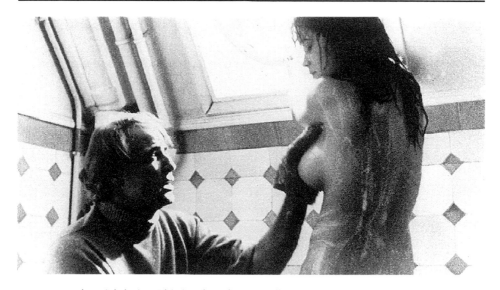

memory and social duties. This is what they initially have. This breeds an excitement and the freedom unleashes their true sexual natures and suppressed selves.

Jeanne starts off full of excitement and passion. Her fascination for Brando/Paul is oblique, fetishistic but quite overwhelming. She progresses/digresses to fear. Why? Does Paul (as some critics claim) brutalize her? Clearly he frightens her, but how? Certainly towards the film's demise it is obvious that it is what he is presenting that is so unsettling. And it is what she believes he is presenting or offering her. Hence, she is frightening herself. She is relating him to her own dark fantasies. She is projecting onto him, because he is so without identity. For me one of the most interesting questions arising from the film is: whether she kills him because through learning more of his identity he thus loses the "emptiness" she requires in order to project her fantasy or ideal onto him? Or whether, as she follows him deeper into her own dark fantasies and collective unconscious nature – she fears the force of that inside her? The side of her that houses her "shadow" (as Jung named the figure that is the opposite of ego), or animus (her male counterpart side), or ideal sexual partner born of unleashed passion. And if she feels repulsion towards him – is it because she suddenly sees him as "object" and mortal (realising the contractual obligations inherent in an adult sexual relationship), or because he is bred from within the side of her to which her conscious social self is opposed?

For me, it is not merely a case of Jeanne wanting to remove herself from a man and their illicit affair which repulses her, but to remove that integral part of herself.

At one point in the film Brando and Schneider enact a perverse parody of the "Little Red Riding Hood" fairytale. The young girl meeting the wolf. A young girl coming face to face with rampant bestiality. Her own, as yet, uncovered/unborn sexuality. In an earlier scene Schneider crawls in just like a cat and there is a great sense of her feline erotic nature.

Brando in the "Red Riding Hood" scene delivers a long monologue. He tells her about his past; his adolescence. He is so sincere, apparently so involved in his story, we believe him. It is a revelation: It was *he*, after all, who so adamantly insisted on anonymity.

Jeanne: "You've been 'ad. *I don't want to know anything about your past, baby.*"
Paul: "So you think I was telling you the truth?"
[He plays a few bars on his harmonica]
"Maybe."

We don't know if he genuinely slipped up and revealed something and then tried to cover up his mistake; or if he was lying all the time to prove a point.

She flutters her arms like a butterfly and throws the bedsheet over him. During the following dialogue he intermittently plays harmonica whilst she is speaking.

Jeanne: "I am a Red Riding 'ood and you is the wolf."
Paul: "Gggrrr!"
[She explores his body as he lies supine]
Jeanne: "What big arms you 'ave."
Paul: "All the better to squeeze the farts out of you"
Jeanne: "What long nails you 'ave."
Paul: "All the better to scratch your ass with."
Jeanne: "What a lot of fur you have."
Paul: "All the better to let your crabs hide in."
Jeanne: "Ohh, what a long tongue you 'ave."
[Holding onto his tongue with her fingers]
Paul: "The better to... stick in your rear, my dear."
Jeanne: "And this. What's this for?"
Paul: "That's your happiness and my... my ha-penis."
Jeanne: "Peanuts?"

[He lists a long collection of slang names for penis]

Perhaps the two scenes which best demonstrate this "dark" sexuality are the two anal sex scenes. Here both characters step beyond "normal" barriers towards extremes and social taboos; reconciling themselves with the very real corners of the collective unconscious, the suppressed areas of their psyches and their immorality.

As she enters the apartment he orders her to fetch the butter. As they sit on the floor she finds a secret cubby-hole in the floorboards. He makes an analogy between the secret hole and the opening of her trousers.

"Maybe there's gold."

Paul: "Are you afraid?"
Jeanne: "No."
Paul: "You're always afraid."
Jeanne: "No; but maybe there's family secrets."
          [In reference to the inside of the cubby-hole]
Paul: "Family secrets? I'll tell you about family secrets. I'm going to tell you about the family. That holy institution, meant to breed virtue into savages."

Then using the butter (a vivid golden colour) as a lubricant, he turns her over and anally penetrates her. All the time renouncing and denouncing:

"The holy institution ... holy family ... church of good citizens ... the children are tortured ... first lie ... repression ... freedom is assassinated ... you fucking family ... you ... fucking ... family ..."

He makes her repeat this dissertation after him until he climaxes.

Jeanne's admission of what he really represents to her comes in a slightly later scene. She tells him about her boyfriend Tom and how much "in love" they are. He derides her and says the best fucking she will ever find is right there in the apartment (with him). That's where all the mysteries are. Maria then falters and exclaims passionately that Tom doesn't frighten her. Again Paul sneers at her accusing her of wanting to build herself a fortress to hide in – so she won't ever have to be alone or afraid. But that she will always be alone and will never be free until she looks death in the face. Goes right up into the "ass of death" – the "womb of fear" – then maybe she'll be able to find him. (Him whom she dreams of; her animus; the part of herself she is projecting onto Paul.)

Jeanne screams back from her very guts:

"But I find this man. He's you. *You're that man.*"

He then requests that she cut all the nails from her right hand and put her fingers into his anus. Whilst she does this he describes various obscene things he would like her to do for him. Ecstatically, she agrees to all his fantasies; hugely and darkly excited she asks for more and more.

Symbolically within the film there are many threads which support and run parallel to each other. Of course there is the film itself which cuts to both Jeanne and Paul's previous relationships (with Rose and Tom) and the new subsequent relationship between them. This structure itself is indicative of a duality – a binary opposition between ego and alter-ego; social self and hidden dark self. Frequently throughout the film, mirrors play an integral part in the setting. We often see Paul or Jeanne's reflections as they speak to one another. We see reflections of the interior or inner self. Sometimes the use of

mirrors is such that there is a spatial feeling of looking far inside to the corners of the psyche. Or the unreality of the apparent self.

Paul's razor is quite an emphatic object. It is the very same one that Rose used to commit suicide. When Jeanne, rifling through his pockets, finds it – there is a terrible sense of foreboding and danger. Something terrible about him and his past. A feeling that whilst conventional safety (within the order of marriage and family) can be so unsafe – there is another, greater danger. A danger of the unknown. That of letting go and facing your fear and threat. He tells her that the razor could belong to a madman. There is one powerfully menacing shot as he sharpens the barber's razor on a belt. Due to the camera angle we see Jeanne's naked breasts in the foreground seeming horribly close to the swinging blade in the background. Again the atmosphere is electric with the force of their "other" selves. We see him within the context of murderer – the man with the razor that recently killed a woman – but also as a saviour. He who could save her from the charade and facade of social conventionality.

At this point in the film Jeanne claims, as she finds out a little about him, that this is a beginning. The start of a proper relationship is what she means. He answers that it is not a beginning – it is a finish. At the end of the film he says the opposite. When she tells him that it is over – he asserts that it is just starting. It has gone full circle, in effect. They dance the Last Tango with Paul's pants around his kness, making a mockery of the ultimate erotic dance.

Paul's pursuit of Jeanne at the end of the film produces a feeling of claustrophobia and panic. He relentlessly chases her back to her mother's apartment. Here it is interesting to note that it is to the family home that she runs to for "safety". As he approaches her in a mocking and self-derisive manner (pointedly, wearing her father's army cap) he claims that he loves her and wants to know her name. The final straw. He knows that he is pushing her into an irrevocable situation. A conscious reality for Jeanne where before it had been fantasy or dream. As he stands so close in front of her, hiding the gun she is holding from us, as viewer (importantly her father's gun), she murmurs her name and shoots him. He walks slowly away, over to the balcony where he opens the doors and steps out.

"Our children ... our children ... will remember."

His last words. He looks up at the sky for a while and then dies curled up in a foetal position. A peaceful position. Emphatically it is the first symbol of birth or pre-life in the entire film. The symbol for the start of a fresh narrative or sentence structure to complement the full stop that initiated the film.

So, Jeanne kills her obverse of ego, life instinct and convention. Her dead man. The conclusionary scene demonstrates her death instinct projected out and onto Paul – to reaffirm her own life. And that this was Paul's wish, his concept of the love he claimed, is highly likely. Such did he breed in the darkness of her that her ego, repulsed, revolted against the threat he presented.

Jeanne – repetitive monologue:
"I don't know who he is.
 I don't know his name.
 He followed me in the street.
 He tried to rape me.
 He's a madman.
 I don't know who he is.
 I don't know his name.
 I don't .....
 ......"

The End

TORTURED LOOKS

Dario Argento And Visual Displeasure

Ray Guins

INTRODUCTION

Whether crawling along a floor or tracking up the sides of a building, Dario Argento's sinister and ever restless camera draws fervent devotees. To accompany his wandering eye, Argento also provides rich, idyllic scenes in which to view. Well known motifs include: the ever famous black leather gloves, resplendent red hues of blood, glistening knife blades, masked killers, eerie aggressive soundtracks, tortured eyes, and of course murder. His quarter century of film directing partly locates itself neatly into a horror "sub-genre" known as the *giallo*. This term, first made famous by Italian director Mario Bava, literally means "yellow" and stems from Italian crime books which were traditionally bound in yellow covers. Whereas traditional horror and mystery films emphasise a struggling yet surviving protagonist who overcomes tragedies or solves the horrific conundrum, the *giallo* places equal (if not more) importance on the actual method of killing as well as solving the crime. Argento has however, imbued the *giallo* with a distinctive aura all his own.

His characters usually suffer from a repressed libido. They grow twisted and deranged, leading to total immersion into madness. Male characters are ill-suited to traditional notions of the phallocentric hero. That is, they lack the power and the authority commonly associated with men in horror films. Female characters also defy simple categorisation. Both genders partake in killing, both become victims. And in some cases, the murderer's gender is revealed during the closing minutes of the narrative. When a crime is dissolved, a sense of unsettlement lingers because Argento denies the sense of emotional release associated with horror films. Boundaries between good and evil are so unclearly demarcated that one is left to wonder which position has really been conquered while the films' protagonists are frequently left both mentally and physically scarred. Finally, by means of recurring motifs and a dynamic gaze, Argento's *giallo* builds intricate webs of subjectivity between the characters and spectators of his films.

I choose here to discuss **Profondo Rosso** and **Opera** in relation to psychoanalysis and feminist film theory because these two fascinating texts most clearly illustrate the relationship of subjectivity to "fetishisation" and the gaze. As briefly mentioned earlier, Argento uses his camera to a dynamic end. The use of point of view shots (I-camera) have virtually become a trade mark of "slasher" films that reached their peak during the mid-'80s. The I-camera is used in order to illustrate the killer's visual perspective. Argento takes this process to extreme measures by constantly switching the point of view between characters. In some cases the viewer is unsure who is doing the looking. And once a visual perspective is established the possessor of sight is punished for looking. Punishment is dealt by torturing the spectating eye of both characters in the film and audiences watching the film. Argento leaves the characters amongst a paradox of sight, both the characters and human spectators are forced to look while at the same time castigated.

FETISHISM

Whether female or male, killers in **Profondo Rosso** and **Opera** surround themselves with fetish objects. Freud (1977) states that the fetishised object acts as a substitute for the male "penis" which the castrated woman wishes to possess. Rather than adopt Freud's notion of penis=phallus, Lacan holds that the phallus is a symbolic structure. This Weedon (1987) describes as a Lacanian reworking of Freud ultimately ending in the phallus as the "signifier of sexual difference, which guarantees the patriarchal structure of the symbolic order" (Weedon 1987:53). Stam *et al* (1992) distinguish Freud and Lacan's positions by asserting that fetishism does not pertain to a real woman without a penis, but to a "structure in which symbolic relations, already constituted as meaningful, are put into play" (Stam *et al* 1992:149). Argento stresses the phallus by visually dwelling on fetishised objects. To illustrate, in **Opera** the camera investigates the killer's "tool box" and gently tracks the blade of a huge knife from the bottom to the top thus illustrating its enormity and power. **Profondo Rosso** shares a similar scene as the camera slowly tracks over marbles, bits of thread and toy dolls before stopping at a switchblade. The camera then proceeds to erotically inspect the switchblade, exploring along its slender shaft ending at the tip of the blade. Such emphasis on phallic signifiers highlights their purpose, i.e. to penetrate.

The traditional *giallo* demands that one observe the numerous murders, thus placing strict attention on acts of violence. I consider this a film fetishisation of murder (most prominent in **Opera**) which surpasses traditional notions of object fetishism of which Argento makes free and frequent use. In some cases Argento wants the spectator to witness the knife going in and out of the body or simply view the knife in the body. Creed (1986) comments that the action of stabbing a knife into a woman is to symbolise a sexual act. For example, during the scene at Carlo's primary school Carlo stabs Gianna with a switchblade. Marc finds Gianna resting upright against a wall complete with knife in stomach. The knife is left intact, so the viewer can see that she has been penetrated. However, Argento's knife is not gender specific. It penetrates both male and female bodies at the hands of both male and female killers. In other words, both men and women battle for control of the phallus.

A variety of readings have been forwarded to account for the phallic significance of murder. To cite an instance, Creed (1986:71) states that:

> "Woman's body is slashed and mutilated, not only to signify her own
> castrated state, but also the possibility of castration for the male. In the
> guise of a "madman" he enacts on her body the one act he fears most
> for himself, transforming her entire body into a bleeding wound."

If the victim is a woman, body mutilation is to signify her existing castrated state. Whereas if the victim were a man and the killer a woman, her actions are to be read as attempts to castrate the male by possessing the phallus and using it against her victim.

Creed (1993) argues that the fear men possess from castration has forced them to identify woman as the castrating agent. Due to Lacan's emphasis on the phallus as symbolic and not actual in the form of the penis, neither women nor men can obtain the phallus. The quest for phallus possession is an attempt to create the mythical unified whole that we lack. (Sarup, 1993).

In **Profondo Rosso** the young Carlo watches his mother stab his father. After the stabbing, the symbolic knife is left at the feet of Carlo, he then clutches the knife in his own hand. In a symbolic exchange of power, Marta uses the phallus signifier to free herself from the oppressive father figure. Then, the dying father gathers enough strength

Profondo Rosso

to pass the phallus in the form of the knife onto his son. Unsure how to respond, Carlo stares at the knife. Freud (1977) claims that the child witnessing his parents engaging in coitus develops a sadistic view of sex in which a power relation exists where the stronger partner forcefully penetrates the weaker. Carlo's primal trauma could then be considered the murderous act which carries a more literal and lethal version of parental sexual signification.

One learns that Carlo chooses men as his preferred sexual partners. During Marc's discovery of this fact, Carlo taunts; "Now you know I'm a faggot" (U.S. version) and "Now you know that I have perverse sexual practices" (Italian version). Carlo's lifestyle causes a conflict within himself. According to Lacan, Carlo sees himself in his father as other, hence identifying with his father's castrated state. Marta destroys the symbolic reserved for the father and through murdering other people attempts to possess the phallus. Carlo now has his mother entirely to himself, but rejects her out of fear of castration choosing to remain among men.

Two additional motifs used to connote Carlo's childhood experience while recreating Marta's murderous experience are toy baby dolls and the eerie nursery rhyme. Both act as signifiers for the killer and their murders. Before Amanda Righetti is scalded she finds a toy baby doll hanging from a noose in her house. In **Profondo Rosso**, Marta uses a mechanical doll marking the threat of death to Professor Giordani. He is further symbolically castrated by having his teeth bashed out on a marble mantle. Silverman (1983) forwards Lacan's notion that a child's play toys are used as an object to suffice

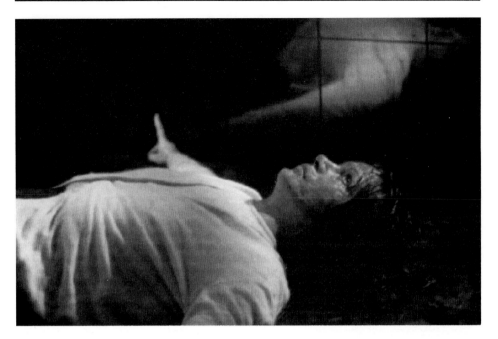

Profondo Rosso

their missing component. The killer's use of the dolls confuses matters, because under ordinary circumstances, the toys would be equated with Carlo, but Marta uses them to mark death. Dolls might be viewed as a form of confession by Marta for the murdering of Carlo's father. In discussing fetishism, Freud (1977) states that a fetish object is adopted due to the overwhelming horror of seeing the absence of the penis from the woman. Objects that come to be fetishised act as a substitute for one's lack. Creed (1993) goes on to state that the object in question does not necessarily have to be a "penis-symbol". The object in question is appropriated as the last object in the child's visible field before he views the woman's genitals. A baby doll was present during the murder Carlo was witness to. Marta has stolen fetish objects from Carlo and uses toys and music to recreate the original murder scene. Recreating the murder scene allows Marta to unleash the madness she represses. The music might serve as an example of Freudian displacement. Marta actually plays the song before killing. This process provides the film with a nostalgic feel because the music continually acts as mnemic traces foreshadowing the revelation of a horrible childhood.

THE GAZE, VISION AND SPECTATOR
The camera itself possesses a phallic quality. Balun (1991) reveals that the serpent-like movement of Argento's camera takes the viewer through winding tunnels, up twisting staircases, into dark damp passageways, penetrates mutilated bodies, and allows the spectator a killer/killed point of view. Forceful activity on the part of Argento's camera demands attention on the part of the spectator. Such a camera coupled with Argento's directorial intention is masculine and sadistic. The camera is powerful. It serves as

Opera

authority over the spectator's experience. We are nearly as subject to Argento's wilful camera as Betty to Santini's sadism. Under this analysis, Creed (1993) would be correct in noting that horror films which promote identification foster a masochistic form of looking. Because Argento draws the viewer into his film and once in, punishes them for watching. The spectating subject as associated with the cinematic apparatus witnesses the killer's deeds while his or her field of vision is infiltrated to construct and maintain the masculine gaze.

Connecting the spectating subject's process of identification to the actual act of looking is what Metz (1975) refers to as primary cinematic identification. Viewer perception is directed by camera movements. Point of view shots allow spectators to witness (first hand) the killer's actions. Usually as Stam *et al* (1992) illustrates, the point of view shot creates an empty space thus allowing the cine-spectator to occupy as otherness. Argento exceeds this type of identification by taking spectators into the killer's psyche. By showing their pulsating brain, one visually experiences the killer's adrenalin rush. The camera itself builds upon this experience by mimicking the pulsating motion of a throbbing brain.

Betty and Carlo are victims of visual childhood trauma. However, other characters in **Profondo Rosso** and **Opera** suffer the consequences of a curious eye. Most notably, Mira (Betty's stand-in mother figure), who is shot point blank as she peers into a peephole to catch a glimpse of the killer. The spectator actually views the bullet (slow motion close-up) fired from a gun, pass through the peephole and blast through Mira's eye socket only to exit out the back of her head. The killer punishes those who attempt to capture him/her in the gaze. The killer attempts to free him or herself from surveillance by going

Un Chien Andalou

to its source – the vulnerable eye.

The destruction of eyes in the film is not distinct to Argento. Other Italian horror directors such as Lucio Fulci use the delicate organ as a "money shot" in their films.

One of the greatest eye mutilation scenes ever to appear in film, would no doubt have to be Buñuel's **Un Chien Andalou** (1928). Williams (1994) argues that what makes the slicing of the eye appear gruesome and horrific is that the camera allows the spectator to actually watch the event in its entirety without editing right before the tragic moment. The eye itself is the ideal organ for destruction. Williams (1994) reminds us that the organ itself is grotesquely vulnerable and highly sensitive. In these respects, the eye is very similar to the penis. Both are exposed organs, very sensitive. If looking being fostered in Argento films is masculine, then hurting the eye could be equated with castration. The eye itself houses characteristics such as tears, protein deposits, and discharge that lend themselves to elements of disgust that are also common in horror films, namely associated with a monster. Presenting his theory of horror, Carroll (1990) holds that in order for a film to be considered a member of the horror genre it must possess the element of disgust. Eyes by their nature are already regarded as horrific, to actually witness the organ's destruction generates further fright and commentary on spectatorship.

It has already been established that eyes play an important role in Argento films. What remains to be explored is whether what they see generates the attention they suffer. One aspect of sight is Argento's use of his camera. McDonagh (1991:8) describes:

> Unrestrained by strictly narrative concerns, the camera reflects no point of view save its own as it creeps across the facade of a sharply angled building for a startling two and a half minutes or hovers over two girls in a baroque swimming pool (**Suspiria** 1977), their pale legs floating like seaweed beneath the water's rippling surface.

Opera

What distinguishes Argento from other directors is that his camera continues to film where others stop. In regards to point of view, I have to disagree with McDonagh, the camera does indeed reflect various points of view – only for a limited amount of time in relation to characters. For example, the point of view is shared between killer and victim. But the point of view is also adopted by others not immediately engaged in struggle such as: ravens, other characters and unknown voyeurs. This allows the spectator access to various perspectives of cinematic identification.

Argento's own privileged position as a director, is his personal vehicle of representing his own desires. For example, he characterises his "look" by constituting Betty as an object of the desiring gaze. Betty is looked at from a voyeuristic (perverse) perspective by Santini, the camera, and the spectator. Whereas her way of seeing is more scopophilic i.e. intended to be pleasurable. My support for claiming that Argento's camera maintains the phallocentric gaze comes from Argento himself. He is known for his infamous statement, "I like women, especially beautiful ones. If they have a good face and figure, I would much prefer to watch them being murdered than an ugly girl or man". (Clover 1987:111). What stands out in Argento's statement is the word "watch". His ocular obsession with "watching" beautiful women is shown to the spectator so that we can "enjoy" and accept his sadistic, voyeuristic pleasures as our own. The act of looking is strongest in **Opera**. The film is strongly absorbed with seeing and what is seen (Martin, 1991). The character of Betty is physically attractive. Her appearance is what the killer comes to fetishise as a signifier of his lack. In two scenes Betty is abducted, bound, gagged and forced to watch Santini murder his friends. Santini himself is also a deranged pawn of vision. He also was forced to succumb to the gaze of his lover, who happened to be Betty's mother. She would seduce Santini into killing other women while she

Opera

watched. Her appetite for sadism grew and becoming more and more selfish, she wouldn't allow Santini to touch her. He eventually kills Betty's mother. Santini constructs Betty's role as Lady Macbeth (Betty's mother was also an opera singer) as his lost other that has returned for him to win back. He hopes that by forcing Betty to watch, she will come to adopt the desires of her mother.

In the area of ideology, Argento's camera is very much masculine hence maintaining the male sexual gaze that Mulvey (1975) describes in her article "Visual Pleasure In Narrative Cinema". The gaze incorporates both men and women by showing the spectating subject how women are to be looked at. The masculine gaze attempts to legitimise itself by constituting its vision as the desire of the human spectator. Thus as Kaplan (1983) explains the gaze forces the spectator to identify with men while placing women in opposition. A particular scene of **Opera**, specifically focuses on Betty as both watcher and watched. The subject of violence is unclear. Betty's eyes are forced open by notorious needles, forcing her to watch the killer's deeds. The point of view and reverse shot used in this scene supports Mulvey's claim that spectatorship is from an active male perspective that watches a passive – in this case bound, tortured and displayed – female. Betty is purely meant to be watched, the fact is enforced by Santini placing her in the display case. The spectator watches Betty and watches Betty watch Santini. Mulvey also states that the three looks – "the camera, the characters, and the spectator produce a specific, eroticised image of the woman, naturalising the 'masculine' position of the

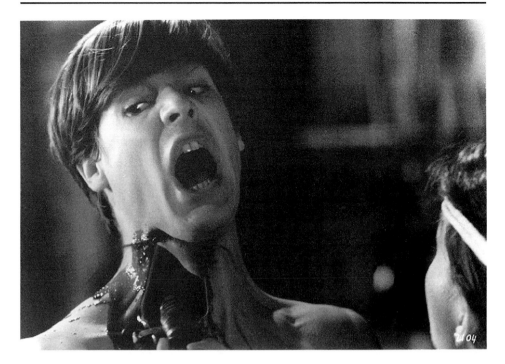

Opera

spectator and the pleasures that entails" (Stam *et al* 1992:175). Betty's point of view is distorted by the needles taped to her lower lids. This is the very perspective that Argento allows the spectator. We watch Betty as she at the moment would be watching us. Argento also uses these scenes as playful commentary on those fans who watch horror films through covered eyes. He professes to hate when people turn their heads or cover their eyes during the gory scenes of his films. Williams (1994) comments on this scene:

> Her eyes bleed a little, the real violence comes from the fact that she cannot close them. Who is the focus of the violence is not clear, others are being killed, but Betty's violation is primary – she is made to watch, on penalty of losing her eyes themselves, which is worse then the deaths taking place before her.
>
> (Williams 1994:16).

This scene's creepy content ranks among the most brutal and powerful shots in the film. Although Stephen's death was malicious and bloody, it was fast-paced. Stephen was in a sense an easy victim. He offers little resistance. The slaying of Julia takes on a new dimension. She puts up a fight and when she is eventually defeated – after subjecting the killer's face to her gaze – her death still manages to cause Santini aggravation. She swallows the bracelet. Santini has to slowly and with detail cut open her throat to retrieve it as her lifeless eyes stare aimlessly. Incidentally, Betty remains tied and tortured during the entire scene. Creed (1993) believes that scenes which appear horrific unsettle the "unified self" of the viewer. The spectator may break identification and sight by turning away or covering their eyes. Betty isn't so fortunate.

SUBJECTIVITY: CHARACTER IDENTITY – ROLE OF ILLUSION AND MIRROR STAGE

Betty's pain and agony stem from having to watch. Marc's dilemma is having to remember the vital clue that he saw the night of Helga's murder. Marc searching for the eerie illusion of his subconscious reveals itself to be a reflection in a mirror. McDonagh (1991) describes the scene in Helga's apartment:

> The hallway of Helga Ulman's apartment is lined with small, mostly round canvasses: they depict a veritable sea of Munchian faces, pale, ghastly, and anguished. In a niche is a mirror in a frame, and in this mirror Marc sees Marta's chalky face, surrounded by reflections of the painted faces hers so resembles.
> (McDonagh 1991:118)

When the police arrived at Helga's apartment, he was certain that the police had moved one of the paintings. Marc begins to investigate the crime believing the lost clue to be a painting, that somehow will reveal the missing clue. In an ironic way, Marc is partially correct. A child's drawing does reveal Carlo, who is covering up for his mother. Only when Marc returns to Helga's apartment and stands in Marta's position, does he identify with her reflection.

The mirror stage in Lacanian psychoanalysis marks the point when the child attempts to identify with its reflection in the mirror (Weedon 1992). Laplanche and Pontalis (1973) define the mirror stage: "the infant perceives in the image its counterpart or in its own mirror image – a form (Gestalt) in which it anticipates a bodily unity which it still objectively lacks" (Laplanche & Pontalis 1973:251). Observing itself in the mirror or another person (the mother's face) the child recognises objects that are different than he or she. This acknowledgment lends itself for identifying one as a self. Thus the child comes to recognise itself from another. The process of identifying with the ideal image is the child's first attempt to supplying meaning to its lack (Grosz 1990). The use of mirrors in **Profondo Rosso** coincides with the Lacanian theory of identity.

Black (1993) argues that the use of mirrors in **Profondo Rosso** is to emphasise the criticalness of illusion. Entering Helga's apartment in an attempt to remember. Marc spies the mirror which he didn't realise was there. Marc stands in the position that Marta stood in on the night of the murder. The spectator sees Marc's reflection placed in the same painting as was Marta's ghostly reflection. Marc stares at his reflection identifying with the image, he sees himself cast as the murderer. Marc sees himself in the murderous other. After Marta attacks and is decapitated, the film ends with Marc staring into a pool of blood. The viewer is left watching Marc's reflection in the crimson pool. Carlo once occupied this position. He however, gazed into his father's blood, Marc stares into his mother's. Marta may in fact be dead, but Marc's reflection leads us to ponder if the event has turned him into a madman. Has Marc chosen his identity by assimilating the image of the other as his own? The reflective pool and Marc's narcissistic gaze may very well transform the image of otherness into a reflection of what Marc has now accepted as the self.

The mirror image draws parallels between Marta, Marc, and Carlo. Marc and

Profondo Rosso

Carlo have an emotional relationship. Both men suffer from an uncertain and "unbalanced" sexuality. Carlo's lifestyle causes him disgust and despair in the eyes of his other. Marc who also seems to be sexually repressed views sex and for the most part, women, as dominating. McDonagh (1991) states that both Marc and Carlo are reduced to helpless impotent characters. Carlo is constantly drunk, falling down. He seeks help and direction from Marc. Marc appears to express genuine fatherly concern for Carlo and enjoys his company. The character Gianni proves to be Marc's sexual other. She is forceful, up front and a very sexual character. Marc being ineffectual is completely dominated by Gianni. She controls and intimidates him. During their second meeting, Gianni tells Marc that at the present time she doesn't have a boyfriend. Marc doesn't express interest, nevertheless, she selects him as her lover.

Argento purposely illustrates their unbalanced power relation. She beats him at arm wrestling in an answer to Marc's comment that women are physically weaker. Gianni saves Marc from the burning house. Marc is further humiliated by the fact that Gianni always drives and her passenger seat is positioned lower so that Marc can barely see over the dash board. The women in Marc's world, one a murderer and the other "sex crazed", act as constant reminders of Marc's symbolic castration. One being the castrator and the other a reminder of the women's castrated state.

Betty also suffers a similar fate. During a "needle" scene, Santini holds a mirror up to her field of vision, so that she can view her tortured state. At this stage in the film Betty is horrified and disgusted at her appearance. She resists by trying to look up. Betty is refusing to adopt the mirror image as her identity. At the end of the film, Betty freely stops and watches Santini repeatedly stab Marco. Betty could have continued to run while Santini was preoccupied with Marco, instead she elected to remain and once again watches Santini's gruesome performance. After Santini finishes, Betty acts as if this sight has awakened a secret sadistic part of her that makes her just like her mother (she plays the role in order to escape from Santini). The text never reveals Betty's self-proclaimed reasons for describing herself as "frigid" or a "disaster in bed". Before the murders begin she seems quite content in her position. After being subjected to the brutality and throughout the rest of the film, she naturally warms to Marco – a known sadist. Marco expresses his sadism by directing horror films.

Her changing attitude seems to lead the viewer to believe that Betty is more like her mother than she realises. The case is further complicated by the fact that Argento decided to release the film with two different endings. In one ending, once Santini is apprehended, in an almost too convincing and highly exaggerated performance, Betty assures the spectator that she loves life, and proceeds to free a trapped lizard. She claims the world is hers to love. The other version ends when Santini is restrained by Interpol. The dual endings, one with Betty heading towards insanity and the other allowing her to maintain her faculties allows the spectator to draw his own conclusions. Whether or not she desires the lust crimes of her mother is uncertain.

CONCLUSION

In reflection, the end result is a corpus of film texts simultaneously exploring and creating the relationship of spectatorship to film subjectivity. Argento's film technique, especially his camera, extend to the spectator perspectives frequently ignored by other directors. His sadistic gaze operates to position the spectator within the madness. Numerous uses of point of view shots and emphasis on mirror images allows the spectator not only the opportunity to witness brutality, but to actually lose and define themselves while adopting a role. Thus identifying with the scopic division of watcher and watched as well as violator and victim. These films consequently inhabit a special niche in the history of film along with such precedents as Hitchcock's **Vertigo**, which allows the spectator to experience vertigo. However, this identification privilege reserved for Hitchcock's protagonists is also extended to Argento's villains. We experience the dark and evil aspects of film subjectivity as poignantly and directly as the good, that is, when Argento bothers to differentiate the two. Spectators are juggled back and forth, uneasily "resting" at the film's conclusion. Stunningly executed murders are now open to cinematic spectators via access to visual facilities and the anonymity of the black gloves which wield the flashing blades. The overvaluation of eyes, knives and various other objects including the female body, fetishises the way spectatorship is constructed as part of the cinematic apparatus. In effect, these films serve as a kind of twisted presentation of relationships between what we are shown and what the discourse of the film tells us we see.

BIBLIOGRAPHY
Balun, C. (1991), "Dario Argento: Face To Face", *Deep Red*, Special Edition, Number 7.
Black, A. (1993), "Deep Red", *Necronomicon*, 3, p15–21.
Carroll, N. (1990), *The Philosophy Of Horror*, Routledge, New York and London.
Clover, C. J. (1987), "Her Body, Himself: Gender In The Slasher Film", *Representations*, p20, (Fall).
Creed, B. (1986), "Horror And The Monstrous Feminine – An Imaginary Abjection", *Screen*, 27(1):44–72 (January–February); (1993), *The Monstrous Feminine*, Routledge, London and New York.
Freud, S. (1977), *On Sexuality: Three Essays On The Theory Of Sexuality And Other Works*, Penguin, Harmondsworth.
Grosz, E. (1990), *Jacques Lacan: A Feminist Introduction*, Routledge, London and New York.
Kaplan, A. (1983) *Women And Film: Both Sides Of The Camera*, Methuen, London.

Laplanche, J. and Pontalis, J–B. (1973), *The Language Of Psychoanalysis*, W.W. Norton, New York.

Martin, J. (1991), "Dario Argento: A Deep Red Opera", *Fantasy Film Memory*, Gothic, Paris.

McDonagh, M. (1991), *Broken Mirrors/Broken Minds: The Dark Dreams Of Dario Argento*, Sun Tavern Fields, London.

Metz, C. (1975), "The Imaginary Signifier", *Screen* 16(2):14–76 (Summer).

Mulvey, L. (1975), "Visual Pleasure And Narrative Cinema", *Screen* 16(3):6–18 (Autumn). Sarup, M. (1993) *An Introductory Guide To Post-Structuralism And Post-Modernism*, University of Georgia Press, Athens.

Silverman, K. (1983), *The Subject Of Semiotics*, Oxford Press, New York.

Stam, R., Burgoyne, R. and Flitterman-Lewis, S. (1992), *New Vocabularies In Film Semiotics*, Routledge, London and New York.

Weedon, C. (1987), *Feminist Practice And Post-Structuralist Theory*, Blackwell, Oxford.

Williams, L. R. (1994), "An Eye For An Eye", *Sight & Sound* 4(4):14–16 (April).

HERSCHELL GORDON LEWIS

Compulsive Tales And Cannibal Feasts

Mikita Brottman

*Herschell Gordon Lewis's **Blood Feast** provides the definitive source, some would argue, for the narrative of the contemporary slasher film. Has the time possibly come for a re-assessment of the Wizard of Gore?*

Often given the dubious credit of being the founder of the exploitation film, the inspired and inspiring Dr. Herschell Gordon Lewis, "The Wizard of Gore", has currently been relegated to the nethermost ranks of drive-in, B-movie, and schlock directors. Whilst it may be true that Lewis's later films, like his hillbilly movies such as **Moonshine Mountain** or his 1972 strip-joint movie **The Gore-Gore Girls**, might be lacking the fiendish inventiveness of **The Gruesome Twosome** (1967) or the infamous **Blood Feast** (1963), there is something in Lewis's best films that demands a re-evaluation of this much maligned and oft ridiculed mogul of the drive-in shocker.

Not many people know that Lewis originally began his career as a professor. With a PhD in English Literature, he soon realised that academe was neither creative nor profitable enough for one with his colourful and ambitious imagination, and alongside the now-infamous porn director David F. Friedman, he entered the world of B-movie, drive-in nudie cuties, eventually hitting the target with a rip-off of Russ Meyer's **The Immoral Mr. Teas**, entitled **The Adventures Of Lucky Pierre** (made in 1961, in just 4 days, with Lewis as director and cameraman and Friedman as producer and soundman). The commercial success of **Lucky Pierre** prompted a follow-up, **Boin-n-g!** (1963), a film about the making of a softcore B-movie, with two actors portraying Lewis and Friedman. Whilst most of Lewis's gore films were commercially successful and many of them, especially **Two Thousand Maniacs** (1964) and **Colour Me Blood Red** (1965) have subsequently become cult classics, it is his cheap and nasty saga **Blood Feast** (1963) for which Lewis is now best remembered, when he is remembered at all.

Blood Feast is the story of a lame Egyptian caterer, Fuad Ramses, who stalks and slays a selection of nubile young girls for their body parts, all in the service of the Egyptian goddess Ishtar. His fiendish masterplan goes awry when he decides to re-stage the cannibal feast of Ishtar at the home of his final victim-to-be, Suzette Fremont, whose fiancé is in the police force and hot on Fuad's tail. After a frenzied chase (during which Ramses, played by Mal Arnold, forgets which leg he's supposed to be limping on), he's rounded up by the police, captured, and crushed to death in the steel jaws of a garbage truck, "like the garbage he was".

Lewis was professionally frustrated with the way death was presented in the horror movies of the 1950's: the way characters were dying quietly and silently, with a smile on their face. There's none of this beating about the bush in **Blood Feast**. Ramses' first victim is knifed to death in the bath and her "Legs Cut Off!", as the next morning's headline vividly exclaims. The second victim, enjoying a secret liaison with her boyfriend in a motel, undergoes the removal of her meaty tongue (actually an ox's tongue smothered in cranberry jelly, so grotesquely enormous that one critic was prompted to suggest that it looked like it had come out of a giraffe). The third victim is slaughtered

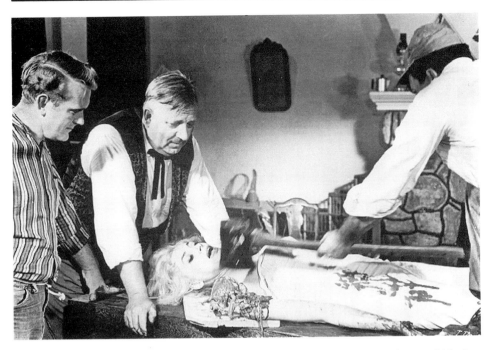

Two Thousand Maniacs

while courting on the beach and her heart pulled out, still beating (of course), and the first victim is followed, flayed alive and skinned. The final victim, Trudy Sanders, is kidnapped on her way home, tied up and whipped to death, her blood collected in a golden goblet to be used as a sacrifice to the goddess Ishtar.

Of course **Blood Feast** is hammy, of course it's a spoof, and of course it's all a pile of schlock. Lewis used the crew left over from a recently-finished nudie-cutie movie, and chose an Egyptian theme because he and Friedman just happened to be staying at the Suez motel in north Miami beach, which had as its gimmick, an enormous, garishly painted model of the Sphinx, flanked on either side by two ridiculous looking, life-size camels. Never one to ignore a free prop, Lewis gave his script – such as it was – an Egyptian flavour, and nine days later **Blood Feast** was ready for release. The actresses went home, the film reels were sent off to be developed – but two things were never the same again. The first was the sheets Lewis used in the tongue-pulling scene, which were indelibly stained with the Wizard's special blood solution, part-gelatin, part jam ("Axion in its original formula used to do the trick", complained Lewis, "but funnily enough they changed the formula so it wasn't so good"). The second thing that changed indelibly was the history of the slasher movie, which has never been the same again.

Carol J. Clover has argued in a footnote to her analysis of gender in the slasher film, *Men, Women And Chainsaws*, that **Blood Feast** is in fact the definitive source for the slasher movie. All the classic elements are there: the semi-motiveless, disfigured psychopath who stalks and slays a series of teenage girls, one by one, until he is overcome by the bravery of the "final girl", who survives him. The murders are always

Blood Feast

different in technique and always graphic, and they always occur during a moment of socially reprehensible behaviour (generally a courting scene). Finally, the killer is "explained" and "buried" by the representatives of justice and ethics (police, psychiatrist or parents), who are responsible for the re-establishment of the social order.

Lewis, normal-sized tongue firmly in cheek, described **Blood Feast** as "Aristotelian", and Aristotelean it certainly is. Limited, like most subsequent slasher movies, to the classical narrative unities of time, place and action, the film establishes a framework, pattern and structure to which all slasher movies have ever since, however unknowingly, adhered. As many writers on the horror film have testified, the continuous popularity of sequel after sequel within slasher cycles suggests that what the fans of such movies are looking for is not just a similar narrative, but the *same* story, told over and over again, without variation. Anthropologists have often drawn attention to the way in which a culture is compelled to repeat and re-live its most significant traumas and conflicts, again and again, through the repetition of representation – something which critic Barbara Creed refers to as "a descent into the foundations of the symbolic construct". Freud has much to say about the way we, as a culture, devote a great deal of time to re-telling the narratives of our unconscious lives. From the number of imitations it has spawned, and from the lasting nature of these imitations, **Blood Feast** seems to be one of these narratives. This backs up the suggestion that the reason for the multiplicity of slasher sequels relates to the fact that their victims are destined never to learn the lessons required of them: don't go into the cellar, don't look in the closet, don't go out after dark...

Lewis left the film industry after some embarrassing legal trouble concerning an illegal abortion referral agency, and now lives happily in a beautiful home in Fort Lauderdale, Florida, where he is a keen tennis player and well-liked member of the local country club. The days of ox tongues and cranberry jelly are far behind him, and very few of his friends and colleagues know him as the "Wizard of Gore". But it is for his wizardry that he will be remembered – for his magically fiendish weaving of a tale to be told and re-told, in virtually the same form, again and again: a gory stain on the sheets of cinema history that no updated formula can ever remove.

THE BRIDE OF FRANKENSTEIN

Sexual Polarity And Subjugation

Carol Jenks

In the narrative of the classic horror film, the problem of the female body reaches its crisis as both the site of danger and desire (dangerous because of desire, mysterious, unknowable), and the threat of an intolerable eruption of carnality that would be uncontainable by the boundaries marked out by the male order. The narrative action can literally take place through or upon the female body – in **Dracula** (1930), the moment of death by impalement is not seen, but undergoes an extraordinary process of transference on to the spellbound figure of the heroine, the vampire's prospective bride, as ("saved") she awakens jerking and shuddering into life. By an exact reversal, in **Dracula's Daughter** (1935), the vampire's flesh (that of a woman and beyond that a lesbian woman), must be seen to be pierced, penetrated, as she is shot through the heart with a phallic arrow. In **Mad Love** (1935) Peter Lorre can only feel the passion of the title for a fetish object, a statue. When the real woman replaces it he attempts to strangle her with her own hair: this Pygmalion cannot endure Galatea coming to life. The veritable sign of life that she exhibits is a cut, a wound that reveals her as a woman – like all of them, she bleeds.

These are attempts to subdue or contain the female body, excessive merely because the horror film can push them to a degree of violence not equalled in any other genre. But **The Bride Of Frankenstein** has a different project – total erasure, gynocide. A mythic novel, written by a woman who equated two creative acts (those of writing and giving birth), about a man who, fleeing from repressed homosexuality on the one hand and the taboo of incest with the female on the other, creates life without recourse to the channel of the female body – this novel has been appropriated (myths being infinitely adaptable) as a gay male fantasy of a world without women, the "world of gods and monsters" dreamed of by Dr. Praetorious. With spiralling irony, the fantasy can only turn in on itself, condemned to reproduce (literally) the structures from which it tried to escape, exploding at last in auto-destruct.

The initial male/female structures of the film can be summed up by the word monsterism (Karloff's creature as the original product of the flight from woman becomes a symbol of this). The order is one of a polarity so extreme that the female body is profaned by male desire and that body's own desires are unfathomable, certainly not readable by the male. (What does a woman want?). The famous prologue possesses an exemplary clarity, although it has traditionally been regarded by critics of the horror movie as redundant if not actively embarrassing, presumably because of its outrageous high-camp quality. Mary is sewing pattern embroidery, an activity both a metonymic substitute for and a "feminised" version of the act of writing (Shelley, by contrast, really is seen writing), yet one that establishes her as the phallic (needle) woman who controls language and narrative. It also anticipates by inversion her manifestation within her own narrative as the Bride, whose neck is adorned with stitch-scars. She works herself into her own design, stitches herself into her own story – which is not her own story. It belongs not to Mary Shelley but to the gay man James Whale, directing the actress Elsa Lancaster, impersonating her, just as Byron's reminiscences of "her" *Frankenstein* are actually flash-

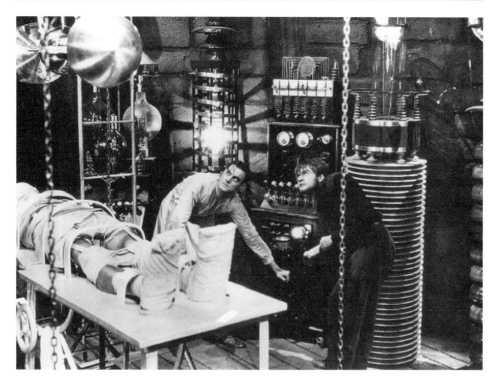

Frankenstein

backs to Whale's 1931 film version. This suggests both an acknowledgement of the way in which his own fantasy derived from and had become intertwined with Mary's original, and also, perhaps, a partial disavowal of that fantasy, which he may not have wished to face the full implications of, by still, in and through the film's fiction, "attributing" it to Mary.

Byron finds it strange that such an "angelic" creature ("Am I?" is the sardonic comment) should wish to write of horrors. Did he perhaps expect her to write "love stories", she demurs; looking directly at the two men she throws down her challenge – "with such an audience, why shouldn't I write of monsters?". (This is the repressed "frustration and wrath" Whale told Lancaster was the key to Mary's character). Byron goes to kiss her (needle) hand – deflection of threat – and she springs up, exclaiming "you pricked me": the violation of the male touch makes her bleed. She stands, in her trailing white dress which looks like a bridal gown, between Shelley and Byron, in a tableau which will be repeated exactly when she appears as the Bride between Frankenstein and Praetorious as they make ready to deliver her to her mate (a real monster), from whom she will recoil again, in an eternal return.

In an oppressively dark film, there are only four areas of shimmering silver/white: Mary/the Bride's clothes and Elizabeth's two negligées, chiffon and satin, worn in scenes with Frankenstein. This pearl-like glow points up one of the film's more peculiar undertones – the untouchable, "sacred" nature of the female body. Awe curdles into fear

and hatred. In this film, men and women are each other's monsters.

The final solution to the problem of woman is propounded by Dr. Praetorious, whose entry into the narrative is brilliantly contrived through sound. Elizabeth declares that she can "see" a figure in black (antithesis, of course, of her white) coming to endanger Frankenstein – she collapses into hysteria and her shrieks of laughter become mingled with and then overlaid by heavy knocking. The opposition between her and Praetorious ("a very queer-looking old gentleman") for the possession of Frankenstein, the entirely passive object of desire, is set up unequivocally. Admittedly, there seems to be no contest (Elizabeth's one attempt to oust Praetorious is when she has just secured Frankenstein by marriage) – Praetorious has no difficulty in inducing him to leave Elizabeth in the middle of the night, by a proposition that is, more or less, come and look at my etchings – the miniature people.

These were created by incubation in glass bottles "from seed", as he expresses it, i.e. semen – the realisation of his dreams of birth by male means alone, abolishing the need for women as agents in procreation. The miniaturised version of Henry VIII, true to his heterosexually lecherous nature, escapes Praetorious' vigilance for a moment, in order to climb out of his confining bottle and attempts to get at his equally miniature spouse. Praetorious, noticing this, picks him up with a pair of sugar tongs and secures him back in the jar by placing a cup and saucer on top of it, remarking prissily "that should keep you quiet for a while". Even, apparently, among a new, albeit small, race, heterosexuality cannot be eradicated, but at least it can be severely policed.

Praetorious' proposal to Frankenstein, that "together" they create life, has obvious sexual overtones – which would have been clearer had the film's original project,

squashed at script stage (presumably by the censor), gone through. In that, Praetorious was to murder Elizabeth and use her spare parts to create the Bride. Instead, he contents himself with kidnapping her and threatening to kill her, to ensure Frankenstein's co-operation, which is finally given with a mixture of backsliding hesitancy, hysteria and extreme erotic excitement once the process has begun, "shall we put the heart in now?". And so the Bride is created entirely by phallic equipment, shooting out orgasmic sparks of electricity, without even the aid of a surrogate womb i.e. a tank (a device which, filmically, came in with the Hammer cycle and continues to this day courtesy Kenneth Branagh's recent version).

The new Eve, however, is still irreconcilably different, other, from her creators – they have even inscribed her outwardly and visibly with the mark of the wound she bears, the threat she represents, the scars of castration upon her surrogate orifice, the throat. And she turns out to be a new Lilith, who, recoiling like a snake, screams her rejection of the touch of her preferred mate. The new order is over before it can begin, collapsing in on itself, imploding through the device of the mysterious lever in the laboratory which, if pulled, will destroy everything. This is usually taken as a gratuitously overdetermined mechanism for bringing about the end of the film – actually it is the visible sign of the built-in weight of self-destruction the fantasy of **The Bride Of Frankenstein** contained within itself from the start. Elizabeth, whom we last saw tied up Perils-of-Pauline style, reappears miraculously with the unconscious organising logic of a fantasy, to drag Frankenstein away to safety and heterosexuality, re-established with offhand perfunctoriness as he embraces her, murmuring "Darling, darling" while they watch the laboratory explode – "Tumescence Tower literally blows its top", in the words of Raymond Durgnat. The end. Their endlessly interrupted wedding night can now take place, though Elizabeth was warned to beware the event. We understand why, even if she doesn't.

    The Bride Of Frankenstein is not merely a very bizarre but a very black fantasy (though never recognised as such). Between men and women there is nothing but incomprehension and repulsion, but the dream of a world without women proves untenable. Checkmate. There is no way out of this sexual fix – or perhaps one. Praetorious made a fundamental mistake, which he unwittingly articulated – he wished to change the method of transmitting the existing order, but not the order itself, "Male and female, he created them both, if you like your bible stories". He remains trapped in the fix of the impossible male/female polarity. "'Male' and 'female' are concepts we need to learn to refuse... we need to pose the question, analyse, understand, refuse – refuse to be heterosexual and homosexual, the opposite sex and a sex at all" (Stephen Heath, *The Sexual Fix*, p156). **The Bride Of Frankenstein** poses no such question, it does not even know (the flaw in the fantasy) it can be asked. Nevertheless, it is suggestive, funny and subversive enough (in embryo) to have provided, forty years later (and mixed in with **The Old Dark House**), the starting point for the film that most ecstatically sets out to break down all the boundaries and structures of sexuality by and through which most of us are forced to live – **The Rocky Horror Picture Show**.

FRIGHTMARE

Peter Walker's Psycho-Delirium Classic

Leon Hunt

In the *Aurum Encyclopedia*'s entry for **Frightmare**, it soon becomes apparent that we aren't going to get much in the way of analysis. After a plot summary, the writer expounds on the importance of the "body in pieces" fantasy and its place in 1970's horror, with its new emphasis on bodily dismemberment, cannibalism and zombies.

Fair enough, but there's a catch. This fantasy, we are told, has a "social grounding" in American horror, thus legitimising "classics" such as **The Texas Chainsaw Massacre** and George Romero's zombie movies, but European horror films featuring superficially similar imagery are merely "cynically trying to cash in on the phenomenon".

That, say, the Italian cannibal movies might belong to other traditions with other imperatives is not considered; nor is the problem of lumping "European Horror" into a homogenous mass. Instead, all is sacrificed to this clumsy grafting of psychoanalysis onto social history (how exactly does the question Watergate + Vietnam = Images of Dismemberment happen and why?).

As for British Exploitation, the films of Walker, Warren, McGillivray etc; not only have no "social grounding", they have no reason to exist. I think we can do better than this.

To be fair, the *Aurum* isn't alone in not quite knowing what to do with these films. The two best histories of British horror, David Pirie's and Peter Hutchings', are predominantly Hammer-centred, and Pirie is, in any case, writing before this period. Nor did audiences exactly take these films to their hearts on their original release. Indeed, it's always seemed odd that someone as apparently hardbitten as Walker – McGillivray likens him to a car salesman – should make the transition from sex to horror just as British audiences were moving in the opposite direction.

In 1974 when Walker and McGillivray began their collaboration, the British sex film was making its biggest commercial breakthrough – this was the moment of Robin Askwith, not Sheila Keith, of window cleaners and plumber's mates, not cannibals and homicidal catholic priests. Yet the films do seem to be enjoying a small scale rediscovery after the recent Britfest and Leicester's British Exploitation conference, and it's worth considering why films like this appeared when they did.

If the unrest in America does go some way to explaining the confrontational nature of its 70's horror films, it isn't difficult to see why Britain in the early 70's might produce films marked by an unremitting bleakness – these are among the grimmest horror films ever made. 1974 was marked by power cuts, escalating IRA bombing campaigns on the British mainland (the Birmingham pub bombing being the worst) and violent reprisals, picket line violence and the growing spectre of the National Front.

With panics over mugging and other violent crime, Britain was becoming a "Law and Order" society, a context exploited in at least two of Walker and McGillivray's films, **The House Of Whipcord** (their "Festival of Light" movie, if you like) and **House Of Mortal Sin**. The "bad crowd" Debbie hangs around with in **Frightmare** are like the kind of ultra-violent delinquents roaming through the New English Library landscape of Richard Allen's *Skinheads* and Mick Norman's *Hells Angels*.

It's difficult to imagine these films being made at any other time and they take on greater resonance with hindsight. Patrick Barr in **Whipcord** is like Ted Heath, the hardliner in decline (the miners saw him off for good that year), while Barbara Markham's Mrs Wakehurst and Sheila Keith's sadistic Walker (!) are like the scarier, even more hardline Thatcher waiting in the wings.

In **Frightmare** too, "Mad Sheila" is uncannily Thatcher-like – the voice that hardens and rises in volume when you least expect it, the demented quality of her eyes. Dorothy Yates, **Frightmare**'s cannibal, is the wicked stepmother incarnate (an idea I shall explore in more detail later) – Thatcher's first major splash into public consciousness was the termination of free milk in schools. What more of a wicked stepmother could there be than a "milk snatcher"?

There are precedents for these films. What the 70's are to the 60's, Walker is to someone like Michael Reeves. **Witchfinder General** and, in particular, **The Sorcerers** (whose old couple – he's weak; she's mad, bad and dangerous to know – anticipate the Yates' in **Frightmare**) introduce a key shift in British horror, a narrative in which an old, metaphorically cannibalistic generation preys on "Youth" at what should be the moment of its liberation.

This theme is present in some of the more ambitious Hammer films (especially those of Peter Sasdy or written by Christopher Wicking), but also in oddities like **Night After Night After Night** (1969), where a pre-**Whipcord** psycho judge dons leather and a bizarre Beatles wig to both vicariously explore and exterminate the world of permissive London. **Night** can't decide which is most monstrous between pathological repression and

unchecked liberation, hence the thuggish "swinger" in the film who becomes the Judge's counterpart and key suspect. This generation-gap horror hardens in the 70's.

Reeves' films are cynical, but they're angry with it – Ian Ogilvy's characters are would-be bohemians (even in **Witchfinder**) who discover that "liberation" isn't going to be so simple. Walker's films have lost hope altogether, but accept that this is how things are. On the face of it, **Frightmare**'s "don't-release-the-mentally-ill-ever" refrain makes it look like the right wing flipside of the Whitehouse-baiting **House Of Whipcord**. But what seems most significant is that young psychiatrist Graham (Paul Greenwood) is still talking about the effectiveness of out-patient treatment for former cannibals about ten minutes before having his cranium explored with a Black-and-Decker.

In 1951, the year of the Festival of Britain, Michael Frayn defined two important types in British cultural life – the herbivores (middle-class, Labour-voting do-gooders) and the aggressive, acquisitive carnivores, quite happy to prey on those weaker than themselves. Charles Barr has argued that Ealing studios celebrated the British herbivore, Peter Hutchings that Hammer were attracted to the carnivore, embodied not just by Dracula and Frankenstein but also by such ruthless, no-nonsense puritans as Van Helsing and the Duc De Richleau.

In the 1970's, the carnivores got hungrier – this was the time of the New Right – and the herbivores were the domesticated remnants of 60's hippies; social workers, the sort of school teachers who insisted that their pupils use their first names. The latter are the "heroes" of the Walker-McGillivray films, and they're easy pickings for the hungry "new right" – you don't get much more carnivorous than Dorothy. Even the sort of

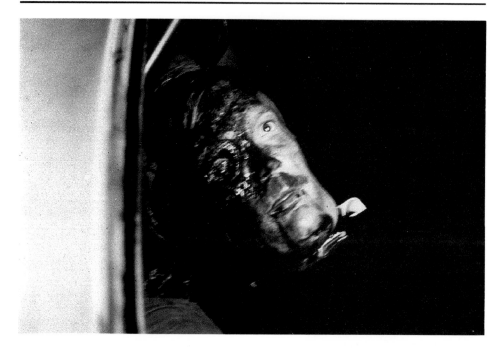

hoodlums the tabloids were always warning us about are no match for her – Debbie's biker boyfriend is bloodily despatched in a stable. It may sometimes take on some unattractive forms, but if this cynicism isn't "socially grounded" I don't know what is.

The narrative of **Frightmare** is like a violent fairy story combined with Freud's "Family Romance". In the latter, a child imagines that their parents are not biological but adoptive; the "real" parents are "better", probably belonging to a higher social class – with some variation, this is like Debbie's desire for parents who will "naturalise" her violent urges.

The film begins in 1957 as Dorothy and husband Edmund (Rupert Davies) are imprisoned for her gory crimes and his largely protective complicity. With this linking of scandal and "disturbing", boundary-crossing crime, the film invites memories of the Moors murderers (if Jack the Ripper is recuperable for English tourism, Brady and, in particular, Hindley surely aren't; killing women is British, killing children isn't). We're talking Wicked Stepmothers again – while Brady was largely acknowledged as the instigator, Hindley's gender, her "violation of the maternal", has made her an undying tabloid "Other" whose monstrousness has never been questioned, whose recuperation is utterly out of the question. The cinema won't touch it with a barge pole, but this is a central British horror mythology, a story to be told over and over again. It's a distinctly British conception of the Monstrous Mother, and **Frightmare** is the ripest tapping of it (in a sense, Dorothy is probably as much like Hindley as most movie Elizabeth Bathorys are like the "real" Bloody Countess).

In the present, Jackie (Deborah Fairfax) lives with her delinquent half-sister Debbie (Kim Butcher) – Debbie is Dorothy's daughter, raised in an orphanage and supposedly ignorant of her infamous parents; Jackie is Edmund's daughter from an earlier marriage. This is a very loaded family romance, in more ways than one. Dorothy is using Tarot cards and ads placed in *Time Out* to lure her victims to her farmhouse, and their deaths form the gory set-pieces that are the main focus of the few existing accounts of the film – pokers, pitchforks and drills are, shall we say, memorably deployed, but the film's most terrifying images are usually the close-ups of Dorothy's face as she drills away (Walker's attempt to make a horror star of Sheila Keith may not have worked out, but she doesn't exactly waste the opportunity).

Initially, Jackie mediates with her father and step-mother, bringing bloody placebos from the butcher shop to keep Dorothy's old urges at bay (the audience may notice a therapeutic flaw here before psychiatrist Graham explains it to her). But, by the end of the film, the family is reconstructed – Debbie has been working with Dorothy, unknown to Edmund, and comes home to claim her rightful place, her carnivorous heritage, if you like. In the final scene, homicidal mother and daughter close in on Jackie as Edmund's divided loyalties keep him watching from the sidelines (they aren't equally divided – he does lock the door behind Jackie).

What if Snow White's Wicked Stepmother had a "real" daughter, one who was very much her daughter in every way? That is Debbie, Juliette to Jackie's Justine. McGillivray's reminiscences about working with Walker suggest that Debbie was as much the conceptual centre of the film as the sensational cannibalism "hook" – Walker's original idea was the duplicitous daughter, sparked off by Jane Greer's character in Jacques Tourneur's **Out Of The Past/Build My Gallows High**. But Debbie isn't presented as duplicitous in the sense of a "bad" girl passing for "good", unlike the later **Schizo** (1976) – it's more a question of the nature and degree of her transgressiveness.

Initially seen as no more than a "delinquent" – Graham draws on sociological notions of lack of "roots" and "background" to explain her behaviour – Debbie is just mummy's little girl. "I've always known," she says mockingly when Edmund asks when she discovered the identity of her parents – "She's so grown up, isn't she," says Dorothy admiringly. Edmund is doubly disempowered, a fact reinforced by some offscreen violence preceding Jackie's arrival (his face is badly bruised). "We both feel closer to Deborah," he tells his doomed elder daughter with a mixture of admonishment and apology; "They have a lot in common, you know." Neither are "containable" within rational discourse – the explanation for the Dorothy's "condition" (forced to eat her pet rabbit during the depression) gives more weight than Debbie's "rootlessness". Dorothy's Tarot cards actually work – she's onto Graham even before Debbie confirms his identity – and her mocking references to visiting woodland animals reinforce the fairytale quality of her "gingerbread" farmhouse.

Frightmare is the most relentless and excessive of the 70's "Country House" horror films, a sub-genre which includes **Whipcord, Horror Hospital, Exposé** and **Satan's Slave**, the dark counterpart of the sex comedy's suburban utopia (I'm grateful to Ian Conrich and Ian Hunter for different formations of this idea). Ealing's "Greenleaf" England has rotted and turned ugly; an earlier generation of herbivores have developed a taste for real meat (like all those "angry" writers of the 50's who defected to the right). In this film, one can't separate this reading from the misogynist, if compelling, conception of Dorothy and Debbie – as is often the case with unruly Exploitation, you have to take the rough with the smooth, and these films display no warmth for anyone. Walker maintains an apparently hostile silence and McGillivray refuses to take them seriously, but for all sorts of reasons, the time for their reconsideration seems to have arrived.

THANA AS THANATOS

Sexuality And Death In Ms 45: Angel Of Vengeance

Xavier Mendik

Let us call the "maternal" the ambivalent principle that is bound to the species, on the one hand, and on the other stems from an identity catastrophe that causes the Name to topple over into the unnameable that one imagines as femininity, non-language or body[1].

Following the work of French Psychoanalyst Jacques Lacan, theorists such as Julia Kristeva have sought to understand the relationship between language, the drives of the unconscious and the depiction of gender in cultural representations. This paper seeks to argue that these advances in psychoanalysis and linguistics prove crucial tools in comprehending images of horror, and in particular provide a method of analysing the Abel Ferrara film **Ms 45: Angel Of Vengeance** (1981).

While recapitulating the Freudian notion of adult sexuality as premised on infantile drives, the importance of Lacan's work remains the emphasis he placed on the role of language in the process of sexual maturation. Not only does the Oedipal trauma force the child to assume a position of gendered stability, but this mechanism is concurrent with the child's gradual exposure to the processes of speech.

By terming the sphere of discourse the "symbolic", Lacan points to language's attempt to repress these primary drives through the provision of a battery of terms and labels designed to "police" sexuality. Specifically, Lacan notes how the symbolic attempts to regulate sexual difference through the ideological privileging of "masculine" terms such as the phallus as signifier's of identity, virility and control. These remain sharply differentiated from the status of terms used to define female sexuality, confirming Lacan's belief of interrelations between language and patriarchy.

If, in the symbolic, identity is governed by the dominance of a male language then Kristeva terms the period of early infancy as the realm of the maternal. Importantly, this primary period before speech is also marked by the infant's ambivalent conception of its own identity, as well as its overwhelming dependence on the mother. By giving the child a name, access to the language system and a gendered identity, what the symbolic ultimately seeks to repress is this infantile fascination with the mother.

However, as Kristeva implies, this primary maternal power (or "semiotic" as Kristeva terms it) threatens to re-emerge in later life, and is evidenced in certain forms of modernist literature. For instance in the works of writers such as James Joyce and George Bataille, the semiotic is evidenced by features such as the subversion of established forms of language presentation, as well as the concentration on acts of excessive physiological acts.

Firstly, the subversion of established forms of discourse is important because it replicates the infant's attempts to grapple with a language system that it can not yet master:

> Once upon a time and a very good time it was there was a moocow
> coming down the road and this moocow that was coming down along
> the road met a nicens little boy named baby tuckoo...[2]

The opening paragraph of *A Portrait Of The Artist As A Young Man* replicates the infant's uncoordinated use of language through the construction of nonsense words as well as the re-ordering of established codes of syntax and grammar.

Although the use of nonsense words and repetitions in the opening paragraph of the book are revealed to be a nursery rhyme sung to the central character Stephen Dedalus, Maud Ellmann has argued that it establishes a pattern whereby the narrator's access to established patterns of speech are displaced.

As she notes in the article "Disengaging Dedalus", although the tale is supposed to be an autobiography of a writer, Stephen is revealed as a character whose access to both language and a stable notion of identity is made problematic. As a consequence, the whole of the narrative is plagued by doubts as to the validity of Stephen's identity and recollections.

The problematic definition of self that occurs in Joyce's novel extends beyond the subversion of the dominant modes of discourse to include the second element of the semiotic: an excessive concentration on disturbing acts of physiology. According to Ellmann, Joyce's novel exposes a tension between "litter and letters" by linking Stephen's tenuous mastery of language with a concern that filth will overwhelm his identity[3].

Once more the basis for this trauma can be found in infancy. Kristeva relates it not only to the ethereal sense of self that the infant experiences but also to the fascination with elements of bodily waste such as urine and excreta that are of concern to the child.

Although this transgressive preoccupation with elements of filth and waste matter become submerged via the "civilizing of the self" that the symbolic ensures Barbara Creed has argued that these infantile pleasures of flesh and decay are replicated in the horror genre. Here the dissolution of both language and identity occurs through the horror texts concentration on the human form as a site of destruction, mutilation and physiological corruption.

Arguably it is both the destruction of established modes of discourse as well as the concentration on extreme physiological acts that places **Ms 45: Angel Of Vengeance** in the category of the semiotic. The film deals with a mute central female protagonist who after being raped by two differing attackers begins to stalk the city streets in order to both seduce and then victimise men.

As if to underscore the narrative's concentration on acts of decay and the disturbing, its worth noting the name of the heroine Thana, which derived from the Greek term *"thanatos"*, makes clear reference to her status as a signifier of death. The "death" to which Thana refers is the annihilation of language, this being implicit in the fact that she is literally unable to speak or enter into discourse. The structure of the narrative confirms this silence through the subversion of the soundtrack at pertinent points of the text.

If Thana's world is revealed to be a silent sphere, then the film explicitly codes this inability to communicate as a "female" space. This is foregrounded in the sequences shot at Thana's apartment, in which any referent on the soundtrack is absent.

Importantly, the major references to discourse that do occur in this silent world are primarily masculine and coded as a form of assault against the female body. This pattern is initiated with the entry of one of Thana's rapists into her apartment. The silence of the space is further disrupted by Phil the inquisitive male dog, who constantly interrupts Thana's attempts to dispose of the body of the rapist after she manages to overpower

and kill her attacker.

This pattern of a verbal male assault is reciprocated in Thana's interactions with both her work colleagues as well as her intended male victims. In particular Thana's lascivious employer who divides his on-screen presence between subjecting his female workers to verbal "assaults" for the quality of their work as well as using discourse as an attempt to seduce them.

If the film genders its use of sound to create a polarity between female silence and male hostility the pattern is also prominent in Thana's attempts to kill one male victim whom she picks up in a bar. The man engages in a long dialogue (split between two locations of the bar and the park bench outside it) of the steps leading up to his discovery of his wife engaging in extra-marital sex. At the point when Thana is about to shoot him, he reveals that he was horrified when he discovered that his wife's lover was another woman and as a result strangled her cat[4].

Although Thana's gun jams when she is at the point of dispatching this character, he snatches the weapon and proceeds to kill himself. Importantly the moments leading up to his death are marked by a cacophony of sound (his narration and the direct sound of the city scape which surrounds the pair) with the soundtrack reverting to silence at the point when he turns the gun on himself. If this sequence provides a further division between gendered zones of discourse, silence and their relation to aggression, then it is a strategy which culminates in the final sequence of the film. Here Thana (having been bullied into attending a fancy dress party by her employee), goes on the rampage and shoots the male guests attending[5]. The soundtrack shifts between dialogue between the

guests before being re-mastered to distort the sound of the human voice at the point when Thana attacks[6].

While clearly replicating the semiotic effect through its subversion of established codes of language, Ferrara's film also replicates the infantile fascination with elements of filth and waste matter that Kristeva identifies.

Her analysis defines as "abject" waste matter and bodily fluids such as excreta, urine, saliva and menstruational blood which are seen as disgusting and offensive to the civilized and the symbolic precisely because they evoke this primary period before the establishment of language and identity.

According to Creed in *The Monstrous Feminine* what such bodily fluids also evoke is ultimately the power of the mother in this "primitive" era. Evoking Kristeva's term "primary mapping", Creed argues that the mother becomes abject by association. Not only is she the agent who is primarily responsible for providing the infant with training skills for their own physiology, but she is traditionally coded as being the "carer" who disposes of their waste substances. As Creed argues, by trading on images of waste matter such as vomit, excreta and in particular blood, as well as the constant depiction of body in differing states of decay, what the horror film does is expose:

> ...a split between 2 orders: the maternal authority and the law of the father. On the one hand these bodily wastes threaten a subject that is already constituted, in relation to the symbolic as whole and proper. Consequently, they fill the subject – both the protagonist in the text

Bad Lieutenant

and the spectator in the cinema – with disgust and loathing. On the other hand, they also point to a time when a fusion between the mother and nature existed, when bodily wastes... were not seen as objects of embarrassment and shame[7].

From the opening of **Ms 45: Angel Of Vengeance**, Thana becomes equated with abject elements of waste, filth and decaying flesh. It is interesting to note that during the first rape scene, her attacker forces her into a garbage strewn side street, not only sexually assaulting Thana, but pushing her face in the dirt. This establishes a pattern whereby the female protagonist becomes equated with "filth". Indeed, it is Thana's shambolic appearance subsequent to the first assault that provokes her second attacker into an attempted rape before she manages to overpower him[8].

Prior to these attacks, Thana has clearly been coded as virginal and only subsequently adopts a "guise" of adult sexuality as a means to snare her intended male victims. Extending her status as a site of "filth", it could be argued that one of the waste products associated with her assault is vaginal blood.

As Creed has argued, the role of female body fluids such as menstrual blood has a long cultural history that is mirrored in horror cinema. Her analysis of De Palma's **Carrie** (1977) indicates how the central character becomes recast as a site of abjection after menstruating in the high school's communal shower room. As Creed notes, the revulsion of Carrie's (female) peers links both into long standing taboos that surround the passage of "feminine blood", as well as reciprocating an infantile inability to control one's own physiology.

If the use of blood as a metaphor for the filthy female form is implicit in the

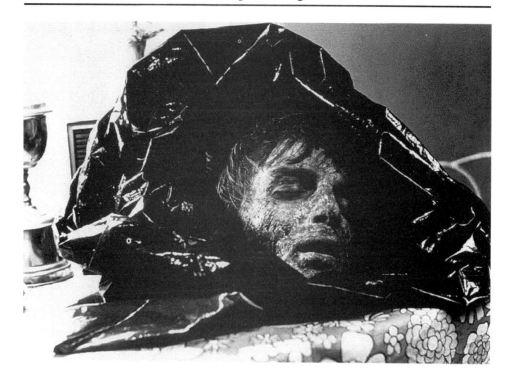

attacks that Thana experiences, then they are coded much more explicitly in Ferrara's later **Bad Lieutenant** (1992), where the text's central investigation centres on the rape of a nun whose attackers use her own vaginal blood to smear obscenities on the walls of the church where she is attacked.

Most explicitly, Thana becomes associated with the semiotic processes of the abject through the murder and dismemberment of the second rapist who attacks her. Once more this can be related to the taboos against waste matter, as exemplified by what Kristeva sees as the universal proscription against the corpse (which Creed sites as the ultimate abjection). As she notes, this is the ultimate point where identity and the ability to enter into discourse are displaced, with any former sense of "self" being eroded as the body begins to rot.

Thus, if the symbolic works to construct the individual as a unified subject, it is pertinent that Creed concludes that the horror film deconstructs this unity via its preoccupation with images of the corpse. Indeed, the unity of identity that the symbolic offers is rendered disparate by Thana's actions, not only dismembering the corpse, but discarding pieces of his flesh in differing areas of the city. Once again, these actions become linked with issues of hygiene and bodily care. Indeed, it is marked that a radio news report that discusses the police discovery of these body bits (as well as Thana's subsequent male victims) links the events to an impending city wide strike by *sanitation* workers.

However, while **Ms 45: Angel Of Vengeance** establishes Thana as a signifier of death and decay, what is important is that this representation is not constructed in isolation, but functions to draw parallels with other female characters in the text. In

particular she is linked to an elderly female landlady, who is introduced into the narrative in an abrupt shot change between Thana killing the rapist with an iron[9]. This interchange proves pertinent because as with Thana, the landlady is coded as inhabiting a dead and decaying world. Indeed, the exploratory shots of her apartment reveal it to be cluttered with the memorabilia of a "dead" past. Equally, the image of the old woman constantly intervenes on Thana's proximity to the bodily remains[10]. For instance, in one instance her face is superimposed over the plug hole through which Thana is attempting to flush away the remains of the corpse), while also appearing in her dreams as a distorted figure.

The construction of the landlady as an overbearing, excessively over-made-up hag provides another link between Thana and the realm of decay and abjection. As Creed argues, by exposing the semiotic link between the infant and the mother, the horror film also explores the tensions implicit in the child's desire for separation from this powerful figure:

> By refusing to relinquish her hold on her child, she prevents it from taking up its proper place in relation to the symbolic. Partly consumed by the desire to remain locked in a blissful relationship with the mother and partly terrified of separation, the child finds it easy to succumb to the comforting pleasure of the didactic relationship[11].

Noting the construction of "monstrous" maternal figures in texts such as **Carrie** and **Psycho** (1960), Creed notes that these texts often construct mothers as archaic or aggressive figures who threaten the autonomy of their offspring.

Although not a biological mother to Thana, the landlady's overbearing presence in her life indicates another example of the text's subversion of symbolic identity via the

equation between death, decay and the female subversion of language. If the text features a concerted attempt to abuse female protagonists either through discourse or physical violence, then this phallic discourse is ultimately displaced through the functioning of this semiotic strand, which points to a zone of archaic female resistance.

NOTES

1. Kristeva, "Stabat Mater", p161.
2. James Joyce, p3.
3. An early example of this occurs when Stephen is pushed into a ditch by bullies at school. The narration stresses the character's horror as he experienced "...the cold slime of the ditch covered his whole body" (p11).
4. As the feline has been traditionally been equated with the feminine, this narration provides a further example of the link between male discourse and aggression.
5. In her analysis of the film Clover notes how the victims at the party seem to be linked by their use of discourse as means to "appropriate" female sexuality. These include two men who have been discussing buying under-age girls for intercourse from central America, as well as Thana's employer who introduces her to colleagues at the party as "a protegé of mine" (Clover p141).
6. As if to confirm Thana's status as a signifier of death, the party is a Halloween ball where the imagery of annihilation is over-coded in many of the costumes that the guests wear.
7. Creed, p13.
8. Indeed, Thana's next male victim after her attacker is a street hustler who attempts to pick up her up before trapping her in a garbage-strewn ally.
9. The fact that the landlady is cooking eggs at the point of her introduction is also pertinent. As

Kristeva has argued, many sources of abjection revolve around foods and their ingestion. This recalls the infant's inability to control its own physiology in relation to such substances. Equally the ingestion of food stuffs also references primary phases of development such as those revolving around the oral pleasures that the child experiences from contact with areas of the mother's body (such as the breast). Ultimately the link between abjection and food in the film is achieved via the fact that Thana minces the remains of her attacker's body and feeds it to the landlady's dog.

10. The text makes further equations between the female body and the construction of physiological decay in a sequence which reveals that some of the discarded remains of the rapist's body have been added to the accumulation of packages and rags of a female tramp. As well as being marked by her filthy appearance, the itinerant is also distinguished by her infantile babble and mumbling. Even the recollections of the feminine in the film seem to be connected with the image of filth and waste matter. This is foregrounded in the monologue that Thana is exposed to by the victim she picks up a bar. It is noticeable that he recalls having to illicitly enter an apartment via the *garbage* entrance, in order to spy on his wife being unfaithful.

11. Creed, p12.

BIBLIOGRAPHY.
Clover, Carol J: *Men Women And Chainsaws*. London, British Film Institute 1992.
Creed, Barbara: *The Monstrous Feminine*. London, Routledge 1993.
Joyce, James: *A Portrait Of The Artist As A Young Man*. London, Penguin 1992.
Kristeva, Julia *The Kristeva Reader* (Toril Moi, Ed). London, Blackwell 1989.
Ellmann, Maud: "Disremembering Dedalus: A Portrait Of The Artist As A Young Man" in Young, Robert (Ed) *Untying The Text*. London, Routledge 1981.

CLOCKS, SEAGULLS, ROMEO & JULIET

Surrealism Rollin Style

Andy Black

"A grandfather clock is of no interest – a vampire woman getting out of this clock at midnight, that's me!"

—Jean Rollin

"Dreams and life – it's the same thing; or else it's not worth living."
—From Rollin's **Les Enfants Du Paradis**

As any viewer who is acquainted with **Le Frisson Des Vampires** in the former case, or *any* of Rollin's surrealist fantasies (and that's basically his whole *oeuvre*!) in the latter case will testify, the above quotations encapsulate Rollin's filmic *raison d'être*, symbolised in his kaleidoscopic costumes, decadent characters and nebulous romanticism.

Whilst the Frenchman's early career focused on his now trademark vampire sex "epics" such as **Le Viol Du Vampire**, **La Vampire Nue** and **Requiem Pour Un Vampire**, and encompassed moulding corpses in **Zombie Lake**, masturbatory couplings in **Hard Penetrations** and grotesque gore in **Les Raisins De La Mort**, recent years have been somewhat less than vintage for the mercurial Rollin.

However, times, they are a changin' as the man said and perhaps the halcyon days are due to return with the release of **Les Deux Orphelines Vampires (Little Orphan Vampires)** in 1996 – Rollin's first vampire film for some 10 years.

The master's well-documented love of the old French magazine serials or *Feuilletons* shines through with the film being the first to be adapted from his long line of successful *romans de gare* (station novels) – a unique brand of French "pulp fiction", which also includes *Anissa*, *Les Voyageuses*, *Les Pillardes* and *Les Incendiares* in this particular vampire novel series.

With **Les Deux Orphelines Vampires**, Rollin revisits his obligatory two female vampire leads – Louise and Henriette here – and favoured gothic graveyard milieu as the duo of blind vampires ("clack, clack, clack, clack went the two white sticks") await nightfall when their sight (and more importantly, their appetite for blood) returns and they seek out new victims.

The vamps, with their dual personalities alternating effortlessly between good and evil, mirror the equally diverse nature of those Sadean characters Justine and Juliette, an irony not lost on Rollin to be sure.

Having tracked down the ubiquitous Rollin recently, here follows our lengthy dialogue:

You have stated that the poet Corbière and the artists Druillet and Trouille are among those who have inspired your work – in what way?

Corbière was a poet of the sea. And the sea is most important to me. My first short film was an evocation of Corbière on a beach near Dieppe. I was young, no money, no material etc. But I was there, on that strange beach covered in stones, deserted, with just

Jean Rollin

the *falaise* and the seagulls. And in my mind, I said: "One day I'll come back here with all the possibilities for a real shoot. For me, now, after six or seven films shot on that beach, it is mixed with the remembrance of Corbière. Druillet has nothing to do with my work, he is just a friend. After the shooting of **Le Viol Du Vampire** I ask all my friends who can take a pencil to do an image for the poster. Druillet brought (an image) which immediately became the film's poster. Clovis Trouille paints, I think, as I film. When I see some of his paintings, it seems to me that they could be photos from one of my films. The same strange arrangements of the elements, romantic-expressionist protagonists, expression of the imagination. As for Magritte, Trouille paints people and objects in a realistic, ultra-realistic manner. It's the arrangement between the elements which forms the surrealist way. Paintings like *Stigma Diaboli*, *La Violée Du Vaisseau Fantome* [The Raped One From The Haunted Ship – could be the title from a Rollin film!], *L'Heure Du Sortilege* and so on could absolutely be images from my mind and my films. They are part of the "mystery of the imagination" I like so much. If you look at a painting like *Mon Tombeau* [My Grave] it can recall many images from **Le Viol**, **Le Frisson** or **Requiem**.

What influence did the likes of Georges Franju and Luis Buñuel have on your career?

It's the same kind. Buñuel shot visions like Trouille did paintings, or Magritte. We can take some images off for film, those images speak for themselves. They are independent of the story, they are the voice of Buñuel himself. So, in a film so banal in appearance like **Susana** or even **El**, everything is shown by the vision of the artist. Personally, I am jealous of an extraordinary vision I saw in one of Buñuel's last French films, I don't remember which one but: a man closes a coffin, and some gold hairs from the dead girl inside are visible. Such imagery leaves me full of exaltation. There are many such images in Buñuel films. Franju is the author of the greatest film of the genre, **Les Yeux Sans Visage**. Perfection of the script, of the actors, of the light, of everything. I was haunted during many, many years by the end, Edith Scob walking in the park with her face covered by the white mask, and the white birds and that music... I have tried to find that atmosphere of dream, poetry and madness in many of my films. Same reflections about **Judex**. It's a serial, like a serial. For me, where the cinema is near the surrealist poetry, near the primitive mind of childhood, it is the serial. My remembrance as a child is of the serials I saw after school every Wednesday – **Zorro Fighting Legion, Mysterious Docteur Satan, G-Men Versus The Black Dragon**, etc. I think I personally have shot two serials: **Viol Du Vampire** and **Les Trottoirs De Bankok**. Here a critic said; "Rollin has done with **Bankok**, the same film as his first one, **Le Viol**, twenty-five years after." And it's true! **Bankok** is a kind of "Fu-Manchu" and the film was improvised to a great degree like **Le Viol**. When I was shooting it, I was in the same mind that I was for **Le Viol**. I was twenty years old again!

*Your first fantasy film **Le Viol Du Vampire** was considered daring for the time and released during a turbulent period in French history – in what way did this film and the critical reaction to it, shape your future career?*

Le Viol was a terrible scandal here in Paris. People were really mad when they saw it. In Pigalle, they threw things at the screen. The principal reason was that nobody could understand the story. But there is a story, I swear it! Now, after such a long time, I think the principal reason is that the film was supposed to be a vampire story. The audience knew only Hammer's vampires and my film disturbed their classical idea of what such a film had to be. And outside it was the revolution, so people were able to exteriorise themselves. The scandal was a terrible surprise for me. I didn't know that I had made such a "bizarre" picture. For me, it was so simple! In all the country, throughout France, the film was a scandal. In my area, a little village, the priest said to his audience in church that they must not see the film on release at their local cinema... I was the devil. And even the fans of such films were disillusioned and the critics wrote horrors about me. A great newspaper, *Le Figaro*, wrote: "this film is certainly made by a group of drunk people, probably medical students. It's a joke". I thought that my career was finished. But many people came to see *that* scandalous film and the producers asked me to do a second one. **La Vampire Nue** was not so delirious. But I kept one element from **Le Viol**, the mystery, like in the old serials...

Vampires burst from grandfather clocks, lovers are speared on the same stake – you are noted for your imagery not your narratives – is this fair comment?

The answer is this. The imagery in my films is certainly more important than the story itself. But the stories are done to provoke such images. In a certain way, the stories are "mad love" stories and the images are surrealist visions. The mixture of both makes my films.

La Vampire Nue

Le Frisson Des Vampires

In some ways your films break gender stereotypes – often two females are the lead players – is this a conscious attempt at "sexual equality" or a male reaction in showing seductive figures, often engaged in lesbian activities, or something else?!!

Why the girls? I really don't know. Maybe a psychoanalyst can tell! Even in my books, *Les Demoiselles De L'Etrange* are two, *The Vampire Orphans* of course and many more. About the love scenes, I must confess that, for me, I prefer to see (and show) two girls naked rather than a girl and a man. For me, a naked girl is more interesting, for sensuality and for poetry (a naked girl is *always* poetry), to put her in a clock or in a chimney, or anywhere except a bed. Using things for unexpected uses is the base of all surrealist painting. See Max Ernst, Marcel Duchamp. When Duchamp painted *Nude Walking Down A Stair*, it's no more a simple stair. It became *the* stair with a nude on it. Understand? My clock is no more a simple clock, it's a clock with the vampire girl in it [**Le Frisson**], then the girl killer hides in it [**Killing Car**]. It's become Rollin's clock!!

Regained memory and lost innocence also appear to be central themes in your work – why?

Every man is, consciously or not, researching, remembering his childhood. When I was a child, there was no TV, only movies. I saw so many films... with the innocent eyes of a child. Maybe I am trying to recapture these moments and make films with the same eyes I had to see **Mysterious Docteur Satan** or **Jungle Jim**...

These childhood memories would include such recurring locations as Dieppe beach?

As I said I was fascinated by that strange beach. I have seen many beautiful beaches in my life, but this one, I don't know why, for me represents mystery itself. It's a surrealistic beach. Three elements: the *falaise*, the sea and the *mouettes* [seagulls].

How have you enjoyed working with such actresses as Brigitte Lahie, Marina Pierro and Françoise Pascal?

Brigitte is a pleasure to work with. She is quiet, she really likes to act, to play, and she does what is required of her role. When I took her for **Nuit Des Traquées** I was sure she would be great in the scene where she becomes insane slowly. And that sequence was the most important in all of the film for me. And I was right. Brigitte in that part was *émouvante*. Marina Pierro is Italian. Her temperament is fiery. It was good for such a character in the film. Françoise Pascal is very professional. Working with her was interesting because, to the contrary of most girls I'd directed before, she really was into the story, trying to bring ideas, to discuss what I had in mind. Her performance in the film is great. If she can find such roles to play she can go far, but what became of her?

Lèvres De Sang is widely regarded as your best film – which is your own favourite and why?

I have no favourite. Maybe the next one! **Lèvres De Sang** is certainly my best script. The story was really good, based on the childhood memories that the hero had forgotten. Every person is sensitive to such a story. Everybody has had a childhood love at some time, and in the film the childhood love came true! Of course I like **Le Viol** because it was so attacked! But I have a little love for **Requiem** and for **Bankok**. But the best one is **The Orphan Vampires**, probably.

La Rose De Fer has been described as a horror version of Romeo And Juliet – do you agree with this description?

One day, a stupid journalist, who understood nothing of my films in general and **La Rose** in particular asked me: "But at the end, what is that film about? What did it mean?" and I answered: "What! You don't see it's my version of *Romeo And Juliet*? You have the boy and the girl and the cemetery and the family trying to separate them! But maybe it's true as you can see the film like that – but for me it was just a joke.

La Vampire Nue is a personal favourite of mine for its dramatic use of colour, costumes and fetishistic imagery – it was also your first film in colour – how much of a difference did the use of colour make in your approach to the film?

After **Le Viol** I had to make a more classical film. So in place of the delirious images of **Le Viol** I tried to put some mystery into **La Vampire Nue**. Mystery of the strange people, the strange girl who is not really a vampire, and mystery with the locations in Paris I found. Places had great importance for me in that film. For example, I like the strange meeting in the beginning between the girl and the boy (my brother Olivier) under the pale

Virgin Among The Living Dead

light. Nothing special, only elements of everyday, except the girl with her strange costume, but the bizarre atmosphere is there. Why? Which? What? I don't know but the mystery is there.

You have been roundly condemned by critics for your excursions into pornographic/ hardcore films – what is your response to such criticism?

I shoot X-films to have sufficient money to be able to live. I don't like the films but to make them can be amusing. I remember that period with pleasure. I liked the people I was working with, it was always one or two day shoots, very funny, a good friendly atmosphere. But no interesting films, that's all I can say.

You worked on **Zombie Lake** *– segments of which appeared in Jess Franco's* **Virgin Among The Living Dead** *– how did you get involved in this project?*

I technically shot **Zombie Lake** because Jess Franco, who was supposed to do it, had disappeared! The producers phoned me one Sunday when I was asleep and asked; "Can you shoot a zombie film tomorrow morning for two weeks?" and I said "Yes". I haven't seen the sequence in **Virgin** as I haven't seen that film, so I don't know if it's my sequence. But it's true I shot a sequence of zombies running after a girl for the same producer separately, and I don't know what was done with that footage, so maybe that's

Living Dead Girl

in **Virgin**.

Your later living dead/zombie films such as **Les Raisins De La Mort** *and* **The Living Dead Girl** *are very different in their approaches the former with almost USA-style gore scenes,*

Living Dead Girl

the latter more psychological as well as sanguinary. What were your intentions in each of these films?

Raisins is probably my greatest commercial success. It's sold everywhere (except in England!). Because it's more like what is expected by the audience. The idea was to do a "living dead" film with the same horrors you would find in a Romero film, but with a different story. Romero's style is "claustrophobic", the people are holed-up in a house surrounded by the zombies. I try the contrary approach; people are running in a vast countryside area, and, most importantly, my zombies are in part living, with consciences, they know what they are doing but can't stop themselves. So the sequence where the actor becomes mad and cuts the head off his girlfriend, telling her at the same time that he loves her, is very dramatic! And such a dramatic construction was not possible with the unconscious zombies in Romero's film and many others.

For **The Living Dead Girl** it's also the memories that interest me. The girl came back to life and now inhabits her former château, in her own room, and finds her childhood toys and other souvenirs come back one by one. It's very emotional, very dramatic. And that for me, was the most interesting part of the film. The memories of the two little girls, the music box. And the end before one girl kills and eats the other one, she reminds her of when they were little girls. The massacre is a kind of love scene, like the killing with the axe in **Les Raisins**. The two sequences are from the same idea.

*How did you get involved with **Emanuelle 6** and was it an enjoyable/rewarding* *experience?*

In **Emanuelle 6**, I like the character of the little savage girl. I was thinking of Yoko, the girl in **Bankok** for that, but she had disappeared at that moment. I directed a part of the film in France. It was a job with no problems. I like to shoot "erotic softcore films", it's a rest for me.

Fascination is another highly regarded film of yours – there's a startling opening contrast of upper-class costumed ladies drinking blood from wine glasses in an abattoir. What was the thinking behind this and how do you explain your own fascination with vampires?

My idea at the beginning was to give Brigitte Lahie a costume from the beginning of this century! And to make a film practically entirely in a château. The first image of the script was the girls drinking in the slaughterhouse. That was inspired by a short story called "The Glass Of Blood" by Jean Lorrain, an author of that period. The rest is my idea, from that: all the film shot in the château and just three people in most of the scenes. And Brigitte in a château dressed in 1900 costume period!

*Can you tell me about three of your films which have never been available within the UK – **Les Trottoirs De Bankok**, **La Femme Dangereuse** and **Perdues Dans New York**?*

I have spoken of **Bankok** before. **Femme Dangereuse (Killing Car** is the real title) is a kind of strange thriller. There is a mysterious Asian girl, really so beautiful you should see her, killing people, nobody knows why. In a moment, she jumps from inside a clock to shoot! It's a minor film, but I like it, it's real B-movie style as in the good old times! **Lost In New York** is a one-hour film for TV. It's a kind of resumé of everything personal I've put in my other films. It's really shot in New York for the greatest part, and, of course, on the beach near Dieppe.

*Your latest film **Little Orphan Vampires** sees you reunited with one of your earlier collaborators – Lionel Wallman – how do you rate the film compared with your previous works and what are the key elements?*

Lionel Wallman is an old friend and he knows me very well. So, it's always a pleasure to collaborate with him. This latest film is a little different. For the first time, I had a little money and time to work with the actors before shooting. The construction is the real construction of a film, and not an improvisation. It was easy, because the script is based upon the book. Maybe for the first time, I think it's a real movie and not a strange patchwork of eroticism, violence, blood, horror and Rollin's obsessions like before.

With elaborate figures such as Batgirl, we seem assured of more of your trademark outré costumes and images though?

The batgirl is an idea which was not in the book. It's one of the very rare supernatural moments in the film. The film is realist.

Your novels in this series run to five now – are there plans to produce film versions of

Le Frisson Des Vampires

these and have you a UK distributor for **Little Orphan Vampires** *yet?*

If this film is a success, of course the idea is to make a sequel with the five books. Having just finished the film recently the first thing we did was to mail a video to Redemption Films... every country is free...

Little Orphan Vampires *marks your return to the vampire genre after a ten year hiatus – why return to it now?*

It's not really exact. There is a vampire sequence in **Lost In New York** and the girl in **Killing Car** is a kind of vampire... but real vampires? Because of the five books. The idea was to put on screen the first one and then the others. Now I have in my mind a little vampire film totally set in the ruins of a medieval château... very low-budget but a classical vampire story with beautiful locations.

You acted in **Trepanator** *as a mad doctor – how did this come about and did you enjoy the experience on the other side of the camera?*

As this was directed by Norbert Moutier and he is an old friend and writes many articles in France about my films, to act for him was very funny, and I also appear in his last film, **Dinosaurs From The Deep**.

You have a regular team of actors and technicians who are your friends – how important are they to the unique style and spirit of your films?

They know me and I know them. They trust me and that is great. Without my crew it's impossible to make such low-budget films.

*"Dreams and life – it's the same thing, or else it's not worth living" – quoted from your own **Les Enfants Du Paradis**. Your own philosophy?*

There are many beautiful images hidden inside the head of each human being. The idea is to take them and show them outside.

INDEX OF FILMS

Page number in bold indicates an illustration

you have just read
necronomicon 1
a creation book
published by:
creation books
head office:
83, clerkenwell road, london ec1, uk
tel: 0171-430-9878 fax: 0171-242-5527
e-mail: creation@pussycat.demon.co.uk

creation books is an independent publishing organisation producing fiction
and non-fiction genre books of interest to a young, literate and informed
readership. your support is appreciated.

*creation products should be available in all proper bookstores; please ask your
local retailer to order from:*
uk & europe: turnaround distribution, 27 horsell road, london N5 1xl
tel: 0171-609-7836 fax: 0171-700-1205
usa: subterranean company, box 160, 265 south 5th street, monroe, or 97456
tel: 503 847-5274 fax: 503-847-6018
canada: marginal, unit 102, 277 george street, n. peterborough, ontario k9j
3g9
tel/fax: 705-745-2326
australia & nz: peribo pty ltd, 58 beaumont road, mount kuring-gai, nsw 2080
tel: 02-457-0011 fax: 02-457-0022
japan: charles e tuttle co. inc., 21-13 seki 1-chome, tama-ku, kawasaki,
kanagawa 214
tel: 44-833-1924 fax: 44-833-7559

other film books from creation:
deathtripping an illustrated history of the cinema of transgression
by jack sargeant: isbn 1 871592 29 1, £11.95/$16.95
inside teradome an illustrated history of freak film
by jack hunter: isbn 1 871592 41 0, £11.95/$16.95
house of horror an illustrated history of hammer films
edited by jack hunter: isbn 1 871592 40 2, £12.95/$19.95
fragments of fear an illustrated history of british horror movies
by andy boot: isbn 1 871592 35 6, £12.95/$17.95
killing for culture an illustrated history of death film
by david kerekes & david slater: isbn 1 871592 20 8, £12.95/$17.95
desperate visons 1 the films of john waters and george & mike kuchar
by jack stevenson: isbn 1 871592 34 8, £11.95/$17.95

a full colour catalogue is available on request